Radical Christian Writings

And what shall I more saye, the tyme wold be to short for me to tell . . . of the prophetes, which thorowe fayth subdued kyngdoms, wrought righteousnes, obteyned the promyses, stopped the mouthes of Lyons, quenched the violence of fyre, escaped the edge off the swearde, off weake were made stronge, wexed valient in fyght, turned to flyght the armees of the alientes . . .

Wother were racked, and wolde not be delivered, thatt they myght receave a better resurreccion. Wother tasted off mockynges, and scourgynges, moreover off bondes and presonment: were stoned, were heawen asunder, were tempted, were slayne with sweardes, walked uppe and doune in shepes skynnes, in gotes skynnes, in nede, tribulacion, and vexacion, which the worlde was not worthy of: They wandred in wildernes, in mountaynes, in dens and caves of erth. And these all thorow fayth obtayned good reporte, and receaved not the promes, god providynge a better thynge for us, that they without us shulde not be made parfect.

Wherefore lett us also (seynge that we are compased with so gret a multitude of witnesses) laye awaye all that preseth us doune, and the sinne that hangeth on us, and let us runne with pacience, unto the battayle that is set before us, lokynge unto Jesus, the auctor and fynnysher of oure fayth, which for the ioye that was set before hym, abode the crosse, and despysed the shamee and is sett doune on the right honde off the throne off God.

Hebrews 11:32–12:2 from William Tyndale's translation of the New Testament (1526)

. . . words and writings were all nothing, and must die, for action is the life of all, and if thou dost not act, thou dost nothing.

Gerrard Winstanley, *A Watch-Word to the City of London and the Armie*, 1649

# Radical Christian Writings

*A Reader*

*Edited by*
Andrew Bradstock
*and*
Christopher Rowland

Copyright © Blackwell Publishers Ltd 2002
Editorial matter and arrangement copyright © Andrew Bradstock and Christopher
Rowland 2002

The moral right of Andrew Bradstock and Christopher Rowland to be identified as
authors of the editorial material has been asserted in accordance with the
Copyright, Designs and Patents Act 1988.

First published 2002

2 4 6 8 10 9 7 5 3 1

Blackwell Publishers Ltd
108 Cowley Road
Oxford OX4 1JF
UK

Blackwell Publishers Inc.
350 Main Street
Malden, Massachusetts 02148
USA

*British Library Cataloguing in Publication Data*

A CIP catalogue record for this book is available from the British Library.

*Library of Congress Cataloging-in-Publication Data has been applied for*

ISBN 0-631-22249-9        (hbk)
ISBN 0-631-22250-2        (pbk)

Typeset in 10$^1/_2$ on 12$^1/_2$ pt Bembo
by Best-set Typesetter Ltd., Hong Kong
Printed in Great Britain by T.J. International, Padstow, Cornwall

This book is printed on acid-free paper.

# Contents

# Preface

When we started out on the task of making this collection we had a relatively clear idea of what we would include in it. Both of us have greatly profited from studying those great radicals of the Christian tradition, Gerrard Winstanley and Thomas Muentzer, and having found echoes of the themes with which they were concerned elsewhere in the Christian tradition, we thought others would like to study them too. That was the easiest part of our task. We were, however, deeply aware that there were many areas where our competence even to *discover* what might be included in our collection needed to be buttressed by advice from friends and colleagues, and to this end we wrote around to many in these islands and elsewhere for advice. To say that we were overwhelmed by the response would be an understatement. The numerous suggestions, the sympathy for our project and the wisdom that was shared should mean that there are fifty names on the cover of this book not just two. We gladly put on record our indebtedness to:

Natasha Barr, Tony Benn, Brad R. Braxton, Henry Chadwick, David Constantine, Mark Corner, Andrew Dawson, Susan Dowell, Katy Ellis, Moby Farrands, Paul Fiddes, Stephen Finamore, Ian M. Fraser, Peter Garnsey, Andrew Goddard, Tim Gorringe, Mary Grey, Margaret Halsey, Elaine Hobby, Janet Hodgson, Anita Holmes, Ros Hunt, Claire Jowitt, Paul Joyce, John Kent, Alan Kreider, Christopher Lamb, Caroline Lee, Ken Leech, Ian Linden, Diarmaid MacCulloch, Lucia McGuckin, David McLellan, David McLoughlin, Sara Maitland, John Mantle, Henry Mayr-Harting, John Medcalf, Leslie Milton, John Morrill, Stuart Murray, Gillian Nicholls, Judy Powles, Rosemary Pugh, Bridget Rees, Marjorie Reeves, Mena Remedios, Jenny Richardson, Roger Ruston, Jane Shaw, Mike Simpson, Graeme Smith, Elizabeth Stuart, R. S. Sugirtharajah, Michael Taylor, Mark Thiessen-Nation, John Vincent, John Webster, Tom Weinandy, Louise Welcome, Angela West, Alan Wilkinson, and Alex Wright.

In addition we wish to record our special thanks to Gerard Mannion, who advised us particularly on the modern period, Tim Horner, Tony Dancer and Jean Alexander, who each played a vital role in tracking down many of the pieces included here, undertaking preliminary readings of the texts, listing secondary sources, preparing draft introductions, and many other tasks. We are also grateful to the British Academy for the grant which made it possible to have their assistance.

We were overwhelmed in another sense also, for it became clear to us quite early on that the task which we had set ourselves was much larger than we had at first imagined. As we make this collection available, we do so with a sense of humility and insufficiency. There is a lifetime's work tracking and assembling material from different disciplines which reflect even some of the practices and ideas to be found in this book. The sheer variety, theological insight, and breadth of the material that we have considered convinces us that here are resources both for the history of Christian theology and contemporary belief and practice, which have been neglected for too long.

This is *not* a collection of writings about "grassroots Christianity." It is a collection of radical writings. In class terms few of the writings in this book are by people without formal education: Blake, Bunyan, and Sojourner Truth are just a few examples. A book of witnesses to Christianity "from below" would have a very different feel to it. It would need to depend on oral testimony, given that many of those whose views would be represented would have not been able to write themselves (hence the importance here of *The Narrative of Sojourner Truth*, which, in many ways, parallels what we have in the New Testament gospels, where the writings are about Jesus rather than by him).

This collection may be a small, faltering step in the direction of remedying an omission which has existed for too long, but if it is able to put some of the writings it contains, and the remarkable people who penned them, on the theological map, and stimulate discussion of them in the seminar room, the pew, the house-group and the pub, our efforts will not have been in vain.

# Acknowledgments

The editors and publishers gratefully acknowledge the following for permission to reproduce copyright material:

Augsburg Fortress, for 'Credo'. Reprinted by permission from *Against the Wind* by Dorothee Soelle, translation copyright © 1999 Augsburg Fortress; Jeremiah: The World, the Wound of God by Daniel Berrigan. Copyright © Augsburg Fortress; 'Mary and Martha' reprinted by permission from *The Window of Vulnerability* by Dorothee Soelle, translation copyright © 1990 Augsburg Fortress;

Bowerdean, for Herbert McCabe, 'The Class Struggle and Christian Love' in Rex Ambler and David Haslam (eds), *Agenda for Prophets: Towards a Political Theology for Britain*. Published by Bowerdean, 1980;

Cairns, for Alan Ecclestone, 'The Parish Meeting at Work' in *Firing the Clay: Articles and Addresses* compiled by Jim Cotter. Published by Cairns, 1999;

Cambridge University Press, for Gustavo Guitiérrez, translated by Judith Condor, 'The Task and Content of Liberation Theology' in C. Rowland (ed) *The Cambridge Companion to Liberation Theology*, 1999;

CFWM, for Ian M. Fraser, 'Christian Grassroots Communities in Europe' in Derek Winter (ed.), *Putting Theology to Work*, CFWM, 1980;

Christian Action Journal, for Kenneth Leech, 'The Rebel Church in the Back Streets – Where are we now?' in *Christian Action Journal*, Spring/Summer 1996;

The Christian Century, for Martin Luther King, Jr. "Letter from Birmingham Jail," June 12, 1963, pp. 767–73;

CIIR, for 'The Kairos Document' in *Challenge to the Church: A Theological Comment on the Political Crisis in South Africa*. The Kairos Document. Published by CIIR, 1985;

T & T Clark Ltd., for Argula von Grumbach, *A Woman's Voice in the Reformation*;

DLT, for John Rowe, *Priests and Workers: A Rejoinder*, 1965, pp. 16f, 65f;

Emory University, for Ann Trapnel, 'The Cry of a Stone', copyright © Emory University, 1996 and Anne Wentworth, 'The Revelation of Jesus Christ' copyright © Emory University 1996;

Epworth, for John Vincent, *OK Let's Be Methodists*. Published by Epworth, 1984;

Franciscan Press, for Peter Maurin, 'What the Catholic Worker Believes' in *Easy Essays*. Published by the Franciscan Press, 1977;

Aruna Gnanadason, "Women's Oppression: A Sinful Situation," in V. Fabella and Mercy Amba Oduyoye (eds.), *With Passion and Compassion: Third World Women Doing Theology*, New York, 1988, pp. 74–5;

Carlos Mesters, 'God's Project', translated by The Theology Exchange Programme;

Mowbray, for Sara Maitland, *Angel and Me*. Published by Mowbray, 1995;

Orbis Books, for *Voice of the Voiceless: The Four Pastoral Letters and Other Statements* (Maryknoll, NY: Orbis Books 1985); Marie Dennis, Renny Golden, Scott Wright, *Oscar Romero: Reflections on his Life and Writings*. Published by Orbis Books, 2000; Philip Berryman, *The Religious Roots of Rebellion*. Published by Orbis Books, Maryknoll, NY and SCM Press, London 1984; Robert Ellsberg (ed) *By Little and Little: The Selected Writings of Dorothy Day*. Published by A. Knopf, 1983;

Pilgrim Press, for Carter Heyward, 'Liberating the Body', in *Our Passion for Justice: Images of Power, Sexuality and Liberation*. (Cleveland: The Pilgrim Press, 1984) 140–5. Copyright © 1984 The Pilgrim Press; Thomas Hanks, 'Matthew and Mary of Magdala: Good News for Sex Workers' in *Take Back the Word: A Queer Reading of the Bible*. Robert E. Goss and Mona West (eds) (Cleveland: The Pilgrim Press, 2000) 187–8, 189–90, 193–4. Copyright © 2000 The Pilgrim Press. Used by permission.

The Solentiname Community, "Nicaraguan Peasant Mass," in *Nicaraguan Perspectives*, trans. Sylvia Mullaly and Tony Ryan, based on *Misa Campesina Nicaragüense*, Ministry of Culture, Managua, Nicaragua, 1981;

Taylor and Francis, for John Petrie, *The Worker Priests*. Published by Routledge and Kegan Paul, 1956;

Skotaville, for Sigqibo Dwane, *Issues in the South African Theological Debate: Essays and Addresses in Honour of the Late James Matta Dwane*;

SCM Press, for Chung Hyun Kyung, *Struggle to be the Sun Again*. Published by SCM Press, 1991; Jacques Ellul, The Presence of the Kingdom. Published by SCM Press 1951;

Camilo Torres, *Love and Revolution*, Cape, 1971, pp. 327–32;

Unlock, for their diagram;

Word, for William Strongfellow, *An Ethic for Christians and Other Aliens in a Strange Land*. Published by Word, 1973;

Worldview, for Stanley Hauerwas, 'Messianic Pacificism: Non-resistance as a defense of a good and just social order' in *Worldview* 16(6), June 1973.

The publishers apologize for any errors or omissions in the above list and would be grateful to be notified of any corrections that should be incorporated in the next edition or reprint of this book.

# Christianity:
# Radical and Political

The Gospel of Jesus Christ, announcing the arrival of the kingdom or reign of God, offered a radical and subversive challenge to the world, its powers and authorities. The subversive aspect of the nascent Christian movement was recognised by people in Thessalonica who, hearing that Christians were proclaiming "another Jesus" and acting against the decrees of Caesar, accused them of "turning the world upside down" (Acts 17:6).[1] Throughout Christian history – and particularly at times of crisis and social upheaval – there have emerged writings which, reflecting the values of the Kingdom, have engaged in searching critiques of the political order and promoted change in social and economic relations, most commonly by advocating or enacting equality of wealth, power, gender, or status. This collection brings together in one volume examples of such writings from various periods of Christian history, arranged chronologically and with short introductions and explanatory notes. No attempt has been made to represent every century, and where there are gaps in the coverage this is because little appears to have survived from a particular era.

Fifteen years or more of study of individuals and groups whose views and stories are largely ignored by the major textbooks have persuaded us of the urgency of the task of redressing the balance in the presentation of Christian political thought; and our decision to consider how we might bring the "radical tradition" to greater prominence led to a period of consultation with friends and colleagues, for whose advice and help we are extremely grateful. As a result of this consultation we found ourselves faced with much more material than could be easily encompassed within the pages of even a substantial book, though if nothing else this confirmed our suspicion that the flow of radical ideas through 2000 years of Christian history, however it might appear, could be best described as a stream than a trickle. Not that we have found it easy to define exactly what we have been looking for, and one of our responses to the oft-asked question, "What do you mean by 'radical'?", has been to give an account of the process of our collection. It started with a

[1] The connection is brilliantly captured in the title of Christopher Hill's landmark book about the seventeenth-century English radicals, *The World Turned Upside Down*, Harmondsworth: Penguin, 1972.

shared interest in the writings of Thomas Muentzer and Gerrard Winstanley, and moved from a conviction that what they were saying was an authentic and largely ignored expression of the Christian faith, to a growing realization that theirs were not lone testaments to their distinctive perspective. Back and forth in time we found ourselves stumbling across others who shared their sentiments, and our project was under way.

There *is* an appeal to the roots: to Jesus and the early church as paradigms of what Christian polity and action should be about. Frequently, this expresses itself as a critique of false religion, which places institutions and rituals above the needs of people: this theme runs from the earliest text through to the most recent in this collection. A few of the writings included here exemplify the more violent dimension of radicalism: being so convinced of the godlessness of contemporary culture and institutions they consider it necessary to uproot them by force – though there are more witnessing to protest through the way exemplified by Jesus himself, resistance even unto death.

But even this kind of focus does not really encapsulate the basis of our selection. That is best understood by reference to the life and work of people like Muentzer and Winstanley,[2] whose careers exemplify several features which are catalysts for our choice of material. Their sense of vocation is such that they believe that they are called, in an apocalyptic sense, to a form of preaching and activity which is explicitly contrary to received wisdom and practice. In this the scriptures form a resource for them as they see their own activity in the light of the struggle between the forces of light and the forces of darkness (apocalyptic images, unsurprisingly, have a potent resonance for them). What one finds is not merely abstract reflection, therefore, but exposition of understandings which are based on an active engagement to see another kind of order at work in the world, the realization of God's kingdom on earth. What impressed us was that again and again, similar themes and convictions emerged, suggesting to us that there was some kind of "radical tradition." And yet the word "tradition" hardly adequately describes what is going on here. Even if historically connections can be made between the various writings represented in this book, that sense of destiny and vocation, which characterized so many of those who wrote them, often meant that there was little awareness on their part of indebtedness to others. Of course, there are exceptions, as, for example, when radicals borrow the ideas of Joachim of Fiore; and the Anabaptists created their sense of tradition as they told their own stories by relating them to the martyrologies of the early church in texts like the *Martyrs' Mirror* or the *Hutterite Chronicle*. Yet even what appears to be an explicit borrowing on the part of a writer is done so unconsciously as the impression is given of the Spirit moving afresh in each generation.

Christianity has always been radical *and* political. Such radicalism is apparent in the discussions which Jesus of Nazareth is reported to have had with some

---

[2] In the case of Winstanley it would be more accurate to speak of *a part* of his career as there is evidence that for most of the latter part of his life he lived as a conforming and relatively respectable member of southern English society.

intellectuals of his day in which he harked back to the life of Paradise as a criterion for judging a contemporary legal question about divorce (Mark 10:6). That
"back to basics" is characteristic of much else in the New Testament writings as
writers sought to explain and make sense of their experience and convictions in
relation to the roots of the tradition of which they were a part. Similar appeals to
the roots of Christianity are undertaken by many of the writers included in this
book, as they seek to appeal to or be inspired by the foundation texts of major
ancestors in the faith, particularly the gospel stories of Jesus.

The foundation narratives of Christianity tell of a man who fell foul of a colonial power and its surrogates, and for well over two hundred years the religion
developed in the shadow of a deep-seated ambivalence to empire. Its own rhetoric
demanded allegiance to another commonwealth: Christian discipleship was not like
joining a religious society whose demands were only temporary; it was all-
consuming and utterly demanding. Conversion could be dramatic, a demanding
and totally transforming experience. In the Epistle to Donatus 3–4, Cyprian speaks
of "lying in darkness and gloomy night remote from truth." His experience of
baptism echoes Pauline language in that he speaks of "putting off the old humanity" (Eph. 4:22) and witnessing the transformation of innate characteristics. Such
ideas are perhaps not surprising: what is, however, is the way in which a previous
style of life is questioned and abandoned. Cyprian writes of "learning thrift" after
a life of banquets and sumptuous feasts, of donning simple attire after being used
to expensive clothes of glittering gold and purple. Conversion involved a different style of life with values at odds with mainstream culture. It meant belonging
to a group where elite values and goods were widely shared and were the hall-
mark of the community: wisdom, religiosity, wealth and power, which had been
the preserve of the few, were now available to all through the divine spirit.

Emerging Christianity until the time of Constantine was characterized by such
a sectarian spirit. The period of preparation to become a member of the church
(the catechumenate) was long and thorough. At the heart of the baptismal experience was the clear message of a transfer from one dominion to another involving the acceptance of Jesus Christ as king of kings and lord of lords. What is so
striking about the New Testament texts is that they were written by people who
had little or no political power, with a vision of the world which was at odds with
the prevailing ideology. Yet their counter-cultural stand did not mean that they
ended up writing utopian tracts which were far removed from their everyday
reality. We may not like their apparent collusion with slavery, or some of the less
inclusive sentiments which seem to encourage the subordination of women, but
there are enough indications of an impatience with the status quo to suggest that
they propounded and expected a different kind of understanding of and way of
living in the world.

Christians were a different sort of people, not from one particular race or background, committed to a different kind of life and culture, more often than not at
odds with the wisdom of the age. Their faith was thoroughly political, therefore,
though doubtless never uniformly so, and if from the first those non-conforming
instincts were strong, there was inevitably going to be a tension between the radical

demands of the teacher who lived the life of a mendicant and the more settled, predictable existence of those who sought some kind of accommodation with the powers that be. Nevertheless, until the time of Constantine, Christianity remained a different kind of culture more or less at odds with the politics of the age. That is not to deny that once it become the religion of empire its inclusive rhetoric could easily be used to serve rather different ends as it offered the social cement of a fragmenting empire. The radical slogan of Galatians 3:28, "there is neither Jew nor Greek, slave nor free, male nor female" has a rather different ring when it might serve as the vision of an inclusive, cosmopolitan empire.

From the very first Christianity's theological instincts were radical in the strict sense of that word. The Pauline reflection on the significance of Jesus Christ includes a comparison with the first human and the assertion that in the person of Christ there had been a complete reversal of the negative effects of a fallen creation. Similarly, in their approach to the religious tradition of which they were a part, early Christian writers took a radical approach and asserted that the very foundations of the religion had been changed and the traditions which had provided the resource for life were either questioned or relativised in the light of new wisdom.

Nowhere is this radicalism more evident than in the fourfold story of Jesus in the New Testament. Mark's gospel has become a favourite source for a radical Christian theology in recent biblical study,[3] though its story is essentially that of the other gospels too. Jesus bursts on the margins of Israel's life coming from Galilee, not Jerusalem, the capital city, which becomes a place of rebellion. It is on the margins of "normal" life that Jesus is to be found, near the sea, in the desert, in the country rather than the town. Jesus challenges convention (1:40; 2:23ff; 5:25; 7:19) and a culture of status and customary practice and institutions. While the disciples want to sit and rule just like the kings and mighty of the world, Jesus offers a baptism of suffering (10:42f). In common with the other synoptic gospels Mark has a twofold account of Jesus dealing with and speaking of children (9:33ff; 10:13ff). Children do not have high social status. That Jesus should advance them as models for discipleship and put a child at the center challenges contemporary culture. At the climax of its life of Jesus the economic, institutional, and spiritual power of the Temple is destroyed at the moment of Jesus' death and replaced by a "counter-culture" based on service.

In the story of the early church in the Acts of the Apostles, Stephen represents one of the most radical voices in the New Testament. The powerful speech which precedes his stoning, which suggests that the construction of the Temple marked an actual act of rebellion, is a daring use of Scripture; in the context of Second Temple Judaism, it must have been seen as a monstrous act of blasphemy and sacrilege, making comprehensible the charges brought against Stephen according to Acts 6:14. The quotation of Solomon's words about the Most High not dwelling in houses made with hands merely precedes a ringing indictment of the "stiff-necked people" and a link between present rebelliousness in rejecting Jesus, the prophet like Moses who was to come, and the history of similar disobedience.

---

[3] F. Belo, *A Materialist Reading of the Gospel of Mark*, Maryknoll, 1981; C. Myers, *Binding the Strong Man*, Maryknoll, 1988; K. Wengst, *Pax Romana and the Peace of Jesus Christ*, London, 1988.

In the early Christians' reflection on Jesus' life and in their articulation of the worship of God, the Temple, the sacred building, played little part save as a way of talking about the building of human community: it is rather the reign of God which is the cenral concern, the witness to the ways of God's justice and the hope of heaven on earth anticipated in the common life of small groups of men, women, and children who began to explore a variant way of being God's people. The individuals and groups who appear in the following pages are not those whose message is proclaimed and lived in fine buildings or elaborate liturgies. Indeed, such activity seemed to be at odds with what the heart of the Christian message was about. As was the case for much of the early church's existence, homes and small spaces were the loci for the active agency of the divine spirit, a point nowhere better exemplified than in the document of the Swiss Anabaptists (p. 90).

Christianity is about deeds not words, famously exemplified by the text "faith by itself, if it has no works, is dead." These words come from the Letter of James (2:17), much neglected and famously derided by Luther as "an epistle of straw." The epistle highlights characteristic features of Christian identity, however, in its emphasis on humility (1:9) and the need for the demonstration of faith in good works (2:18). The criticism of those who practise differentiation between individuals on the basis of class is held up to ridicule (2:1–7). This flies in the face of that universal tendency in early Christianity to question the limitation of elite goods to the rich, wise, and mighty of the world. James's words "Has not God chosen the poor in the world to be rich in faith and to be heirs of the kingdom that he has promised to those who love him" (2:5) are as explicit a testimony as anywhere in the New Testament of the peculiar privilege granted to the poor to discern and inherit the kingdom of God. Towards the end of the letter the writer returns to his critique of the rich with a stinging denunciation, owing much to the material in the Sermon on the Mount and echoing passages like Amos 2:6–8 and 5:10–19. Here we have that insight into the contemporary social evils which led to exploitation of day labourers and the enjoyment of the fruits of the earth by the few at the expense of the many (5:1–6), sentiments echoed in the words of Ball, Muentzer, Winstanley, and others.

The Apocalypse, the book of Revelation, stands on its own in the New Testament, though its contents are echoed elsewhere in the New Testament (e.g. Mark 13; Matthew 24–25; Luke 21 and II Thess. 2). Its visionary character is of importance.[4] This book has been a resource for different kinds of interpretation in the history of Christianity. On the one hand have been those who have pored over its images and tried to calculate the details of future history (usually making use of the other prophetic books of the Bible also). On the other, Revelation has offered space for women as well as men to enable their vocations as visionaries and mystics to flourish. For women it has meant that they have been able to emerge as persons in their own right, in the midst of a society permeated with

---

[4] C. Rowland *The Book of Revelation*, New Interpreter's Bible, vol. xii, Nashville: Abingdon, 1998.
[5] On women visionaries see S. Elm, *'Virgins of God': The Making of Asceticism in Late Antiquity*, Oxford: Oxford University Press, p. 32, and G. Jantzen, *Power, Gender and Christian Mysticism*, Cambridge: Cambridge University Press, 1995.

patriarchy. Prophets and the mystics have found in Revelation an inspiration to explore a ministry denied by much else in scripture and tradition.[5] Teresa of Avila, Catherine of Sienna, and Hildegard of Bingen, like the male radicals who turned to Revelation, found in this allusive text a licence to resist received religion and practice precisely because a canonical text opened a door for an experience of God which enabled them to transcend the boundaries imposed by what was conventionally possible. It is that kind of visionary inspiration, found in the call of Gerrard Winstanley, in the prophetic vision of Anna Trapnel, and in the peculiar genius of William Blake.

The Apocalypse does not allow its readers to accept the world as it is. But it enables them to view their present situation from a completely different perspective, that of the Risen Christ. It is a text which seeks to summon to a change of heart and life-style by resisting the power of Empire and the ethos of the age. Revelation 13 and 17 bring out most clearly, perhaps inevitably, the character of the state. State or society is not a neutral enterprise devoid of conflict of interest or human self-aggrandizement. Apocalyptic "unveiling," drawing as it does on the prophetic symbolism of empire from Daniel, unmasks the reality of life where violence and oppression are the cornerstones of the might of an apparently benevolent empire. A passage like this is the cornerstone of the critique of empire throughout Christian history. Its radicalism is its concern to lay bare the roots of this oppression in the deep-seated conflict between good and evil. In many of the extracts which are contained in this book we shall consider those who have found in apocalyptic symbolism a tool that has enabled the oppressed to find and maintain a critical distance from an unjust world with the real prospect of a reign of justice, though we shall always need to remember that the apocalyptic symbols have served the needs of the politically powerful as well.

The identification of a radical strand within early Christianity should not lead us to suppose that early Christianity was either homogeneous in its radicalism or revolutionary in its activism. As the Pauline letters indicate, the new converts, particularly those in the urban environment of the cities of the Empire, had to learn a degree of accommodation with the world as it was, without, somehow, abandoning the stark call to discipleship of the teacher from Nazareth. What is remarkable about the letters of Paul is the way in which this Christian activist maintained the counter-cultural identity of these isolated groups by his travelling and writing, much as the Anabaptist leader Menno Simons was to do fifteen hundred years later. In another respect too, consolidating Anabaptists like Menno Simons are inheritors of the Pauline radical spirit more than Muentzer, or even Winstanley. The strange thing about Paul is that the energetic innovator and founder of the Gentile church should have been the one who above all sowed the seeds of the acceptability of the world order as it is and passivity towards it. Nevertheless, as recent study has reminded us, there is at the heart of the emerging Christianity a distinctive identity in which elite goods and privileges (wealth, power, holiness, and knowledge) ceased merely to be the prerogative of an elite but were open to all within the common life of the Christian communities.[6] It comes as no surprise,

[6] G. Theissen, *A Theory of Primitive Christian Religion*, London: SCM Press, 1999, pp. 81–118.

therefore, that in the history of Christianity many have often looked to the radical Paul as a basis for appeals for radical change as the examples of Augustine, Luther, and Karl Barth indicate. Excessive concentration on Paul's theological ideas detracts from Paul's activism, not least the task which occupied the last years of his career: the collection for the poor in Jerusalem which has few obvious parallels in the ancient world (Rom. 15:26; 2 Cor. 8–9).

The New Testament has many contradictory strands. These are well represented in Luke–Acts. Luke–Acts was probably written to churches which were relatively affluent. They had tasted of the good news of justification by faith and life in the Spirit and needed to be reminded that there was more to faith than mere religion, and most important of all Luke wanted them to take seriously "the option for the poor."[7] Nevertheless according to Acts 10 the account of Cornelius' conversion leaves open the question of what kind of life was expected of the newly converted Gentile soldier. Quite a remarkable omission given that in the following century there was widespread doubt about whether a Christian should sign up for military service.[8] Tensions exist both between the New Testament documents, and, in the case of some writings, this attitude may exist within the same document. Such a tension between what was politically and theologically possible and what needed to be held onto, to be heeded whenever possible within the severe constraints posed by historical circumstances, is part of the story of Christian radicalism. Some individuals were more inventive than others in the ways in which they dealt with this conundrum. There were martyrs who brooked no compromise or found there was no alternative but to die for their faith.[9] But there were those who sought the freedom within the status quo to pursue their goals, as we find particularly with the sixteenth-century Familists (p. 94). In many ways their ingenuity and their knack for survival bespeaks of that same divine spark that kept the faith alive in the early years of the Christian church. Such were ways to maintain the commitment to Christ's Kingdom in the midst of a political and economic order of an age which demanded compromise.

## Identifying the Radical Strand in Christian Theology

It is evident from various writings of the New Testament that the suspicion of wealth and power in texts like the book of Revelation and the letter of James continued ancient traditions in the prophecies of Amos and the Torah itself, where care for the widow, orphan, and the stranger and the severe critique of inequity, led to a remarkable voice of social protest. When such texts are put alongside the indifference to wealth and status in the gospels, the hints of an egalitarian communitarianism in parts of primitive Christianity begin to emerge (Acts 2:44, 4:32). This was later to take the form of the emergence of monasticism. The solitary

---

[7] P. L. Esler, *Community and Gospel in Luke–Acts*, Cambridge: Cambridge University Press, 1986.
[8] See, e.g., M. Hornus, *It is Not Lawful for Me To Fight*.
[9] D. Boyarin, *Dying for God*, University of California, 1999.

voices in the wilderness grew into an integral part of church and society prompt-ing their own renewal movements in the later Middle Ages pioneered by people like Bernard of Clairvaux and Francis of Assisi, who in their turn sought to recap-ture the original vision of Jesus. The various monastic rules are part of the necessary background to many of the practices and beliefs to which the sources in the book bear witness.[10] The counter-cultural vision of the emerging Christian identity is nowhere better exemplified than by the commitment to martyrdom, the deep roots of a Christian vision of protest, where the practical implementation of an alternative style of life and the promotion of a common life of equality under God began to take shape. Such strands of radicalism have been part of the rich fabric of Christianity.

## The Critique of False Religion

Throughout many of these texts there is a heartfelt cry against acts of injustice and inhumanity, whether at an individual or societal level. This is often linked with a critique of a false religion in which the preservation of institutions and traditional rituals are elevated above the needs of people. The woes of Jesus (e.g. Matthew 23:23) against the pietists of his day for tithing mint and cumin but neglecting the weightier matters of the divine law are echoed in many of our pieces. The cri-tique of inhumanity is linked with the perception of a false religion which main-tains the status quo and is in danger of masking injustice. These are themes which emerge from the earliest text to the most recent in the collection.

## Hope for a New Order

It is hardly surprising that hope for a new world features in many of these texts. Nevertheless this hope differs quite markedly from the character of hope within other areas of Christian tradition. In many of our texts we are concerned with a hope for this world rather than some transcendent realm. Ken Leech exemplifies this when he writes, "the fundamental division within the Christian world . . . did not run along denominational lines but rather divided those Christians in all tra-ditions who believed that the kingdom of God involved a hope for the transfor-mation of this world and its structures, and those who did not" (see below p. 329).

There emerges in Christian history a clear difference between those who pore over the detail of texts like Revelation in order to be able to map out the narra-tive of the end of the world, and those who are inspired by the apocalyptic texts to see their own visions and to offer a prophetic challenge to the communities of their day (such as Anna Trapnel and William Blake). The former group of

---

[10] On this see, e.g., P. Brown, *The Body and Society*; R. Lane Fox, *Pagans and Christians*, London, 1987; P. Rousseau, *Pachomius: The Making of a Community in Fourth Century Egypt*, University of California, 1985; and D. Chitty, *The Desert a City*, Oxford, 1966.

interpreters tend to use Revelation to point forward, the latter find its words an empowering conviction for the present moment of crisis, the Kairos. The coming reign of God is not merely an article of faith for the future but is in some sense already present, either in the life of the prophetic group, called to implement or proclaim, or as a phenomenon within the historical process which demands a response and interpretation, what is known as "reading the signs of the times." Paul's mission to the Gentiles, Jesus' journey to Jerusalem, Muentzer's holy war against the impious, and Winstanley's communist experiment of digging all evince this same imperative to act to fulfil the hope for a new order in the present.

## The Present as the Decisive Moment in the Divine Purposes

There is the conviction that the present moment is one of utmost significance within the whole gamut of history. It is a time of crisis and a moment of opportunity (a point made with particular force in The Kairos Document, pp. 285–304). As a result commitment rather than detachment is necessary, and action (and in the case of a few writers this may involve violence). This kind of attitude conditions the way apocalyptic and prophetic texts are interpreted and their hopes construed.

There is frequently a high premium placed on prophetic charisma, as the visionary or prophet sees things which contradict received wisdom and claims authority to take decisions and inaugurate actions, which, in the view of those who wield political power, are of a highly controversial kind.

There is often an intense awareness of God's presence and a conviction that God or Christ indwells and empowers. The divine indwells the human as well as the process of history, and there is often an intimacy of interaction between the human and the divine in enabling the understanding of God's purposes to be known. This is often manifested in the doctrine of the Spirit and the conviction that the believer is closely identified with Christ.

## The Prophetic Politics of Equality

Early Christianity was dominated by the belief that the coming of God's reign on earth was imminent and that signs of that were already to be seen in the activity of the Christian communities, all of whom equally had tasted of the prophetic spirit. Acts 2:17 encapsulates this conviction; it is a verse which has kindled the enthusiasm of later generations also:

> And in the last days, it shall be, God declares, that I will pour out my Spirit on all flesh, and your sons and daughters shall prophesy, and your young men shall see visions, and your old men shall dream dreams.

The reorganization of status, relationships, wealth, knowledge and power relations, among women as well as men, and different races, was all part of a different ethos, an anticipation of a commonwealth which would be operative throughout the universe. To the extent that Christians began to implement these deep-seated convictions, they were not merely utopian dreamers but practitioners of the kingdom-life amidst a political reality which seemed to militate against its fulfilment. Many of our texts bear witness to the practice of that hope, not mere theorization about it. That is true of the earliest Christian, and later Anabaptist, texts, all of which bear witness to movements that in the various facets of their social life promoted the democratization of what had hitherto been elite privileges and values: holiness, knowledge, wealth, and power. The account of the conversion of Cyprian brings this to the fore, and the critique of privilege and wealth found in the *De Divitiis* harks back to the uncomfortable sayings of Jesus with which the Christian church has always struggled. They were also to be the source of much grief when Francis of Assisi insisted that they form the bedrock of the rule of his new order, as the debates between the mainstream, and Spiritual, Franciscans make plain.

## Use of Scripture

The author of the *De Divitiis* criticizes those who use sophisticated scriptural interpretation to allow them to avoid the plain meaning of the text, for example by looking to the examples of wealthy men from the Old Testament rather than the words and example of Christ. Nevertheless elsewhere we find a use of the tradition in which interpreters refuse to be content with the letter but pierce to the real meaning of the text. In the case of some writers this attitude may manifest itself as a rejection of the priority of Scripture and a subordination of it to the inner understanding which comes through the Spirit. The meaning of Scripture and tradition is subordinated to experience as a prior "text" which must be the necessary condition of the way in which Scripture is read (see the example of Early Baptist worship, pp. 105–6).

There is a democratic, participative emphasis on the ability of all those open to the Spirit of God to understand the meaning of Scripture. This can come without access to the wisdom of the experts. As early Anabaptist testimony indicates (see below p. 91), I Corinthians 14 is a passage that is an important witness not only to what went on but also how spontaneity and a participation in a spiritual discipline might be conducted. It is a chapter in which the validity of congregational openness to the Spirit and the need for discernment and mutual edification sits uneasily alongside clear, peremptory apostolic instruction. According to Acts 2, when Peter preached on the day of Pentecost it was about a promise of the spirit being poured out on to "all flesh," not just apostles. Women as well as men, old as well as young would prophesy, a reason for the visionary and prophetic vocation to women demonstrated in several examples (pp. 144 and 153).

At the Reformation writers like Erasmus and Tyndale both stressed the importance of ordinary people reading the Bible. They viewed this text as one that spoke to, and informed, people whether or not they had spent years studying it. In the basic ecclesial communities of contemporary Latin America the Bible has often been the means of enabling literacy. Through it people are taught to read, and that matches the way in which the Bible functions in the early modern period in Britain (see p. 308 on the work of "Unlock"). It was the tool for the education of ordinary people, enabling a Bunyan or a Blake to read, write, and, as important, to reflect on the world in a way which enabled them to glimpse something of the way of God.

In much of the interpretation going on in the texts cited in this book we are not dealing with the kind of analytical exegesis that is typical of modern acade-mic writing, in which the intention of the author and attention to the precise meaning of words and phrases predominate. Instead, we see a rather oblique rela-tionship with the Scriptures in which the words become the catalyst for discern-ment of the divine way in the present. It is, as some recent Brazilian popular educational material from Bahia puts it, "enabling one to look at the world with new eyes." The wisdom of experience is as much the vehicle of the Holy Spirit. What counts is not so much what the text meant to Isaiah, Jesus or Paul, but what import these words may have in the circumstances of the present. In this regard Karl Barth is close to the view of the radicals: "why should parallels drawn from the ancient world be of more value for our understanding of the epistle than the situation in which we ourselves actually are and to which we can therefore bear witness."[11]

The claim to be able to understand the scriptures without recourse to learned divines is a repeated theme throughout this collection. It is one that is deeply rooted in the Christian tradition, going back to the words of Jesus and the remark-able testimony to spirit-inspired exegesis, standing in need of the insights of the learned, which is evident in Paul's words in I Corinthians 2. Patterns of biblical exegesis which have emerged in parts of Latin America over the last twenty years offer a more recent example of the way in which the practical faith of the non-professional reader can be resourced by a mode of reading of the scriptures which does not need (even if it is often supported by) sympathetic intellectuals.[12]

The perspective on Scripture surveyed in this book has a long pedigree in Chris-tian theology. It is particularly evident in, for example, the mid-seventeenth century English writer, Gerrard Winstanley's, words, that ordinary people will have direct experience of God. Action will be the context of knowledge of the divine will. According to Liberation Theology understanding comes through action. Theology is the "second act," paralleling Winstanley's words that "action is the life of all." Scripture then acts as confirmation of that intuitive knowledge of God. The radi-cals in Christianity stress the presence of God in the persons of the poor and also active in history. From Paul's letter to the Galatians, where the meaning of Scrip-ture and the tradition is subordinated to experience of the Spirit, to the use of the Bible in the basic ecclesial communities in late twentieth century Latin America, the emphasis is on experience as a prior "text" which must condition the way in which Scripture and tradition are read and the "signs of the times" interpreted, the more clearly to discern the Kingdom's coming.

---

[11] K. Barth, *The Epistle to the Romans*, Oxford: Oxford University Press, 1933, p. 12.
[12] See Gerald West, *The Academy of the Poor*, Sheffield: Sheffield Academic Press, 1999.

# Chapter 1

# Justin (ca. 100–ca. 165) and Cyprian (ca. 300)

**Justin,** First Apology **(mid-second century)**
**Cyprian,** Epistle I to Donatus **(third century)**

In the early centuries of the Christian church preparation for baptism was a crucial part of enabling the transition from the dominant culture to another culture patterned on the way of Christ. Baptism marked the moment of transition but the catechumenate was the way in which a candidate for baptism was prepared for this moment. Nowhere is this more clearly demonstrated than in two conversion accounts, the first by the influential second century writer Justin and the second by the third century North African bishop, Cyprian. The latter's account is of his own conversion from an aristocratic lifestyle to a different pattern of behavior. What is striking about this is not so much the intellectual character of faith but the struggle to acclimatize to different patterns of behavior. According to the Gospel of Mark, Jesus had told his disciples that their life should differ from contemporary culture (Mark 10: 42ff). What was required was to live as Jesus' followers taught and lived, a pattern of life which by all accounts was impressive and attractive to pagans. In the catechumenate, candidates for baptism learned how to live differently.

In Justin's account of his conversion the sense of oppression by larger powers and the release which fellowship in the Christian community afforded are brought out. This situation required an exorcism of the principalities and powers. The importance of such ideas is at the heart of William Blake's theology (see pp. 165–71) and has been a feature of recent radical theological writing by William Stringfellow (see below pp. 255–60) and more recently W. Wink, *Naming the Powers*, Philadelphia: Fortress, 1984; *Unmasking the Powers*, Philadelphia: Fortress, 1986; *Engaging the Powers*, Philadelphia: Fortress, 1993.

Source

C. C. Richardson, *Early Christian Fathers*, New York: Macmillan, 1970, pp. 249–50 and *http://www.ccel.org/fathers2/*

Further reading

A. Kreider, *The Change of Conversion and the Origin of Christendom*, Harrisburg: Trinity, 1999.
R. Lane Fox, *Pagans and Christians*, Harmondsworth: Penguin, 1986.
W. Meeks, *The Origins of Chrisian Morality*, New Haven: Yale, 1993.

## Justin Martyr, *First Apology* 14

[The demons] struggle to have you as their slaves and servants, and . . . they get hold of all who do not struggle to their utmost for their own salvation – as we do who, after being persuaded by the Word, renounced them and now follow the only unbegotten God through his Son. Those who once rejoiced in fornication now delight in self-control alone; those who made use of magic arts have dedicated themselves to the good and unbegotten God; we who once took most pleasure in the means of increasing our wealth and property now bring what we have into a common fund and share with everyone in need; we who hated and killed one another and would not associate with men of different tribes because of [their different] customs, now after the manifestation of Christ live together and pray for our enemies and try to persuade those who unjustly hate us, so that they, living according to the fair commands of Christ, may share with us the good hope of receiving the same things . . . The teachings of Christ were short and concise, for he was no philosopher, but his word was the power of God.

## Cyprian, *Epistle I to Donatus* 3–4

While I was still lying in darkness and gloomy night . . . and remote from truth and light, I used to regard it as a difficult matter, and especially as difficult in respect of my character at that time, that a man should be capable of being born again . . . and that a man quickened to a new life in the laver of saving water should be able to put off what he has previously been . . . How, said I, is such a conversion possible, that there should be a sudden and rapid divestment of all which, either innate in us has hardened in the corruption of our material nature, or acquired by us has become inveterate by long accustomed use? These things have become deeply and radically ingrained within us. When does he learn thrift who has been used to liberal banquets and sumptuous feats? And he who has been glittering in gold and purple, and has been celebrated for his costly attire, when does he reduce himself to ordinary and simple clothing? . . .

But after that, by the help of the water of new birth, the stain of former years had been washed away, and a light from above, serene and pure, had been infused into my reconciled heart – after that, by the agency of the Spirit breathed from heaven, a second birth restored me to a new person; – then in a wondrous manner, doubtful things at once began to assure themselves to me . . . What before had seemed difficult began to suggest a means of accomplishment, what had been thought impossible, to be capable of being achieved.

# Chapter 2

# *The Acts of Paul and Thecla* (second century)

Evidence about women's involvement in the corporate life of the people of God from all periods of church history is difficult to come by. What is particularly striking about the Montanist movement which came to prominence in the second half of the second century CE is the important position it gave to women and its millenarian beliefs, though reconstruction of its history and beliefs is not easy (see C. Trevett *Montanism: Gender, Authority, and the New Prophecy*, Cambridge: Cambridge University Press, 1996). An important role was given to women in the earliest phases of the movement. Montanism probably represents a protest against greater ecclesiastical organization dominated by men. The church had narrowed the options open to women. In the case of the role of martyr women could still exercise significant influence, as is evident from the *Martyrdom of Perpetua and Felicity*.

The Acts of Paul and Thecla is part of a cycle of legendary material reflecting stories in the Acts of the Apostle possibly dating from toward the end of the second century CE. Tertullian in his treatise on baptism relates how the priest who wrote the apocryphal acts of Paul was dismissed for writing such fictitious literature (Tertullian, *On Baptism* 17 where Tertullian rejects this work as an authority for a woman to teach and baptize). *The Acts of Paul and Thecla* recount how Thecla, as a well to do young woman betrothed to be married, became an enthusiastic follower of Paul's teaching. She found herself on the verge of death but escaped miraculously. The story contrasts with some of the grim realism of the martyr stories which were circulating roughly contemporary with it, in which men and women find themselves having to choose between the imperium of Jesus and that of Caesar and suffering dreadfully for it (see H. Musurillo *The Acts of the Christian Martyrs*, Oxford: Oxford University Press, 1972 and the way in which such martyr texts provided the foundation for the understanding of Christian identity reflected in the Mennonite *Martyrs' Mirror*). The stories in *The Acts of Paul and Thecla* are reminiscent of the tales of miraculous escape we find in the canonical Daniel (e.g. Daniel 3 and 6) and deserve to be compared with the apocryphal book of Susannah where a narrative of a woman on trial is to be found. What is remarkable about *The Acts of Paul and*

*Thecla* is the way in which Thecla functions as a Christian teacher and missionary, and baptizes herself just before she expected to die for her faith.

## Source

J. K. Elliott, *The Apocryphal New Testament*, Oxford: Oxford University Press, 1993, pp. 365–72.

## Further reading

W. Schneemelcher, *New Testament Apocrypha*, London: Lutterworth, pp. 353–64.
R. Ruether and E. McLaughlin, *Women of Spirit. Female Leadership in the Jewish and Christian Traditions*, New York: Simon and Schuster, 1979, pp. 37ff, 74ff.
D. Sawyer, *Women and Religion in the First Christian Centuries*, London: Routledge, 1996.

## The Acts of Paul and Thecla

7.   And while Paul was speaking in the midst of the church in the house of Onesiphorus a certain virgin named Thecla, the daughter of Theoclia, betrothed to a man named Thamyris, was sitting at the window close by and listened day and night to the discourse of virginity, as proclaimed by Paul. And she did not look away from the window, but was led on by faith, rejoicing exceedingly. And when she saw many women and virgins going in to Paul she also had an eager desire to be deemed worthy to stand in Paul's presence and hear the word of Christ. For she had not yet seen Paul in person, but only heard his word.

8.   As she did not move from the window her mother sent to Thamyris. And he came gladly as if already receiving her in marriage. And Thamyris said to Theoclia, 'Where, then, is my Thecla (that I may see her)?' And Theoclia answered, 'I have a strange story to tell you, Thamyris. For three days and three nights Thecla does not rise from the window either to eat or to drink; but looking earnestly as if upon some pleasant sight she is devoted to a foreigner teching deceitful and artful discourses, so that I wonder how a virgin of her great modesty exposes herself to such extreme discomfort.

9.   'Thamyris, this man will overturn the city of the Iconians and your Thecla too; for all the women and the young men go in to him to be taught by him. He says one must fear only one God and live in chastity. Moreover, my daughter, clinging to the window like a spider, lays hold of what is said by him with a strange eagerness and fearful emotion. For the virgin looks eagerly at what is said by him and has been captivated. But go near and speak to her, for she is betrothed to you.'

10.   And Thamyris greeted her with a kiss, but at the same time being afraid of her overpowering emotion said, 'Thecla, my betrothed, why do you sit thus?

And what sort of feeling holds you distracted? Come back to your Thamyris and be ashamed.' Moreover, her mother said the same, 'Why do you sit thus looking down, my child, and answering nothing, like a sick woman?' And those who were in the house wept bitterly, Thamyris for the loss of a wife, Theoclia for that of a child, and the maidservants for that of a mistress. And there was a great outpouring of lamentation in the house. And while these things were going on Thecla did not turn away but kept attending to the word of Paul.

11.    And Thamyris, jumping up, went into the street, and watched all who went in to Paul and came out. And he saw two men bitterly quarrelling with each other and he said to them, 'Men, who are you and tell me who is this man among you, leading astray the souls of young men and deceiving virgins so that they should not marry but remain as they are? I promise you money enough if you tell me about him, for I am the chief man of this city.'

12.    And Demas and Hermogenes said to him, 'Who he is we do not know. But he deprives the husbands of wives and maidens of husbands, saying, "There is for you no resurrection unless you remain chaste and do not pollute the flesh."'

13.    And Thamyris said to them, 'Come into my house and refresh yourselves.' And they went to a sumptuous supper and much wine and great wealth and a splendid table. And Thamyris made them drink, for he loved Thecla and wished to take her as wife. And during the supper Thamyris said, 'Men, tell me what is his teaching that I also may know it, for I am greatly distressed about Thecla, because she so loves the stranger and I am prevented from marrying.'

14.    And Demas and Hermogenes said, 'Bring him before the Governor Castellius because he persuades the multitude to embrace the new teaching of the Christians, and he will destroy him and you shall have Thecla as your wife. And we shall teach you about the resurrection which he says is to come, that it has already taken place in the children and that we rise again, after having come to the knowledge of the true God.'

15.    And when Thamyris heard these things he rose up early in the morning and, filled with jealousy and anger, went into the house of Onesiphorus with rulers and officers and a great crowd with batons and said to Paul, 'You have deceived the city of the Iconians and especially my betrothed bride so that she will not have me! Let us go to the governor Castellius!' And the whole crowd cried, 'Away with the sorcerer for he has misled all our wives!', and the multitude was also incited.

16.    And Thamyris standing before the tribunal said with a great shout, 'O proconsul, this man – we do not know where he comes from – makes virgins averse to marriage. Let him say before you why he teaches thus.' But Demas and Hermogenes said to Thamyris, 'Say that he is a Christian and he will die at once.' But the governor kept his resolve and called Paul, saying, 'Who are you and what do you teach? For they bring no small accusation against you.'

17.    And Paul, lifting up his voice, said, 'If I today must tell any of my teachings then listen, O proconsul. The living God, the God of vengeance, the jealous God, the God who has need of nothing, who seeks the salvation of men, has sent me that I may rescue them from corruption and uncleanness and from all pleasure, and from death, that they may sin no more. On this account God sent his

Son whose gospel I preach and teach, that in him men have hope, who alone has had compassion upon a world led astray, that men may be no longer under judgement but may have faith and fear of God and knowledge of honesty and love of truth. If then I teach the things revealed to me by God what harm do I do, O proconsul?' When the governor heard this he ordered Paul to be bound and sent to prison until he had time to hear him more attentively.

18.  And Thecla, by night, took off her bracelets and gave them to the gate-keeper; and when the door was opened to her she went into the prison. To the jailer she gave a silver mirror and was thus enabled to go in to Paul and, sitting at his feet, she heard the great deeds of God. And Paul was afraid of nothing, but trusted in God. And her faith also increased and she kissed his bonds.

19.  And when Thecla was sought for by her family and Thamyris they were hunting through the streets as if she had been lost. One of the gatekeeper's fellow slaves informed them that she had gone out by night. And they examined the gate-keeper who said to them, 'She has gone to the foreigner in the prison.' And they went and found her, so to say, chained to him by affection. And having gone out from there they incited the people and informed the governor what had happened.

20.  And he ordered Paul to be brought before the tribunal, but Thecla was riveted to the place where Paul had sat whilst in prison. And the governor ordered her also to be brought to the tribunal, and she came with an exceedingly great joy. And when Paul had been led forth the crowd vehemently cried out, 'He is a sorcerer. Away with him!' But the governor gladly heard Paul speak about the holy works of Christ. And having taken counsel, he summoned Thecla and said, 'Why do you not marry Thamyris, according to the law of the Iconians?' But she stood looking earnestly at Paul. And when she gave no answer Theoclia, her mother, cried out saying, 'Burn the wicked one; burn her who will not marry in the midst of the theatre, that all the women who have been taught by this man may be afraid.'

21.  And the governor was greatly moved, and after scourging Paul he cast him out of the city. But Thecla he condemned to be burned. And immediately the governor arose and went away to the theatre. And the whole multitude went out to witness the spectacle. But as a lamb in the wilderness looks around for the shep-herd, so Thecla kept searching for Paul. And having looked into the crowd she saw the Lord sitting in the likeness of Paul and said, 'As if I were unable to endure, Paul has come to look after me.' And she gazed upon him with great earnestness, but he went up into heaven.

22.  And the boys and girls brought wood and straw in order that Thecla might be burned. And when she came in naked the governor wept and admired the power that was in her. And the executioners arranged the wood and told her to go up on the pile. And having made the sign of the cross she went up on the pile. And they lighted the fire. And though a great fire was blazing it did not touch her. For God, having compassion upon her, made an underground rumbling, and a cloud full of water and hail overshadowed the theatre from above, and all its con-tents were poured out so that many were in danger of death. And the fire was put out and Thecla saved.

23.   And Paul was fasting with Onesiphorus and his wife and his children in a new tomb on the way which led from Iconium to Daphne. And after many days had been spent in fasting the children said to Paul, 'We are hungry.' And they had nothing with which to buy bread, for Onesiphorus had left the things of this world and followed Paul with all his house. And Paul, having taken off his cloak, said, 'Go, my child, sell this and buy some loaves and bring them.' And when the child was buying them he saw Thecla their neighbour and was astonished and said, 'Thecla, where are you going?' And she said, 'I have been saved from the fire and am following Paul.' And the child said, 'Come, I shall take you to him; for he has been mourning for you and praying and fasting six days already.'

24.   And when she had come to the tomb Paul was kneeling and praying, 'Father of Christ, let not the fire touch Thecla but stand by her, for she is yours'; she, standing behind him, cried out, 'O Father who made the heaven and the earth, the Father of your beloved Son Jesus Christ, I praise you that you have saved me from the fire that I may see Paul again.' And Paul, rising up, saw her and said, 'O God, who knows the heart, Father of our Lord Jesus Christ, I praise you because you have speedily heard my prayer.'

25.   And there was great love in the tomb as Paul and Onesiphorus and the others all rejoiced. And they had five loaves and vegetables and water, and they rejoiced in the holy works of Christ. And Thecla said to Paul, 'I will cut my hair off and I shall follow you wherever you go.' But he said, 'Times are evil and you are beautiful. I am afraid lest another temptation come upon you worse than the first and that you do not withstand it but become mad after men.' And Thecla said, 'Only give me the seal in Christ, and no temptation shall touch me.' And Paul said, 'Thecla, be patient; you shall receive the water.'

26.   And Paul sent away Onesiphorus and all his family to Iconium and went into Antioch, taking Thecla with him. And as soon as they had arrived a certain Syrian, Alexander by name, an influential citizen of Antioch, seeing Thecla, became enamoured of her and tried to bribe Paul with gifts and presents. But Paul said, 'I know not the woman of whom you speak, nor is she mine.' But he, being of great power, embraced her in the street. But she would not endure it and looked about for Paul. And she cried out bitterly, saying, 'Do not force the stranger; do not force the servant of God. I am one of the chief persons of the Iconians and because I would not marry Thamyris I have been cast out of the city.' And taking hold of Alexander, she tore his cloak and pulled off his crown and made him a laughing-stock.

27.   And he, although loving her, nevertheless felt ashamed of what had happened and led her before the governor; and as she confessed that she had done these things he condemned her to the wild beasts. The women of the city cried out before the tribunal, 'Evil judgement! impious judgement!' And Thecla asked the governor that she might remain pure until she was to fight with the wild beasts. And a rich woman named Queen Tryphaena, whose daughter was dead, took her under her protection and had her for a consolation.

28.   And when the beasts were exhibited they bound her to a fierce lioness, and Queen Tryphaena followed her. And the lioness, with Thecla sitting upon her,

licked her feet; and all the multitude was astonished. And the charge on her inscription was 'Sacrilegious.' And the women and children cried out again and again, 'O God, outrageous things take place in this city.' And after the exhibition Tryphaena received her again. For her dead daughter Falconilla had said to her in a dream, 'Mother, receive this stranger, the forsaken Thecla, in my place, that she may pray for me and I may come to the place of the just.'

29.  And when, after the exhibition, Tryphaena had received her she was grieved because Thecla had to fight on the following day with the wild beasts, but on the other hand she loved her dearly like her daughter Falconilla and said, 'Thecla, my second child, come, pray for my child that she may live in eternity, for this I saw in my sleep.' And without hesitation she lifted up her voice and said, 'My God, Son of the Most High, who are in heaven, grant her wish that her daughter Falconilla may live in eternity.' And when Thecla had spoken Tryphaena grieved very much, considering that such beauty was to be thrown to the wild beasts.

30.  And when it was dawn Alexander came to her, for it was he who arranged the exhibition of wild beasts, and said, 'The governor has taken his seat and the crowd is clamouring for us; get ready, I will take her to fight with the wild beasts.' And Tryphaena put him to flight with a loud cry, saying, 'A second mourning for my Falconilla has come upon my house, and there is no one to help, neither child for she is dead, nor kinsman for I am a widow. God of Thecla, my child, help Thecla.'

31.  And the governor sent soldiers to bring Thecla. Tryphaena did not leave her but took her by the hand and led her away saying, 'My daughter Falconilla I took away to the tomb, but you, Thecla, I take to fight the wild beasts.' And Thecla wept bitterly and sighed to the Lord, 'O Lord God, in whom I trust, to whom I have fled for refuge, who did deliver me from the fire, reward Tryphaena who has had compassion on your servant and because she kept me pure.'

32.  And there arose a tumult: the wild beasts roared, the people and the women sitting together were crying, some saying, 'Away with the sacrilegious person!', others saying, 'O that the city would be destroyed on account of this iniquity! Kill us all, proconsul; miserable spectacle, evil judgement!'

33.  And Thecla, having been taken from the hands of Tryphaena, was stripped and received a girdle and was thrown into the arena. And lions and bears were let loose upon her. And a fierce lioness ran up and lay down at her feet. And the multitude of the women cried aloud. And a bear ran upon her, but the lioness went to meet it and tore the bear to pieces. And again a lion that had been trained to fight against men, which belonged to Alexander, ran upon her. And the lioness, encountering the lion, was killed along with it. And the women cried the more since the lioness, her protector, was dead.

34.  Then they sent in many beasts as she was standing and stretching forth her hands and praying. And when she had finished her prayer she turned around and saw a large pit full of water and said, 'Now it is time to wash myself.' And she threw herself in saying, 'In the name of Jesus Christ I baptize myself on my last day.' When the women and the multitude saw it they wept and said, 'Do not throw

yourself into the water!'; even the governor shed tears because the seals were to devour such beauty. She then threw herself into the water in the name of Jesus Christ, but the seals, having seen a flash of lightning, floated dead on the surface. And there was round her a cloud of fire so that the beasts could neither touch her nor could she be seen naked.

35.   But the women lamented when other and fiercer animals were let loose; some threw petals, others nard, others cassia, others amomum, so that there was an abundance of perfumes. And all the wild beasts were hypnotized and did not touch her. And Alexander said to the governor, 'I have some terrible bulls to which we will bind her.' And the governor consented grudgingly, 'Do what you will.' And they bound her by the feet between the bulls and put red-hot irons under their genitals so that they, being rendered more furious, might kill her. They rushed forward but the burning flame around her consumed the ropes, and she was as if she had not been bound.

36.   And Tryphaena fainted standing beside the arena, so that the servants said, 'Queen Tryphaena is dead.' And the governor put a stop to the games and the whole city was in dismay. And Alexander fell down at the feet of the governor and cried, 'Have mercy upon me and upon the city and set the woman free, lest the city also be destroyed. For if Caesar hear of these things he will possibly destroy the city along with us because his kinswoman, Queen Tryphaena, has died at the theatre gate.'

37.   And the governor summoned Thecla out of the midst of the beasts and said to her, 'Who are you? And what is there about you that not one of the wild beasts touched you?' She answered, 'I am a servant of the living God and, as to what there is about me, I have believed in the Son of God in whom he is well pleased; that is why not one of the beasts touched me. For he alone is the goal of salvation and the basis of immortal life. For he is a refuge to the tempest-tossed, a solace to the afflicted, a shelter to the despairing; in brief, whoever does not believe in him shall not live but be dead forever.'

38.   When the governor heard these things he ordered garments to be brought and to be put on her. And she said, 'He who clothed me when I was naked among the beasts will in the day of judgement clothe me with salvation.' And taking the garments she put them on.

And the governor immediately issued an edict saying, 'I release to you the pious Thecla, the servant of God.' And the women shouted aloud and with one voice praised God, 'One is the God, who saved Thecla', so that the whole city was shaken by their voices.

39.   And Tryphaena, having received the good news, went with the multitude to meet Thecla. After embracing her she said, 'Now I believe that the dead are raised! Now I believe that my child lives. Come inside and all that is mine I shall assign to you.' And Thecla went in with her and rested eight days, instructing her in the word of God, so that many of the maidservants believed. And there was great joy in the house.

40.   And Thecla longed for Paul and sought him, looking in every direction. And she was told that he was in Myra. And wearing a mantle that she had altered

so as to make a man's cloak, she came with a band of young men and maidens to Myra, where she found Paul speaking the word of God and went to him. And he was astonished at seeing her and her companions, thinking that some new temptation was coming upon her. And perceiving this, she said to him, 'I have received baptism, O Paul; for he who worked with you for the gospel has worked with me also for baptism.'

41.    And Paul, taking her, led her to the house of Hermias and heard everything from her, so that he greatly wondered and those who heard were strengthened and prayed for Tryphaena. And Thecla rose up and said to Paul, 'I am going to Iconium.' Paul answered, 'Go, and teach the word of God.' And Tryphaena sent her much clothing and gold so that she could leave many things to Paul for the service of the poor.

42.    And coming to Iconium she went into the house of Onesiphorus and fell upon the place where Paul had sat and taught the word of God, and she cried and said, 'My God and God of this house where the light shone upon me, Jesus Christ, Son of God, my help in prison, my help before the governors, my help in the fire, my help among the wild beasts, you alone are God and to you be glory for ever. Amen.'

43.    And she found Thamyris dead but her mother alive. And calling her mother she said, 'Theoclia, my mother, can you believe that the Lord lives in heaven? For if you desire wealth the Lord will give it to you through me; or if you desire your child, behold, I am standing beside you.'

And having thus testified, she went to Seleucia and enlightened many by the word of God; then she rested in a glorious sleep.

# Chapter 3

# Pelagius (late fourth and early fifth centuries CE)

On the Christian Life
On Riches

Pelagius' reputation as the foe of Augustine so dominates interest in him that the wider theological and ethical concerns easily get lost. Nevertheless that more optimistic view of human betterment which is evident in the teachings of Pelagius and his followers suggests the possibility of human betterment and the reform of this world. Such perfectionism is an ongoing feature of Christianity, not least among its radical exponents down the centuries. In antiquity such views were linked with the kind of perfectionism inherent in the emerging monastic practices. Pelagius' sentiments expressed in his outline of what constitutes a Christian life probably seems to be the stuff of orthodox Christianity to a modern reader, but the prioritization of action is a feature of many of the texts in this collection.

By far the most radical text dealing with the subject of wealth in Christian antiquity is the document *De Divitiis (On Riches)*, which was either written by Pelagius or one of his disciples in the fifth century. Pelagius was a British theologian who achieved fame as the target of Augustine of Hippo's theological ire for suggesting that it was essential for Christians to practise good works as part of their path to salvation. The *De Divitiis* is criticized by Augustine (*Letters* 156, 157, see B. R. Rees, *Pelagius*, p. 173). It offers a potent critique of wealth and property, even if it stops short of advocating community of goods. Nor does it suggest that the possession of wealth is wrong. It is rather something which is likely to lead to sin. Nevertheless wealth is seen as the result of covetousness and theft, and is the cause of violence. Wealth causes difference of status between rich and poor and blinds the rich to the equality of humanity shared by both. Like other writers the author of *De Divitiis* appeals to the equal share of nature. The author criticizes those who use fanciful scriptural interpretation to allow them to avoid the plain meaning of the text and dismisses those who look to the examples of wealthy men from the Old Testament in preference to the example of Christ. There is a pointed comment on the double standards which are applied by those who want to avoid the plain sense of the scriptural text. The writer rejects the notion that it is more important to have one's life straightened before giving away one's wealth. A link is made between wealth and political power. The rich are the ones who seek to sit on the tribunals, such as the one before which Christ stood when he was on trial, which provokes devastating critique of the consequences of such political involvement.

In the emerging Christendom, post-Constantine, *De Divitiis* offers a clarion call to Christians to look closely at their profession of faith and to note the discrepancy between their beliefs and their practice. *De Divitiis* tackles the views of an imaginary opponent. The argument is quite simple: wealth is an obstacle to salvation. It takes a much harder line than is found in Clement of Alexandria's *Quis dives salvetur? De Divitiis* is evidence that the subversive challenge of the foundation documents of the Christian church were to haunt an organization, particularly at those times when its place in the social fabric seemed most snug and secure. It took the writing of what came to be regarded as a heretical school to remind mainstream Christianity of the sharpness of Jesus' challenge about wealth and property.

## Source

B. R. Rees, *Pelagius. Life and Letters*, Woodbridge: Boydell, 1998, pp. 123–4, 174–211.

## Further reading

R. S. T. Haslehurst, *The Works of Fastidius*, London: Westminster House, 1927.
C. Avila, *Ownership. Early Christian Teaching*, Maryknoll: Orbis, 1983.
P. D. A. Garnsey and C. Humfress, *The Evolution of the Late Antique World*, Cambridge: Orchard, 2001.
M. Hengel, *Property and Riches in Early Christianity*, London: SCM Press, 1974.
A. Kessler, *Reichumskritik und Pelagianismus: die pelagianische Diatribe de divitiis*, Freiburg: Universitätsverlag, 1999.
J. A. Ryan, *Alleged Socialism of the Church Fathers*, Saint Louis: Herder, 1913.
G. de Sainte Croix, *The Class Struggle in the Ancient Greek World*, London: Duckworth 1981.

## *On the Christian Life*

13, 6.    And I read that our Saviour said in a certain passage: Not every one who says to me, Lord, Lord, shall enter the kingdom of heaven, but they who do the will of my Father who is in heaven (Mt. 7:21). Without doubt those who called him Lord believed in Christ; but it is not for this reason – that they confess with their lips him whom they deny by their deeds – that the gate of the heavenly kingdom is opened to them. The apostle has also said that God is denied by deeds no less than by words: They profess to know God, but they deny him by their deeds (Tit. 1:16). And in the gospel the Lord says: On that day many will say to me, 'Lord, Lord, did we not cast out demons in your name, and do many mighty works in your name?' And I will declare to them, 'I never knew you; depart from me, all you evildoers' (Mt. 7:22,23). They are said to have believed to the extent that they also performed good works in the name of the Lord, but their faith alone will not profit them, because they have not done works of righteousness. So, if faith only profits, why are those who are judged not for their faithfulness but for having done nothing that is good delivered along with Satan's angels to the fires of hell for ever, as it is written: And the King will say to those at his left hand, 'Depart from me, you cursed, into the eternal fire prepared for the devil and his angels; for I was hungry and you gave me no food' (Mt. 25:41,42). Surely he did not say to them, 'Because you did not believe in me'; hence it is possible to understand that they are to be damned not because of unbelief but on account of their lack of good works.

14, 1.   Let no one therefore deceive another or mislead him: unless a man has been righteous, he has not life; unless a man has kept Christ's commandments in all things, he cannot share with him; unless a man has despised worldly things, he shall not receive those which are divine; unless he has spurned human things, he cannot gain possession of those which are heavenly; and let no man judge himself to be Christian, unless he is one who both follows the teaching of Christ and imitates his example. Do you consider a man to be a Christian by whose bread no hungry man is ever filled, by whose drink no thirsty man is refreshed, whose table no one knows, beneath whose roof neither stranger nor traveller comes at any time, with whose clothes no naked man is covered, by whose help no poor man is sustained, whose good deed no one experiences, whose mercy no one knows, who imitates the good in no respect but rather mocks and insults them and does not cease to persecute the poor? Let such a thought be far from the minds of all Christians, let it be impossible that one who is such a man should be called a son of God.

2.   *He* is a Christian who follows the way of Christ, who imitates Christ in all things, as it is written: He who says he abides in him ought to walk in the same way in which he walked (1 Jn. 2:6). *He* is a Christian who shows compassion to all, who is not at all provoked by wrong done to him, who does not allow the poor to be oppressed in his presence, who helps the wretched, who succours the needy, who mourns with the mourners, who feels another's pain as if it were his own, who is moved to tears by the tears of others, whose house is common to all, whose door is closed to no one, whose table no poor man does not know, whose food is offered to all, whose goodness all know and at whose hands no one experiences injury, who serves God day and night, who ponders and meditates upon his commandments unceasingly, who is made poor in the eyes of the world so that he may become rich before God, who is held to be without fame among men so that he may appear renowned before God and his angels, who is seen to have no feigning or pretence in his heart, whose soul is open and unspotted, whose conscience is faithful and pure, whose whole mind is on God, whose whole hope

is in Christ, who desires heavenly things rather than earthly, who spurns human possessions so that he may be able to possess those that are divine. Listen then to what is said to those who love this world and take pride and pleasure in the present time: Do you not know that friendship with this world is enmity with God? And whoever wishes to be a friend of this world makes himself an enemy of God (Jas. 4:4).

## On Riches

6, 1.   . . . Note carefully, I beg you, what a great sign of arrogance and pride it is to want to be rich when we know that Christ was poor, and to take upon ourselves any of the power that comes with lordship, when he took on the outward form of a servant, as it is written: Have this in mind among yourselves, which is yours in Christ Jesus, who, though he was in the form of God, did not count equality with God a thing to be grasped, but emptied himself, taking the form of a servant (Phil. 2:5–8). Surely everyone who is called a Christian professes that he is Christ's disciple, and Christ's disciple should follow his teacher's example in all things, so that in the deportment and conduct of the pupil his manner and doctrine may be in accord with that of his master.

2.   What pattern of Christ is revealed in such a rich man? What likeness to him is shown in such a possessor of wealth? How can poverty be compared with affluence? What has humility in common with pride? What similarity is there between the man who has nothing and the man who has superfluous possessions? I shall say no more about material fortune; but let us see if the rich man's way of life has any similarity with that of Christ. There is none that I can see: the one is haughty, the other downcast; the one is proud, the other humble; the one is full of fury, the other of gentleness; the one is angry, the other long-suffering; the one is boastful, the other self-effacing; the one abhors the poor, the other embraces them, the one abuses them, the other extols them. The rich, with that vainglorious and proud spirit in which they covet for themselves the glory of this world, are sometimes accustomed to solicit earthly power and to take their seat upon that tribunal before which Christ stood and was heard. How intolerable is the presumption of human pride! You may see the servant sitting where the master stood, and judging where he was judged. What is this, Christian? What is this, disciple of Christ? This is not the pattern given by your teacher. *He* stood humbly before the tribunal; *you* sit on the tribunal, above those who stand before you, propped up by your pride, perhaps about to judge a poor man. *You* ask the questions, *he* was heard; *you* judge, *he* was subjected to the judge's decision; in your presumption *you* utter your judgement, in his innocence *he* received it, as if guilty; *he* said that his kingdom was not of this world, but to *you* the glory of a worldly kingdom is so desirable that you procure it at vast expense or acquire it with unworthy and wearisome servitude and flattery.

3.   And all the time you convince yourself that it is from God that you receive what, in fact, you either procure with your ill-gotten gains or acquire at the price

of shameful sycophancy and oft-repeated acts of obeisance, bowing your head to the ground and addressing as 'Lord' one whom you scorn, while he, the trafficker in offices, also scorns you; and sometimes you glory in being called 'honourable', though the only true honour is that which is paid to moral character, not that acquired by money or shameful servitude. Before your eyes human bodies, of a like nature to yours, are battered with a scourge of lead or broken with cudgels or torn apart with claws or burnt in the flames. Yet all this your holy eyes can bear to witness and your Christian disposition permits you to watch – and not only to watch but even to exercise the authority given you by your exalted rank and administer the torture yourself in the place of the executioner. I find the spectator quite loathsome enough; what am I now to say of the one who gives the orders? Reflect with me, earthly judge: does some hardening of the heart render you immune and exempt from the suffering endured by one who is of the same nature as yourself, or does the pain of his human body somehow fail to penetrate to the feelings of your human heart? . . .

5.   What is the reason, I beg you, for so great a discrepancy between persons who are called Christians by the same name and are bound by solemn obligation to the same religion that some of them engage in such unholy acts of cruelty that they are not afraid to oppress, rob, torture and, finally, kill, while others are so frightened by their feelings of compassion and sense of duty that they fear to be lacking in mercy to those whom the others have destroyed without any fear at all. It is worth giving careful consideration to what causes such diversity in men of the same faith. Has the same law of Christian conduct not been given to all who are called Christians? Or are they perhaps bound by two kinds of commandments different from each other, one by which some are by necessity bound to fulfil the obligations of compassion and sense of duty, the other by which others are given leave to perform acts of irresponsible cruelty? Or is a cooler fire made ready in hell for those whom it pleases to commit cruel acts and a hotter one for those who must practise godliness? We know that we are 'one body', in the words of the apostle (1 Cor. 12:13); if we are truly one, then we should act as one. There is no room for such variety in the same people. Let us search the scriptures and weigh up with serious and careful thought which law we should adhere to and then choose one of these two alternatives, either to be compassionate or, shocking though it may be to hear, to live a life of professed cruelty, if that is what is expedient in our opinion. . . .

7, 1.   . . . the most skilful physician of our souls everywhere condemns the lust for riches which he knows to be the occasion of sin and would have us shudder at what is harmful, knowing that we are more easily detached from sin if its cause forsakes us.

2.   That is why he says in the Psalms: Put no confidence in extortion, set no vain hopes on robbery; if riches increase, set not your heart upon them (Ps. 62:10). Someone will say, 'In this passage he appears not to have been warning us against riches in general but specifically against seeking after them.' Yes, but what else is the chief source of riches but extortion and robbery? I can give a most convinc-

ing proof of this fact by pointing out that we know that nearly all those who were once poor and whom we can now see becoming rich can become so only by extortion and robbery.

3. 'That,' you will say, 'may be true of those who were once poor and have become rich; but what of those whom we know to have become rich as the result of inheriting their parents' wealth and are properly described as 'born rich'? They certainly appear to be able to possess riches acquired not by extortion but by just inheritance; but I was talking not so much of the possession of riches as of their source, since I think that they can hardly have been acquired without some injustice.

4. 'How can you know the source of these riches,' you will say, 'when you do not know when they started?' I know the present from the past, and I also understand what I have not seen from what I see. If you were to ask me how men or herds or flocks or all the manifold variety of living things were born a thousand years ago, I would reply that it was in every case by coition. And if you were to say to me, 'How can you know that?', I would reply that I infer the past from the present and that I am confident that every effect which I see to have a certain cause now had the same cause then too, when I was unable to see it.

5. 'So riches are sinful?' Well, I do not say that they are sinful in themselves but I do think that for the most part they are the result of sin. And if you are willing to discuss the matter with me in a peaceable spirit and not in anger and to cease to defend in a contentious manner the possessions with which you have fallen in love, and, setting aside all inclinations to perverseness, to listen to the voice of true reason in a calm and serene frame of mind, then perhaps I might be able to prove to you that it is wicked to hang on to riches with too tight a hold.

8, 1. Does it seem just to you then that one man should have an abundance of riches over and above his needs, while another does not have enough even to supply his daily wants? That one man should relax in the enjoyment of his wealth, while another wastes away in poverty? That one man should be full to bursting-point with expensive and sumptuous banquets far in excess of nature's habitual requirements, while another has not even enough cheap food to satisfy him. That one man should possess a vast number of splendid houses adorned with costly marble statues in keeping with the instincts of his vanity and pride, while another has not even a tiny hovel to call his own and to protect him from the cold or the heat? That one man should maintain countless possessions and enormous expanses of land, while another cannot enjoy the possession even of a small portion of turf on which to sit down? That one man should be rich in gold, silver, precious stones and all kinds of material possessions, while another is harassed by hunger, thirst, nakedness and all kinds of poverty? Add to this the fact that we can see evil men abounding in excessive wealth and good men struggling with need and destitution, which makes us even more suspicious of the unfairness of this thing called riches.

2. 'What then?', you say, 'Do not riches come from God?' Whatever can be justly defended comes from God; but anything that is the result of injustice does

not come from God, because whatever is bestowed on us by God as its origin ought to be free from all suspicion of having an unjust origin. So we must first prove that there is no injustice in riches and only then can we believe that they come from God. Surely we can agree that God is equitable and just, nay more, that he is the source of all equity and justice. First I ask what theory of justice, what principle of equity permits one man to enjoy the freedom of plenty and another to suffer the constraints of need. And if we know that some are rich by God's decree, while others are poor, how is it that we can sometimes see their positions reversed and very often undergoing a change to the opposite? How many poor men we know who were once rich, how many again who were once poor and are now rich! If these things had been so ordered at the beginning by God's decree, none of them could have changed to the opposite.

3.   I beg you, therefore, to set aside all spirit of contention and to surrender and abandon your defence of the possessions that you love and reflect upon my words with a sincere and unprejudiced mind, examining the force of my remarks not as an advocate of your own cause but as a searcher after truth. If God had decreed that there should be inequality in all things, surely he would have made an unequal distribution of the gifts of his creation to all men and would not have allowed men whom he wished to be unequal in respect of his lesser gifts to be equal in respect of his greater gifts, and those who ought to be unequal in every respect would not be receiving to an equal degree the benefits of the sky, the earth or any element. Reflect then how those elements serve the needs of the human race which are distributed not according to men's judgement but by God's will, and you will then be able to infer a few truths from many and to understand lesser truths from greater. Observe whether the rich man enjoys the benefit of this air of ours more than the poor, whether he feels the sun's heat more or less, or, when rain is given to the land, whether larger drops descend on the rich man's soil than upon the poor man's, whether the glowing lights of the moon or the stars serve the rich man more than the poor. Do you not see then that we possess equally with others all the things which are not under our control but which we receive by God's dispensation, and on unjust and unequal terms only the things which are entrusted and subjected to our own rule for the sake of free choice and to test our righteousness?

4.   But, to say no more on those matters, let us turn to the mysteries of the sacraments and consider if any inequality can be found in them which affects the situation of the human race. Let us see if there is one law for the rich and another for the poor, if the former are reborn by one kind of baptism and the latter by another, if they do not obtain the same pardon for sin and the same sanctification of righteousness, if they are not all endowed with the one spirit, if they do not feed on the communion of the same altar and drink of the one holy draught. But if God the Dispenser's indulgence towards mankind is found to be equally distributed in things material and spiritual alike, it now begins to become clear that this inequality in the dispensation of riches must be ascribed not to divine favour but to human injustice. For why would God want men to be unequal in the lesser things, when he has made them equal in the greater? Is it not perhaps more fitting

that he who receives the gifts of heaven without discrimination should also obtain the benefits of this world on equal terms with you? For I assume that the Holy Spirit should be preferred to all the honours and riches of this world. Do you suppose that he who is worthy to possess along with you that which is greater is unworthy to possess that which is less?

5.   I ask you to answer this question too, you who think that riches are given by God: to whom do you suppose he gives them, the good or the bad? If to the good, why is it that the bad have them? If to the bad, why do the good have them? If both to the good and to the bad, why do the majority, whether good or bad, not have them? But if you say that riches are bestowed by God on the good but by the devil on the bad, I shall first ask why all good men do not rejoice in this gift of God's; secondly, I shall add that it is no great boon if God seems to bestow on the good what the devil can present to the bad . . .

10, 1.   In what manner then are we to imitate Christ? In poverty, if I am not mistaken, not in riches; in humility, not in pride; not in worldly glory; by despising money, not by coveting it. And what are the commandments of the new covenant that we are to keep? First and foremost, those by which the occasion of sin is to be removed through contempt of riches. That is why you will find that the Lord gave no commandment to those who desire to follow him and to offer themselves as his disciples, which was of higher priority than to despise riches and the world, as he demonstrated to the man who offered himself on one occasion as his follower how he might follow him in the way he ought to follow, by saying: Foxes have holes, and the birds of the air have nests; but the Son of Man has nowhere to lay his head (Mt. 8:20). That is to say: see whether you are able to be such a disciple that you can follow such a master; for it is easier for a poor man to follow a poor man, since the rich man rejects him, being ruled by his pride. Let there be an end to false allegory, now that we are furnished with the truth and now that it is not the approval of the reader that we are seeking but his improvement, it is not the ingenuity of the writer that is being presented to us but the truth of his subject matter that is being proclaimed.

2.   Likewise elsewhere: If you would be perfect, go, sell all that you possess and give to the poor, and you shall have treasure in heaven; and come, follow me (Mt. 19:21). You can see that not even this man is given permission to follow along the road to perfection until he has sold all that he has and distributed it to the poor. 'But,' you will say, 'it is his sins that he has to sell, not his property.' And where will he find a purchaser stupid enough to buy *them* – unless, perhaps, it be the person who understands the passage in such a sense? I do not know who is going to spend money in order to purchase something which is nothing but a nuisance even if you possess it free of charge. 'But,' you say, 'the devil will buy it.' I ask you, what price will the vendor get for it from *him*, and how will he distribute to the poor what he does get from him? 'Well then, it was a statement referring to the Jewish people as a whole, and the young man merely represented them symbolically.' Is the Jewish people the only one which is wealthy, the only one which riches can hinder, to which the kingdom of heaven opens its doors? 'He was rich,'

you will say, 'in the commandments of the law, and therefore he is commanded to divide them up and sell them off separately.' Here too I ask who will buy them, or why he is bidden to sell at a price what he had received free of charge? This is how they discuss the passage quoted and argue about it and debate it, simply because they prefer to watch jealously over their riches than to keep Christ's commands, and love money more than the glory of the kingdom.

3.   The Lord says the same thing again elsewhere: Unless a man renounce all that he has, he cannot be my disciple (Lk. 14:33). What will you say in this instance? I suppose you will say that he is ordered to renounce his sins, not his property. But is a man able to strip off all his sins *before* becoming Christ's disciple? If so, what more has he to gain by taking Christ as his Master? Or in what respect will he be in need of Christ's teaching if he has already become righteous through his own efforts? But I ask you this, 'Are sins possessed, or do they possess us?' If *they* are possessed, it will be possible to understand this saying to refer to them: Every man who does not renounce all his possessions cannot be my disciple (Lk. 14:33). But if, on the other hand, they possess *us*, no kind of reasoning permits us to interpret as referring to possessors what was actually said about possessions. To make it even clearer that our sins possess us rather than are possessed by us, listen to the Lord himself, when he says: Every one who commits sin is a slave to sin (Jn. 8:34). A slave, as I see it, does not possess but is possessed. And if that is so, whether you want or do not want to be rich, you have to understand the passage as referring to worldly goods.

4.   But when it has been established by clear reasoning that the statement refers not to sins but to worldly goods, they are in the habit of turning to another interpretation: they say, 'Of course these words have to be understood as referring to worldly resources but the command was given not to all men for all occasions but to certain men on certain occasions, that is, to the apostles, who had to follow their Lord in a variety of places and at that particular time when the Christian religion was putting forth its first shoots and believers were being continually harassed by the storms of persecution to such an extent that they were unable to remain in their own lands or retain their own possessions. Thus it was necessary for them to bow before the assaults of their persecutors and to distribute all their possessions, lest they lose all by being forced into flight. But now, when nearly all men are Christians through the Lord's graciousness and even kings and potentates have to submit their necks to Christ's yoke, times are peaceful and calm and we are safe from all the troubles of persecution; so it is not necessary for anyone either to distribute or sell his property, since it was not so much the needs of his religion as the stress of persecution that demanded this of him.' How ingenious the greedy can be! They never want for a reply in order to prevent the loss of what they love! But, in fact, the light of plain reasoning will establish that such an interpretation is incorrect.

5.   In answer to the first part of the interpretation which they now wish to adopt — namely, that the apostles alone were told to distribute all their possessions — I ask, 'When that young man approached the Lord and sought his advice as to what good he had to do in order to be able to earn the reward of eternal life,

was the number of the apostles complete at the time when those words were spoken?' I think it was already complete. Why then did Christ also say to him: If you would be perfect, go, sell all that you possess and give to the poor, and you shall have treasure in heaven; and come, follow me (Mt. 19:21), if only the apostles had to do this? And in the case of those who, in the Acts of the Apostles, undoubtedly sold all their possessions, some of them laying the price of what they sold at the apostles' feet, while others distributed them to the poor themselves, why were they willing to do this if they knew that only the apostles had to do it? Or if in their ignorance they supposed that an instruction given to particular individuals was really intended to be applied generally, then their inexperience ought to have derived enlightenment from the apostles' knowledge and an action resulting from ignorance to have been prevented on their authority from being done by those who came after them. But what if that act was not only not forbidden but laid down as approved and commended for posterity to imitate? If others were not supposed to do it, it ought to have been stopped right at the outset and no written record of it preserved for posterity to follow . . .

10.   Will you then say, 'Riches are not from God'? But who was it then that made gold and silver? Who placed precious stones in the earth which he had created? By whose decree was the earth founded? Or whose command was it that brought all things forth? Was it not God's? Who will deny this, unless he is either foolish or ungodly? Yet we should not think that all riches are from God merely because all those things are his which, when piled up in one heap, are called 'riches'. For, according to my earlier definition, I say that riches are not gold or silver or any other created thing but the superfluous wealth that is derived from unnecessary possessions. Whether this wealth comes from God, who must be believed to be the source of equity and justice, I leave you to decide for yourself. For it is agreed that God created the things which we have just mentioned along with the rest of his creation, yet not in order that one man should become wealthy by the possession of unlimited affluence while another is tormented by excessive poverty, but that all should possess impartially and with equal rights what the source of all justice has granted them.

11, 1.   Let the supporters of riches now reflect on these utterances, asking themselves whether riches alone have been overlooked by him who has impressed on others the need to observe whatever he had ordered the apostles to do. Perhaps you say: 'The command was given because of the critical circumstances of that time, in that men who had to avoid the unremitting attacks of persecution were unable to keep their possessions.' First I shall ask where have you read this, or what text of scripture has given you evidence to the effect that believers of this period distributed all their possessions as a result of flight or persecution. Or how did churches come to be founded in Jerusalem and throughout other cities, if all men had to forsake their property? It remains only for you to say that the churches were founded by foreigners and that the persecutors had more mercy on strangers than citizens!

2.   Well, yes, I shall agree with you that fugitives would have to distribute estates, houses or anything else which could be regarded as immovable for the

simple reason that they would be unable to carry them around with them through different countries. But were they unable to take money with them or carry it around? Or was it something of a hindrance to the fugitives, since a man would be more convinced of the need to flee or betake himself to foreign parts if the abundance of his resources enabled him to feel less anxious about meeting his expenses? If they sold their houses or lands or any other possessions which they disposed of for the sake of flight, why did they lay down the price of what they had sold at the apostles' feet, when they ought rather to have kept back enough to help them in their flight, having distributed all their possessions under that obligation? . . .

12, 1.   Let us then turn to that notorious statement which lovers of this world believe that they can present as a reasonable argument, when they maintain, under the pretext of upholding godliness, that the counsels of perfection in the gospels ought by no means to be kept. For they say, 'If all men are willing to distribute their possessions and to keep nothing at all for themselves, where would we then find works of godliness and compassion to perform, when the supply of objects to which to direct them have been exhausted?' Or, 'How are the poor to be sustained, where are guests to be entertained, from what source are the hungry to be fed, the naked covered and the thirsty given drink, if worldly wealth is lacking?' Great indeed is their love of compassion and godliness, if they care more for the poor than for God! And I would that they really cared for the poor and not rather for riches, which they try to defend on the pretext of helping the poor and under the pretence of being obliged to practise godliness, not realizing that some are in need because others have more than they need. Get rid of the rich man, and you will not be able to find a poor one. Let no man have more than he really needs, and everyone will have as much as they need, since the few who are rich are the reason for the many who are poor.

2.   But what sense is there in striving to achieve something which the 'perfect' were never bidden to do, while being unwilling to do what *was* bidden? We were told to possess nothing; but those who possess nothing were never given any command with regard to works of mercy. Observe then how wrongheaded and inconsistent it is to neglect to do what we have been bidden to do for the sake of something which we have not been bidden to do, and so to seem to be afraid to implement an order which was not given merely to avoid doing what was! Thus you say, 'If I have become poor, how can I give alms?' – as if you were ever bidden to give alms when you have nothing or to possess superfluous riches so as to be able to be always giving them. The apostles too ought then to have given this reply to the Lord when he either called the poor 'blessed' or laid down that the rich could not possess the kingdom of heaven, had they not been thinking rather of Christ's command than of the riches which are defended only as a means of helping the poor.

3.   You ask therefore, 'Who will there be any longer to do works of mercy, if all are striving to climb to the highest stage of perfection by renouncing their possessions?' But why do you not envisage the possibility that all men are able to

attain to the highest stage both of fulfilling the obligations of compassion and of achieving perfection, especially as you know that it is only by degrees that each individual advances and makes progress in faith? Surely we can see that there are two classes of people in the Church, though all confess the same Lord – the catechumens and those who, after being catechumens, are cleansed and sanctified by the divine laver – and no one can be a candidate for baptism without first having been a catechumen. And though there must be these two classes, yet both are pressing on to the same end; for they either cannot or ought not to belong to the same class for the reason that it is quite clear that there were two classes from the beginning. Why then do you not hold the same opinion in the matter of compassion and perfection, that is, that we have first to attain to all the stages required by the obligations of compassion, yet nevertheless try to climb to the heights of perfection, and not abandon the highest stage of compassion because we are all striving to reach perfection, since, as I have said, the higher stage of perfection is reached only by degrees? To take an example from ordinary life, there are many classes in an orator's school but all are hastening to reach the highest. Yet the lower classes are not entirely empty because everyone is striving to reach the highest.

4.   You are afraid that, if you renounce riches, if you renounce all the resources of this world, there will be no one to do works of compassion. Are you then the only possessor of property in the whole world, so that you fear that you can have no successor? I do not want you to defend your avarice on the pretext of compassion or with the excuse of helping the poor. Achieve your aim and climb from the lower class to the higher; your place will not be left empty: whenever a man has been baptized or becomes a catechumen, his place will be filled.

13, 1.   Perhaps you say, 'And where shall I get food to enable me to live, if I have renounced all my possessions?' Ah, I can now see the reason why perhaps riches are boldly defended and the purpose served by the other arguments: it is, of course, our little faith, which we strive in vain to conceal under the pretext of compassion, while refusing to believe the Lord's promise when he says: Do not consider what you shall eat or what you shall drink or what you shall wear. For the gentiles seek these things; and your Father knows that you need them all. But seek first the kingdom of God and his righteousness, and all these things shall be set before you (Mt. 6:31–33). And he confounds our little faith by citing the example of the birds of the air and the lilies of the field. And lest with your customary perversity in interpretation you should judge that this was said for the benefit of the apostles alone, he added, 'For the gentiles seek these things' – not 'other Christians besides the apostles' . . .

14, 1.   'But,' you will say, 'it will be a source of confusion, if the man who has been accustomed to give to others now receives from them.' If you were afraid of confusion, why were you so willing to give your allegiance to one whose mysteries are such a source of confusion to this world? For his birth and Passion and the whole course of his life after taking upon himself human form cause more than a modicum of confusion to unbelievers. But the Lord says of such things: Whoever shall confound me before men, I will also confound before my Father who is in heaven (Mt. 10:33). So you can see that we are ashamed to keep God's commandments not because of the obligation to do works of compassion but on account of men's confusion. We are too wise in matters of the flesh and are influenced by the understanding of the human mind more than by the force of the divine, and for this reason we make a serious and weighty mistake. We are ashamed of the whole way of life of Christ and his disciples, and yet we suppose that we belong to Christ; we are confused by their humility, poverty, shabby clothing and cheap and simple fare, by their mean treatment at the hands of this world, the abuse, the derision, the insults, by all those things, in fact, which we know to have been a cause for rejoicing not only to Christ himself but also to his apostles.

2.   On the other hand, we glory in pride, in riches, in splendid clothing, in agreeable food, in the nobility of this world, in the transitory praises of men. Anyone who has come to us poor after the pattern of Christ, of whom it is written that 'he had no comeliness or beauty, but his face was despised' (Is. 53:2), is provoked, mocked and ridiculed in the manner of the Jews and, like him whose form and likeness he bears, is judged to be a deceiver and a traitor. But if anyone, however unbelieving and encompassed by a variety of sins and wrongdoing, comes to us distinguished in appearance and clothed in splendid apparel befitting his rank, he is given pride of place over all the poor, however holy their lives, contrary to the apostle's command, and this world's style is preferred to the pattern of Christ (cf. Jas. 2:1–3). But we believe that, by carrying on practices of this kind, we are following the mind and example of Christ, and we are 'confused', I suppose, in our attitude to all those things in which the example of Christ is portrayed, while glorying in all those which are appropriate to the honour of this world! We do firmly believe that our teachers, after Christ, are his apostles. Why then are we ashamed to live by the example of those whose disciples we profess to be?

15, 1.   'But it is better for me to live off my own resources rather than set my hopes on another's.' So far as human wisdom goes, it is indeed rated better; but by the standards of the divine wisdom I think that the apostles, who were sustained by others' wealth, were better than those who retained their own possessions. 'Then why,' you will say, 'does the apostle Paul say: Remember the word of Jesus, for he said. It is more blessed to give than to receive (Acts 20:35)?' But why is it then that we read that both he and his apostles received? Were those who gave more blessed than those who received? If it is more blessed to give than to receive, Paul received from the Macedonians, as he himself testifies, saying: For my needs were supplied by the brethren who came from Macedonia (2 Cor. 11:9). And if it is more blessed to give than to receive, then we must accept that the Macedonians were more blessed than Paul, since we know that they gave to him. What do we have to say about that young man who is commanded to distribute all his possessions? Not only would our Lord not have given him such an order but he would even have prevented him from carrying it out of his own volition lest, after distributing all his resources, he would no longer have the means of giving, if, that is, it was always better to give than to receive; for it is not right for us even to suspect from Christ's teaching that he would have placed in a less blessed state those who could have attained a greater one. How can that young man be told: If you would be perfect, go, sell all that you possess (Mt. 19:21), if it is more blessed to give than to receive, for the way of perfection is seen to lie where the greater state of blessing is to be found? . . .

16, 1.   But if we are to believe that the man who gives always attains the highest blessedness and yet he will not always be able to give unless he remains rich, why does God so often criticise the rich and eulogize the poor, since the latter, being able to attain to a higher state of blessedness, are more worthy to be praised? 'But it is the *evil* rich that he blames,' you will say. Did you then read: Woe to you *evil* that are rich! (cf. Lk. 6:24)? Or what need was there to add the label 'rich' at all, if he were not passing his judgement of condemnation upon them because of their riches? If he was rebuking the evil of men specifically, he would simply have said, 'Woe to you that are evil!' And if he is criticising not the rich in general but only the evil that are rich, he ought to have praised the rich that are good, if there are any such men to be found anywhere. And if you want his words, 'Woe to you that are rich!' to refer only to the evil rich, then he ought to say also of the good that are rich, 'Blessed are the rich'. He says quite clearly that there are men who are blessed but they are the poor (cf. Lk. 6:20); if he had said, 'Blessed are the rich', then he would have been seen to be reducing to an even lower state the very class of men whom he pronounces blessed for being the opposite.

2.   At this point I believe you will say, 'He praises the *good* poor'. Why then did he add the label 'poor', if he knew that no special mark of goodness was attached to poverty? For just as he would never have named riches in his statement of censure if he had not seen that they were worthy of censure, so too he would never have named poverty in his commendation of blessedness if he had felt that it was not aid to the attainment of goodness. I suppose that, in fact, the Word of God had left out from his utterance words which, if added, would have led to the censure of the evil and commendation of the good! Omitting the names of those attributes which, in some men's judgement, can neither hinder nor help, he would have said, 'Woe to you that are murderers or adulterers or greedy for plunder or idolaters or slaves to any other kind of vice or sin!' Why does he leave out all other sins and misdeeds and name only riches as an object of censure, as one who knows that they are frequently the cause of all our faults? Again, why does he omit the names of all the other virtues in praising the beatitudes and name only poverty, if he did not know that it is the source of *all* our virtues? And if he is not specifically addressing his censure to riches and his commendation to poverty by extolling it, he ought somewhere to have praised the rich and censured the poor. Since, however, he both censures the rich in general and commends the poor in general, he plainly and clearly demonstrated that, by the authority of his judgement, he both condemned the greed for riches and extolled the name of poverty.

17, 1.   I wish to add also something that no wise man will be able to dispute, namely, that it is difficult to acquire riches without committing every kind of evil. They are procured by calculated lies or clever theft or fraudulent deceit or robbery with violence or barefaced falsification. They are frequently accumulated by plunder of widows or oppression of orphans or bribery or, much more cruel still, by the shedding of innocent blood. If that is so, how can we imagine that something which is acquired by such a variety of crimes has the sanction of God? Far, far from our thoughts be a notion so ungodly! For God either forbids all the crimes mentioned above if they have not yet been committed, or condemns them when they have been perpetrated. So we can have no grounds whatsoever for regarding as conferred by God wealth which has been acquired by means which he forbids.

2.   'The wealth which I have amassed,' you will say, 'has accrued from legacies inherited from a variety of people.' This too can be most sinful if, by shutting out lawful heirs, you possess the goods of others which could have come to you only by employing deception or violent pressure. But let that pass, and let us suppose that nothing of the kind occurred and that they were bestowed on you freely and willingly: a just man always refuses to keep what has been given to him by an unjust will, and it is an unjust gift if it is bestowed on an heir who is no relation and poor parents are possibly excluded from inheriting.

3.   Hence the Lord deservedly censures and condemns excessive wealth, since he saw greed for it to be the cause of sin. For what wise or sensible man would doubt that greed is the occasion of all evils, the root of crimes, the fuel of wrong-doing, the source of transgressions? Because of it no one can live in safety or travel without fear on land, sea or anywhere else for that matter. It is through greed that we have pirates on the ocean waves, highwaymen on the roads, burglars in towns and villages, and plunderers everywhere; it is greed that motivates fraudulent practices, pillage, falsehood, perjury, false witness, cheating, ungodly and cruel acts and every conceivable kind of misdeed. For its sake the earth is daily stained with innocent blood, the poor man is stripped of his property, the wretched man is trodden underfoot and not even widows or orphans are spared. Greed drives men to spurn God's law almost every moment of the day and to outrage heaven's decrees by committing transgressions of all kinds one after the other; on account of it modesty is often assaulted, chastity over-powered, and shameless lust given free rein to revel in its forbidden pleasures; in order to satisfy it, parricide is often committed in thought or by deed, since a man will wish for his parents' death or even bring it about, when he is in haste to acquire riches and is driven to extremes by the force of his impatience and greed.

4.   For the sake of wealth men also learn to commit accursed acts of unspeakable, unmentionable wickedness and ungodliness and rush into the study and practice of arts which are both disgraceful and criminal. In the search for riches morals are often ruined, souls are destroyed, and every good feature of human nature is profaned. In a word, how many rich men are free from pride, arrogance, haughtiness and disdain? What man is there, however gentle, humble, patient, kindly and moderate in his poverty, who does not become puffed up with haughtiness, swollen with pride, inflamed with anger and goaded into madness as his riches increase?

When does a man of substance remember the frailty of his human condition? When does he not forget himself to such an extent that he imagines that he is not mortal? Or how can he ever realise what he is, when, from his proud and exalted position of eminence, he no longer deigns to know those who share his own human nature?

5.   And so, in his wretchedness, in his desire to cease to be the man he is, the worse he becomes the better he thinks he is, and, overwhelmed by the sheer mass of his evil deeds, makes himself the slave of sins which are perhaps as great as the riches of which he is the master. He despises the needy man, who is maybe as much richer than himself in moral integrity as he is poorer in worldly wealth, and in his lowly state cannot find consolation even in the contemplation of his Lord. Listen to him saying, 'Just look at him, outcast, ragamuffin, and baseborn; and *he* is the one who dares to say anything in the presence of people in *our* position and, in his rags and tatters, to discuss *our* morals and conduct and to try to disturb *our* consciences and force them to recognize the truth by rational debate!' As if the rich alone were permitted to speak, and riches, rather than thought, had the right to reason out the truth!

18, 1.   It is not in vain, then, that the Lord uses every opportunity to criticize and condemn riches, knowing, as he does, that greed for riches is the seedbed of all crimes. Nor was it without due cause that he as good as closed the entrance to the heavenly kingdom to rich men by his use of an analogy to illustrate the extreme difficulty which faced them, since he saw that they were entangled in all kinds of evil: It is easier for a camel to go through the eye of a needle than for a rich man to enter the kingdom of heaven (Mt. 19:24), he said. What need have we to debate any further a passage whose meaning is absolutely clear – unless it is necessary to remind rich men to recognize that they will be able to possess the glory of heaven only if they find a needle large enough for a camel to pass through its eye, and a camel so small that it can go through the very narrow entrance provided by such a needle? Or if this proves to be something which is quite impossible, how will it ever be possible to accomplish something which is by definition still more impossible? Only, perhaps, if the rich man makes a proper distribution of his wealth so as either to become poor or to leave himself with just enough to live on, and then strives to enter where a man of substance cannot.

2.   'But,' you will say, 'the reference is not to a camel, which cannot possibly go through the eye of a needle, but to a ship's hawser!' What an intolerable excess of ingenuity a man is forced to employ by his love of riches if he has to betake himself to names for ship's ropes in order to avoid being compelled to diminish his abundant supply of worldly resources! How blessed this ingenuity would be if only he could exercise such mental effort for the love of God! But a mind pre-occupied with worldly attachments has no room for heavenly love. However that may be, this is a very inadequate argument and will never help the rich man's cause. As if it were any more possible for such a large rope to pass through the eye of a needle than it is for that very large animal, the camel! You have still failed

to give enough thought to your examination of this matter, nor have you yet found an adequate form of defence which will enable you to live immune from punishment outside the heavenly abode. What help are you going to get from ships, whose gear is on such a huge scale? You will have to apply your ingenuity rather to a search through the weaver's stores to see if you can discover a thread there which is called 'a camel'! Such human folly must be subjected to at least a modicum of derision, however much one has to feel sorry for its wretchedness, so that men may realise that arguments which only succeed in provoking men to laughter will carry no weight with God.

3.   'But the difficulty involved in the definition given above,' you say, 'the Lord tempered, nay rather, removed entirely by a later reply when he said: What is impossible with men is possible with God (Lk. 18:27),' Certainly it is 'possible' not only for rich men with all their paraphernalia and faults to be received into heaven but also camels as well! If we are dealing with what is 'possible with God', we shall find no man who is excluded from his kingdom, because nothing can be found which is impossible with God. But how can the earlier utterance stand, when either it ought not to have been delivered at all, if it was going to be rescinded later by the exercise of God's power, or, if it had to be delivered, it ought never to have been possible to render it meaningless?

4.   It remains for us to try to interpret the meaning of the saying that what is seen to be impossible with men is possible with God. When the Lord denied admittance to the heavenly kingdom both to the man who was rich in possessions of every kind and to the man whose riches consisted of money only, on hearing his words of judgement, the disciples were smitten with the grief that comes with despair: they were not yet in possession of full and perfect knowledge, since among them rich men were by Jewish custom considered to be of great importance, because they were often seen to be performing works of compassion in proportion to the excessive wealth which they owned; nor did they yet know that a man who infringes even one commandment is held to be transgressing the whole law in accordance with the Lord's utterance.

5.   So they reconsidered the matter amongst themselves and said, 'If so difficult an illustration denies entry to the heavenly kingdom even to those who find it possible to fulfil every obligation of godliness by using their abundance of wealth in order to do so, what are we to think of the poor, who have not the means to enable them to perform works to compassion?' Their reply shows that this is what they thought. Thus they say, 'Who then can be saved?' (Mt. 19:25; Mk. 10:26; Lk. 18:26), as if no man can be saved if the rich could not or as if the rich alone constituted the whole human race, though the poor are much more numerous and scarcely one wealthy man can be found among a thousand who are needy. That is why his reply to that young man is: What is impossible with men is possible with God (Lk. 18:27), that is, 'What seems to human thought to be impossible, that anyone can be saved without an abundance of riches, is made much more possible with God in his wisdom: a humble and holy poverty gives him much greater pleasure than the proud and sinful ostentation of riches, and even the good which is found in the possession of riches can be difficult to achieve without the

accompaniment of evil, since it is performed not so much for the sake of deserving God's mercy as in order to acquire glory in the eyes of men.'

6. 'But,' you will say, 'God denied to the rich the kingdom of heaven, not the attainment of eternal life, because the man who is denied possession of the heavenly kingdom is not at once cut off from eternal life in consequence, since life is possible with or without a kingdom: for every man who reigns lives but not every man who lives also reigns.' My first question addressed to you is, 'Where do you find mention of this life which you locate outside the kingdom?', and the second, 'Can these men be saved who will have life without having the kingdom?' You say, 'I believe they can be saved.' Then why do the apostles say, 'Who then can be saved?', if they know that only the kingdom was denied to the rich? By this it is clearly and manifestly shown that where the kingdom is, there is life also, and that where life is, there is salvation also, and that when there is no salvation, there is also neither life nor kingdom, and those who are outside the limits of the kingdom cannot be saved.

7. 'But the word "camel",' you will say, 'refers to the gentiles: for in their case, though corrupted by every kind of vice and devoid of all virtue, yet because, like camels, they have bowed down and surrendered themselves to Christ's faith, it is foretold that they will have an easier passage through the eye of the needle, meaning the path of the narrow way to the kingdom than will the rich man, that is, the Jewish people.' But I have already argued earlier that the rich man cannot possibly be identified as the Jewish people; so now let us see whether the gentiles can properly be described as the camel. I ask first what reason requires us to obscure such an important issue by introducing a different nomenclature, and what prevented the gentiles from being called by their own name, and what was the motive for calling them by another. You say that it is because, like the aforesaid animal, they were distorted by their various crimes and sinfulness. Then there was no wickedness in the Jews, I suppose; or, if there was, why are they too not designated by an illustration which employs the same comparison? Or, I would like to know, why is this comparison with a camel appropriate to men who are corrupted by sin and vice? 'Because its body is not straight,' you will say, as if there were any animal which can be drawn in a straight line without any curve or bend in its bodily outline, especially one which is supplied with a variety of differently shaped limbs. And although it has a multiplicity of curves and bends, yet it is straight in its nature, and if it has of its own nature what it does have, it is without fault. And if it is without fault, how can it possibly be compared with a man whose corruption is the result not of his nature but of his free will?

8. 'Why then,' you say, 'does the Lord himself sometimes compare men to animals, for example, the Canaanites to dogs (Mt. 15:26), Herod to a fox (Lk. 13:22), the apostles to sheep (Mt. 10:16), and evil men and false prophets to wolves (Mt. 7:15)?' These comparisons refer not to bodily shape but to similarity of character, which even in animals themselves is controlled by a decision taken on a natural impulse. But you rightly call Herod a fox and the Canaanites dogs and the rest by the names by which they are called by the Lord; where, however, do you read that the gentiles are called camels, so that you have to call them by that same

name too? But if it is nowhere so written, how dare you adopt for your own use something which lacks the sanction of any scriptural authority? From what text have you learned that the needle's eye has to be understood to mean 'the narrow way'? And if that is the true interpretation, how is the camel, that is, a people corrupted by all sorts of sin and wickedness, to tread it, when on the authority of the Lord's utterance it is ordained that it is for the few persons who are righteous? For either the gentiles in their wickedness and sinfulness will be the camel and, however long they remain so, will be unable to enter upon the narrow way or, if they rid themselves of all their errors of unbelief and wickedness and become worthy to begin the journey along the track marked out for the straight way, then it will be no longer possible to call them 'the camel'.

9.   Now that we have explained the interpretation by which, according to the way in which some people understand it, it was the gentiles who were designated by the name of the aforesaid animal, it will follow that in this passage, whether in literal truth or according to an allegorical device, a camel is unable to pass through the eye of a needle.

10.   Again, what reason have we for believing that, when the narrow way and the kingdom of heaven have been conjoined and connected the one with the other, the Saviour then proceeded to separate them from one another? For if the needle's eye is 'the narrow way', why does he then say, 'it is easier for a camel to go through the eye of a needle than for a rich man to enter the kingdom of heaven'? When he says that the one thing is 'easier' than the other, he is making a total distinction between them, and, if it is such a very great distinction, then it cannot be applied to the narrow way, since it is conjoined to the heavenly kingdom, not separated from it.

11.   We must now consider the reason why those who are accustomed to discuss nearly all the Old Testament in allegorical and mystical terms but to understand the precepts and actions in the New Testament in a more literal and simple sense, on the grounds that the actions of the Old Testament figures foreshadowed the truth of those which are depicted in the New, yet in the sole matter of riches either forget or change their previous practice by reversing the process and using things done under the law to defend riches and by interpreting them simply and without mystical imagery; and why at the same time they strive to conceal the precepts of the gospel under a cloak of allegorical obfuscation with no regard for the simple, literal truth, as if in this instance alone the New Testament were a figure containing allusions to the Old, when we know that the Old offers an image of the New in every respect. For they want the riches of Abraham and David and Solomon and the rest to be understood literally; but when they read something about contempt of riches in the gospel, they exert themselves to adulterate its meaning by employing a metaphorical treatment of it, although, as we have already stated, it is more fitting to allegorize the commandments of the law than those of grace – unless, of course, they are trying by this means not so much to reinforce the scriptures as to defend the quality of their own way of life and, through false interpretation of the law and the use of every stratagem which their natural wit can devise, to protect what they love, not so much ordering their conduct accord-

ing to the precepts of the gospel as modifying their understanding of the commandments of the gospel to suit their habitual actions. What they want is not so
much to submit their way of life to the law as to subordinate the law to the way
in which they conduct their own lives, not to live as they have been commanded
to do but to adapt the commandments to the manner in which they live. Yet not
only will such an interpretation not help its authors but we have to believe it to
be a positive hindrance to them, since by it they are shown to be not only transgressing but also debasing the commands of heaven . . .

19, 7.   But I shall grant you that it is possible for you to have riches – riches, of
course, which have come to you by an inheritance from your parents honestly
acquired – in such a way that their possession involves no infection by sin but
rather supplies you with the means to do good works and not a cause of misdeeds. Let it be admitted that you may be a man of such virtue and goodness,
such discernment and good sense, that you are the only, or almost the only, person
or one of the very few persons able to turn to your own advantage the thing
which is the cause of permanent damage to the salvation of others. How many
are there who are as circumspect and prudent as you seem to be and so realize
that they ought not to acquire wealth for themselves by evil means and, if it comes
to them by honest means, try to use it in performing works of compassion and
obligation? *You* have riches which have been honestly acquired and possess them
in the right way, *you* perhaps have not obtained them unjustly but possess them
justly. But *others* cannot see how you acquired them or how you possess them;
they can only see that you have them, not how you got them or how you use
them. And since they only want to imitate what they see, they will commence to
seek riches by any means, fair or foul, and to commit many crimes in order to
appear your equals or superiors in the extent of their possessions, and so your
wealth will now become not so much an occasion of virtue as a cause of sin.

8.   'But for me,' you will say, 'it will be the means of doing good works.' A
means of doing good works for you indeed but for very many a means of doing
bad! And I no longer know if any good will come to you from something which
is a cause of death for many. We can place little value on the goodness of something which kills many, while it is supposed to be profiting one. How much more
valuable will your action be, if, by distributing all your possessions, you perform a
work which is good in three different ways! First, it will be a work of compassion because, when you have distributed all your possessions, you have to be considered as having reached perfection; secondly, by leaving nothing for yourself, you
will not only be depriving all men of an occasion of sin but also be setting an
example of virtue; thirdly, by distributing all your worldly resources, you are climb-
ing the ladder of perfection.

9.   What then am I saying? That, acting on our advice, you should hate the
riches left you by godly parents, amassed by grandparents, great-grandparents, great-
great-great grandparents and great-great-great-great-grandparents and acquired
with no sin incurred by themselves and no hurt or pain inflicted on others? Far
from it! Nay rather, I encourage you to love such riches; for everything that a man

loves faithfully he longs to keep as a permanent, not a temporary, possession. If you love your patrimony, then act in such a way that you may be able to retain it as an eternal inheritance. And if you really wish to do that, transfer it from earth to heaven while you have time, since whatever remains in this world must be destroyed when the world comes to an end. Therefore, whatever you transfer to heaven while you live you will, in fact, possess for ever; but whatever you leave here you have lost. Remember the maxim that says: Justify your soul before death; for there is no seeking of dainties in the grave (Sir. 14:16); and elsewhere: Before judgement, examine yourself (Sir. 18:20). I count as noble and praiseworthy and to be preferred to all by virtue of his wisdom the man who so restrains himself by meditating on life and death that he sends all his possessions on before him and thus arranges for all his property to cease with himself. Of him, I think, it is written: The ransom of a man's life is his wealth (Pr. 13:8). 'But how,' you will say, 'can earthly things be transferred to heavenly places?' By those, to be sure, of whom it is written: Go, sell all you possess and give to the poor, and you will have treasure in heaven (Mt. 19:21) . . .

20, 1.   But I must not ignore either the excessively subtle and refined ingenuity of those who think themselves religious and are reckoned to be despisers of the world by themselves and by ignorant people, because they go about in more lowly attire, taking no pleasure in possessing ornaments or gold or silver or in display of more costly metal, and yet keep all their possessions hidden away in their treasuries and, motivated by sheer greed, retain possession of what they disdain to use in the eyes of men merely in order to enjoy a worthless reputation.

2.   'But I have sons,' you will say, 'for whom I want to keep all my possessions.' Why then do you feign contempt for something out of respect for religion when you are really protecting it out of consideration for your children? Or why do you applaud yourself and indulge in self-congratulation as if you were doing something original in making your sons heirs to all your possessions, when even unbelievers are in the habit of doing just the same? Perhaps you suppose that you are conferring some benefit on God by bestowing on your children rather earlier a gift which you were without doubt bound to leave them some day? What then are we saying? That you should completely disinherit your sons? Far from it! Rather, that you should leave them no more than their nature requires. For how can you be said to love them, if you are seen to confer on them something which will only harm them? What has been seen to be detrimental to your interests can be equally detrimental to theirs: for either it was not detrimental to you and you are vainly pretending to despise it, or, if it was detrimental to you, you ought not to confer it on them, since no one wishes those whom he loves to possess something which he knows to be detrimental to himself. And so, either you do not love your sons, if you want to give them things which are not in their interest, or, if you do love them, it is certain that you do not regard what you want to give those whom you love as not in their interest.

3.   On the contrary, as we have said above, it is for the sake of winning glory among men that you pretend to despise as worthless what, deep down in your

heart, you cherish as the supreme good. For, when our last hour overtakes us, we shall profit nothing from a famous progeny with numerous offspring or from the possession of substantial wealth derived from fertile land spreading far and wide through all the regions of the world or from the scores of houses which our excessive pride and arrogance have erected or from the manifold elegance and splendour of our costly garments or from the ostentatious display of our high offices and honours: to all of us, we know not when that end will come when no man will receive for himself anything save the fruit of his works, be they good or bad. Gold, silver and the sparkling jewels of precious stones will profit us nothing when the day long ago fixed by God begins to glow and the very elements begin to crackle in the flames. Of that day the prophet bears witness, saying: The day of the Lord is great and dazzling, and who can endure it (Joel 2:11)? And the blessed apostle Peter: But the day of the Lord will come like a thief, and then the heavens will pass away with a loud noise, and the elements will be dissolved with fire (2 Pet. 3:10) . . .

6. 'But,' you will say, 'folly and knavery are to be found among the poor as well.' Yes, but no one covets poverty, and it is easier for the poor man to divest himself of such feelings than it is for the rich man, since poverty not only does not provide the raw materials for sin but in most cases renders it impossible, as the scripture says: A man may be prevented from sinning by his poverty (Sir. 20:21). Observe then which is the better choice – what prevents sin, or what sometimes compels it. For we have demonstrated earlier on the authority of a divine utterance that a rich man can only with difficulty be a stranger to sin. Let us rather seek those riches in which we may be worthy to share with the assent of Christ and his angels.

# Chapter 4

# Joachim of Fiore (1135–1202) and Peter Olivi (1248–1298)

**Joachim of Fiore,** Liber Figurarum **(twelfth century)**
**Peter Olivi on Poverty and the Role of St. Francis**
**(thirteenth century)**

Joachim of Fiore used Revelation as a way of understanding history and thereby emboldened groups and individuals to see themselves as being part of the imminent eschatological events. There are two basic threads which run through Joachim's hermeneutic: everything which happened in the Old Testament has its own actuality in time but is also a sign pointing forward to a future happening in the new dispensation which is (or will be a fuller disclosure) of God's purpose for humanity, and a trinitarian reading of history in which a coming third age, that of the Spirit, would be characterized by an outburst of spiritual activity in the form of monastic renewal. That time was imminent. The Book of Revelation, therefore, offered the key to the reading of the Bible as a whole and to the interpretation of history. In his later years Joachim complemented his literary expositions of the Apocalypse with images which encapsulated the heart of his beliefs about history and salvation. The final one of these images is a cross which is used to symbolize the new Jerusalem. It is a plan for the new society of the third age. In Joachim's new Jerusalem people live in their own homes but according to a lay rule, fasting, working with their hands, giving to the poor, and obeying their spiritual fathers. In his recognition of the importance of the laity Joachim's insight was prophetic of future developments when in the age of the friars there were third orders and lay fraternities of various kinds. This extraordinary outline of a future society might be called utopian were it not for the fact that Joachim clearly believed that such a state of bliss on earth was not just a possibility but a future reality. The contemplative life was the highest. Nevertheless the life of the wider world is incorporated into this new society.

Francis of Assisi (1181/2–1226) founded his order of "lesser brothers" (Friars Minor) who were to follow a life of absolute poverty, performing charitable works and providing pastoral care for others, but with special preference for the poor and for all creation. Francis believed this, initially lay, movement to be a rekindling of the life of Christ and his apostles. The more influential the order became, the more it began to adopt more formal structures akin to other religious orders. So, too, did its power increase and with it the opportunities to acquire wealth and possessions. Many friars, including the dying Francis himself, resisted such dilution of their gospel-inspired radical way of life. Those who saw no wrong in modifying the rule of poverty, for pragmatic purposes, were known as the Conventual Franciscans who believed in compromising the absolute rule, so as to allow the community to do its practical work better. Divisions raged between the Conventuals and a minority group, the "Spiritual Franciscans," until Pope John XXII condemned the Spirituals in 1323. Such controversies were fuelled by the work of Joachim of Fiore (ca. 1135–1202), whose interpretation of the Apocalypse was used to give an apocalyptic role for Francis and the Franciscan order.

One of the chief inspirations and spokesmen for the Spirituals was Peter Olivi (ca. 1248–98), a native of Languedoc, in southern France. He became a most accomplished scholar in theology and philosophy. The Franciscans had earlier came to settle upon an understanding of their poverty which saw the Papacy as holding all rights of the order's property. Olivi supported the arguments of those uncomfortable with such a compromise, by arguing that it is not simply the ownership, but the *use* of property by friars which needed careful attention. So any use of goods beyond what was absolutely necessary was sinful and to be condemned. His teaching and writing only served to strengthen further the resolve of the Franciscan Spirituals. In his Treatise *Usus Pauper*, written shortly before his censure in 1283, Olivi tried to show that the Franciscan vow demanded not only lack of ownership but restricted use of property. In an often complex argument he contended that, whatever goods the Franciscans seemed to possess actually belonged to others, not themselves; and that the Franciscans should use these things only insofar as it was necessary to use them and that this limited use was fundamental for the Franciscan rule and so failing to conform to it entailed mortal sin. His commentary on the Apocalypse draws on the apocalyptic tradition inspired by Joachim of Fiore. Olivi follows Joachim's suggestion that the angel mentioned in Rev. 7:2 is a man who heralds a third, spiritual, age. St. Francis is the angel of the opening of the sixth seal, the herald of that penultimate period of reform and unrest which must precede the coming reign of God on earth. Olivi describes him as "the renewer of the evangelical life" which is "to be propagated and glorified in the sixth and seventh periods, and its greatest observer after Christ and his mother." Olivi was accused of heresy and removed from his teaching post in 1283.

## Source

Joachim: Translation by B. McGinn, *Apocalyptic Spirituality*, SPCK, London: 1979, pp. 147–8.

Petrus Iohannis Olivi, *Treatise on Usus Pauper*, ET David Burr, http://www.majbill.vt.edu/history/burr/heresy/beguins/olivi/Olivi_Usus.html
The translation is from the Latin text in *De usu paupere: The Quaestio and the Tractatus*, Florence, 1992.

Unpublished Sources: http://dburr.hist.vt.edu/OliviPage/OliviSouces.html
Flood, David and Gàl, Gedeon, *Peter of John Olivi on the Bible*, St. Bonaventure, NY:
Franciscan Institute Publications, 1997.

## Further reading

D. Burr, *Olivi and Franciscan Poverty: The Origins of the Usus Pauper Controversy*, Philadel-
phia: University of Pennsylvania Press, 1989.
D. Burr, *Olivi's Peaceable Kingdom: A Reading of the Apocalypse Commentary*, Philadelphia:
University of Pennsylvania Press, 1993.
M. Lambert, *The Doctrine of the Absolute Poverty of Christ and the Apostles in the Fran-
ciscan Order, 1210–1323*, New York: Bonaventure, 1994.
B. McGinn, *Visions of the End – Apocalyptic Traditions in the Middle Ages*, New York: Colum-
bia University Press, 1998.
B. McGinn *The Encyclopedia of Apocalypticism Volume 2. Apocalypticism in Western History
and Culture*, New York: Continuum, 2000.
M. Reeves and B. Hirsch-Reich *The Figurae of Joachim of Fiore*, Oxford: Clarendon Press,
1972.

## Joachim's Description of Life in the New Jerusalem in the *Liber Figurarum*

They will sleep with their wives for the sake of having children rather than for
pleasure. At set times or days they will abstain from them by consent to be free
to pray, taking into account the physical constitution and age of the young people
lest they be tempted by Satan . . . They will have food and clothing in common,
and will obey their Master according to the direction an order of the spiritual
father to whom all these orders will be obedient like a new ark of Noah . . . No
idle person will be found among these Christians . . . Let each one work at his
own craft, and the individual trades and workers shall have their own foremen
. . . Food and clothing will be simple as befits Christians . . . Honest and approved
women will spin wool for the need of Christ's poor . . . They will give tithes of
all that they possess to the clerics for the support of the poor and strangers, and
also for the boys who are studying doctrine. They do this so that in case they have
more than they need and the rest have less, at the command of the spiritual father
the surplus will be taken from those who have more and given to those who have
less so that there may be no one in need among them but all things held in
common.

## Olivi's Contribution to the Discussion of Poverty in the Early Franciscan Order

Note, though, the craziness of these people's position. According to them it is perfectly legitimate for us to consume five or six delicate pieces of meat on golden

plates in the refectory every day, simply because it is not illicit for us to do so in the homes of secular persons. Now Christ, when he said "Eat what is placed before you," was speaking of the time when his disciples went out to preach, as is clear from the text. Doing so projected the image of loving poverty and solidarity while avoiding hypocrisy . . .

. . . we could have as many changes of clothing as the burghers have, or all we want short of what kings have. Moreover, we could eat as much as we want as often as we want, perhaps seven meals a day and one or two during the night. We would have summer and winter residences, or three or four in a single city for the same Franciscan community, as the burghers and knights do. We could ride horses and wear shoes all the time. We could wear precious clothing of every color imaginable short of those befitting royal splendour. Who can bear such foolishness? Perhaps they will say an approved custom prevents all these things, but in time the custom could die out and it would all be legal, as with monks or clerics. Further, does violating any approved custom incur mortal sin? Aren't customs often altered into their opposites by civil, ecclesiastical and even monastic law?

## Olivi on St. Francis of Assisi

Just as our most holy father Francis is, after Christ and under Christ, the first and principal founder and initiator and exemplar of the sixth period and its evangelical rule, so he, after Christ, is primarily designated by this angel. Thus, as a sign of this fact, he appeared transfigured in a fiery chariot in the sun in order to show that he had come in the spirit and in the image of Elijah, as well as to bear the perfect image of the true sun, Christ.

I have also heard from a very spiritual man, very worthy of belief and very intimate with Brother Leo, confessor and companion of blessed Francis, something which is consonant with this scripture but which I neither assert nor know nor think should be asserted, namely that both through the words of Brother Leo and through revelation made to him personally, he learned that during the pressure of that Babylonian temptation in which Francis' state and rule will be crucified, as it were, in the place of Christ himself, he will rise again glorious, so that just as he was singularly assimilated to Christ in his life and in the stigmata of the cross, so he will be assimilated to him in a resurrection necessary for confirming and informing his disciples, just as Christ's resurrection was necessary for confirming the apostles and informing them concerning the foundation and governance of the future church. In order that the resurrection of the servant should clearly be distinguished in degree of dignity from the resurrection of Christ and his mother, however, it is said by certain people who are not entirely to be rejected that Christ was resurrected immediately after three days, his mother after forty, and this man after the whole duration of his order up to its crucifixion assimilated to the cross of Christ and prefigured in Francis' stigmata.

# Chapter 5

# Marguerite Porete (d. 1310)

### The Mirror of Simple Souls (ca. 1306)

Most of what is known of her comes from Marguerite Porete's work, *The Mirror of Simple Souls* (*Le Miroeur des simples âmes*), and from records of her trials for heresy. She became a Beguine (women living quasi-monastic lives in society who had close links with Dominicans and Franciscans). They were condemned at the Council of Vienne in 1314 because of their links with the Brethren of the Free Spirit, who were suspected of antinomianism and pantheism. It is not difficult to see why the book caused problems for the ecclesiastical authorities, as during the mystical ascent of the soul she suggests that the soul has attained such a high level that it is "free of all obedience to eternal authority and laws," and "need not concern itself with masses, penance, sermons, fasts or prayer." She makes a distinction between the "little Church" and the "greater church," the former the Church on earth and the latter the community of free souls. Her book was officially condemned and burned in her presence, but she continued to spread her ideas. In 1310 she was declared a heretic and was burnt at the stake in Paris. The short extract that follows anticipates the views which are found in the work of the Reformation radicals and William Blake.

### Source

P. Dronke, *Women Writers of the Middle Ages*, Cambridge, 1982, p. 224.

### Further reading

Biller P. and A. Hudson, *Heresy and Literacy 1000–1530*, Cambridge: Cambridge University Press, 1994.

Porete, Marguerite, *The Mirror of Simple Souls*, translated and introduced by Ellen L. Babinsky with a preface by Robert E. Lerner. Classics of Western Spirituality, New York: Paulist Press, 1993.
Pou y Marti, J.M., *Visionarios, Beguinos y Fraticeles Catalanes*, Madrid: Colegio Cardenal Cisneros, 1991.

## Excerpt from *The Mirror of Simple Souls*

Theologians and other clerks,
You won't understand this book
– however bright your wits –
if you do not meet it humbly,
and in this way Love and Faith
make you surmount Reason:
they are the mistresses of Reason's house.

Reason herself proclaims to us
in the thirteenth chapter
of this book, unashamed,
that Love and Faith make her live:
she never frees herself from them –
they have sovereignty over her,
and she must do obeisance.

So bring low your sciences
Which are founded by Reason,
And put all your trust
In the science conferred by Love,
That are lit up by faith –
And then you'll understand this book,
which by Love makes the soul live.

Chapter 6

# John Ball (d. 1381)

## Sermon

Most of what is known about John Ball is recorded in the unsympathetic accounts of Thomas Walsingham and Sir John Froissart. Froissart notes in his *Chronicles* that Ball was imprisoned three times by archbishops of Canterbury for "assembling the people about him" after Mass on Sundays and preaching radical sermons to them along the lines of the extract here. Ball also believed, according to Froissart, that "at the beginning of the world ... there were no bondmen," and Walsingham credits him with arguing that "servitude had been introduced by the unjust and evil of oppressions of men against the will of God". Against the background of an ever-widening gulf between rich and poor, exacerbated by Archbishop Sudbury's poll tax of 1380, Ball's message had an explosive effect on his devoutly Catholic hearers.

If Ball began expounding a revolutionary gospel in the 1360s or even earlier, it was during the so-called Peasants' Revolt, which erupted in the wake of the poll tax, that his influence reached its peak. Sprung from prison in Kent in June 1381, Ball was found on the Feast of Corpus Christi saying Mass and preaching to the throng at Blackheath on the popular saying, "When Adam delved and Eve span, Who was then the gentleman?" This sermon, Walsingham notes, found high favor with the common people, who were then led by Ball and Wat Tyler to meet the young King Richard and attempt to persuade him of the justice of their case. In the aftermath of the events which followed Ball was captured, tried, and hung, drawn and quartered.

## Source

Christopher Hampton, ed., *A Radical Reader: The Struggle for Change in England, 1381–1914*, Harmondsworth: Penguin, 1984, p. 51.

## Further reading

R.B. Dobson, *The Peasants' Revolt 1381*, London: Macmillan, 2nd edn., 1983.

Charles Poulsen, *The English Rebels*, London: Journeyman, 1984.

Brian Bird, *Rebel Before His Time: The Story of John Ball and the Peasants' Revolt*, Worthing: Churchman, 1987.

Brian Bird, *Colchester Rebel: A Short Study of John Ball*, Colchester: B. Bird, 1984.

Ashok Kumar Singh, *Peasant Revolt and Agrarian Reform*, London, 1997.

## Extract from *"Sermon to the People"*

My good people, things cannot go well in England, nor ever shall, till everything be made common, and there are neither villeins nor gentlemen, but we shall all be united together, and the lords shall be no greater masters than ourselves. What have we deserved that we should be kept thus enslaved? We are all descended from one father and mother, Adam and Eve. What reasons can they give to show that they are greater lords than we, save by making us toil and labour, so that they can spend? They are clothed in velvet and soft leather furred with ermine, while we wear coarse cloth; they have their wines, spices and good bread, while we have the drawings of the chaff, and drink water. They have handsome houses and manors, and we the pain and travail, the rain and wind, in the fields. And it is from our labour that they get the means to maintain their estates. We are called their slaves, and if we do not serve them readily, we are beaten. And we have no sovereign to whom we may complain, or who will hear us, or do us justice. Let us go to the King, he is young, and tell him of our slavery; and tell him we shall have it otherwise, or else we will provide a remedy ourselves. And if we go together, all manner of people that are now in bondage will follow us, with the intent to be made free. And when the King sees us, we shall have some remedy, either by justice or otherwise.

# Chapter 7

# William Langland (1330–1387)

Piers Plowman, **Passus XVII (fourteenth century)**

Langland was probably a cleric in minor orders from the West Midlands area. *Piers Plowman* is in the form of a dream vision as a way for Will to investigate the theory and practice of the Christian life. The character of Piers Plowman in the dream is the link connecting the various visions and events seen by Will.

In the poem before this extract Will has met Abraham, who introduces himself as Faith. He explains the Trinity to Will, but, as a figure from the Old Testament, he is still waiting for the fulfillment of his beliefs. He is waiting, and in his lap he has sheltered thousands, in a sort of limbo, among them Lazarus, who lay at the gate of Dives (Luke 16). Next Will meets Hope. From Mount Sinai he has received the new Law: love thy neighbor as thyself. Will actually finds it easier to believe in the Trinity than in the teaching that he should love his neighbor, when he thinks of the real neighbors he has. They then meet the Good Samaritan and the man who has "fallen among thieves." Faith and Hope, like the priest and the Levite in the New Testament story (Luke 1) "pass by on the other side," and the Samaritan gives immediate practical help. Will continues on the road with him, and from him hears the teaching of practical love, and in the images of the hand and of the candle understands the Trinity better, precisely in terms of such practical love.

The poet, David Constantine, who has made the translation of *Piers Plowman* XVII (below), writes: "I am an unprincipled translator: that is, I let the principle of each translation be dictated to me by the text I am translating. Then I abide by them. The lines I chose seemed to me to be chiefly about incarnation. Thus the extraordinarily physical language – of hand and candle – to render a difficult abstraction, the Trinity. And more than that: the immediate practising of the abstract virtue: Love. Faith and Hope cannot be realised in that way: they are both still waiting, for what is, they believe, they hope, to come. But Love acts in the meantime, in the here and now, on earth, in our real conditions, to help. Christ incarnates God, the Samaritan (and Piers Plowman himself) incarnate Christ: Christ as healer and helper. That incarnating – or you might call it secularizing, humanizing-principle is certainly in Langland, and in accordance with my own beliefs and my own understanding of the needs of the world we live in, I followed and accentuated that principle in my version."

## Further reading

Sir David Lindsay, *Ane Satyre of the Thrie Estaitis*, Edinburgh: Canongate, 1989.

E. Salter, *Piers Plowman. An Introduction*, Oxford: Blackwell, 1969.

K. Kenly-Fulton, *Reformist Apocalypticism and Piers Plowman*, Cambridge: Cambridge University Press, 1990.

## *Piers Plowman*, Passus

### *End of Passus XVI*

'So I have been his herald, here and in Hell
And comforted many who were bowed down with waiting,
Bowed myself and seeking him. And now I hear
Of a man called John the Baptist who has baptized him
And to the patriarchs and the prophets
And to all of us seeking and waiting in the dark
Announces that this is the Lamb of God
Who will take away the sin of the world.'

So said Faith, bent as a hawthorn, white
His head of hair as the hawthorn is in May.
His words were a wonder to me and more still
The roominess of his clothes. Under his heart
He was rocking something and crooning over it
And when I looked I saw that it was Lazarus,
The leper from Dives' gate, and there besides
In his lap lay all the patriarchs and the prophets,
Wailing like babies. Faith asked:
'What are you looking for? What is it you want?'
'To see,' I answered, 'what is in your lap.'
'Look then,' he said, and showed me. Then I said:
'This is a precious gift for somebody.'
'Precious,' he said, 'for nobody. They are all in hock
To the devil and so am I, and nobody
Will come here with the ticket to redeem us,
No one stand surety and get us out.
Out of the devil's pound nobody can bail us
Till he comes, the one they call the Christ,
Who may deliver us from the devil's grip some day
And lay down more for us than we're all worth,
Life for life, that is, his for ours, but until
Such a lord fetch us they must loll in my lap.'

'Alas,' I said, 'that for so long God's mercy
That might mend all of us should be so baulked.'

I wept over his words. Then I saw another man
Hurrying the same road. I enquired of him
Where he was from and what his name was and where
He was bound for, and he answered forthwith.


*Passus XVII*

'I am Hope,' he said, 'a searcher. On Mount Sinai
I was given a rule to overrule all kingdoms.
Here it is in writing.' 'May I see?' I asked.
'Are your letters sealed?' He answered: 'No.
I go about looking for the seal's keeper
And that is Christ, the man they hanged on the tree.
And without that seal, so much is certain,
The kingdom of wrong will endure for ever.'
I said: 'Let me see your letters and know the law.'
He showed his patent. It was a hard stone
And written on it were these words: 'Love thy neighbour
And God.' That was the text, truly.
I took good note of it, and in a bold script
In gold below was added: 'The old law
And the prophets end in these commandments.'
'And is this all your lord's bidding?' I asked.
He answered: 'Yes, and whosoever works
By this writ, ill will never betide him nor
Will death, believe me, enter his soul. Myself
I have saved scores of thousands with this charm.'
[Hope's herald spoke then: 'What he says is true.
See here in my lap are some believers on it:
Joshua and Judith and Judas Maccabeus
And sixty thousand more that you cannot see.']
'Your words are wonderful,' I said, 'but which
Between yours and Faith's are truest and the best
To be believed for life and for the soul?
Faith says he saw the Trinity all one
And yet three separate and all three
One God. He taught me this and cannot count
How many believing it and sorry for their sins
He has saved by it and some are in his lap.
Why bring in a new law when that first
Was enough to bring us safely among the blessed?
And now you come, who have seen the new law, you,
Hope, and have the letters of it but whoever
Gave them you says nothing of the Trinity
But only: Love thy neighbour and love

And believe in an almighty God.
Now a man who leans on only one stick looks
To all of us haler than a man on two.
And for common people there are no easy lessons
But one is always easier to learn than two.
It is hard to believe in Faith but following you
And loving a bad neighbour is harder still
And easier to believe in three sweet persons
As one, in a trinity, than to love and give
Charity to scroungers and good men alike.
Go on,' I said to Hope, 'go on without me.
Whoever learns your law won't keep it long.'

And as we went along thus talking together
We saw a Samaritan riding on a grey mule
And hastening the same road we were bound
Coming from a place called Jericho
And getting along at a jog towards Jerusalem.
Then he, the Samaritan, and Hope and Faith
All came on a man who had fallen under the fists
And the feet of a gang and the way they had treated him
He could not walk or stand or stir a foot
Or a hand nor help himself, their hands
Had stripped him bare as a bone and their boots
As good as killed him and all around there was
No help. Faith saw him first but he, Faith,
Fled to one side and wouldn't go nearer him
Than several arm's lengths. And after Faith
Hope came bustling up that had so boasted
How he with Moses' law had helped thousands
But seeing what the man in the road looked like,
He cowered away, Hope did, as though the sight
Might do the same to him. But the Samaritan,
Seeing it, he dismounted immediately
And knelt close to learn how the man was hurt
And felt for his pulse and through his own fingers
Felt that the life in the man was very low and that
Without help there and then he would die where he lay.
So the Samaritan set to, helping.
Quickly he broached the two bottles he carried,
One of wine, one of oil, and sponging, swabbing,
With hands clever and gentle he brought forth
From under the blood and dirt a human face,
Salving the gashes, binding the head, and in his arms
Bore him then on the mule six or seven miles
To a place for travellers near the new market
Called *Lex Christi*, which is *The Rule of Christ*,
And lodged him there, saying to the landlord:
'Look after him till I come back this way,

See to his wounds, here is the necessary silver
For his keep and care, two pieces, and if
The sum is more I will make it up to you
But now I cannot stay.' And he bestrode his mule
And set off fast the straight way to Jerusalem.

Faith hurried after, to catch him up,
And Hope likewise made terrific speed
To have his conversation on the road to town
And seeing them run I outran both of them
To follow the Samaritan because
That man had shown pity and I begged him
To let me serve him. 'Thank you,' he answered,
'But what I need are companions and friends
Not servants.' I answered: 'Thanks' and told him
How Faith had fled and Hope also had fled
At the sight of the poor man as the thieves had left him.
'Excuse them,' he said. 'What help they might have been
Was very little, neither Hope nor Faith
Could do much for a man with such bad wounds
And even what I did with my wine and oil though that
Saved him, no doubt, so that he will stand up
And step forth again and be hale and strong
What help is it against the boots and the fists?
Not much. For the way the world is now
Who goes about in it, in this wilderness of a world,
On foot or on horseback without fear of the same?
Faith has been lucky, and I myself, and Hope too
Still survives and you by the looks you may be lucky
And some others like you, seekers and followers,
A few. But Outlaw is in the wood, in hiding
He spies on every traveller, who goes ahead
And who falls behind and who is on horseback
And of the riders he is warier than of them on foot.
Seeing Faith, for example, and his companion
And me, a Samaritan, mounted on a horse
Called Flesh, given me by humankind, seeing us
He turned coward, the villain, and hid himself in Hell.
But I will undertake that three days hence
The malefactor will be heavy with chains
And never again trouble travellers going this road.
"O Death," so the script says, "I will be thy death . . ."
And then Faith shall be the forester here
And walk this wood and be the guide to people
Who do not know this country and show them
The way I went and which way forth to Jerusalem.
And Hope shall be a helper at the inn
Where the man lies healing now and all
Those who are feeble and faint and whom Faith cannot

Do anything for Hope shall lead them the way
With love as his patent promises and lodge them
And recover them in God's House till I have
Help for them all. And then I will return
And come again through this country and comfort all
Who crave it and desire it and cry out for it.
For by a child born in Bethlehem Faith
And his fellow Hope will be satisfied.'

'Sir,' I asked, 'shall I then believe
As Faith, bent with the waiting, instructed me
In three who are distinct and everlasting
And all three one God? Faith taught me so
And later Hope bade me love this one God
And all my fellow men, doing to them
As I would be done by, as did our Lord the best.'
'As Faith taught you,' he answered, 'who was
Christ's herald, so firmly believe,
And as Hope bade you I likewise bid you
Love your fellow men as you would be loved by them
And if doubts trouble you or your thoughts
Or others come at you with arguments against this
Show them your hand. For God is like a hand.
See mine, and listen.
      In the beginning
The Father was a fist, the fingers were clenched shut
Until he loved and loving loosened them
And he put forth the hand then as an open palm
Wherever the need was. And the palm is
Wholly the hand, when it opens the fingers
The hand comes into its strength, which is
The power to minister. And in this image
Think of the Holy Spirit: he is the palm.
And the fingers that are free to do and to mend
Thinking of them you may imagine the Son
Who was sent to earth and through the body of Mary
Gave to the Spirit the nature of humankind
So it could taste and touch, and so the Father
Opened and through the fingers and to the very palm
Was let into good and ill in the world of feeling.
So are they all three one, like a hand:
The fist that opens shows the palm and the fingers,
One self and three. And as the hand holds hard
And fast on a thing with fingers into the palm
So Father, Son and Holy Spirit
Hold all the wide world within the three of them
Even the sky and the winds, the water and the earth,
Heaven and Hell and all that there is therein.
And so it is, and this belief is sufficient,

That three things belong to our Lord in Heaven
And though distinct they were never separate
Any more than are the parts of a whole hand.
And as my fist is a full hand folded together
So is the Father a full God, a maker, a shaper,
And in him is all the might for making things.
Think what can be done with the full hand's fingers:
How they can draw and paint and carve and design,
Such craft the fingers have. So Christ may be called
The Father's science and he is as full a God
As the Father is, no less, no better.

The palm is wholly the hand, has power
All of its own, other than the clenched fist,
Other than the cleverness that is in the fingers.
For it is from the palm that movement comes
Through the joints to open the fist, and into the palms,
Into them cupped, comes from the givers of gifts
Whatever the opened fingers have asked for.

Thus is the Holy Spirit neither greater nor less
Than is the Sire or the Son, but of the same strength
And all are one as are my hand and fingers
Clenched and opened, fist and palm, all are
Only a human hand however I turn it.
But hurt someone in the hand, in the middle
Of the open hand when it is lifted to greet,
To bless, to show itself defenceless,
This spoils everything, the fingers made to touch,
Comfort, caress, or fold to have and to hold
Because of the pain in the palm they lose the ability.
When the middle of my hand is pierced through
What can I do then to help or make amends?

By this,' he said, 'I give you an idea
Of the wrongdoing that is beyond forgiveness
That you have heard of, that neither here nor elsewhere
Can ever be made up for, the wrong done
Against the very heart of the hand, against the palms
That put together whole make a bowl of blessing.
This harm against Love's very spirit
Thwarts all the work of God, parent and child,
All the reaching out, all the healing and giving.

The Trinity is like a candle: as wax and wick
Are twined and the candle flame comes forth
Out of the wedding of both and as wax and wick
And warm fire together foster a flame
And a lovely light to labour by in the dark

So do Father and Son and Holy Spirit
Foster faith and hope and love in humankind.
And as sometimes you may see the flame of a candle
Suddenly blown out and only a dot of life
Left red on the wick, no light, no comfort,
So God is reduced by the extinguishing
Of love. So if we are unkind
And spend our spirit on the destruction
Of the life and the love that God made, where shall we
Go looking for mercy? And just as coals
Barely glowing give small comfort to workmen
Awake and labouring through winter nights
But a fire that flames and blazes gives great comfort
Neither can Sire nor Son nor Holy Spirit
Give grace or forgiveness till that Spirit
Begins to brighten and flame when the breath of love
Comes over the coals and God's might and the Son's
Melt into mercy, as you may see in winter
Icicles under the eaves in the warmth of the sun
Melting in a short while to breath and water.

And as the grace of the Holy Spirit melts
All the Trinity to mercy, so let us be merciful.
And as the candle, which is only wax and a wick,
When fire is given to it and it is carried in
To a room where we were sitting in the dark
Lights up a space of cheerfulness
So will Christ in his courtesy, when we beg him,
If we do really repent and make amends
Enter the dark where we were crouched in lovelessness
To forgive and forget. Four hundred winters
You might strike fire from a flint but unless the spark
Has touchwood and tinder waiting for it
You labour in vain. Fire will never flame up
Without a body of kindling. So on us
The Holy Spirit might shower sparks for ever
And we will never kindle if we are unkind.
Pray all you like and make donations,
Do penance night and day and buy up all the pardons,
All the indulgences in Christendom, and be
Still unkind, unloving to humankind,
The Spirit will never listen, cry as you might,
Unkindness quenches it, it cannot shine
Nor burn nor blaze out brightly under
The damps of lovelessness. Rich men, clever men,
Dealers in the world, I ask them
By what rule do they live in the life of the soul?
If they are unkind to human kith and kin
And many are, the point of fire in them

Will never blaze, they will always be blind beacons.
Dives with all his meat and money
Died unkind among so many needing it.
Give where you can, where it will help, for all
The rich like Dives, so ungiving,
Endure a neverending lovelessness.

Unkindness is the contrary that quenches
The grace of the Holy Spirit, God's own nature.
For what love does unkindness undoes
Like those who left that traveller by the wayside bleeding
And took his goods, using their hands
Only to hurt and thieve, so unkindness
Trespasses against the Holy Spirit and puts out life and love
Which are the flame in the body of men and women.
For evey woman and man may be understood
Like the Trinity itself as a candle
In the wedding of wick and wax and the lighting it with a flame
And anyone harming them does harm against
What Christ loved best on earth looking around him.
And this is the worst of sins against the Holy Ghost:
Violence against the flame in every man and woman,
Violence to the face, violence to the open palm
Of humankind to whom Christ in the flesh
Extended love. Where shall they face then,
Where shall they show their faces and to whom,
Asking for mercy, who showed none to the flame
And face of humankind? The human being,
So well shaped, the face and hands so apt
For innocence and lovingkindness
Whoever unmakes that, undoes that work,
Where shall he go with his prayers when he wants pity?'

So saying my Good Samaritan ended. Haste
Came over him, he spurred his horse and like
The whirlwind vanished and I awoke.
And took the road again, shod with the mire of it
And clad in tatters. What had I learned?
That Love must go on alone and do well,
Do better, do the best it can
Without Faith often, often without Hope.

# Chapter 8

# Jan Hus (ca. 1372–1415)

## Letters of John Hus (fifteenth century)

Born in southern Bohemia, Hus was a prominent figure in Prague academic and ecclesiastical life. His writings display the influence of John Wycliffe (ca.1330–84). He emphasized that Christ was the Head of the Church, and that the highest standard for the church was the Law of God: the teachings of scripture and the ancient church. He supported moral reform, from clerical abuses, the sale of indulgences and, especially, simony, to moral reform in society in general extending to the Papacy itself. This led to an important treatise on ecclesiology, *De Ecclesia* (1413). His views concerning authority and obedience in the church and the laity receiving communion under both kinds continued to cause controversy and division long after his death. Hus also argued for radical social and political reform: opposing the right to private property and hierarchical forms of society alike.

He was excommunicated by Pope John XXIII in 1411. When the Council of Constance (1414–17) was called, Hus set out to the gathering to appeal against his treatment, only to find himself on trial for heresy. Refusing to accept the charges or retract his views, on 6 July, 1414, Hus and his books were burned.

His significance is due to the events which followed his death. Seen as a martyr in Bohemia, his teachings inspired the Taborite-led uprisings which overthrew the government of Prague, attempted to develop a new society based on communism and fraternity, and gathered together the lower classes.

The extracts include two letters from Hus. The first, from 1411, sees Hus telling John Barbatus and the people of Krumlov that if those in positions of authority – be it in the church or secular government – command something contrary to the gospel, then Christians have a right and duty to disobey such commands and to oppose such leaders. The second, "To an unnamed monk," seeks to reiterate the Christian tradition of opposing private property, and this at a time when debates surrounding the ownership of property and riches by the church was a highly contentious issue.

## Source

*The Letters of John Hus,* ed. Matthew Spinka, Manchester and Totowa, NJ, Manchester University Press, and Rowman and Littlefield, 1972.

"On Simony" in *Advocates of Reform: from Wyclif to Erasmus,* ed. Matthew Spinka, London: SCM, 1953.

*De Ecclesia,* ET David S. Schaff, New York, 1974.

## Further reading

Bartos, F. M, *The Hussite Revolution, 1424–37,* New York, 1986.
Lambert, Malcolm, *Medieval Heresy,* Oxford: Blackwell, 1992.
Kaminsky, Howard, *A History of the Hussite Revolution*: Berkeley, 1967.
McGinn, Bernard, *Visions of the End – Apocalyptic Traditions in the Middle Ages,* New York: Columbia University Press, 1998.
Spinka, Matthew, *John Hus – a Biography,* Princeton, 1968.

## Letters of John Hus

*To John Barbatus and the People of Krumlov*

Prague
Spring of 1411

Salvation and peace from the Lord Jesus Christ.

Dearly beloved!

I have heard of your tribulation; therefore, 'count it all joy when you fall into various temptations,' for the testing of your constancy. Dearly beloved, I am now beginning to be tested; but I regard it as joy that for the sake of the gospel I am called a heretic and am excommunicated as a malefactor and disobedient. But as a protection of joy there comes to my mind the life and word of Christ as well as the word of the apostles; for we read in Acts 4 that 'Annas the high priest, and Caiaphas, and John and Alexander, and as many as were of the priestly kindred,' having called the apostles, 'commanded them not to speak or teach in the name of Jesus. But Peter and John responding, said to them: Whether it be just in the sight of God to obey you rather than God, judge yourselves. For we cannot but to speak of that we have heard and seen.' When these same chief priests again ordered them not to preach, they said in accordance with Acts 5: 'We ought to obey God rather than men.' Pagans, Jews, and heretics agree in that rule, declaring that God must be obeyed above all.

But alas! the adherents of the Antichrist are blind to that rule, although the holy apostles and the true disciples of Christ are not. Therefore blessed Jerome says in his epistle to the Corinthians: 'If a lord or a prelate commands that which is not contrary to the faith or opposed to Holy Scripture, the servant submits to him; if, however, he commands that which is contrary to them, let him obey the Lord of his spirit rather than of the body.' Further on: 'If what the emperor commands is good, fulfil the will of the command; if evil, reply: God ought to be obeyed rather than men.' Likewise Augustine in Homily 6 on the Lord's words: 'If the authority commands what you ought not to do, then rightly reject the authority in fear of a higher authority. Observe the grades in human affairs: if a procurator orders something, should it be performed when the proconsul orders the contrary? And again, if a proconsul orders something and the emperor orders something else, would you doubt that you must ignore the former and obey the latter? Accordingly, if the emperor orders something else than God, one ought to ignore the former and submit to the latter. Hence we resist the diabolic or human might whenever it suggests what is contrary to God. In such an event we do not resist God's ordinance, but submit to it. For thus God ordained that we obey no authority in evil.' So far Augustine.

To the same subject Gregory, in the last book of *Moralia*, says: 'It is to be known, that no evil must ever be done through obedience.' Likewise the blessed Bernard says in a letter: 'To do any evil whatever, by whomever ordered, constitutes not obedience but disobedience.' Similarly the blessed Isidore, as is read in [*Decretum?*] XI, qu. 3: 'If anyone in authority does or commands to do whatever is prohibited by the Lord; or if he disregards or orders to disregard what is written, he should be reminded of the saying of St Paul, who wrote: Though we or an angel from heaven should descend and preach to you any other gospel than that which we have preached to you, let him be accursed.' And further: 'If anyone prevents you from doing what is commanded by the Lord, or on the contrary commands you what the Lord forbids to do, let him be accursed by all who love the Lord.' Then it follows: 'If anyone in authority states or commands anything beyond the will of God or beyond what is clearly enjoined in the Holy Scriptures, let him be regarded as a false witness of God or as guilty of sacrilege.'

It is obvious from this that those who prohibit preaching are false witnesses and guilty of sacrilege, and consequently excommunicated by the Lord, according to the declaration of the prophet pronouncing excommunication: 'They who wander from Thy commandment are accursed.' As far as my case is concerned, Jerome says in his letter to Rusticus, the bishop of Narbonne: 'Therefore let none of the bishops, puffed up with envy of diabolical temptation, be angry when the priests occasionally exhort the people, or when they preach in churches – as has been said – if they pronounce blessing upon the people. For I would answer him, who would refuse me these things: Whoever does not wish that priests do what God enjoins them to do, let him declare that he is greater than Christ!'

Likewise Bede on the words: 'You shall find an ass tied and a colt with her; loose them and bring them to me. And if any may say something to you, you shall say: the Lord has need of them;' he says: 'Here the Lord mystically instructs the doctors that, if they meet with an obstruction, if someone would not allow sinners to be loosed from the bonds and by the confession of faith lead them to the Lord, they should not then desist from preaching, but the more constantly remind them that the Lord needs such people for the upbuilding of His Church.'

But who could collect all the sayings of the saints who all teach obedience to God rather than to men?

Nevertheless, obstinate men object to it the words of Matthew 23: 'Whatever they bid you, observe!' But instantly their mouth is stopped by the following prohibition which says: 'According to their works do not do!' Therefore in Deuteronomy 24 God says: 'Thou shalt do whatever the Levite priests shall teach you according to what I commanded them.' Notice, that the Lord desires, that the obedient man should obey solely according to His precepts. Hence, also the words of Peter in his I Epistle, chap. 2: 'Servants, be subject to your masters with all fear'; and lower: 'Also to the overbearing.' Nevertheless, be it far from anyone to obey them in evil, for he would thus obey the devil. Hence, the will of God and Scripture teach that the superiors should be obeyed only in things lawful.

Relying on that, I desired in preaching to obey only God rather than the pope or the archbishop and the rest of the satraps opposing the word of Christ: 'Go into all the world', etc. I made this remark so that you may know how to oppose the devil's dogs.


*To an Unnamed Monk*

Prague
28 February 1412

Salvation and grace from the Lord Jesus Christ!

Beloved brother in Christ Jesus!

The basic rule for clerics concerning the owning of property, particularly those who have taken vows, is to possess all things in common, according to Acts 2: 'They had all things in common.' Blessed Augustine deduced therefrom and incorporated in his rule this conclusion: 'This is what we command, that it be observed by those who are residing in monasteries.' And further on: 'Do not claim that any of you has anything of his own.'

Similarly Gregory in the third book of *Dialogus* toward the end ordered the monk, brother Justinus, to be thrown on the dung heap on account of three ducats and commanded the brethren to say: 'Your money perish with you!'

Also St Benedict in his *Rule* says: 'Let no one presume to give or receive anything or to possess anything of his own – anything whatsoever: neither a codex, nor a tablet, nor a stylus – nothing whatsoever. Those who cannot exercise power over their bodies or wills, let them have all things in common. As is written, let no one call anything his own, etc.'

Equally Basil in his *Rule* states: 'If anyone call anything his property, he makes himself a stranger from God's elect and of the love of the Lord, who taught it by word and fulfilled it by deed, and for His friends laid down his life.'

Also St John Cassian, writing to Pope Castorius about the teaching of the holy Fathers in the fourth book of his *Regula*, says as follows: 'Because in other monasteries some things are laxly tolerated, we insist that this rule be most stringently observed, so that no one would dare by a single word to call something his own. It is, therefore, a great crime for any monk to let the word out of his mouth: this is my codex, my tablet, my stylus, my tunic, my shoes, or my cape. In case such a word slips out of his mouth through inadventure or ignorance, he must surely make satisfaction for it by suitable penance.'

Likewise St Francis stated in his *Rule*: 'The rule and life of the Brothers Minor is this: namely, firmly to observe the holy gospel of our Lord Jesus Christ by living without property, in obedience and chastity.' And further in the middle of the *Rule*: 'Brothers, do not appropriate anything to yourselves, either a house, or a place, or any other thing; but as pilgrims and strangers in this world, in poverty and humility serve the Lord, confidently seeking alms.' This is in the *Rule*.

To that same subject blessed Jerome writes in his letter to Heliodorus; also blessed Bernard in his book to Pope Eugenius; and blessed Augustine in his sermon to clerics, of which it is written in *Decretum* XII, qu. 1, c. 17: 'The Lord had a purse.' Also Augustine in his *De opere monachorum*. Also St Thomas in his *Tractatus monachorum*. I have also read, but do not know the passage, where the blessed Bernard said: 'A monk owning a farthing, is not worth a farthing.'

Even if none of these teachers taught anything, every monk is bound by his vow.

I pray, therefore, if you find anything bearing on this anywhere else, send it to me. I also pray that you salute the lord abbot. Receive graciously brother Andrew, the bearer of this letter. If you will be able to do it conveniently, aid him for God's sake, that he could remain with you.

Farewell in Christ!

I write what I had at hand; if I shall have more, I shall write about it sometime later.

A.D. 1412, the second Sunday in Lent.

# Chapter 9

# Lollard Sermon for Christmas Day on Luke 2:1–14 (early fifteenth century)

The Lollards were a movement based on the writings of the theologian John Wycliffe, who emphasized the importance of the Bible and criticized the clergy and the Church. Wycliffe's philosophy and his writings brought him into conflict with the status quo. He actively supported the Crown's temporal authority over the Church in civil matters. His own scholarship questioned the current policies of the Roman Church in the light of research on the Bible, and the Early Church. He published texts in English rather than in Latin. He embarked on a translation of the Vulgate. Copies became available to a large audience in England. At the Council of Constance (1415), Wycliffe and his writings were condemned. Wycliffe's own personal involvement in the Lollard movement is unclear. Lollards preached a reformed doctrine based on Wycliffe's writings. They promoted the popular reading of Holy Scripture in the vernacular and promoted equality of the sexes, including women preachers. The Lollard Bible was banned in 1407. The Church actively continued in its efforts to root out and prosecute Lollard influence wherever it could be found.

The example quoted here is a sermon for Christmas probably written in the early part of the fifteenth century. Its tone exhibits a distinctive perspective on the story of Jesus' birth; it brings out those elements which suggest Christ's identification with the poor and humble rather than those of wealth and power. It is a theme which recurs again in radical Christian writings down to peasant interpretation of Scripture in the modern world (see E. Cardenal, *The Gospel from Solentiname*; and see *Misa Campesina*, pp. 243–6).

Source

G. Cigman, *Lollard Sermons*, The Early English Text Society, Oxford, 1989, pp. 60–1.

Further reading

M. Aston, *Lollards and Reformers: images and literacy in late medieval religion*, London: Hambledon, 1984.
A. Hudson, *The Premature Reformation: Wycliffite Texts and Lollard History*, Oxford: Clarendon Press, 1988.

## Lollard Sermon for Christmas Day on Luke 2:1–14

And Joseph and Mary, though they were of high character, they were poor in regard to worldly goods, and of such worldly men took little notice . . . It was in a crib, between the animals, this blessed maid laid her child when he was born. Here men may see, who look closely, great poverty [revealed] in the attire at this lord's birth. Both poor and rich must learn a lesson from this . . .

Where were the great castles and the towers, with large halls and long chambers, royally adorned with tapestries, bed hangings and extravagant beds and curtains of gold and silk, fit for the birth of so noble an emperor? Where were the royal ladies and worthy gentlewomen, [ready] to attend this worthy empress and be her companions at this time? Where were the knights and squires to render service to this lady, with noble meals, costly attire, and with hot spices and rare drinks of diverse sweet wines?

Instead of the royal castle with rich clothes, she had a stinking stable in the highway. Instead of royal beds and curtains she had no other clothes but such as belonged to a poor carpenter's wife on a journey. Instead of a company of knights and ladies she had poor Joseph her husband and two mute beats. In the face of this must wicked hypocrites be ashamed, who say that they follow Christ in his poverty most nearly of all men on earth, and say that the Christ was born in so poor a place while they dwell in such regal places, [with] halls, chambers, pantries, store rooms, kitchens, stables and all other houses of office, regal enough for the households of a king, prince or duke.

That this blessed child was born in a house open on every side betokens that God will be shut off from no one who will come to his mercy, but is ever open to all who will appeal to him for mercy and grace. Therefore said David, 'The Lord is near to those who call upon him, to those who call upon him in truth'. That is: that he was in this situation betokens that there is no other way to the bliss of heaven but only by the example of his life and teaching. And therefore he says: I am the way the truth and the life.

He was born in this way to give us an example to have ever in mind that all our life we are here but in exile and on pilgrimage, having here no city to dwell in but rather await the bliss of heaven as our own country and proper heritage.

That this blessed child, after that he was born was laid instead of his cradle in a crib among the food of animals, betokens not only that he came to save highly intellectual men and great clerks but also the simple, ignorant and uncultivated who would be devoted to him and keep his commandments. And therefore David spoke in this way: Men and beast thou shalt save, Lord.

And thus whosoever takes good heed of what was said before, he may see somewhat the manner of array of Christ's birth . . . The fourth thing that this gospel speaks concerns those to whom first came the things concerning his birth. They should understand that God did not send his messengers to show his blessed birth to the great emperor of Rome, who was the greatest temporal lord of this world, nor to king Herod, who was king of Galilee, in which country Our Lady dwelt, who was the mother of this blessed child, and in which place he was also conceived. Nor were they sent to the high priest of Jerusalem, who was in those days highest in spiritual dignity. Rather it was as the gospel says: There were shepherds in the same country, watching and keeping the watches of the night over their flock. And lo! The angel of the Lord stood beside them and they feared with a great dread. And the angel said to them. Fear not. Lo! I preach to you about a great joy, which shall be to all people. For this day is born to us a saviour which is Christ, the Lord, in the city of David. And this shall be a token for you: you shall find a child wrapped in cloths and put in a crib.

Here it seems openly in this text that God sent first his message and joyful tidings of his Son's birth to simple, poor shepherds, to show that he was not born into this world to reign over men with worldly excellence and temporal power, but in a poor estate and to lead his life simply, and so to reign through grace virtuously in human souls. And therefore he showed first his birth to poor men of simple occupation. The token that the angel gave to the shepherds whereby they could know about this child proves the same. It was not a token of great excellence and dignity, but a token of great simplicity and poverty. When he said, 'You shall find a child wrapped in cloths and placed in a crib', God said this to show that he is not a respecter of persons. A poor shepherd may be acceptable, or a poor man with a proper occupation if he love God and keep his commandments, whether he be the most exalted person, temporal or spiritual.

So no rich man should despise any poor man because of his poverty or for his simple occupation, if he be virtuous in his living. He should note well how Christ chooses rather poor men for his friends rather than rich. Therefore Saint James said: Did God not choose the poor of this world? [Jas. 2:5]. God often shows the mysteries of Scripture to the simple and those of moderate learning, who are meek; and hides it from the lofty clergy and the intellectuals that are proud of their learning, as the gospel reminds us: 'I declare to you, Father of heaven and of earth, that you have hid these things from the wise and prudent and thou hast made them clear to the humble' [Mt. 11:25].

# Chapter 10

# Girolamo Savonarola (1452–1498)

Compendium of Revelations **(1495)**

Born in Ferrara, Italy, Savonarola was an apocalyptic visionary whose despondence at the moral corruption of the society and church around him led him to run away from home and enter the Dominicans. After initial difficulties, he eventually developed a distinct and most popular style of preaching. He became an erudite biblical scholar and his preaching displayed an evangelical emphasis before such an approach became widespread with the advent of the age of reform. A further innovation was his interpretation of many Old Testament texts, and Exodus in particular, in relation to human liberation in the context of his own age. It was in the city of Florence that he would have most influence and it was near there, in 1485, that he preached his first prophetic sermon, telling of a coming time of trial and hardship for the church, which would later be reformed anew. He was elected prior of the important convent of San Marco in 1491 and set about reforming the practices in the convent, urging a stricter observance of the order's rule. His earlier spell as novice master saw the beginnings of his promotion of biblical and patristic studies which would bear bounteous fruit for generations to come. His prophecy of an invasion of Italy by a king who would wreak God's vengeance across the land as atonement for the people's immoral lifestyles and the corruption of the church eerily appeared to be fulfilled in the eyes of many when Charles VIII of France (1483–98) entered Italy in 1494. With the subsequent decline in power of the Medici family in the city, Savonarola's influence increased to the point where he became the guiding light behind the Florentine Republic, established after negotiations with Charles. His preaching now took on a positive, millenarian character and he attempted to reform Florentine society not simply in terms of personal morality amongst individual citizens, but also institutionally and in terms of social justice. His vision was of a theocratic republic, a Christian Commonwealth which cared for all its needy citizens and resisted the vanities of worldly pleasures. However, his antagonism of the Borgia Pope, Alexander VI, was to eventually lead to his demise, with first excommunication, then his arrest on charges of false prophecy and political intrigue following once

Alexander had succeeded in provoking the fickle Florentine masses to turn against their preacher. Following torture, Savonarola and two companions were put to death on May 23, 1498. He influenced and was in turn influenced by leading humanist scholars of the day and helped shape later reforms and spiritualities on many sides of the reformation divides. His legacy lived on in the shape of his followers, the *Piagnoni* ('Wailers'), throughout Florence for a further half-century.


## Source

Our extract comes from his apologetic *Compendium of Revelations* (Florence, 1495) and recounts his apocalyptic preaching early in his career, as well as indicating his own agenda for ecclesial and societal reform. (Taken from Bernard McGinn, *Visions of the End*, Columbia University Press, 1998, pp. 280–1.)


## Further reading

de la Bedoyère, Michael, *The Meddlesome Friar: the Story of the Conflict between Savonarola and Alexander VI*, London: Collins, 1957.

Macey, Patrick Paul, *Bonfire Songs – Savonarola's Musical Legacy*, Oxford: Clarendon Press, 1998.

McGinn, Bernard, *Visions of the End – Apocalyptic Traditions in the Middle Ages*, New York: Columbia University Press, 1998.

McGinn, Bernard (ed.), *Apocalyptic Spirituality: treatises and letters of Lactantius, Adso of Montier-en-Der, Joachim of Fiore, the Franciscan Spirituals, Savonarola*, London: SPCK, 1980.

Olin, John C, *The Catholic Reformation – Savonarola to Ignatius Loyola*, New York: Fordham University Press, 1992.

Polizzotto, Lorenzo: *The Elect Nation – The Savonarolan Movement in Florence, 1494–1545*, Oxford: Clarendon, 1994.

Ridolfi, Roberto, *The Life of Girolamo Savonarola*, ET by Cecil Grayson, London: RKP, 1959.

Weinstein, Donald, *Savonarola and Florence – Prophecy and Patriotism in the Renaissance*, Princeton: Princeton University Press, 1970.

## From *Compendium of Revelations*

*The Early Stages of Savonarola's Prophetic Career*

Therefore when Almighty God saw the sins of Italy multiply, especially among both ecclesiastical and secular princes, he was not able to bear it any longer and determined to purify his Church with a great scourge. Since, as Amos the prophet says: "The Lord God will not perform his word unless he first reveal his secret to his servants the prophets" (Amos 3:7), for the sake of the salvation of his elect he wished that scourge to be foretold in Italy, so that forewarned, his people might prepare themselves to endure it more firmly. Florence, located in the middle of Italy like the heart in a man, God deigned to choose to receive this message so that from there it might be widely spread through other parts of Italy as we now see fulfilled. He chose me, unworthy and useless among his other servants, to this task. At the bidding of my superiors, God saw to it that I came to Florence in 1489, and in that year on Sunday, August 1, I began to interpret publicly the Book of Revelation in our Church of San Marco. Through the whole of the same year I preached to the people of Florence, continually stressing three things: first, the future renovation of the Church in these times; second, the great scourge that God would bring on all Italy before such a renovation; third, that these two things would come soon. . . .

Among other things, there was one that brought men of genius and learning to admiration, namely that from 1491 to 1494 I undertook continuous preaching upon Genesis through the whole of Advent and Lent, with the exception of one period spent in Bologna. . . . And with God willing and leading me on, I left off with the text, "Make a second and third floor in it" (Gen. 6:16), and began again the next September on the Feast of St. Matthew the Apostle with the following passage, that is, "Behold, I will bring flood waters upon the earth." Since everyone knew that the French king had invaded Italy with his forces, when I began my sermon with these words, that is, "Behold, I will bring flood waters upon the earth," suddenly many were astonished and thought that this passage of Genesis was furnished by God's hidden will for that moment in time. Among these was Count Giovanni della Mirandola, a man unique in our day for talent and learning; he later told me that he was struck with fear at these words and that his hair stood on end.

# Chapter 11

# Defending the Indians

**Antonio de Montesinos (fl. 1510), Advent Sermon (1511)**
**Bartolomé de Las Casas (1474–1566),** Historia de las Indias

Montesinos was one of four Dominican friars who landed on Hispaniola (now Haiti/the Dominican Republic) in 1510, eighteen years after Columbus first arrived there. By this time the subjugation and conversion of the indigenous population was well under way through the *encomienda* system, an institutionalized form of slavery under which, in return for labor and tribute, owners gave their Indians religious instruction. Montesinos' sermon, preached on the Sunday before Christmas 1511, was a deliberate rebuke to his fellow country-people, and probably the first public protest against their treatment of the Indians. His words are taken from a report by Las Casas, also a Dominican friar, who was at that time an *encomendero* himself. Las Casas famously experienced a Damascus-road conversion four years later while on his estate in Cuba, and the second extract, taken from his *History of the Indies*, relates (in the third person) that experience. After turning over his slaves to the Governor of the island and preaching a sermon along the lines of Montesinos', Las Casas shuttled between America and Spain, pleading the Indians' case at the royal court and before leading church figures.

Las Casas' long life is well-documented, and he is today the best-known of the Catholic missionaries who took up the Indians' cause and advocated their evangelization without the use of arms. Little is known of Montesinos, however, other than that he once also spoke out for the Indians at the court in Spain, and died protecting them in Venezuela. The only document to remark upon his historic sermon, outside of Las Casas' writings, is a royal edict ordering him to refrain from preaching.

## Source

L. Hanke, *The Spanish Struggle for Justice in the Conquest of America*, Boston: Little, Brown, 1965, p. 17.

H. R. Parish and F. P. Sullivan, *Bartolomé de Las Casas: The Only Way*, Sources of American Spirituality, New York: Paulist Press, 1992, pp. 186–91.

## Further reading

Gustavo Gutiérrez, *Las Casas: In Search of the Poor of Jesus Christ*, New York, 1993.
Enrique Dussel, *A History of the Church in Latin America: Colonialism to Liberation*, Grand Rapids, Michigan, 1981.

## Advent Sermon (1511)

In order to make your sins against the Indians known to you I have come up on this pulpit, I who am a voice of Christ crying in the wilderness of this island, and therefore it behoves you to listen, not with careless attention, but with all your heart and senses, so that you may hear it; for this is going to be the strangest voice that ever you heard, the harshest and hardest and most awful and most dangerous that ever you expected to hear. . . . This voice says that you are in mortal sin, that you live and die in it, for the cruelty and tyranny you use in dealing with these innocent people. Tell me, by what right or justice do you keep these Indians in such a cruel and horrible servitude? On what authority have you waged a detestable war against these people, who dwelt quietly and peacefully on their own land? . . . Why do you keep them so oppressed and weary, not giving them enough to eat nor taking care of them in their illness? For with the excessive work you demand of them they fall ill and die, or rather you kill them with your desire to extract and acquire gold every day. And what care do you take that they should be instructed in religion? . . . Are these not men? Have they not rational souls? Are you not bound to love them as you love yourselves? . . . Be certain that, in such a state as this, you can no more be saved than the Moors or Turks.

### *Historia de las Indias*

. . . We told how Diego Velásquez, in charge of Cuba for the admiral, marked out five places for settlement where all the Spaniards on the island were to live in groups. There was one already populated, Baracoa. The Indians who lived near each settlement were divided up and given to the Spaniards. Each Spaniard had an itch for gold and a narrow conscience. They had no thought that those natives were made of flesh and blood. They put them to work in mines and at other projects the Indians could accomplish as slave labor, put them to work so promptly, so pitilessly that in a few days' time many native deaths showed the brutality of Spanish treatment. The loss of people on Cuba was quicker, fiercer, during the early period than it was elsewhere. The explanation: the Spaniards roamed the island *pacifying* it. They took many Indians from the villages as servants for themselves. The Spaniards reaped but did not sow. As to the villagers, some fled; some, nervous and fearful, cared only to escape being killed as many another was killed. The fields were picked clean of food and abandoned.

Since greed fed the Spaniards, as I said, they cared nothing for sowing and reaping food; they cared only for reaping gold they had not sown, however they could, eating whatever scraps of food they could scrounge up. And they set men and women to work without food enough to live on, never mind work on, in the mines. It is a true story, one I told elsewhere, that a Spaniard recounted in my presence and in that of several others, as if he were telling a fine way of doing things. He had his allotted Indians raise so many thousand mound-rows. (That is how they grow [the root] cassava bread is made from.) He sent them every third day, or two on, two off, to the fields to eat whatever growth they found. With what they then had in their bellies he made them work another two or three days in the mines. He gave them not another bite to eat. Farm work means digging the whole day, a far harder job than tilling our vineyards and food gardens home in Spain. It means raising into mounds the earth they dig, three to four feet square, three to four hands high. And not with spades or hoes that are provided, but with pole-length, fire-hardened sticks.

Hunger, having nothing to eat, being put to hard labor, caused death among these peoples more quickly, more violently, than in any other place. The Spaniards took healthy men and women to do mine and other work. They left behind in the villages only the sick and the old, left no one to help them, care for them. So the sick and old died from anguish and age as well as from mortal hunger. I sometimes heard, back then when I traveled the island, as I would enter a village, voices calling from inside the huts. When I went in to find out what they wanted, they answered, "*Food!*" "*Food!*" There was not a man or a woman able to stand on two legs that they did not drag off to the mines. As for the new mothers with their small boy and girl children, their breasts dried: they had so little to eat, so much work, they had no milk left, the babies died. That was the cause of the deaths of seven thousand baby boys and girls in the space of three months. The event was described in a report to the Catholic king by a creditable person who had investigated it. Another event also occurred back then. An official of the king got three hundred Indians as his allotment. He was in such a hurry putting them to work in the mines and at the rest of his jobs that at the end of three months only a tenth of those Indians remained alive.

The crushing of Indians took this route and grew in ferocity each day. As greed grew and grew, so did the number of Indian dead. [While this was going on] Padre Bartolomé de las Casas (mentioned briefly above) was very busy looking after his own holdings. As the others did, he sent his allotted Indians to the mines to dig gold, to the fields to plant crops, profiting from his Indians as much as he could, though he was always careful to maintain them well in every way possible, and treat them kindly, and alleviate their hardships. But he took no more care than the others to recall that these were pagan peoples and that he had an obligation to teach them Christian doctrine and gather them into the bosom of the Church.

Diego Velásquez and the group of Spaniards with him left the port of Xagua to go and found a settlement of Spaniards in the province, where they established the town called Sancti Espiritus. Apart from Bartolomé de las Casas, there was not a single cleric or friar on the whole island, except for one in the town of Baracoa. The feast of Pentecost was coming up. So he agreed to leave his home on the Arimao River (accent on the penult) a league from Xagua where his holdings were and go say mass and preach for them on that feast. Las Casas looked over the previous sermons he had preached to them on that feast and his other sermons for that season. He began to meditate on some passages of Sacred Scripture. If my memory serves me, the first and most important was from Ecclesiasticus 34:18ff.:

> Unclean is the offering sacrificed by an oppressor. [Such] mockeries of the unjust are not pleasing [to God]. The Lord is pleased only by those who keep to the way of truth and justice. The Most High does not accept the gifts of unjust people, He does not look well upon their offerings. Their sins will not be expiated by repeat-sacrifices. *The one whose sacrifice comes from the goods of the poor is like one who kills his neighbor. The one who sheds blood and the one who defrauds the laborer are kin and kind.*

He began to reflect on the misery, the forced labor the Indians had to undergo. He was helped in this by what he had heard and experienced on the island of Hispaniola, by what the Dominicans preached continually – no one could, in good conscience, hold the Indians in encomienda, and those friars would not confess and absolve any who so held them – a preaching Las Casas had refused to accept. One time he wanted to confess to a religious of St. Dominic who happened to be in the vicinity. Las Casas held Indians on that island of Hispaniola, as indifferent and blind about it as he was on the island of Cuba. The religious refused him confession. Las Casas asked him why. He gave the reason. Las Casas objected with frivolous arguments and empty explanations, seemingly sound, provoking the religious to respond, "Padre, I think the truth has many enemies and the lie has many friends." Then Las Casas offered him the respect due his dignity and reputation because the religious was a revered and learned man, much more so than the padre, but he took no heed of the confessor's counsel to let his Indians go. Yet it helped him greatly to recall his quarrel later, and also the confession he made to the religious, so as to think more about the road of ignorance and danger he was on, holding Indians as others did, confessing without scruple those who held or wanted to hold Indians, though he did not do so for long. But he had heard many confessions on that island of Hispaniola, from people who were in the same mortal sin.

He spent some days thinking about the situation, each day getting surer and surer from what he read concerning what was legal and what was actual, measuring the one by the other, until he came to the same truth by himself. Everything in these Indies that was done to the Indians was tyrannical and unjust. Everything he read to firm up his judgment he found favorable, and he used to say strongly that from the very moment he began to dispel the darkness of that ignorance, he never read a book in Latin or Spanish – a countless number over the span of forty-two years – where he didn't find some argument or authority to prove or support the justice of those Indian peoples, and to condemn the injustices done to them, the evils, the injuries.

He then made a decision to preach his conclusion. But since his holding Indians meant holding a contradiction of his own preaching, he determined to give them up so as to be free to condemn allotments, the whole system of forced labor, as unjust and tyrannical, and to hand his Indians back to Governor Diego Velásquez. They were better off under the padre's control, to be sure. He had treated them with greater respect, would be even more respectful in the future. He knew that giving them up meant they would be handed over to someone who would brutalize them, work them to death, as someone did ultimately. Granted, he would give them a treatment as good as a father would give his children. Yet, since he would preach that no one could in good conscience hold Indians, he could never escape people mocking back at him, "You hold Indians nonetheless. Why not release them? You say holding them is tyranny!" So he decided to give them up completely.

To get a better understanding of all that happened, it would be right here to recall the close friendship the padre had with a certain Pedro de la Rentería, a prudent, deeply Christian man. We spoke of him earlier somewhat [saying that he was the only encomendero I remember who cared for the Indian soul]. They were not just friends, but partners also in the estate. They received together their allotments of natives. They had decided together that Pedro de la Rentería should go to the island of Jamaica where Pedro had a brother. The purpose: to bring back pigs to fatten and corn to plant, plus other things not found in Cuba since it was cleaned out, a fact already established. For the voyage they chartered a government ship for two thousand castellanos. So, since Pedro de la Rentería was away, and since the padre had decided to give up his Indians and go preach what he felt obliged to preach and thus enlighten those who were deep in the darkness of ignorance, he went on a day to Governor Diego Velásquez. He told him what he thought about his own situation, the situation of the governor, and of the rest of the Spaniards. He stated that no one in that situation could be saved, and he stated that he intended to preach this to escape the danger, and to do what his priesthood required. Thus he was determined to give back his Indians to the governor, to keep charge of them no longer. Therefore the governor should consider them available and should dispose of them as he wished. But the padre asked the favor that the business be kept secret, that the governor give the Indians to no one else until Rentería returned from the island of Jamaica where he was at the moment. The reason: the estate and the Indians they held in common might suffer harm if, before Rentería returned, the person to whom the governor gave the Indians might move in on them and the estate prematurely.

The governor was shocked at hearing such an unusual story. For one thing, that a cleric who was free to own things in the world should be of the opinion of the

Dominican friars – they had first dared to think it and dared to make it known. For another, that the cleric had such a righteous scorn for temporal possessions that, having such a great aptitude for getting rich quickly, he should give it up. Especially since he had a growing reputation for being industrious: people saw him most zealous about his property and his mines, saw other acquisitive qualities in him. But the governor was mainly stunned, and answered him more out of consideration for what touched the padre in the temporal realm than for the danger in which the governor himself lived as top man in the tyranny perpetrated against the Indians on that island.

> Padre, think of what you are doing. No need for scruples! It is God who wants to see you rich and prosperous. For that reason I do not allow the surrender you make of your Indians. I give you fifteen days to think it over so you can come to a better decision. After a fortnight you can come back and tell me what you will do.

The padre replied,

> My Lord, I am most grateful that you want me to prosper, most grateful for all the other kindnesses your grace has done for me. But act, my Lord, as though the fortnight were over. Please God, if I ever repent of the decision I broached to you, if I ever want to hold Indians again – and if you, for the love you have of me, should ever want to leave them with me or give them to me anew – if you accept my plea to have them, even if I wept blood, may God be the one to punish you severely, may God never forgive this sin. I ask your grace one favor, that this whole business be kept secret and that you do not allot the natives to anyone until Rentería returns, so his estate suffers no harm.

The governor promised. He kept his promise. From then on he had a far greater respect for the padre. And concerning his governance, he did many good things that touched on native matters and his own personal conduct, all due to the effect of the padre (as if he had seen him do miracles). The rest of the Spaniards on the island began to change their view of the padre from before, once they knew he had given up his natives. Such an action was considered then and always the consummate proof that could demonstrate sanctity. Such was and is the blindness of those who came out to the New World.

The padre made the secret public the following way. He was preaching on the feast day of the Assumption of Our Lady in that place where he was – [the town of Sancti Espiritus] mentioned earlier. He was explaining the contemplative and the active life, the theme of the gospel reading for the day, talking about the spiritual and corporal works of mercy. He had to make clear to his hearers their obligation to perform these works toward the native peoples they made use of so cruelly; he had to blame the merciless, negligent, mindless way they lived off those natives. For which it struck him as the right moment to reveal the secret agreement he had set up with the governor. And he said, "My Lord, I give you freedom to reveal to everyone whatever you wish concerning what we agreed on in secret

– I take that freedom myself in order to reveal it to those here present." This said, he began to expose to them their own blindness, the injustices, the tyrannies, the cruelties they committed against such innocent, such gentle people. They could not save their souls, neither those who held Indians by allotment, nor the one who handed them out. They were bound by the obligation to make restitution. He himself, once he knew the danger of damnation in which he lived, had given up his Indians, had given up many other things connected with holding Indians. The congregation was stupefied, even fearful of what he said to them. Some felt compunction, others thought it a bad dream, hearing bizarre statements such as: No one could hold Indians in servitude without sinning. As if to say they could not make use of beasts of the field! Unbelievable.

# Chapter 12

# Argula von Grumbach (ca. 1492–1554)

## To the University of Ingolstadt (1522)

Argula von Grumbach came from an aristocratic family but for a time became embroiled in the 1520s in the major debates of the Reformation in Germany. Arsacius Seehoffer of the University of Ingolstadt was arrested for Lutheran views and was forced to recant. This event was about to pass off without too many repercussions when Argula dispatched a letter to the university authorities. It provoked a furious reaction. Argula was called a "female devil" (she was later to be accused of neglecting the upbringing of her children), and her husband was sacked from his civil post. She was forced to write a poem by way of defense of her position in the light of the extraordinary polemic that was directed at her. Argula was clearly indebted to the new impetus given to scripture as the basis for criticism of polity and religion. Hers is (to quote Peter Matheson) "a dialectic between the situation of her own time and the Scripture." She believes herself led by the Spirit to see how God is speaking through the Scriptures to the people of her own day. In this vein her approach, and the sense of vocation which impels her to testify whatever the habits and conventions of her culture, are reminiscent of many others, not least her Anabaptist contemporaries, who come from very different social strata from Argula. The apocalyptic sense which is found also in the writings of Müntzer reflects a sense of struggle between darkness and light, and between human and divine wisdom.

## Source

P. Matheson, *Argula von Grumbach A Woman's Voice in the Reformation*, Edinburgh: T&T Clark, 1995.

Further reading

P. Matheson, *The Imaginative World of in the Reformation*, Edinburgh: T&T Clark, 2000.

## To the University of Ingolstadt

NOW FOLLOWS THE CHRISTIAN LETTER *of the woman we have mentioned, whose name will be found at the end*

THE LORD SAYS, JOHN 12, 'I am the light that has come into the world, that none who believe in me should abide in darkness.' It is my heartfelt wish that this light should dwell in all of us and shine upon all callous and blinded hearts. Amen.

I find there is a text in Matthew 10 which runs: 'Whoever confesses me before another I too will confess before my heavenly Father.' And Luke 9: 'Whoever is ashamed of me and of my words, I too will be ashamed of when I come in my majesty', etc. Words like these, coming from the very mouth of God, are always before my eyes. For they exclude neither woman nor man.

And this is why I am compelled as a Christian to write to you. For Ezekiel 33 says: 'If you see your brother sin, reprove him, or I will require his blood at your hands.' In Matthew 12, the Lord says: 'All sins will be forgiven; but the sin against the Holy Spirit will never be forgiven, neither here nor in eternity.' And in John 6 the Lord says: 'My words are spirit and life . . .'.

How in God's name can you and your university expect to prevail, when you deploy such foolish violence against the word of God; when you force someone to hold the holy Gospel in their hands for the very purpose of denying it, as you did in the case of Arsacius Seehofer? When you confront him with an oath and declaration such as this, and use imprisonment and even the threat of the stake to force him to deny Christ and his word?

Yes, when I reflect on this my heart and all my limbs tremble. What do Luther or Melanchthon teach you but the word of God? You condemn them without having refuted them. Did Christ teach you so, or his apostles, prophets, or evangelists? Show me where this is written! You lofty experts, nowhere in the Bible do I find that Christ, or his apostles, or his prophets put people in prison, burnt or murdered them, or sent them into exile. . . . Don't you know that the Lord says in Matthew 10? 'Have no fear of him who can take your body but then his power is at an end. But fear him who has power to despatch soul and body into the depths of hell.'

One knows very well the importance of one's duty to obey the authorities. But where the word of God is concerned neither Pope, Emperor nor princes – as Acts 4 and 5 make so clear – have any jurisdiction. For my part, I have to confess, in the name of God and by my soul's salvation, that if I were to deny Luther and Melanchthon's writing I would be denying God and his word, which may God forfend for ever. Amen.

Haven't you read the first chapter of Jeremiah, where the Lord says to him: 'What do you see?' He says: 'I see a vigilant rod.' Says the Lord: 'You see correctly, for I am ceaselessly vigilant in order to bring my words to pass.' He asks him again: 'What else do you see?' 'I see a burning pot, and the face of God from midnight.' Says the Lord: 'You have seen correctly; for from midnight every evil will be revealed to every inhabitant of the earth.' The pot burns; and truly you and your university will never extinguish it. And neither the Pope with his decretals, nor Aristotle, who has never been a Christian, nor you yourselves can manage it. You may imagine that you can defy God, cast down his prophets and apostles from heaven, and banish them from the world. This shall not happen. I beseech you, my dear masters, let him stay; have no doubt about it: God will surely preserve his holy and blessed word. As he has hitherto declared; has done in the Old and New Testament, still does, and will continue to do.

God will fall upon you, as the prophet says, Hosea 13: 'They puffed up their hearts and forgot me. I will be to them as a lion in their path. And will fall upon them like a bear who sees her young being stolen.' And Hosea 6: 'I smote them with the words of my mouth. Woe to you! for you have made your counsel without me.' Isaiah 30. And Ezekiel 13: 'Woe to the fools, to those who prophesy according to their own conceits. They see useless things, and teach lies. They say: "The Lord says" when I have neither spoken nor sent them. For a handful of barley and a piece of bread they kill souls which are not dying, and declare souls living which do not live. And they lie to my people, so that they believe their lies . . .'. And what does God say in Ezekiel 33? 'The warning of the Lord was like a cheerful ditty to them until the punishment came, for they did not know that a prophet was among them.' And Jeremiah 48: 'God became the butt of their scorn, as if they had discovered him among thieves.'

Greed has possessed you; you would be much readier to suffer God's word if you did not profit from the publication of the Decretal. The gospel does not pull in so many dollars for its advisers. I have seen how my dear lord and father of blessed memory had to pay twenty gulden for a piece of advice four lines long; not that it did him a cent of good. But what does David say in Psalm 36? 'I have been young and now am old, and have yet to see the children of righteousness having to beg for bread.' I beseech you. Trust in God. He will not desert us, for every hair on our heads is numbered and in his care, as Matthew 10 says. I had to listen for ages to your Decretal preacher crying out in the Church of Our Lady: *Ketzer/ketzer*, 'Heretic, heretic!' Poor Latin, that! I could say as much myself, no doubt; and I have never been to university. But if they are to prove their case they'll have to do better than that. I always meant to write to him, to ask him to show me which heretical articles the loyal worker for the gospel, Martin Luther, is supposed to have taught.

However I suppressed my inclinations; heavy of heart, I did nothing. Because Paul says in 1 Timothy 2: 'The women should keep silence, and should not speak in church.' But now that I cannot see any man who is up to it, who is either willing or able to speak, I am constrained by the saying: 'Whoever confesses me', as I said above. And I claim for myself Isaiah 3: 'I will send children to be their princes; and women, or those who are womanish, shall rule over them.' And Isaiah 29: 'Those who err will know knowledge in their spirit, and those who mutter will teach the law.' And Ezekiel 20: 'I raise up my hand against them to scatter them. They never followed my judgements, they rejected my commandments, and their eyes were on the idols of their fathers. Therefore I gave them commandments, but no good ones; and judgements by which they could never live.' And Psalm 8: 'You have ordained praise out of the mouth of children and infants at the breast, on account of your enemies.' And Luke 10: 'Jesus rejoiced in the Spirit, and said: "Father, I give you thanks, that you have hidden these things from the wise, and revealed them to the little ones".' Jeremiah 3: 'They will all know God, from the least to the greatest.' John 6, and Isaiah 54: 'They will all be taught of God.' Paul in 1 Corinthians 12: 'No one can say "Jesus", without the spirit of God.' Just as the Lord says of the confession of Peter in Matthew 16: 'Flesh and blood has not revealed this to you, but my heavenly Father'.

Do you hear this? That it is God who gives us understanding, not any human being? As Paul, too, says in 1 Corinthians 2: 'Your faith should not be in human wisdom . . .'. You, with your papal laws, will not be able to coerce us, not by a long chalk. We have witness enough from Scripture that they have no right to make laws without God's command, as Jeremiah 23 says. Where, however, it is based in the Bible, the book which contains all God's commands, we will be happy and pleased to accept it. But where it is not, it has no validity for us at all. Or only in so far as it is my duty to spare my weak and foolish brother, until he, too, has been instructed. For God says, Deuteronomy 4: 'Add nothing to my word, and subtract nothing from it'. And Proverbs 30: 'Add nothing to the words of God, lest you be reproved, and be found a liar.' Just before that we find: 'The word of God is a fiery shield to all who put their trust and confidence in him.' Isaiah and Jeremiah: 'The word which I say to you, proclaim to them from my mouth . . .'.

A disputation is easily won when one argues with force, not Scripture. As far as I can see that means that the hangman is accounted the most learned. It's easy to see, though, that the devil has helped to arrange this fine hullabaloo. God will not put up with your ways much longer. In 2 Corinthians 11 Paul says: 'the devil turns himself into an angel of light'. So it is no wonder that confidence tricksters turn themselves into apostles of Christ. Remember Matthew 10: 'There has to be conflict, the son against the father, the daughter against the mother, the bride against the mother in law, and one's servants will become one's enemies.' And John 16: 'The time will come when they will kill you and think that they do God a service. For they know neither the Father nor me.' And Paul in 1 Corinthians 11: 'Conflict must take place, so that those who are approved may be revealed.' Also 2 Corinthians 4: 'If the Gospel is hidden, it is to those who are perishing . . .'.

Ah, but what a joy it is when the spirit of God teaches us and gives us understanding, flitting from one text to the next – God be praised – so that I came to see the true, genuine light shining out. I don't intend to bury my talent, if the Lord gives me grace. 'The gospel', says Christ, Luke 7, 'is preached to the poor, and blessed is the one who is not offended by me . . .'. As Paul says in 1 Corinthians 9: 'I preach the unvarnished gospel, lest I abuse my power.' 'I speak truly to you of the light that shines again in the world'. Psalm 118: 'As your word is disclosed it shines forth and gives understanding to the lowly.' Psalm 36: 'In you is the well of life, and in your light we will see light.' John 2: God sought no human witness, 'for he knew what was in everyone'. John 16: 'The spirit will explain who I am.' John 14: 'I am the way, the truth and the life. No one comes to the Father except through me.' And in John 9 the Lord says: 'I am come for judgement upon this world. So that those who do not see should see, and those who do see should be made blind. The Pharisees said: "Are we blind, then?" The Lord answers: "If you were blind you would be without sin. But if you say: We understand, then your sin stands".' And John 8: 'Whoever abides in my word is my disciple.' And in the same chapter: 'Whoever is of God, hears the word of God. Therefore if you do not hear it you are not of God . . .'. And John 10: 'My little sheep know my voice, but a stranger's voice they do not know and so they do not follow him'. Matthew 24: 'Heaven and earth will pass away. But my words will not pass away'. And Isaiah 40: 'The word of God stands for ever'.

Now I don't find such promises from human beings, or papal laws or utterances. 2 Corinthians 1: 'The word of God in his promises is a Yes which excludes any No.' 'From this word was made heaven and earth and all that is in it, and without it nothing was made.' John 1. And God was the word by which the dead were quickened, the sinner converted, the blind made to see, the lame made straight, the dumb to speak and so on. . . . That is a treasury of salvation, not a pit for cash, like the Decretals. Through it life is promised to us. Matthew 4 and John 6.

I cry out with the prophet Jeremiah, chapter 22: 'Earth, earth, earth! Hear the word of the Lord.' I beseech and request a reply from you if you consider that I am in error, though I am not aware of it. For Jerome was not ashamed of writing a great deal to women, to Blesilla, for example, to Paula, Eustochium and so on. Yes, and Christ himself, he who is the only teacher of us all, was not ashamed to preach to Mary Magdalene, and to the young woman at the well.

I do not flinch from appearing before you, from listening to you, from discussing with you. For by the grace of God I, too, can ask questions, hear answers and read in German. There are, of course, German Bibles which Martin has not translated. You yourselves have one which was printed forty one years ago, when Luther's was never even thought of.

If God had not ordained it, I might behave like the others, and write or say that he perverts (Scripture); that it is contrary to God's will. Although I have yet to read anyone who is his equal in translating it into German. May God, who works all this in him, be his reward here in time and in eternity. And even if it came to pass – which God forfend – that Luther were to revoke his views, that would not worry me. I do not build on his, mine, or any person's understanding, but on the true rock, Christ himself, which the builders have rejected. But he has been made the foundation stone, and the head of the corner, as Paul says in 1 Corinthians 3: 'No other base can be laid, than that which is laid, which is Christ'.

God grant that I may speak with you in the presence of our three princes and of the whole community. It is my desire to be instructed by everyone. Philosophy can avail nothing. As Paul says to the Colossians, chapter 2: 'Be careful of philosophy and the lofty speech of those who are wise in the things of the world.' And what does he say in 1 Corinthians 1: 'God has made human wisdom folly'? In 1 Corinthians 3: 'All the wisdom of the world is folly to God.'

Jurisprudence cannot harm me; for it avails nothing here; I can detect no divine theology in it. Therefore I have no fears for myself, as long as you wish to instruct me by writing, and not by violence, prison or the stake. Joel 2: 'Turn again; return to the Lord. For he is kind and merciful.' The Lord laments in the words of Jeremiah 2: 'They have forsaken me, the well of living water, and have dug out broken cisterns which cannot hold any water.'

With Paul, 1 Corinthians 2, I say: 'I am not ashamed of the gospel which is the power of God to salvation to those who believe.' The Lord says, in Matthew 10: 'Should you be called forward do not worry about what you will say. It is not you who speak. In that same hour you will be given what you have to say. And the spirit of your Father will speak through you.'

I have no Latin; but you have German, being born and brought up in this tongue. What I have written to you is no woman's chit-chat, but the word of God; and (I write) as a member of the Christian Church, against which the gates of Hell cannot prevail. Against the Roman, however, they do prevail. Just look at that church! How is it to prevail against the gates of Hell? God give us his grace, that we all may be saved, and may (God) rule us according to his will. Now may his grace carry the day. Amen.

Dietfurt. Sunday after the exaltation of the holy Cross. The year of the Lord. . . . One thousand five hundred and in the twenty-third year.

My signature.

Argula von Grumbach,
von Stauff by birth.

# Chapter 13

# Thomas Müntzer (1489?–1525)

### Vindication and Refutation (1524)

One of the better-known figures of the so-called "radical reformation," Müntzer was a gifted preacher, pastor, liturgist, and polemicist. A devotee of Luther when the latter issued his first public critiques of the papacy, both soon became the bitterest of foes, their denunciations of each other in print often descending to the lowest levels of personal insult. Glimpses of Müntzer's imaginative invective come through in this extract – note the reference to "the godless flesh in Wittenberg," "Brother Soft-Life," "Dr Liar" (which works as a pun in German), "Father Pussyfoot" and so on – though his concern is not simply to pour scorn on his onetime mentor: rather he seeks to highlight how, since "biblical scholars" only comprehend the letter of Scripture, they know nothing of the movement of the Spirit within the soul, and the true understanding of Scripture and godly life that promotes. This cannot be gained from the study of books, Müntzer affirms, but only by experience, and is often to be found in the "humble folk" whom the biblical scholars despise.

   The full title of the piece from which this extract is drawn is *A highly provoked Vindication and a Refutation of the unspiritual soft-living Flesh in Wittenberg, whose robbery and distortion of Scripture has so grievously polluted our wretched Christian Church*. Published toward the end of 1524, it is clearly a riposte to Luther's *Letter to the Princes of Saxony*, with its exhortation to its readers to crack down hard on "that satan" Müntzer. As such it is by far the most personalized and polemical of his writings, yet in it Müntzer also offers a passionate, scripturally-grounded critique of the way the "lords and princes" exploit the poor through usury, theft, and appropriating to themselves that which God created for all to enjoy. It was to try to overturn this exploitation that he took up the cause of the peasants against the princes the following year. An example of the grievances of the peasants is found in the *Articles of the Peasants of Memmingen* (1525).

## Source

Peter Matheson, ed., *The Collected Works of Thomas Müntzer*, Edinburgh, 1988, pp. 329–35.

Tom Scott and Robert W Scribner, eds., *The German Peasants' War: a history in documents*, Atlantic Highlands, NJ: Humanities Press International, 1991, pp. 78–80.

## Further reading

Gordon Rupp, *Patterns of Reformation*, London, 1969.
Tom Scott, *Thomas Müntzer: Theology and Revolution in the German Revolution*, London, 1989.
Hans-Jürgen Goertz, *Thomas Müntzer: Apocalyptic Mystic and Revolutionary*, Edinburgh, 1993.
Andrew Bradstock, *Faith in the Revolution: The Political Theologies of Müntzer and Winstanley*, London, 1997.

## *Vindication and Refutation* (1524)

The whole of Holy Scripture is about the crucified son of God and nothing else (as is evidenced, too, by all the creatures) which is why he himself explained his ministry by beginning with Moses and going on to all the prophets, showing how he had to suffer and enter into the glory of his father. The last chapter of Luke sets this out clearly. Paul, too, having searched the law of God more penetratingly than all his companions, Gal. 1, says that he can only preach Christ, the crucified, 1 Cor. 1. For he was unable to find in it anything else than the suffering son of God, of whom Matthew 5 says that he did not come to rob the law of its force or to tear up the covenant of God, but on the contrary to complete, explain and fulfil it.

The hate-filled biblical scholars were unable to recognise any of this, for they did not search Scripture with their whole heart and spirit as they ought to have, Psalm 118, and as Christ commanded them, John 5. They were like the monkeys who tried to emulate the cobbler and succeeded only in ruining the leather. And why was this? Because they wanted the comfort of the holy spirit but never once reached the ground [of their soul] through sadness of heart, as one must if the true light is to shine out in the darkness and empower us to be children of God – as is clearly explained in Psalm 54 and Psalm 62 and John 1.

So if Christ is merely accepted on the testimony of the old and new covenants of God but preached without any manifestation of the spirit the result may be much more confusion and monkeying around than the Jews and the pagans caused. Anyone can see with his own eyes that today's biblical scholars do exactly the same as the Pharisees did of old. They boast of their competence in holy scripture, cover every book with their writing and their blots and blether on more and more every day, saying: Have faith, have faith! Yet all the time they deny the source of faith, deride the spirit of God and really believe in nothing at all, as you see. None of them will preach unless they get a stipend of forty of fifty florins. Indeed, the best actually want more than a hundred or two hundred florins, bringing to pass the prophecy of Micah 3: 'The priests preach for the money they get out of it.' They want their peace and their easy life and their lofty status, and yet they boast that they understand the source of faith. In fact, however, they do the absolute opposite, for they scold the true spirit for being an erring spirit and a satan, using Holy Scripture to cover themselves. The very same happened to Christ when he proclaimed by his innocence the will of his father. This was quite abhorrent to the biblical scholars, and quite beyond them, John 5: 6.

You find exactly the same thing continues to our day. When the godless are caught out by the law they declare airily: Oh, it is no longer in force. But when it is explained to them quite correctly that it is written in the heart, 2 Cor. 3 and that one must follow its instructions to discover the right ways to the source of faith, Psalm 36 then the godless man assaults the just man, brandishing Paul in his face, but a Paul so clumsily understood that even children would dismiss it all as a Punch and Judy show, Psalm 63. He still wants to be the wisest man on earth, and boasts that there is none to equal him. What's more he describes all humble folk as deranged spirits and closes his ears as soon as the word 'spirit' is spoken or written. He has to shake his clever head, for, as Proverbs 18 says, the devil cannot abide it when one starts talking to him about the origin of faith, since he has been cast out. So he resorts to deception, 2 Cor. 11. Using the highest register of the musician, the double octave, he sings the following melody from Paul's letter to the Romans, chapter 12: 'One should not bother oneself with such high matters, but adapt them for the humble folk.' He fancies this gruel, but only because he is afraid to breakfast on soup. He commends simple faith, but fails to see what is necessary to have this. That is why Solomon describes a man like this as a numskull, as the 24th chapter of Proverbs puts it: 'The wisdom of God is quite beyond the fool.'

Like Moses, Christ began with the origins and explained the law from beginning to end. Hence he says: 'I am a light to the world.' His preaching was so truthful and so well thought-out that he even captivated the human reason of the godless, as the evangelist Matthew describes in chapter 13 and as Luke, too, indicates in his second chapter. But as Christ's teaching was beyond them and his person and life beneath them they took offence at him and his teaching and had the effrontery to say that he was a Samaritan and possessed by the devil. For their judgement was based on fleshly considerations, which greatly pleased the devil, and they were bound to blurt it out, being in good odour with the world which enjoys being Brother Soft Life, Job 28. They undertook everything with an eye to the world's approval, Matthew 6: 23.

The godless flesh in Wittenberg treats me in exactly the same way when I strive for the purity of the divine law, Psalm 18 by pointing to the beginning of the Bible, to what its first chapter says about the ordering of creation, and explain how all the sayings of the Bible point to the fulfilment of the spirit of the fear of God, Isaiah 11. Also I refuse to tolerate his perverse way of treating the new covenant of God without first dealing with the divine commandments and the source of faith, which one can only reach after chastisement by the holy spirit, John 16. For it is only after the law is understood that the spirit punishes unbelief, which no one can understand until he has first embraced it himself, and as fiercely as the most unbelieving pagan. From the beginning, this is the way in which, testing themselves by the law, all the elect have come to understand their unbelief, Romans 2, 7. I confess Christ with all his members as the fulfiller of the law, Psalm 18, for God's will and work must be completely carried out by observance of the law, Psalm 1, Romans 12. Otherwise no one could distinguish belief from unbelief, except in a counterfeit way, like the Jews, with their Sabbath and Scripture, who never came to understand the true ground of their faith.

All I have done to that wily black crow released by Noah from the Ark as a sign is this: like an innocent dove I have flapped my wings, covered them with silver, which has been purified seven times and gilded my back, Psalm 67, and flown over the carrion on which he likes to perch. How I loathed it! I will let the whole world know his hypocrisy towards these godless rascals, as seen in his book against me. He is, in brief, their advocate. It is quite clear then, that Doctor Liar does not dwell in the house of God, Psalm 15 since he does not despise the godless, but denounces many God-fearing men as devils or rebellious spirits in order to serve the interests of the godless. The black crow knows this very well. He pecks out the eyes of the pigs to turn them into carrion, he blinds these pleasure-loving people. For he is indulgent about their faults in order to eat his fill of their wealth and honours and especially of the fine-sounding titles at their disposal.

The Jews wanted to see Christ insulted and humiliated on every occasion, just as Luther now tries to treat me. He denounces me fiercely and reproaches me with the mercifulness of the son of God and of his dear friends. This is his retort to my preaching about the earnestness of the law, and the punishment of unspiritual sinners. For (even if they happen to be rulers) this is not abolished but is to be executed with the very greatest severity. Paul instructed Timothy (and through him all pastors) to preach this to the people, 1 Tim. 1. He says clearly that (punishment) will visit all who combat and try to subvert sound teaching. No one can deny this. It is stated clearly and unambiguously in Deuteronomy, chapter 13, and Paul pronounces the same judgement against the unchaste sinner. 1 Cor. 5. Although I have had my sermon printed in which, arguing from Scripture, I told the princes of Saxony quite frankly that if they were to avert an uprising they must use the sword: that, in short, disobedience must be punished, and neither great or small would be exempt, Numbers 25.

Despite all this that indulgent fellow, Father Pussyfoot, comes along and says I want to stir up an insurrection. This is how he understands my letter to the mineworkers. He says one thing, but suppresses the most vital point for, as I expounded quite clearly to the princes, the power of the sword as well as the key to release sins is in the hands of the whole community. From the passages in Daniel 7, Revelation 6, Romans 13, and 1 Kings 8 I pointed out that the princes are not lords over the sword but servants of it. They should not act as they please, but execute justice, Deut. 17. Hence it is a good old custom that the people must be present if someone is to be judged properly by the law of God, Num. 15. Why? So that if the authorities try to give a corrupt judgement, Isaiah 10 the Christians present can object and prevent this happening, since anyone spilling innocent blood will be accountable to God, Psalm 78. There is no greater abomination on earth than the fact that no one is prepared to take up the cause of the needy. The great do whatever they please, as Job describes in chapter 41.

The poor flatterer tries to use Christ to cover himself, adducing a counterfeit type of clemency which is contrary to Paul's text in 1 Timothy 1. In his book about trade, however, he says that the princes should not hesitate to join the thieves and robbers in their raids. He suppresses here, however, the basic reason for all theft. He is a herald, who hopes to earn gratitude by approving the spilling of people's blood for the sake of their earthly goods; something which God has never commanded or approved. Open your eyes! What is the evil brew from which all usury, theft and robbery springs but the assumption of our lords and princes that all creatures are their property? The fish in the water, the birds in the air, the plants on the face of the earth – it all has to belong to them! Isaiah 5. To add insult to injury, they have God's commandment proclaimed to the poor: God has commanded that you should not steal. But it avails them nothing. For while they do violence to everyone, flay and fleece the poor farm worker, tradesman and everything that breathes, Micah 3, yet should any of the latter commit the pettiest crime, he must hang. And Doctor Liar responds, Amen. It is the lords themselves who make the poor man their enemy. If they refuse to do away with the causes of insurrection how can trouble be avoided in the long run? If saying that makes me an inciter to insurrection, so be it!

★ ★ ★

*Articles of the Peasants of Memmingen, 24 February–3 March*

1. It is our humble and most sincere request and plea that we may now elect a pastor for ourselves, who will proclaim the divine, almighty, and living Word and holy Gospel, which is a food for our souls, [and do so] purely and clearly, without any human addition, doctrine, or command. We will provide the same pastor with a suitable competency. If such a pastor behaves improperly, then we may dismiss him and take on another in his place, but always with the knowledge of the entire commune. For without proclamation of the divine Word we cannot be saved, as St Paul has shown us.

2. Since we have been forced to pay the tithe, we think that we should not be obliged to give it any more, for the holy New Testament does not oblige us to give it. We will also provide for the pastor's bodily needs.

3. It has hitherto been the usage that we have been held as your poor serfs, which is pitiable, given that Christ has purchased and redeemed us with his precious blood, the shepherd the same as the Emperor. It is not our intention to have no authority, for we will be obedient to all authority appointed by God in all fair

and reasonable matters, and we do not doubt that as Christian lords you will release us from serfdom.

4.   It has been the custom that a poor man did not have the right to catch or shoot game, likewise fish in running water, which is also not permitted us. We regard this as quite unjust and not in accordance with the Word of God, for when the Lord God created man he gave him power over the fish in the water, the birds in the air, and all the animals on the earth, etc. Our request does not apply where someone has [common] water that he has purchased unknowingly, for there one has to exercise Christian concern out of brotherly love.

5.   It is our humble plea and request that since we have hitherto been long and greatly aggrieved by services, which have multiplied and increased from day to day, a gracious consideration might be given to how our forefathers supplied services, but only according to the Word of God.

6.   We request that henceforth we be not burdened by entry-fines, but when a holding is leased for a suitable rent the tenant and his heirs may enjoy the holding without further impositions.

7.   Some villages are aggrieved about the fines for felonies, and request that we may remain by the old usage.

8.   It is our humble request and plea that since some villages are aggrieved about woods, fields, pastures, and other rights which at one time belonged to the communes, these should be returned to them.

9.   It is our diligent plea that when we provide a rent for a feudal lord we should be able to work [our holding] to our best advantage and sell its produce when and where we choose, without hindrance from the feudal lord. If Almighty God sends us a failed harvest or a hailstorm the feudal lord should then remit rent according to the circumstances.

10.   Since some of our holdings are so heavily burdened that we cannot retain them all, we . . . request a reduction of the burdens.

In conclusion, it is our final opinion and wish that if we have presented one or more articles not in accordance with the Word of God, which we do not think we have, then that article will be void. Similarly, where any articles are conceded and subsequently found through the clear evidence of the Word of God to be unjust, then we will not have them. By contrast, if we later find one or more articles contrary to the Word of God, we desire at all times to reveal it to the worthy council, for such action benefits you as our gracious feudal lords as much as us . . .

# Chapter 14

# William Tyndale (1494–1536)

### The Obedience of A Christian Man **(1528)**

In many ways Tyndale stands at the heart of the radical Christian tradition in the English-speaking world, for it was as a consequence of his labors to translate the Scripture into workaday English – and publish it in pocket-size editions – that it became accessible to, as he put it, "the boy who drives the plough." Aware of the social and political repercussions of the common people reading and interpreting Scripture for themselves, conservative forces in the Church – most famously Bishop Tunstall and Sir Thomas More – went to extreme measures to prevent and destroy Tyndale's work (which was in any case forbidden by law). Forced into exile on the continent around 1524, Tyndale produced an English edition of the New Testament in 1526 and of the Pentateuch in 1530. In both cases he eschewed existing Latin translations and used as a basis the original Greek and Hebrew texts. Both volumes had to be smuggled into England, and his New Testament was subjected to seizure and burning on the orders of Tunstall. In 1535, having completed a translation of the historical books of the Old Testament, Tyndale was tricked into arrest and imprisoned in a castle near Brussels. Interrogated for the next sixteen months by Catholic heresy-hunters, he was finally denounced as a heretic, stripped of his priesthood and publicly strangled and burnt.

The *Obedience of A Christian Man* was first printed in Antwerp in 1528, and is liberally sprinkled with quotations from the author's New Testament published two years before. In his book, Tyndale is concerned to refute those (including More) who had accused the reformers of fomenting rebellion, though he also presents, as in the extract below, a justification for his life's work of enabling the common person to know more of the Scripture than the wise and learned.

## Source

William Tyndale, *The Obedience of A Christian Man* (ed. David Daniell), London, 2000, pp. 15–18

## Further reading

David Daniell, *William Tyndale: A Biography*, New Haven and London, 1994.
G. E. Duffield, ed., *The Work of William Tyndale*, London, 1964.
Gerald Hammond, *The Making of the English Bible*, Manchester, 1982.
David Daniell, ed., *Tyndale's New Testament*, New Haven and London, 1989.
David Daniell, ed., *Tyndale's Old Testament*, New Haven and London, 1992.

## From *The Obedience of A Christian Man*

That thou mayest perceive how that the scripture ought to be in the mother tongue and that the reasons which our spirits make for the contrary are but sophistry and false wiles to fear thee from the light, that thou mightest follow them blindfold and be their captive, to honour their ceremonies and to offer to their belly.

First God gave the children of Israel a law by the hand of Moses in their mother tongue. And all the prophets wrote in their mother tongue. And all the Psalms were in the mother tongue. And there was Christ but figured and described in ceremonies, in riddles, in parables and in dark prophecies. What is the cause that we may not have the Old Testament with the New also, which is the light of the Old, and wherein is openly declared before the eyes that there was darkly prophesied? I can imagine no cause verily except it be that we should not see the work of Antichrist and juggling of hypocrites. What should be the cause that we which walk in the broad day, should not see as well as they that walked in the night, or that we should not see as well at noon, as they did in the twilight? Came Christ to make the world more blind? By this means Christ is the darkness of the world and not the light, as he saith himself (John 8). . . .

They will say haply, the scripture requireth a pure mind and a quiet mind. And therefore the lay man because he is altogether cumbered with worldly business, cannot understand them. If that be the cause, then it is a plain case, that our prelates understand not the scriptures themselves. For no lay man is so tangled with worldly business as they are. The great things of the world are ministered by them. Neither do the lay people any great thing, but at their assignment.

If the scripture were in the mother tongue they will say, then would the lay people understand it every man after his own ways. Wherefore serveth the curate, but to teach them the right way? Wherefore were the holy days made, but that the people should come and learn? Are ye not abominable schoolmasters, in that ye take so great wages, if ye will not teach? If ye would teach how could ye do it so well and with so great profit, as when the lay people have the scripture before them in their mother tongue? For then should they see by the order of the text, whether thou jugglest or not. And then would they believe it, because it is the scripture of God, though thy living be never so abominable. Where now because your living and your preaching are so contrary, and because they grope out in every sermon your open and manifest lies, and smell your insatiable covetousness they believe you not, when you preach truth. But alas, the curates themselves (for the most part) wot no more what the New or Old Testament meaneth, than do the Turks. Neither know they of any more than that they read at mass, matins and evensong which they understand not. Neither care they but even to mumble up so much every day (as the pie and popinjay speak they wot not what) to fill their bellies withal. if they will not let the lay man have the word of God in his mother tongue, yet let the priests have it, which for a great part of them do understand no Latin at all: but sing and say and patter all day, with the lips only, that which the heart understandeth not.

Christ commandeth to search the scriptures (John 5). . . .

Christ saith that there shall come false prophets in his name and say that they themselves are Christ, that is, they shall so preach Christ that men must believe in them, in their holiness and things of their imagination without God's word: yea and that against-Christ or Antichrist that shall come is nothing but such false prophets that shall juggle with the scripture and beguile the people with false interpretations as all the false prophets, scribes and Pharisees did in the Old Testament. How shall I know whether ye are that against Christ or false prophets or no, seeing ye will not let me see how ye allege the scriptures? Christ saith: By their deeds ye shall know them. Now when we look on your deeds, we see that ye are all sworn together and have separated yourselves from the lay people, and have a several kingdom among yourselves and several laws of your own making, wherewith ye violently bind the lay people that never consented unto the making of them. A thousand things forbid ye which Christ made free, and dispense with them again for money. Neither is there any exception at all, but lack of money. Ye have a secret counsel by yourselves. All other men's counsels and secrets know ye and no man yours. Ye seek but honour, riches, promotion, authority and to reign over all, and will obey no man. If the father give you ought of courtesy, ye will compel the son to give it violently whether he will or not by craft of your own laws. These deeds are against Christ.

# Chapter 15

# Early Anabaptist Writings

**Anna Jansz (1539): A Hymnic Form of Anna Jansz's Testimony to Her Son (1539)**
The Answer of some who are called Anabaptists **(1536?)**
**Peter Riedemann:** Account of Our Religion **(ca. 1545)**

Anabaptist comes from the Greek meaning "rebaptizer." Anabaptists argued that infant baptism had no valid New Testament authority. For the Anabaptist, the approved method of baptism was a personal pledge of faith of a committed believer coupled with their act of "adult baptism." They rejected what they saw as the corrupt doctrines and practices of the Roman Church, and the only partial reformation of the Protestant Churches of the Reformation period. Anabaptists sought to establish a Christian community based on their concepts of the early New Testaments congregations. For the Anabaptists, baptism was an act of consenting adults, involving a personal pledge of faith on the part of believers who committed themselves to a life of discipleship and of intentional membership in a faith community. They were marked early as enemies of the State and hunted down, imprisoned, or executed. Discipleship was a valued tenet. Anabaptists held the separation of the Church and State, including the abolishment of any State religion. Bearing the Sword" for the state was rejected. Members were often fined or imprisoned for their acts of civil disobedience, the breaking of local codes and laws such as refusing to take public oaths, paying taxes, and the taking up of arms.

Some early Anabaptists prepared for the overthrow of the current ungodly and corrupted world order. In 1534–5, popularly elected Anabaptist leaders transformed the episcopal city of Muenster into a center of militant Anabaptism. After a siege of some months, forces led by the prince bishop recaptured the city, killing thousands of defenders. In contemporary polemic, Muenster came to express the essence of Anabaptism, and served as a reason for suspicion of all Anabaptists. From an early date, however, pacifism had been strongly maintained by Anabaptists; through the leadership of Menno Simons (1496–1560) this view came to predominate even in the area of the movement (Holland and North Germany) where Muensterite tendencies were strongest. By 1560 all surviving strands of Anabaptism, including the Hutterites in Moravia, were committed to a pacifist Christianity.

The story of the various anabaptist groups, persecuted and frequently refugees, yet clinging to their convictions about the radical alternative posed by the gospel, is very much to the fore in the moving testament of Anna Jansz which she bequeathed to her infant son en route to her untimely death at the stake. Anabaptist attitudes about social ethics represented an implicit direct challenge to the ideology of the powerful. Through the vicissitudes of persecution and social ostracism have persisted to the present century movements like the Hutterites and the Mennonites. The extracts included here represent the remarkable labor involved in collecting the testimonies of persecuted anabaptists.

At the Reformation writers like Erasmus and Tyndale both stressed the importance of ordinary people reading the Bible. They saw that in a profound way it spoke to and informed people whether or not they had spent years studying it. Through the Bible people were taught to read. It was the tool of the education of ordinary people, enabling a Bunyan or a Blake to read, write, and as important to reflect on the world in a way which enabled them to glimpse something of the way of God. In this regard there are parallels with the contemporary Basic Ecclesial Communities, where the Bible has often been the means of enabling literacy. The passage, 'The Answer of some who are called Anabaptists to the question why they do not attend church," dating from around 1536, offers evidence of what went on in their meetings and the extent to which there was a different (and challenging) understanding of what it meant to be church. The active participation of all envisioned by I Corinthians 14 is cited. It is a chapter in which the validity of congregational openness to the Spirit and the need for discernment and mutual acceptance are stressed. Outside the Pentecostal Churches, I Corinthians 14 is a passage which has little influence on the life and worship of mainstream churches (except to debar women from preaching or leading worship). Peter Riedemann's *Account of Our Religion* (ca. 1545) comes from the Hutterite wing of Anabaptism and outlines the case for community of goods.

## Sources

Anna Jansz from Thieleman J. van Braght, *Martyrs Mirror*, Scottdale: Herald 1950, pp. 453–4 and C. A. Snyder and Linda A. Huebert Hecht Hecht, *Profiles of Anabaptist Women: Sixteenth Century Reforming Pioneers*, Studies in Women and Religion 3, Waterloo: Wilfrid Laurier University Press 1996, pp. 345–8.

The Answer of some who are called Anabaptists: trans. S. and P. Peachey, in *Mennonite Quarterly* Review, 45 (1971), 11–14.

Account of our Religion, Doctine and Faith Given by P. Riedemann of the Brothers Whom Men call Hutterians, London, 1950, 102–21.

## Further reading

S. Murray, *Biblical Interpretation in the Anabaptist Tradition*, Kitchener, Ontario: Pandora Press, 2000.

C. A. Snyder, *Anabaptist History and Theology: An Introduction*, Kitchener, Ontario: Pandora Press, 1995.

G. H. Williams, *The Radical Reformation*, 3rd edn., Sixteenth Century Essays and Studies, 15, Kirksville: Sixteenth Century Journal Publishers, 1992.

J. M. Stayer, *The German Peasants' War and Anabaptist Community of Goods*, McGill–Queens Studies in the History of Religion, 6, Montreal and Kingston: McGill–Queen's University Press, 1991.

## Anna Jansz (1539)

*AUSBUND*
*The 18th Hymn*

### Another Martyr Song by a Woman Who Took her Leave in Rotterdam Together with her Son

1. There usually is great joy
   When one begets small children
   From the Lord God,
   And instructs them in God's teaching
   About good customs, discipline, and honour,
   So that they honour their parents.

2. Annelein received permission
   To see her son in Rotterdam,
   As her death drew near.
   Isaiah hear my testament,
   My last will before my death
   Now comes from my mouth.

3. I am going on the path of the prophets,
   The martyrs' and apostles' way;
   There is none better.
   They all have drunk from the cup,
   Even as did Christ Himself,
   As I have heard it read.

4. All the priests of the King
   Travelled on this path alone.
   From the beginning they came
   To stand upon this road,
   As God's true sons and children.
   This I have truly understood.

5.  These same children under the altar,
    Who are a great multitude,
    Are described in the Apocalypse:
    How they were killed and murdered
    And executed with the sword,
    Persecuted and banished.

6.  They cried out to God: O Lord!
    Righteous and Truthful One,
    How long until you bring order to the earth
    Among people everywhere?
    And take revenge on only those
    Who with great insolence

7.  Have shed blood everywhere,
    Murdering innocent people?
    Are you willing to punish them
    So they no longer cause dishonour,
    Driving your own out of the land,
    Continuing in their sin?

8.  God gives to all [His children] a white robe,
    And consoles them with the answer:
    To them must still be added
    Those who will also be judged
    Until the number of the pious
    Is filled and completed.

9.  The twenty-four great elders
    Come before God's throne
    And lay down their crowns,
    Honouring the Lamb of God,
    Together with all the heavenly hosts
    Who live under the sun.

10. All of the pious children of God
    Who received the baptism
    Sealed upon their brow
    Also came this way,
    Following the Lamb wherever it went,
    Serving [the Lamb] with desire.

11. Such people must enter this valley,
    And all drink from the bitter cup
    Until the number is fulfilled.
    Zion, the worthy bride of God,
    To whom the Lamb itself is betrothed,
    Who has calmed the wrath of God.

12. Therefore my dearly beloved son,
    May you wish to do my will,

And follow my teaching.
If you know a people who spurn every luxury
And pleasure of this world,
May you wish to join them.

13.   They are despised and rejected
By this wretched world.
They must carry Christ's cross,
And have no secure place
Because they keep God's word.
They often are hunted down.

14.   God lives with such people,
Who are mocked by the world.
Keep company with them.
They will show you the true way,
Lead you away from the path of evil,
Guide you away from hell.

15.   Fear no one; set your life
Completely on the pure teaching.
Set aside your body and earthly goods.
Christ bought you at a dear price,
Delivered you from the eternal fire
With His worthy blood.

16.   May the Lord sanctify you, my son,
Sanctify your conduct.
May you live in the fear of God
Wherever you are in this entire land.
In all the work you may do,
Do not resist God.

17.   Share your bread with the hungry,
Leave no person in need
Who professes Christ.
Also clothe the naked,
Have pity on the sick.
Do not distance yourself from them.

18.   If you cannot always be with them,
Show your good will.
Comfort the imprisoned,
Welcome guests cheerfully into your home,
And don't let anyone drive them out.
Then your reward will be greatest.

19.   Both your hands should be ready
To do the works of mercy,
To give twofold offerings;
This is spiritual and worldly work:

To set the prisoners free, strengthen the weak;
Then you will truly live.

20.   For the rest of what God gives you
You will be taught by the sweat of your brow
By God and the prophets,
To give always to God's people.
May they be happy with you;
Give to them what they ask of you.

21.   Do not let falseness come from you,
Then you may have good hope.
God also will reward you
In His Kingdom in the other world.
He will bestow it twofold;
There should be no doubt of this.

22.   On the one thousand five hundredth
And thirty-first year
Annelein paid with her life,
Which in virtue soft and mild
Was for Christians a beautiful model,
Given in death as well as in life.

Laus Deo


## The Answer of some who are called (Ana)baptists to the Question Why They Do Not Attend the Churches (1536?)

A listener is bound by Christian love (if something to edification is given or revealed to him) that he should and may speak of it also in the congregation, and again thereupon be silent, according to the text which reads . . . When you come together, every one of you has a psalm, has a doctrine, has a tongue, has a revelation, has an interpretation. Let all things be done unto edifying . . . It thus appears further that Paul spoke to the church of God, yea to all Christians whom he in the beginning of the chapter admonished to seek after spiritual gifts, yet most of all, that they may prophesy, prophesying meaning that they receive the meaning from God to share with others . . . [discusses 1 Thess. 5, 1 Cor. 4, Eph. 5] . . . and also Peter, 1 Peter 4, enjoins them to serve one another . . . That all things may be done in the best, the most seemly and convenient manner when the congregation assembles, which congregation is a temple of the Holy Spirit (1 Cor. 6) where the gifts or inner operation of the Spirit in each one (note, in each one) serve the common good (1 Cor. 12, Eph. 4). Note, for the common good . . . When such believers come together, Every one of you (note, every one) has a psalm . . . And it is Paul's intention that if one sitting by or listening receives a revelation or is moved to exercise his spiritual gift or to prophesy, then the first shall hold his peace; and he . . . says that all may prophesy, one after the other, and wants that at all times the spirit of the one who prophesies, or teaches, or preaches first, shall be subject to, and silent before, the one from among those seated or listening who has something to prophesy, and shall not show himself discordant or unpeaceful . . .

And thus . . . they deny that we possess the evangelical order nor would permit us to exercise it (if we did attend their preaching), but teach and presume that we also, as those who err, should remain silent in their preaching regardless of what we would have to speak to edification . . . even though according to 1 Cor. 14 the listeners must judge the preacher's doctrine. All judgement and everything, yes everyone in his conscience, is bound to the preacher and to his teaching, whether it be good or evil . . . And if a prophet or messenger from God came into their congregation (as occurred in apostolic times), being sent of God and of men, he would be compelled to remain silent, or would be persecuted by them, and thereby . . . in the name of love . . . impede the rivers of living water . . . as gifts of the Holy Spirit to the faithful . . .

If anything is revealed to a listener to be spoken to edification in the congregation or to prophesy, even . . . if it does pertain to an error of the minister, this must be treated openly before the congregation which has heard it, and not privately with only the preacher . . . Certainly this opportunity in their congregation is undermined, since no one may speak but the preacher, and thus the congregation is deprived and robbed of all right of judgement concerning matters of the soul, being bound exclusively to the preachers and their understanding, contrary to the word of God. A preacher who verily has the love of God and neighbour, will rejoice in the truth, if someone will kindly correct him before the congregation in things wherein he erred before the congregation . . . Some of the preachers also interpret this passage . . . For you may all prophesy, one by one . . . to mean that it refers not to the entire church but only to the elected ministers, since they are the preachers . . . They infer the same meaning from other words in this same chapter concerning the laity, where they apply the word (lay) to their hearers or sheep, whom they regard as laity, and themselves as those to whom Paul spoke, even though Paul spoke the words 'When you come together' not only to some, but to the whole believing Corinthian church of Christ. We cannot understand the word 'lay' thus . . . There the words (lay or unbeliever) mean nearly the same, and say, 'and there come in those who are lay or unbelievers,' etc., that is to say, into the Christian congregation as, according to our understanding, the Latin text regarding this word (lay) makes still more clear, that it cannot be applied to the true believers or Christian members. Nevertheless let him who thinks otherwise give his proof, for we do not wish to oppose the truth. And even if Paul had meant that the words 'you may all prophesy,' should apply only to the prophets, then prophesying would still not be limited to one person in the congregation only . . . And thus the foregoing words ('When you are come together everyone of you has . . . Let all things be done to edification . . .') undeniably apply to the whole congregation or to all the members of Christ.

## Peter Riedemann: *Account of Our Religion* (ca. 1545)

*Concerning community of goods*

Now, since all the saints have fellowship in holy things, that is in God, who also hath given to them all things in His Son Christ Jesus – which gift none should have for himself, but each for the other; as Christ also hath nought for Himself, but hath everything for us, even so all the members of His body have nought for themselves, but for the whole body, for all the members. For His gifts are not sanctified and given to one member alone, or for one member's sake, but for the whole body with its members.

Now, since all God's gifts – not only spiritual, but also material things – are given to man, not that he should have them for himself or alone but with all his fellows, therefore the communion of saints itself must show itself not only in spiritual but also in temporal things; that as Paul saith, one might not have abundance and another suffer want, but that there may be equality. This he showeth from the law touching manna, in that he who gathered much had nothing over, whereas he who gathered little had no less, since each was given what he needed according to the measure.

Furthermore, one seeth in all things created, which testify to us still today, that God from the beginning ordained nought private for man, but all things to be common. But through wrong taking, since man took what he should not and forsook what he should take, he drew such things to himself and made them his property, and so grew and became hardened therein. Through such wrong taking and collecting of created things he hath been led so far from God that he hath even forgotten the Creator, and hath even raised up and honored as God the created things which had been put under and made subject to him. And such is still the case if one steppeth out of God's order and forsaketh the same.

Now, however, as hath been said, created things which are too high for man to draw within his grasp and collect, such as the sun with the whole course of the heavens, day, air and such like, show that not they alone, but all other created things are likewise made common to man. That they have thus remained and are not possessed by man is due to their being too high for him to bring under his power, otherwise – so evil had he become through wrong taking – he would have drawn them to himself as well as the rest and made them his property.

That this is so, however, and that the rest is just as little made by God for man's private possession, is shown in that man must forsake all other created things as well as this when he dies, and can carry nothing with him to use as his own. For which reason Christ also called temporal all things foreign to man's essential nature, and saith, "If ye are not faithful in what is not your own, who will entrust to you what is your own?"

Now, because what is temporal doth not belong to us, but is foreign to our true nature, the law commandeth that none covet strange possessions, that is, set his heart upon and cleave to what is temporal and alien. Therefore whosoever will cleave to Christ and follow Him must forsake such taking of created things and property, as He Himself also saith, "Whosoever forsaketh not all that he hath cannot be my disciple" [Mt. 16:24–6]. For if a man is to be renewed again into the likeness of God, he must put off all that leadeth him from him – that is the grasping and drawing to himself of created things – for he cannot otherwise attain God's likeness. Therefore Christ saith, "Whosoever shall not receive the kingdom of God as a little child shall not enter therein," or, "Except ye overcome yourselves and become as little children, ye shall not enter into the kingdom of heaven" [Mt. 18:1–5].

Now, he who thus becometh free from created things can then grasp what is true and divine; and when he graspeth it and it becometh his treasure, he turneth his heart toward it, emptieth himself of all else and taketh nought as his, and regardeth it no longer as his but as of all God's children. Therefore we say that as all the saints have community in spiritual gifts, still much more should they show this in material things, and not ascribe the same to and covet them for themselves, for they are not their own; but regard them as of all God's children, that they may thereby show that they are partakers in the community of Christ and are renewed into God's likeness. For the more man yet cleaveth to created things, appropriateth and ascribeth such to himself, the further doth he show himself to be from the likeness of God and the community of Christ.

For this reason the Holy Spirit also at the beginning of the church began such community right gloriously again, so that none said that aught of the things that he possessed was his own, but they had all things in common; and it is his will that this might still be kept, as Paul saith, "Let none seek his own profit but the profit of another," or, "Let none seek what benefiteth himself but what benefiteth many." Where this is not the case it is a blemish upon the church which ought verily to be corrected. If one should say, it was so nowhere except in Jerusalem, therefore it is now not necessary, we say, Even if it were nowhere but in Jerusalem, it followeth not that it ought not to be so now. For neither apostles nor churches were lacking, but rather the opportunity, manner and time.

Therefore this should be no cause for us to hesitate, but rather should it move us to more and better zeal and diligence, for the Lord now giveth us both time and cause so to do. That there was no lack of either apostles or churches is shown by the zeal of both. For the apostles have pointed the people thereto with all diligence and most faithfully prescribed true surrender, as all their epistles still prove today. And the people obeyed with zeal, as Paul beareth witness – especially of those of Macedonia – saying, "I tell you of the grace that is given to the churches in Macedonia. For their joy was the most rapturous since they had been tried by much affliction, and their poverty, though it was indeed deep, overflowed as riches in all simplicity. For I bear witness that with all their power, yea, and beyond their power, they were themselves willing, and besought us earnestly with much admonition to receive the benefit and community of help which is given to the saints; and not as we had hoped, but first gave themselves to the Lord, and then to us also, by the will of God" [2 Cor. 8:1–5].

Here one can well see with what inclined and willing hearts the churches were ready to keep community not only in spiritual but also in material things, for they desired to follow the master Christ, and become like Him and one with Him, who Himself went before us in such a way, and commanded us to follow Him.

# Chapter 16

# The Family of Love

**Hendrick Niclaes,** Introduction to the Holy Understanding of the
Glass of Righteousness **(ET 1574)**
Terra Pacis. A True Testification of the Spiritual Land of Peace

The *Family of Love*, or *Familists*, was a radical Christian movement found throughout Europe in the sixteenth and seventeenth centuries. It was founded, ca. 1540, in
East Friesland, by a wealthy and devout merchant, Hendrick Niclaes (1502–80). A
visionary since childhood, Niclaes stressed the need to imitate Christ. He was deeply
influenced by the mystical *Theologica Germanica* and the German humanist and
radical reformer Sebastion Franck (ca. 1499–ca. 1542).

Niclaes was accused of haboring Lutheran and Anabaptist sympathies at different times, but he professed the orthodoxy of his teachings vigorously until his death.
His many writings display mystical and pantheistic leanings. The Familists espoused
a revolutionary and communistic model of society, governed by an egalitarian ethic,
although the movement adopted a hierarchical structure in its efforts to form a radically moral community which sought to follow Christ as truly and fully as possible,
and to lead all humanity to salvation. Niclaes believed in a church which could overcome the schisms prevalent across the Europe of his time and was convinced that
this time was the "last age" (the age of "the Spirit" predicted by Joachim of Fiore).
Niclaes wrote of a new "Sacred order" coming to pass on Earth and although he
stressed the importance of understanding that the "kingdom of God is within
you," he also wrote of it coming to pass on the Earth in his millenarian work *Ordo
Sacerdotis*. He urged followers to adopt a strategy of adhering to the practices of
the local denomination, wherever they found themselves (known as Nicodemism,
after the secret follower of Jesus in John 3). He came to believe he had become
one with the divine – "Godded with God" – and preached a doctrine whereby Christ
would enter the soul of the true follower, thereby leading them, also, to such divin-
isation. Niclaes believed he had a mission to announce the final judgment which
would soon be upon the world. His works are frequently illustrated with elaborate
apocalyptic imagery. Niclaes believed the Fall had torn asunder the union between

the human person and God and, despite Christ's death bringing about the opportunity for reconciliation with God, superstition, obsession with ceremony and outward signs of religion, all served as proof that few of his contemporaries were truly following the path of Christ. Niclaes rejected literalism in biblical interpretation and likewise forms of Christianity based upon any "pseudo-philosophy" or "good knowledge." Instead, he stressed the importance of the spiritual aspect of Christianity, be it in the Bible or doctrine or morals.

His movement shared some similarities with the Anabaptists (such as an emphasis upon the spirit of scripture over the letter, a belief in the Messianic character of their mission, the importance of holiness and unimportance of outward ceremony and the rejection of justification by faith alone), and he influenced many pietists and the Quaker movement in England. It was committed to a universalistic doctrine of salvation rare for both its time and any other: salvation was open even to Jews and Muslims. The movement's followers in England influenced many radical political groups in the seventeenth century. In England it attracted the poorer classes, whilst on the continent, members tended to belong to the wealthier and hence educated and literary classes. The movement died out in the seventeenth century, though it proved more resilient in England.

The first extract comes from Niclaes' *Introduction to the Holy Understanding of the Glass of Righteousness* (ET 1574), part of his influential work of edification (*Spiegel der Gerechtigheid – The Glass of Righteousness*, first printed in Antwerp in the late 1550s, but never fully translated into English). The selection sets out the importance of core Familist beliefs including the emphasis upon the Kingdom of God being "within you" and the transformation of the self that this realization brings, leading to those actions which will serve to build up the "community of love." Furthermore, Niclaes displays his universalism toward the end of the extract, warning Christians not to forget that their "statutes and ordinances" are not those of the God of Israel. Thus divisions amongst the human family are to be shunned.

The second extract helps illustrate how completely Niclaes wanted to transform society. He contrasts society with the land of Ignorance. The radicalism is evident in the stress on the *inner revolution: the utopia is of the Soul*; the true enemy is evil, sin, and apathy. Familists sought to build their Utopian community away from the limelight and so avoid the attentions of and persecution by the authorities.

## Sources

Chapter XXII (from *Cambridge University Library, Rare Books*, bound with *The Prophecy of the Spirit of Love*, printed London: Giles, Calvert, 1649; Cambridge University Library ref.: B125:2.9.Reel 1153:20. Complete copies in *Bodleian Library, Oxford* and *Union Theological Seminary Library, New York*).

Chap XXVII – *Terra Pacis. A True Testification of the Spiritual Land of Peace* (which is the Spiritual land of *Promise*, and the Holy City of *Peace*, or the Heavenly *Jerusalem*) and of the holy and spiritual *people* that dwell therein, as also of the walking in the Spirit, which leadeth thereto. Samuel Satterthwaite at the Sign of the *Sun* on *Garlick Hill*, 1649. (Transcribed from Bodleain Tanner 504 [2].)

Further reading

A. Hamilton, *The Family of Love*, Cambridge: Cambridge University Press, 1981.
A. Hamilton, *Cronica, Ordo Sacerdotis, Acta HN: Three Texts on the Family of Love*, Leiden: E. T. Brill, 1988.
C. W. Marsh, *The Family of Love in English Society, 1550–1630*, Cambridge: Cambridge University Press, 1993.
N. Smith, *Perfection Proclaimed – Language and Literature in English Radical Religion, 1640–60*, Oxford: Oxford University Press, 1989.
A. C. Thomas, *The Family of Love or the Familists*, 1893.
E. Troeltsch, *The Social Teaching of the Christian Churches*, New York: Harper, 1960.

## An Introduction to the *Glasse of Righteousnesse*

. . . 2.   Some strive for the Kingdom of God, or inward life of Christ (which is called the new Man:) and suppose that it is this or that, or that it is here-hence or therehence after the outward appearance; for to come or to be obtained.

3.   Others think, that it shall be first found and obtained, after the death of the Creature. Yea, the Principallest of the Learned in the Letter: who will forsooth be the understandingest in the Scripture, do maintain such a ground of Beleefe?

4.   O God! How long shall the Scripture through the false and unright light or sight, be yet set forth and taught?

5.   It is doubtles plainly and clearly enough written, that the Kingdom of God is inwardly within us. He is in the middest of you whom ye know not: The same is he, that baptizeth with the Holy Ghost.

6.   But many (as it well appeareth) know him not. For he, who is the very Image of God; or the Christ, and the Kingdom of the glory of God, hath his going down in us, inwardly: and suffereth the Death of the Crosse, for the Sinnes cause.

7.   Nevertheless, if any man be baptized inwardly in the death of Christ, and with his like Death, be, until his burying, planted into him, the same ariseth also with Christ, and liveth. For then, inwardly is Gods Kingdom of Heaven even in him, and not specially, here or there, as among these, or among those: but the Kingdom of God is here and there: among these, and among those: namely, in every one, in us. Howbeit unknown to many, as is already said.

8.   Now if the Kingdom of God be within us, and that we (as the Scripture saith) beleeve in Christ, then ought we, after the Councel of the Wisdom, and of the holy understanding, to seeke it inwardly there: for even thither shall it come, and so be fouud inwardly within us.

9.   But who so seeketh it only at the hands of another, and doth not attend the coming thereof inwardly, according to the direction of the holy word and service of love, the same shall in no wise find it.

10.   For this cause men are not in the seeking of the Kingdom of God, to despise the Councel and Service of the holy word, which under the obedience of the Love, teacheth and directeth rightly to the same; but, with lowly hearts to give good eare thereunto.

11.   Therefore believe the truth, and follow the Councel of the Scriptures, seeke and ye shall find, Turn yon about, and become as little Children, and not subtile, cunning, or wise in your own selves. For who so receiveth not the Kingdom of God as a Child, he shall not enter therein.

12.   Wherefore it is all to no purpose, to set ones mind upon anything, that is above in the Heaven, or that is beneath under the earth: either what people, this or that is: or where hence Christ shall come, or not: or with what outward appearance the Kingdom of God cometh.

13.   For behold, if ye find not the Kingdom of God and his Righteousnes, inwardly in your soules, and the forme of Christ in his glory, appeared not in your inwardness, then shall ye be constrained to misse, or be without the Kingdom of God and Christ; and shall likewise not eat the bread from Heaven with Christ, in the Kingdom of God his Almighty Father.

14.   Therefore seek it, where it is to be found: and take right regard, whether it cometh: hunger and thirst ye after it. Nevertheles, hast you not after it, out of your own chusing, through mis-understanding; but go ye from one vertue to another.

15.   Posses ye your soules with patience, have regard on the coming of Christ, contend not any more, and strive no longer with flesh and blood.

16.   Let it once suffice that ye have contended and wrangled for the Scriptures cause: rather now endeavour you, in obeying of the requiring of the service of love, to receive or put on the gracious word of the Lord in your hearts, and labor ye for the unity of the love. For in such a sort shall the Kingdom of God come.

17.   Now when you have thus received or put on the serviceable gracious word of the Lord, the true Christ after the flesh, in your hearts or inwardness, then apply your selves therewithal, in your inwardness, to the good being which the gracious word of the Lord requireth in his service, for to overcome in like manner with Christ, every thing that is against him, to the intent his enemies, for a footstoole; may be laid under his feet.

18.   And when you exercise your selves herein, be ye likewise baptized in the death or Christ, (that is, in his patience) and with his like death or patience be ye planted into him: and so overcome ye through the belief, with the like crosse or patience of Christ, the sin, death, flesh, and the world, Devill and Hell, and all sensuality, which ariseth out of your own wisdom of the flesh: and be ye likewise in your inward man; renewed unto righteousnes, in the Resurrection of Jesus Christ. Lo, thus doth the Scripture teach us, if it were but rightly understood.

19.   When we are now passed through this, and have through the death of Christ, even until his Resurrection, overcomed all those deadly things, then have we peace with God the Father, and stand firm in the love, which is the end or fulfilling of all the spiritual Testimonies. And therein is comprehended the perfection . . .

. . .

24.   Furthermore, see that ye humbly, with meditation to God, apply your selves out of the inclination to love, to read, or to heare the Glasse of

Righteousnes; and consider or mark the life which is witnessed and set forth in the same. Behold there in the spirit of your understanding, the everlasting unchangeable Statutes and Ordinances of Almighty God, which also shall remain unchangeable for ever. For that which is there witnessed, is such an upright life, as the man is created unto, for to live therein. In which Statutes and Ordinances, the Lords people have lived from the beginning.

25.   Yea, such a Life, Statutes and Ordinances, are a delight and joy to all upright hearts and Prophets, to live therein: and they have heretofore born witness thereunto, that in time to come, men should live in them. For through the truth, they saw into the life of peace in the love; and that through the life of peace in the love, every thing is made perfect, and therein standeth firme, or abideth stedfast.

26.   That verily is the life which is true, and that life is the light of men, and the head of the holy Commonalty. Who so goeth out of it, cometh to the death, blindnes and darknes.

27.   But the soules of those that live therein, are blessed in the Lord. For such people doth God require, as do walk in his Ordinances (that is to say, in the life and peace of love), and do love the only God from the heart.

28.   Lo, it is the true God, that requireth such upright Righteousnes: and he himself cleaveth to his Righteousnes; his Statutes and Ordinances, everlastingly. For he is the spirit of his life, the life of his word, the word of his Spirit, the God of Abraham, the God of Isaac, and the God of Jacob, or Israel.

29.   That verily is the true life of peace, and love: and the Statutes and Ordinances, are the same upright righteousnes, which the holy Fathers have lived and walked in.

30.   The same Statues and Ordinances of the holy Fathers were by Moses renewed, and witnessed unto a life before all people. And that life was through Jesus Christ (being risen from the Dead, and ascended into Heaven) published unto all people for a Gospel, because they should live therein. And unto all that believed thereon, was the Resurrection from the dead, and the everlasting life, witnessed and promised through Jesus Christ.

31.   In sure and firm hope whereof, the upright Beleevers have rested in the Lord Jesus Christ, till the appearing of his coming, which is now in this day of the love, revealed out of the heavenly beeng, with which Jesus Christ, the former Beleevers of Christ; who were fallen a sleepe, rested, or dyed in him, are now also manifested in Glory.

32.   For Christ in the appearing of his comming, raiseth his deceased from the dead, to the intent that they should reign alive, with him over all his enemies: and condemneth all the ungodly, which have not liked of him.

33.   This is the joyful Message, published to the Gentiles, whereby as fellow Heires in the Testaments of promise; they are bidden and called to the house of Jacob, and to the Citizenship of Jerusalem, To the intent, they should depart from the brutishness of their errors, and from the sundry intanglements of their Idolatries, and turn them to the God of Israel, for to serve him only, and to live in his Statutes and Ordinances, through the belief.

34.   Which Righteousnes is required out of the Law: and is now in this last time openly and evidently witnessed out of the inclination of love, and through the insight of the same upright life, to a view of the upright righteousnes, which the man is created unto: and to a demonstration, whereunto, or to what end or fulfilling, God hath given his promises, and made his Covenant with the Fathers.

35.   Behold hereunto (namely, to that which we bear witness of) is the Calling of the Gentiles made, who are out of grace, called thereunto, for to serve with the Stock of Abraham, one God in one manner or Righteousnes.

36.   Lo, these are the promises, which were committed to the Jewes in the Circumcision: And Jesus Christ, the safemaking word of the Lord is amongst them, for the truth of Gods sake become a Minister of the Circumcision, to confirme the promises made unto the Fathers, that the name of the God of Abraham might be magnified likewise among the Gentiles. And for the mercies sake towards the Gentiles, is the Grace of life published also to the Gentiles, to the intent, they should praise God, and know the God of Israel, and his Ordinances.

37.   Which God and his righteousnes, we do now know in the love, through the spirit of truth, which according to the spirit, leadeth us into all truth: that is, into all love, according to the promises. For the love is the band of perfection. By which Band, we are sealed and confirmed for ever in the same perfection, to the intent, that Gods Glory, his Covenant and promises, may likewise abide firme, from everlasting to everlasting, Amen.

38.   Behold the same God of Israel (who out of his Grace, prepareth and bringeth all this unto us) is the God, that hath made Heaven and Earth, the Sea, and all that is therein. He it is that doth wonders, who neither breaketh his promises, nor forgetteth his Covenant: who also suffereth not his Law and Righteousnes to be trodden down for ever: but he setteth up the Children of Israel, his beloved: Not for their Righteousnes; but for their Fathers sakes, towards whom he had a desire, according as he promised, and spake the same in times past, by the mouth of his holy Prophets.

39.   Therefore have regard unto the everlasting unchangeable God, being an invisible living God: the God that hath made you, created every thing that liveth and hath breath. He it is, which was, which is, and which is to come: who liveth everlastingly, and shall still continue. And so is also his Life, Law, or righteousnes.

40.   Wherefore give heed unto the thing that is right and reasonable, and shall continue for ever: glasse your selves in the glasse of Righteousnes, and therein behold according to the spirit, the upright life, and the Lords Statutes and Ordinances, which stand firm in God for evermore.

41.   Let not the matter in any wise seeme too slender or too small unto you. For though the Righteousnes whereof we testifie, be no eloquent speech, and that the same seemeth to be but as a small brooke, yet is it notwithstanding a bottomless Sea, which all Rivers do run into. And whatsoever can be uttered concerning the Righteousnes (were it even by so great multitudes of Bookes, as is the sand by the Seaside) it is every whit comprehended or grounded in the very same.

42.   Who so liveth therein, or in the obedience of the same life the gracious word, loveth the same life, and with a lowly and humble heart, applieth himself

obediently thereunto, such a one shall become wise in the hidden wisdom of God.
For the obeying of the requiring of the service of the gracious word of the Lord,
and of the Law of his Statutes and Ordinances, doth make the man wiser, than all
his chosen Masters or Teachers: and in that manner commeth he to the holy understanding of the godly wisdom.

43.    Hereunto let us be minded from the heart, ye dearly beloved, and regard ye
the kind mercy of God shewed on us, out of his love. For such a perseverance or clear-
ness of the healthful or safe-making Beeing, is shewed unto us worthy in open sight,
& hath in these last dayes, given us to know his requiring in our spirit and understanding, to a right distinguishing of life, and death, to the intent, that we who are yet
in peril of death, & do suffer grief & heavines for the sins cause, should conceive hope
towards such an healthful life, and rejoyce us in the Godlines.

44.    Therefore let no man be negligent in such an appeared Grace; but every
one give God the Honour, and so sigh over his wretchednes, that he may be
reformed of his errors.

45.    O ye Children of men, ye that have named your selves before the time,
or much too soone, with the name of Christ, or with the name of Israel: Lay away
from you your vain boasting, repent, and amend you, and betake your selves to
the love and her service, that ye may be saved.

46.    Do not think in your hearts, that ye yet remaining, without the gracious
word and his service of love; do nevertheless stand sure in Gods Covenant: or that
ye may not have transgressed nor forsaken the Covenant of your God.

47.    Think not also that ye are before God (howsoever after your conceit, ye
have hallowed your selves) any worthier, than all other Heathen are, which are
without you. For truly, ye are subject with them all unto vanity, misunderstanding, and destruction and alike, covered under the darknesses, not knowing, what
wayes ye all walk. For your own righteousnes is strange and unknown before the
God of Israel: inasmuch as the same is not his life of righteousnes, nor yet his
Statutes and Ordinances.

48.    Therefore ye, which live and walk without the Doctrine and Service of
the gracious word, are even altogether, touching the inward man; one manner of
people with all Heathen, although outwardly ye have sundry several sorts of good
Services or Ceremonies; but truly they are to no advantage or unity unto you, but
to all controversie and division: they are not to the life, but much rather to a death,
and destroying one of another.

## From *Terra Pacis*

### Chapter XXVII

This City (named *God's Understanding*) hath very strong and invincible Wall,
Fortresses or Bulwarks, wherewith she is walled and fortified against all her
enemies: Therefore can no man climb over into this city, nor get the same by violence, with any gain-fighting, neither yet deceive her with subtlety.

2.    The Walls or Bulwarks of this City are named *A free mind of the True Being*.

3.    And upon these walls, there is a prudent Watchman or Espyall, which over-seeth all what is present, or shall come, namely Life and Death, the Preservation and Destruction.

4.    His Sight reacheth from the rising of the Sun, even unto her going down.

5.    He beholdeth the highest of the midday and the deepest of the darkness of the midnight.

6.    This Watchman or Espyall is named '*The beginning and the end.*'

7.    He hath also two eyes (a right, and a left eye) wherewith he overlooketh all things, namely Good and Evil, Light, and Darkness.

8.    The eyes are named, *Wise Forsightfulness*.

9.    With the right eye, he looketh into all things, wherein the Life, the Rest and Peace standeth firm forever: but with the left Eye whereabout the Death, the Unquietness, the Confusion or Destruction proceedeth.

10.    This Watchman serveth to a false keeping of this City, and of those people likewise that dwell therein. Therefore he keepeth always a diligent Watch; he never sleepeth nor slumbereth, but is still sounding and playing his Song upon his Trumpet: and all those that dwell in the same City do hear the sound of his Song.

11.    His Trumpet where-thorow he playeth his Song, is named *After this time no time more*.

12.    Seeing then that the same time is the last time, the everlasting Rest of all the children of God, and the heavenly kingdom it self, therefore soundeth the Watchman also out of the Same last time, (as out of the last Trumpet) the sound or noise of the everlasting Life; after the which there is no life more to be waited for; for the same life continueth for evermore.

13.    The Song which he playeth and soundeth out thorow his Trumpet (with the sound of the everlasting Life) is named *Unity in the Love*.

14.    With which noise of the Song, the people do hold themselves in unity in the Love, whose Fortresses or hold is not to be overcome. therefore also soundeth the Song in this matter.

## Chapter XXVIII

We have a strong City run thither apace,
Which doth advance us in all vertue right,
Upright in Peace, is always her race,
Therein now take your joy and delight.
2.    God's understanding is her noble name,
Builded with Truth and Faithfulness sure,
There is true love as beseemeth the same,
Thence never flyeth god's Spirit most pure.
3.    With the true Spirit of God's free mind,
She is wall'd to endure in eternity;
4.    The power of God (hear this now I say)
That's the Defence (Understand the Effect)

From trouble and grief to keep us always,
That is our refuge, and doth us protect.
5.   Ye Princes elected of God, and new born
Regard and love well our City of Peace;
God's wrath is not there, nor cause why to morn;
The death lieth there, swallowed up and doth cease.
6.   Behold such a Song singeth or playeth the Watchman upon the walls; and the people of the City, do rejoyce them with unspeakable joy; and do likewise (all of them together) sing a dancing song, dancing (with great joy) to a thankful lauding of God for their freedom. And they sing in this manner:


## Chapter XXIX

Rejoyce all now pleasantly, For joy our ears doth fill:
Chear up your hearts courageously,
Be glad, *O Sions hill*.
For lo, the new time doth appear,
That has been writ of long;
And is insight to view full clear,
Wherefore rejoyce with Song,
ye Remnant (God's Inheritance)
Be joyful in the City;
Cast fear out of Rememberance,
And sing this dancing Ditty.
2.   For North and South, ye Righteous,
Come, blow the horn apace;
From East and West extoll even thus,
your voyce, and make solace.
For here's *Emmanuel* our King,
Against that fierce *Babel*:
Therefore, now let your trumpets ring,
For he will her expel.
Their hearts are all dismaid now quite,
Sound up your Trumps apace:
Think now on God both day and night,
And discord from you chase.
3.   Now is the last Cup fill'd also,
Over *Babels Kingdom high*,
To stagger and strive like drunkards, lo,
that's now her Melody.
Her Wisdom with her Practises,
That comes now all to shame:
And is no more of worthiness,
than for a laughing game.
In God's Precepts most pure and right,
Rejoyce you in every Land:
His Light doth shine in us full bright,

And under him we stand.
4.   Now is the Kingdom of the Beast,
Made dark, be glad therefore:
the Light of Truth even here doth rest,
Triumphing evermore.
His kingdom eke do we possess,
The Truth doth make us free;
And sets our hearts in quietness,
With god at one are we.
Whole Love is unto us we finde
(that do obey her voyce)
As is the head to's memebers kinde,
God's Life doth us rejoyce.
5.   His shut Paradise wherein we mought
Not come, is op't now fine:
The tree of Life is sprouted out,
Whole fruit is medicine.
Drink now the wine of Love most pure,
With joy and merry cheer,
God's Riches that always endure,
Are never wanting here.
Fore-sightfully with wariness,
See that you leade your life,
As do the wise, And seek no less,
To flie Dissentious strife.
6.   Now swallowed up lie death and sin,
With their folly great and vain:
The Devil and Hell, whose bands we were in,
The mockery appears now plain.
The heavenly Bread, or ghostly food,
That same our souls doth nourish.
The Kingdom of the new man, pure,
That is our God doth rise,
Is now with us, here present, sure,
In upright heavenly wise.

7.   A peaceable Kingdom have we now here,
As Scriptures said before:
Here is no wailing, nor mourning there,
Vex ye your hearts no more,
but now with us associate,
For in the heavenly being,
Is our King: he doth illuminate
Us all, as is agreeing.
To Scripture, where we reade the same,
Rejoyce therefore and sing
This new-land Song unto the Name
Of him our heavenly King.

8.   Ye Princes of our God most high
(Ye people of the Lord)
Which do agree in unity,
Come all with one accord,
your joy increase, and eke fulfill,
The truth receive also:
God's Spirit is on the path, and will,
Rebuke the world, his foe,
Of her self framed righteousness:
And th'arrogant wise ones are
(With their contentious spitefulness)
Laid down in silence once more.

# Chapter 17

# Early Baptist Worship

## Letter from Hugh and Anne Bromehead (1609)

Baptists were considered subversive and heretical in the first half of the seventeenth century. In part this was due to their being identified in the popular mind with the continental Anabaptist movement of the previous century, and in part a consequence of their reluctance to baptize their children into the established church, a clear threat to its hegemony. Baptist practice was only to baptize those old enough to understand the nature and purport of the ceremony, and to enter into it voluntarily. As this extract shows, they also profoundly challenged the idea that learning and scholarship were necessary for understanding the meaning of Scripture: in their gatherings it was only after their books are laid aside, and prayer engaged in, that exposition of the word could begin. Further, this exposition was not the responsibility of only one ordained "authority," but as many as were so led by the Spirit could "propound" and "prophesy."

    This insight into the pattern of early Baptist worship is taken from a letter sent in 1609 by Hugh and Anne Bromehead to a relative. The church they describe is the one generally thought to have been the first English Baptist church, that established by John Smyth and other exiles in Amsterdam that same year. Smyth, who pastored the church, had been an Anglican clergyman until performing the decidedly Anabaptist ritual of re-baptizing himself and other believers in the community. It was one of Smyth's followers, Thomas Helwys, who returned home in 1612 to set up the first Baptist church on English soil. In a gloss on the Bromeheads' comments about worship in Smyth's church, Helwys once remarked that "all books, even the originals themselves, must be laid aside in the time of spiritual worship."

## Source

Ernest A. Payne, *The Fellowship of Believers: Baptist Thought and Practice Yesterday and Today*, rev. edn., London, 1952, pp. 92–3.

## Further reading

B. R. White, *The English Baptists of the Seventeenth Century*, Didcot, 1996.
D. M. Himbury, *British Baptists: A Short History*, London, 1962.
J. F. McGregor and B. Reay, eds., *Radical Religion in the English Revolution*, Oxford, 1986.
W. H. Burgess, *John Smyth, the Se-Baptist*, 1911.

## Letter from Hugh and Anne Bromehead (1640)

The order of the worship and government of our church is:

I.   We begin with a prayer, after read some one or two chapters of the Bible; give the sense thereof and confer upon the same; that done, we lay aside our books and after a solemn prayer made by the first speaker he propoundeth some text out of the scripture and prophesieth out of the same by the space of one hour or three quarters of an hour. After him standeth up a second speaker and prophesieth out of the said text the like time and space, sometimes more, sometimes less. After him, the third, the fourth, the fifth &c., as the time will give leave. Then the first speaker concludeth with prayer as he began with prayer, with an exhortation to contribution to the poor, which collection being made is also concluded with prayer. This morning exercise begins at eight of the clock and continueth unto twelve of the clock. The like course of exercise is observed in the afternoon from two of the clock unto five or six of the clock. Last of all the execution of the government of the Church is handled.

# Chapter 18

# Thomas Helwys
# (ca. 1550–ca. 1616)

## A Short Declaration of the Mistery of Iniquity (1612)

In 1612 Thomas Helwys established England's first General Baptist Congregation. Having become embroiled in the controversy against infant baptism whilst a member of the separatist church in Amsterdam, he had been excommunicated from the English church in 1609. Although fiercely defensive of his own (Baptist) version of Christianity, and not afraid of being sharp with his opponents (particularly in his advocating of believer's baptism), Helwys equally was steadfast in his insistence upon defending religious liberty – even for those same said opponents. The extract is said to mark the first time that a plea for religious liberty was made in English and a costly plea, too, for it is said to have ultimately led to its author's death. The work itself is divided into four parts:

1  On Roman Catholicism's use and abuse of power and Anglicanism's adoption of Rome's methods of persecution;
2  Asserts that King James may have absolute power over his subjects, but none at all with regard to their conscience. Anglicanism should not be forced upon people via the sword;
3  Highlights inconsistencies in Puritanism, particularly those who preach the peace of the church whilst disturbing it at the same time;
4  Attacks separatists, and, again, infant baptism. As well as stressing freedom of conscience, the work, as a whole, advocates a "two realms" theology, separating church and state.

Source

Thomas Helwys, *A Short Declaration of the Mistery of Iniquity*, London: Kingsgate Press, 1935 (copy of original presented to King James in 1612, now in the Bodleian Library, Oxford).

## Further reading

Thomas Helwys, *Objections Answered*, Amsterdam, New York: Theatrum Orbis Terrarum Da Capo Press, 1973.

Thomas Helwys, "Persecution of religious judg'd and condemn'd in a discourse, between an Antichristian and a Christian . . . to which is added, An humble supplication of the King's Majesty . . . ," 1615, in *Tracts on Liberty of Conscience and Persecution*, ed. E. B. Underhill, 1846.

W. H. Burgess, *John Smyth the Se-Baptist, Helwys and the First Baptist Church in England*, 1911.

D. G. Mullen, ed., *Religious Pluralism in the West*, Oxford: Blackwell, 1998.

W.T. Whitley, *Thomas Helwys of Gray's Inn & Broxtowe Hall, Nottingham*, London: Kingsgate Press, 1936.

## A Short Declaration of the Mistery of Iniquity (1612)

We still pray our lord the kind that we may be free from suspect, for having any thoughts of provoking evil against them of the Romish religion in regard of their profession, if they be true and faithful subjects to the King for we do freely profess, that our lord the King hath no more power over their consciences than ours, and that is none at all: for our Lord the King is but an earthly King, and if the Kings people be obedient & true subjects, obeying all humane laws made by the King, our lord the King, can require no more. For men's religion to God, is betwixt God and themselves; the King shall not answer for it; neither may the King be judge between God and man. Let them be heretics, Turks, Jews or whatsoever, it appertains not to the earthly power to punish them in the least measure. This is made evident to our lord the king by the scriptures. When Paul was brought before Gallio deputy of Achaea and accused of the Jews for persuading men to worship God contrary to the law, Gallio said unto the Jews: if it were a matter of wrong or an evil deed, O ye Jews, I would according to right maintain you, and he drave them from the judgement seat (Acts 18:12, 17), shewing them that matters of wrong and evil deeds, which were betwixt man and man appertained only to the judgement seat and not questions of religion.

# Chapter 19

# The Levellers

**John Lilburne (1615–57),** The freeman's freedom vindicated **(1646)**
**Colonel Thomas Rainborow (d. 1648), The Putney Debates (1647)**
**A Petition of Women (1649)**

Of all the radical movements and sects which emerged in the 1640s, the Levellers were the most organized: with their manifestoes, petitions, mass demonstrations and lobbies of Parliament, they in some ways foreshadow our modern political parties. A central Leveller tenet was the fundamental equality of all, both male and female, and this led them to argue, as a consequence, for greater democracy at all levels of government and society. The term "Leveller" was something of a misnomer, for most who took that name eschewed "the levelling of men's estates," that is, communism. They did, however, call for an (albeit limited) extension of the franchise, not least during their debates on government with the Army leadership in Putney church in 1647.

Levellers subscribed to no one religious view, though their affirmation of the equality of all, as these extracts from Lilburne and the women's petition show, was drawn in part from the Creation narratives in Scripture: God created both male and female in God's own image, and therefore (as Rainborow also asserts) no one is to have authority or dominion over another save by the consent, freely given, of the one ruled.

Lilburne was the best-known of the Levellers, though not their only leader. He was responsible for several of their more influential writings, despite being in and out of prison for much of his later life. His wife Elizabeth was much respected in her own right, though either she or another leading Leveller, Katherine Chidley, might have drafted the Petition of Women (unless one shares the view of Woodhouse that it was probably not composed by women at all). Though sympathetic to the Levellers, and a spokesperson for their position at Putney, Rainborow's formal connections with the movement are uncertain.

## Sources

Andrew Sharp, ed., *The English Levellers*, Cambridge: Cambridge University Press, 1998, pp. 31–2.

C. H. Firth, ed., *The Clarke Papers*, vols. I and II, London, 1992, p. 301.

A. S. P. Woodhouse, ed., *Puritanism and Liberty*, London, 1938, pp. 367–9

## Further reading

H. N. Brailsford, *The Levellers and the English Revolution*, London, 1976.
A. L. Morton, Freedom in Arms: a Selection of Leveller Writings, London, 1975.
Christopher Hill, *The World Turned Upside Down*, London, 1972.
G. E. Aylmer, ed., *The Levellers in the English Revolution*, London, 1975.
Pauline Gregg, *Free-Born John*, London, 1961.
J. F. McGregor and B. Reay, eds., *Radical Religion in the English Revolution*, Oxford, 1986.

## *The Freeman's Freedom Vindicated* (1646)

*A postscript, containing a general proposition*

God, the absolute sovereign lord and king of all things in heaven and earth, the original fountain and cause of all causes; who is circumscribed, governed, and limited by no rules, but doth all things merely and only by His sovereign will and unlimited good pleasure; who made the world and all things therein for His own glory; and who by His own will and pleasure, gave him, His mere creature, the sovereignty (under Himself) over all the rest of His creatures (Genesis 1: 26, 28–9) and endued him with a rational soul, or understanding, and thereby created him after His own image (Genesis 1: 26–7; 9: 6). The first of which was Adam, a male, or man, made out of the dust or clay; out of whose side was taken a rib, which by the sovereign and absolute mighty creating power of God was made a female or woman called Eve: which two are the earthly, original fountain, as begetters and bringers-forth of all and every particular and individual man and woman that ever breathed in the world since; who are, and were by nature all equal and alike in power, dignity, authority, and majesty – none of them having (by nature) any authority, dominion or magisterial power, one over or above another. Neither have they or can they exercise any but merely by institution or donation, that is to say by mutual agreement or consent – given, derived, or assumed by mutual consent and agreement – for the good benefit and comfort each of other, and not for the mischief, hurt, or damage of any: it being unnatural, irrational, sinful, wicked and unjust for any man or men whatsoever to part with so much of their power as shall enable any of their parliament-men, commissioners, trustees, deputies, viceroys, ministers, officers or servants to destroy and undo them therewith. And unnatural, irrational, sinful, wicked, unjust, devilish, and tyrannical it is, for any man whatsoever – spiritual or temporal, clergyman or layman – to appropriate and assume unto himself a power, authority and jurisdiction to rule, govern or reign over any sort of men in the world without their free consent; and whosoever doth it – whether clergyman or any other whatsoever – do thereby as much as in them lies endeavour to appropriate and assume unto themselves the office and sovereignty of God (who alone doth, and is to rule by His will and pleasure), and to be like their creator, which was the sin of the devils', who, not being content with their first station but would be like God; for which sin they were thrown down into hell, reserved in everlasting chains, under darkness, unto the judgement of the great day (Jude verse 6). And Adam's sin it was, which brought the curse upon him and all his posterity, that he was not content with the station and condition that God created him in, but did aspire unto a better and more excellent – namely to be like his creator – which proved his ruin. Yea, and indeed had been the everlasting ruin and destruction of him and all his, had not God been the more merciful unto him in the promised Messiah (Genesis 3).

From my cock-loft in the Press Yard, Newgate

19 June 1646. *Per me* John Lilburne

## The Putney Debates (1647)

. . . for really I thinke that the poorest hee that is in England hath a life to live as the greatest hee; and therefore truly, Sir, I thinke itt's cleare, that every man that is to live under a Governement ought first by his owne consent to putt himself under that Governement; and I doe thinke that the poorest man in England is nott att all bound in a stricte sence to that Governement that hee hath not had a voice to putt himself under . . .

## A Petition of Women (1649)

Sheweth, that since we are assured of our creation in the image of God, and of an interest in Christ equal unto men, as also of a proportionable share in the freedoms of this commonwealth, we cannot but wonder and grieve that we should appear so despicable in your eyes as to be thought unworthy to petition or represent our grievances to this honourable House. Have we not an equal interest with the men of this nation in those liberties and securities contained in the *Petition of Right*, and other the good laws of the land? Are any of our lives, limbs, liberties, or goods to be taken from us more than from men, but by due process of law and conviction of twelve sworn men of the neighbourhood? And can you imagine us to be so sottish or stupid as not to perceive, or not to be sensible when daily those strong defences of our peace and welfare are broken down and trod underfoot by force and arbitrary power?

Would you have us keep at home in our houses, when men of such faithfulness and integrity as the four prisoners, our friends, in the Tower, are fetched out of their beds and forced from their houses by soldiers, to the affrighting and undoing of themselves, their wives, children, and families? Are not our husbands, o[u]r selves, our children and families, by the same rule as liable to the like unjust cruelties as they?

Shall such men as Capt. Bray be made close prisoners, and such as Mr. Sawyer snatched up and carried away, beaten and buffeted at the pleasure of some officers of the Army; and such as Mr. Blank kept close prisoner, and after most barbarous usage be forced to run the gauntlet, and be most slave-like and cruelly whipped? And must we keep at home in our houses, as if our lives and liberties and all were not concerned?

Nay, shall such valiant, religious men as Mr. Robert Lockyer be liable to law martial, and to be judged by his adversaries, and most inhumanly shot to death? Shall the blood of war be shed in time of peace? Doth not the word of God expressly condemn it? Doth not the *Petition of Right* declare that no person ought to be judged by law martial (except in time of war) and that all commissions given to execute martial law in time of peace are contrary to the laws and statutes of the land? Doth not Sir Ed. Coke, in his chapter of murder in the third part of his *Institutes*, hold it for good law (and since owned and published by this Parliament) that for a general or other officers of an army in time of peace to put any man (although a soldier) to death by colour of martial law, it is absolute murder in that general? And hath it not by this House in the case of the late Earl of Strafford been adjudged high treason? And are we Christians, and shall we sit still and keep at home, while such men as have borne continual testimony against the injustice of all times and unrighteousness of men, be picked out and be delivered up to the slaughter? And yet must we show no sense of their sufferings, no tenderness of affections, no bowels of compassion, nor bear any testimony against so abominable cruelty and injustice?

Have such men as these continually hazarded their lives, spent their estates and time, lost their liberties, and thought nothing too precious for defence of us, our lives and liberties, been as a guard by day and as a watch by night; and when for this they are in trouble and greatest danger, persecuted and hated even to the death, should we be so basely ungrateful as to neglect them in the day of their affliction? No, far be it from us. Let it be accounted folly, presumption, madness, or whatsoever in us, whilst we have life and breath we will never leave them nor forsake them, nor ever cease to importune you, having yet so much hopes of you as of the unjust judge (mentioned, Luke 18), to obtain justice, if not for justice' sake, yet for importunity, or to use any other means for the enlargement and reparation of those of them that live, and for justice against such as have been the cause of Mr. Lockyer's death.

And therefore again we entreat you to review our last petition in behalf of our friends above mentioned, and not to slight the things therein contained because they are presented unto you by the weak hand of women, it being a usual thing with God, by weak means to work mighty effects. For we are no whit satisfied with the answer you gave unto our husbands and friends, but do equally with them remain liable to those snares laid in your Declaration, which maketh the abetters of the book laid to our friends' charge, no less than traitors, when hardly any discourse can be touching the affairs of the present times but falls within the compass of that book; so that all liberty of discourse is thereby utterly taken away, than which there can be no greater slavery.

# Chapter 20

# John Milton (1608–1674)

The Tenure of Kings and Magistrates **(1649)**
Eikonoklastes **(1649)**
Sonnet XV **(1655)**

John Milton towers over the seventeenth century as poet, political activist, and apologist for the commonwealth. The execution of Charles I in 1649 led to a spate of political writing by Milton which is reflected in the extracts contained in this book. In some respects his writing seems out of place in the context of the Leveller and Digger writings. He was suspicious of the enthusiasm and intellectual calibre of the radical biblical interpreters of his age and was by no means at one with some of the more radical spirits of his day (this is explored in Christopher Hill, *Milton and the English Revolution*, London: Faber, 1977). Nevertheless he stands as one of the foremost apologists of non-conformity (his apology for divorce and his case for the disestablishment of the churches are other examples of his independence of approach in matters ecclesiastical and political). His theological and political instincts link him closely with Winstanley (he was less sympathetic to some of the pragmatic maneuverings of the Levellers with whom in other respects he has much in common also). After the restoration of the monarchy he produced his great poems *Paradise Lost* (1667) and *Paradise Regained* (1671). He was part of that generation which had to come to terms with "the experience of defeat" (see C. Hill, *The Experience of Defeat*, London, 1985). Another figure with whom he has close links is Blake who both recognized him as a kindred spirit but also as an errant ancestor of the radical cause whose views and attitudes needed to be redeemed (this in large part is the subject-matter of Blake's epic poem *Milton* in which the spirit of the older poet invades Blake and the younger poet recapitulates and redeems the views and practice of his spiritual ancestor). It is no accident that Blake's most famous lines are to be found as a preface to some versions of *Milton* (see below p. 170).

Milton became the chief apologist for the Commonwealth which led him to write *Eikonoklastes*, a response to a hagiography of the "martyred" king Charles I, entitled *Eikon Basilike*, which had been something of a publishing sensation and attracted enormous support for the royal ideology. Milton's propagandist instincts are everywhere apparent as he reacts to contemporary royal ideology. The testament of the king which glorified his divine monarchy and offered an apology for his actions during the prolonged struggle with parliament is at times an ill-tempered demolition of a position which Milton himself finds utterly distasteful. The *Eikonoklastes* concludes with a brief exposition of verses from the Apocalypse which predict the end of monarchy using the apocalyptic images of the Beast and Babylon as Winstanley and Blake were to do later. *The Tenure of Kings and Magistrates* was written at the time of the trial and execution of Charles I. In it we find Hebrew Bible passages treated to support the biblical attitude to monarchy, which is then taken further with an examination of famous passages connected with Christianity and state power (Matthew 22 and Romans 13: 1ff).

In 1655, after hundreds of Waldensians were massacred. Milton wrote an official protest on behalf of Cromwell's Government. His sonnet was inspired by an incident in 1655, when the Duke of Savoy, sent an expedition against the Waldensians. The Waldensian Church was founded by Pietro Valdo at the beginning of the thirteenth century. The movement was officially condemned and its adherents excommunicated. An underground network of contacts meant believers were able to meet for worship. The following has been offered as a list of their views during early centuries of the movement: the decay of the Church of God down the centuries; the centrality of the Scriptures; criticism of the papacy; the right to preach publicly; suspicion of oaths; and no obligation to fast or to keep holy days. The Waldensians were persecuted just like the Anabaptists (the Waldensians are commemorated in the Anabaptist *The Martyrs Mirror* as their spiritual ancestors).

## Sources

M. Dzelzanis, *Milton Political Writings*, Cambridge: Cambridge University Press, 1991, pp. 105–11.

"Eikonoklastes", *The Complete Prose Works of John Milton*, New Haven: Yale University Press, 1962, pp. 335–601.

## Further reading

P. Stephens, *The Waldensian Story*, Lewes: The Book Guild, 1998.
E. Cameron, *The Reformation of the Heretics*, Oxford: Clarendon Press, 1984.
A. J. Wylie, *History of the Waldensians* Rapidan, Virginia: Hartland, 1996.

## *The Tenure of Kings and Magistrates* (1649)

So while Christ denied that it was the right of kings to impose excessively heavy dues upon freemen, certainly he even more clearly denies that it is the right of kings to plunder, ravage, murder and torture their own citizens and especially christians. Since he seems to have discussed the right of kings elsewhere too in this manner, certain people began to suspect that he did not consider the licence of tyrants as the right of kings. For it was not for nothing that the Pharisees tested out his mind with questioning of this kind. When they were about to interrogate him concerning the right of kings, they said that he cared for no-one, and did not respect the character of men; and it was not for nothing that he grew angry when this kind of inquiry was proposed to him, Mat. 22. What if someone wished to approach you insidiously and seize on your words, to elicit from you what would be to your harm, question you about the right of kings under a king? Would you grow angry with anyone who questioned you about this? I don't suppose! Hence then observe that his opinion about the right of kings was not agreeable to kings.

The same point is to be gathered most clearly from his answer, by which he seems to repel his examiners from him rather than instruct them. He asks for a coin of the tribute. He says, 'Whose image is this?' 'Caesar's.' 'Render then to Caesar the things that are Caesar's, and the things that are God's to God.' Rather, who does not know that those things which belong to the people should be given back to the people? Render to all men what you owe them, says Paul, Rom. 13. So not all things are Caesar's. Our liberty is not Caesar's, but is a birthday gift to us from God himself. To give back to any Caesar what we did not receive from him would be most base and unworthy of the origin of man. For if upon beholding the face and countenance of a man, someone should ask whose image is that, would not anyone freely reply that it was God's? Since then we belong to God, that is, we are truly free and on that account to be rendered to God alone, surely we cannot, without sin and in fact the greatest sacrilege, hand ourselves over in slavery to Caesar, that is to a man, and especially one who is unjust, wicked and tyrannical?

Meanwhile he leaves open what things are Caesar's and what God's. But if this coin was the same as that double drachma customarily paid to God, as it certainly was later under Vespasian, then indeed Christ has not lessened the controversy, but complicated it; since it is impossible to render the same thing at the same time to God and Caesar. But he showed what things were Caesar's; that coin of course, stamped with the image of Caesar. So what profit do you gain from this, apart from a denarius, either for Caesar or yourself? For either Christ gave Caesar nothing but that denarius, and asserted everything else was ours, or if he gave to Caesar all money inscribed with Caesar's name, now in contradiction with himself, he will give almost all our property to Caesar; as he declared openly, both in his own name and that of Peter, that they did not pay to kings a mere double drachma out of obligation [Mt. 17:24]. In short the reasoning you rely on is weak; for coins bear the portrait of the prince, not to show that it is his property but to show that it is valid, and so that nobody may dare to tamper with a coin marked by the prince's portrait. But if an inscription alone had the power to establish right of kings, kings would immediately make it so that all our property belonged to them, merely by writing their names on it. Or if all our possessions already belong to them, which is your belief, that coin was not to be rendered to Caesar because it bore Caesar's name or portrait, but because it was already Caesar's before by right, even if it was not stamped with any portrait. From this it is clear that Christ in this passage wanted not so much to remind us so obscurely and ambiguously of our duty towards kings or Caesars, as to prove the wickedness and malice of the hypocritical Pharisees. Moreover when the Pharisees reported to him at another time that Herod was preparing an ambush against his life, did they get a humble or submissive reply from him to take back to the tyrant? Rather he said, 'go and tell that fox', implying that kings do not plot against their own citizens by right of kingship, but in the manner of a fox.

'But he submitted to death beneath a tyrant.' And how could he possibly, except under a tyrant? 'He suffered death under a tyrant'; so he might be a witness and defender of all the absolutely unjust acts of royal right! You are an extraordinary reckoner of morals indeed! And Christ, although he made himself a slave to free us, not to put us under the yoke, still behaved in this manner; and did not yield anything to royal right except what was just and good.

Now let us come at length to his teaching about this matter. The sons of Zebedee, who aimed at the greatest authority in the kingdom of Christ, which they imagined would soon be on earth, were reproved in this way by Christ, so that he might at once impress upon all christians what kind of right of magistrates and civil power he wanted to set up amongst them. 'You know', he said, 'that the princes of nations are rulers over them, and great men exercise authority over them; but it will not be so amongst you. Rather let whoever wishes to be great amongst you be your attendant; and whoever wishes to be first among you, be your slave.' Unless you were mentally deranged, could you have believed this passage illustrates your side of the case, and that by these arguments you win us over to consider our kings as masters of all? May we meet with such enemies in war, who stumble into the camp of the enemy as you usually do, as if into their own camp, blindly and without arms (although we know well enough we can conquer them even when they are armed). In your madness you are always accustomed, like this, to set out what is most hostile to your cause as if it lent it the strongest support. The Israelites kept asking for a king 'such as all those nations had'. God advised them against it, using many words which Christ has summarized briefly in this speech: 'you know that princes of nations are rulers over them'. Yet when they asked for one, God gave them a king, although he was angry. Christ, so that the christian people should in no way ask for one to be their ruler, like the other nations, prevented them with the warning, 'among you it will not be so'. What could be said more clearly than this? Amongst you there will not be this proud rule of kings, even though they are called by the plausible title of Euergetes and benefactors. But whoever wishes to become great among you (and who is greater than the prince?) 'let him be your attendant': and whoever wishes to be 'first' or 'prince' (Luke 22) 'let him be your slave'. And so that advocate whom you rail at was not wrong, but had Christ as his authority, if he said that a christian king is the servant of the people, as every good magistrate certainly is. But a king will either be no christian at all, or will be the slave of all. If he clearly wants to be master, he cannot at the same time be a Christian.

## *Eikonoklastes*

So much he thinks to abound in his own defence, that he undertakes an unmeasurable task; to bespeak *the singular care and protection of God over all Kings*, as *being the greatest Patrons of Law, Justice, Order, and Religion on Earth.* But what Patrons they be, God in the Scripture oft anough hath exprest; and the earth it self hath too long groan'd under the burd'n of thir injustice, disorder, and irreligion. Therefore *To bind thir Kings in Chaines, and thir Nobles with links of Iron*, is an honour belonging to his Saints; not to build *Babel* (which was *Nimrods* work the first King, *and the beginning of his Kingdom was Babel*) but to destroy it, especially that spiritual *Babel*: and first to overcome those European Kings, which receive thir [227] power, not from God, but from the beast; and are counted no better then his ten hornes. *These shall hate the great Whore*, and yet *shall give thir Kingdoms to the Beast that carries her; they shall committ Fornication with her*, and yet *shall burn her with fire*, and yet *shall lament the fall of Babylon*, where they fornicated with her. [*Rev.* 17. & 18. chapt.]

Thus shall they be too and fro, doubtfull and ambiguous in all thir doings, untill at last, *joyning thir Armies with the Beast*, whose power first rais'd them, they shall perish with him by the *King of Kings* against whom they have rebell'd; and *the Foules shall eat thir flesh.* This is thir doom writt'n, [*Rev.* 19.] and the utmost that we find concerning them in these latter days; which we have much more cause to beleeve, then his unwarranted Revelation here, prophecying what shall follow after his death, with the spirit of Enmity, not of Saint *John.*

He would fain bring us out of conceit with the good *success* which God hath voutsaf'd us. Wee measure not our Cause by our success, but our success by our cause. Yet certainly in a good Cause success is a good confirmation; for God hath promis'd it to good men almost in every leafe of Scripture. If it argue not for us, we are sure it argues not against us; but as much or more for us, then ill success argues for them; for to the wicked, God hath denounc'd ill success in all that they take in hand.

He hopes much of those *softer tempers*, as he calls them, and *less advantag'd by his ruin, that thir consciences doe already* gripe them. Tis true, there be a sort of moodie, hot-brain'd, and alwayes unedify'd consciences; apt to engage thir Leaders into great and dangerous affaires past retirement, and then, upon a sudden qualm and swimming of thir conscience, to betray them basely in the midst of what was cheifly undertak'n for their sakes. Let such men never meet with any faithfull Parlament to hazzard for them; never with any noble spirit to conduct and lead them out, but let them live and die in servil condition and thir scrupulous queasiness, if no instruction will confirme them. Others there be in whose consciences the loss of gaine, and those advantages they hop'd for, hath sprung a sudden leake. These are they that cry out the Covnant brok'n, and to keep it better slide back into neutrality, or joyn actually with Incendiaries and Malignants. But God hath eminently begun to punish those, first in *Scotland*, then in *Ulster*, who have provok'd him with the most hatefull kind of mockery, to break his Covnant under pretence of strictest keeping it; and hath subjected them to those Malignants, with whom they scrupl'd not to be associats. In God therfore we shall not feare what their fals fraternity can doe against us.

He seeks againe with cunning words to turn out success into our sin. But might call to mind, that the Scripture speakes of those also, who *when God slew them, then sought him*; yet did but *flatter him with thir mouth, and ly'd to him with thir tongues; for thir heart was not right with him.* And there was one, who in the time of his affliction trespass'd more against God; *This was that King Ahaz.*

He glories much in the forgivness of his Enemies; so did his Grandmother at her death. Wise men would sooner have beleev'd him had he not so [229] oft'n told us so. But he hopes to erect *the Trophies of his charity over us.* And Trophies of Charity no doubt will be as *glorious* as Trumpets before the almes of Hypocrites; and more especially the Trophies of such an aspiring charitie as offers in his Prayer to share Victory with Gods *compassion*, which is over all his works. Such Prayers as these may happly catch the People, as was intended: but how they please God, is to be much doubted, though pray'd in secret, much less writt'n to be divulg'd. Which perhaps may gaine him after death a short, contemptible, and soon fading reward; not what he aims at, to stirr the constancie and solid firmness of any wise Man, or to unsettle the conscience of any knowing Christian, if he could ever aime at a thing so hopeless, and above the genius of his *Cleric* elocution, but to catch the worthles approbation of an inconstant, irrational, and Image-doting rabble; [that like a credulous and hapless herd, begott'n to servility, and inchanted with these popular institutes of Tyranny, subscrib'd with a new device of the Kings Picture at his praiers, hold out both thir eares with such delight and ravishment to be stigmatiz'd and board through in witness of thir own voluntary and beloved baseness.] The rest, whom perhaps ignorance without malice, or some error, less then fatal, hath for the time misledd, on this side Sorcery or obduration, may find the grace and good guidance to bethink themselves, and recover.

## Sonnet XV (1655)

*On the Late Massacre in Piedmont*

> Avenge O Lord thy slaughtered saints, whose bones
>   Lie scattered on the Alpine mountains cold;
>     Ev'n them who kept thy truth so pure of old
>     When all our fathers worshipped stocks and stones,
> Forget not: in thy book record their groans
>   Who were thy sheep and in their ancient fold
>   Slain by the bloody Piedmontese that rolled
>   Mother with infant down the rocks. Their moans
> The vales redoubled to the hills, and they
>   To Heav'n. Their martyred blood and ashes sow
>   O'er all th' Italian fields where still doth sway
> The triple Tyrant: that from these may grow
>   A hundredfold, who having learnt thy way
>   Early may fly the Babylonian woe.

# Chapter 21

# Gerrard Winstanley (1609–1676)

Truth Lifting Up Its Head Above Scandals **(1648)**
The New Law of Righteousness **(January 1649)**
The True Levellers Standard Advanced **(April 1649)**
A Watch-Word to The City of London and the Armie **(August 1649)**
A New-yeers Gift for the Parliament and Armie **(January 1650)**
Fire in the Bush **(March 1650)**
The Law of Freedom in a Platform **(1652)**
**An Additional Digger Text from Iver, Buckinghamshire:**
A Declaration **(May 1650)**

Between 1648 and 1652 Winstanley wrote more than twenty radical politico-religious tracts, the majority taking the form of reflections on and apologias for the "Digger" colony he helped to instigate on St. George's Hill in Surrey in April 1649. The Diggers – or True Levellers as they were also known – were arguably the most revolutionary of the movements which emerged in England in the 1640s and '50s, having a vision not just to improve the lot of the hungry and landless through the cultivation of the commons, but to create a communist – that is, moneyless and propertyless – society of the kind they believed had existed before the Fall. Like Ball and the Levellers, Diggers held the Earth to have been originally a "common treasury" for all to share, with the practice of buying and selling the land, which allowed some to become rich and others to starve, constituting the Fall from which humanity stood in need of redemption. True freedom could not be enjoyed by all until the land was held again in common, and it was this vision which inspired Winstanley and the Diggers to occupy St. George's Hill and invite all to join them. The practice of Digging soon spread to many parts of the south and Midlands, but the hostility of local landowners ensured no colonies survived for long – though it is arguable that, had the movement not been suppressed, the "commonwealth" then being fashioned under Cromwell might have been more literally that. The *Declaration* from Iver is an example of a writing from one of the colonies inspired by the Surrey Diggers.

*Truth Lifting Up Its Head* and *The New Law of Righteousnes* are the last of Winstanley's pre-Digger tracts, and mark a transition in his thought: whereas his previous writings had been largely mystical and devotional in character, these demonstrate a concern also to understand the roots of the economic and material struggles facing humankind. *The New Law* is also the first in which he outlines his revolutionary programme for a more just and peaceful socioeconomic order. Some commentators have argued that Winstanley's growing commitment to political struggle led him to abandon his earlier mystical beliefs, but the evidence of this tract is that theological convictions profoundly inspired his project to make the earth once more a "common treasury." These extracts also demonstrate some of the typical features of Winstanley's use of Scripture: current events are viewed through the lens of scriptural types and illuminated by them. It is a form of interpretation which is evident in many parts of the New Testament, for example the use of Balaam and Jezebel in the book of Revelation and the actualizing of Israel's story in the life of the Corinthian community in I Corinthians 10.

*The True Levellers Standard*, published just days after the start of the St. George's Hill occupation, is very much a "manifesto" of the Digger movement, Winstanley setting out in this work a systematic defence of the project. *A Watch-Word*, *A New-yeers Gift* and *Fire in the Bush* were penned after the Diggers were forced to leave St. George's Hill and resettle at Little Heath, Cobham. The extract here from *The Watch-Word*'s "Preface" contains some of Winstanley's finest prose, including his reflection on the importance of action *vis-à-vis* writing, and challenge to those "ashamed and afraid" of his work to understand it for what it is. *The Law of Freedom*, Winstanley's last and only known post-Digger tract, differs from the others in taking the form of a blueprint for the society he would like to see established in the England of his day. He is still concerned, however, to expose the selfishness of the clergy and false doctrines they peddle.

Winstanley's impatience with clergy who live off the tithes of the people and oppress them with their doctrine – which he shared with many of his radical contemporaries and those of other generations – comes through in these extracts. So, also, do other themes in his writings, such as his preference for the term "Reason" to God; the priority of experience over book-learning; the importance of visions as vehicles for divine disclosure; and the identification of the recovery of "communist" society and the return of Christ: for Winstanley, the Second Coming takes the form of Christ "rising up in sons and daughters" and drawing them back into a spirit of true community.

## Source

G. H. Sabine, ed., *The Works of Gerrard Winstanley*, New York, 1965, pp. 105–6, 127, 179–81, 184, 190–1, 193, 196–7, 238–9, 251–4, 257–8, 260–2, 315–16, 373–4, 463–7, 470, 473–4, 566–7.

Andrew Hopton, ed., *Digger Tracts 1649–50*, London: Aporia Press, 1989, pp. 31–3.

## Further reading

D. W. Petegorsky, *Left-Wing Democracy in the English Civil War*, London, 1940 and Stroud, 1995.

Christopher Hill, *The Religion of Gerrard Winstanley*, Oxford, 1978.

T. Wilson Hayes, *Winstanley the Digger*, Cambridge, MA and London, 1979.

Timothy Kenyon, *Utopian Communism and Political Thought in Early Modern England*, London, 1989.

James Holstun, *Ehud's Dagger: Class Struggle in the English Revolution*, London and New York, 2000.

George M. Shulman, *Radicalism and Reverence: The Political Thought of Gerrard Winstanley*, Berkeley, 1989.

Christopher Rowland, *Radical Christianity: A Reading of Recovery*, Cambridge, 1988.

Andrew Bradstock, *Faith in the Revolution: The Political Theologies of Müntzer and Winstanley*, London, 1997.

Andrew Bradstock, ed., *Winstanley and the Diggers 1649–1999*, London and Portland, OR, 2000.

David Boulton, *Gerrard Winstanley and the Republic of Heaven*, Dent, 1999.

### *Truth Lifting up its Head Above Scandals* (1648)

. . . the Spirit Reason, which I call God, the Maker and Ruler of all things, is that spirituall power, that guids all mens reasoning in right order, and to a right end: for the Spirit Reason, doth not preserve one creature and destroy onother; as many times mens reasoning doth, being blind by the imagination of the flesh: but it hath a regard to the whole creation; and knits every creature together into a onenesse; making every creature to be an upholder of his fellow; and so every one is an assistant to preserve the whole: and the neerer that mans reasoning comes to this, the more spirituall they are; the farther off they be, the more selfish and fleshy they be.

Now this word Reason is not the alone name of this spirituall power: but every one may give him a name according to that spirituall Power that they feel and see rules in them, carrying them forth in actions to preserve their fellow creatures as well as themselves.

Therefore some may call him King of righteousnesse and Prince of peace: some may call him Love, and the like: but I can, and I doe call him Reason; because I see him to be that living powerfull light that is in righteousnesse, making righteousnesse to be righteousnesse; or justice to be justice; or love to be love: for without this moderater and ruler, they would be madnesse; nay, the selfewillednesse of the flesh; and not that which we call them.

Lastly, I am made to change the name from God to Reason; because I have been held under darknesse by that word, as I see many people are; and likewise that people may rest no longer upon words without knowledge; but hereafter may look after that spirituall power; and know what it is that rules them, and which doth rule in and over all, and which they call their God and Governour or preserver. And this I hope will be a sufficient accompt why I alter the word. . . .

. . . neither reason nor Scripture allowes any man to speake any words, but what he knowes positively to be truth. And he that spends constructions thereupon, speaking from his imagination, he speaks from the flesh and devill, and so he makes himself to be a traytor to the father, in holding forth that to be truth which is no truth. And a thief, robber, and unrighteous dealer with the Prophets and Apostles: First, in taking their words as his own: and secondly, in expounding their meaning, and so putting his own meaning upon their words.

But yet he that hath the same spirit, may speak the same word, where the Father hath given him the same sight and experience: for no man can safely tell another, this is a positive truth of God, till he have the same testimoniall experience within himself as the penmen of Scripture had: and this I am sure all that stand up to teach by way of office have not; therefore it is clear, that the power that sets up such teachers is not from the Father commanding, but from the flesh; being suffered by the Father for a time, that when he comes to throw downe his enemies, flesh may be shamed, and he honoured.

That man that cannot speak the testimony of the Father, no other way, but from his book as he reads, or from the mouth of another what he heares: as the publike teachers doe, speakes by hearsay and not from experience, and so declares himself to be a false Christ, a false prophet, that runs to teach others, before he have any discovery of God within himself.

## *The New Law of Righteousnes* (January 1649)

The man of the flesh, judges it a righteous thing, That some men that are cloathed with the objects of the earth, and so called rich men, whether it be got by right or wrong, should be Magistrates to rule over the poor; and that the poor should be servants nay rather slaves to the rich.

But the spiritual man, which is Christ, doth judge according to the light of equity and reason, That al man-kinde ought to have a quiet substance and freedome, to live upon earth; and that there shal be no bond-man nor begger in all his holy mountaine.

Man-kinde was made to live in the freedome of the spirit, not under the bondage of the flesh, though the lordly flesh hath got a power for a time, as I said before; for every one was made to be a Lord over the Creation of the Earth, Cattle, Fish, Fowl, Grasse, Trees, not any one to be a bond-slave and a beggar under the Creation of his own kinde. Gen. 1: 28.

That so every one living in freedome and love in the strength of the Law of Righteousnesse in him; not under straits of poverty, nor bondage of tyranny one to another, might al rejoyce together in Righteousnesse, and so glorifie their Maker; for surely this much dishonoured the Maker of all men, that some men should be oppressing tyrants, imprisoning, whipping, hanging their fellow creatures, men, for those very things which those very men themselves are guilty of; let mens eyes be opened, and it appears clear enough, That the punishers have and doe break the law of equity and reason, more, or as much as those that are punished by them.

When every son and daughter shall be made comfortable to that one body, of Jesus the anointed, and the same power rules in them, as in him, every one according to their measure, the oppression shall cease, and the rising up of this universal power, shal destroy and subdue the selfish power. Phil. 3: 21.

But this is not done by the hands of a few, or by unrighteous men, that would pul the tyrannical government out of other mens hands, and keep it in their own heart [hands], as we feel this to be a burden of our age. But it is done by the universall spreading of the divine power, which is Christ in mankind making them all to act in one spirit, and in and after one law of reason and equity. . . .

When this universall law of equity rises up in every man and woman, then none shall lay claim to any creature, and say, *This is mine, and that is yours, This is my work, that is yours*; but every one shall put to their hands to till the earth, and bring up cattle, and the blessing of the earth shall be common to all; when a man hath need of any corn for cattle, take from the next storehouse he meets with. Act. 4: 32.

There shall be no buying nor selling, no fairs nor markets, but the whole earth shall be a common treasury for every man, for the earth is the Lords. And man kind thus drawn up to live and act in the Law of love, equity and onenesse, is but the great house wherein the Lord himself dwels, and every particular one a severall mansion: and as one spirit of righteousnesse is common to all, so the earth and the blessings of the earth shall be common to all; for now all is but the Lord, and the Lord is all in all. Eph. 4: 5, 6.

When a man hath meat, and drink, and cloathes he hath enough, and all shall cheerfully put to their hands to make these things that are needfull, one helping another; there shall be none Lord over others, but every one shall be a Lord of him self, subject to the law of righteousnesse, reason and equity, which shall dwell and rule in him, which is the Lord; *For now the Lord is one, and his name and power one, in all and among all.* Zech. 14: 9.

Their rejoycings and glory shall be continually in eying and speaking of what breakings forth of love they receive from the Father, singing *Sions* songs one to another; to the glory of him that sits upon the throne, for evermore.

This universall freedom hath never filled the earth though it hath been foretold by most of the Prophets. This is the glory of *Jerusalem*, which never yet hath been the praise of the whole earth. And this will be no troublesome businesse, when covetousnesse, and the selfish power is killed and cast out of heaven, and every one is made willing to honour the King of Righteousnesse in action, being all of one heart and one mind: Truly we may well call this a new heaven, and a new earth, wherein dwells righteousnesse. And that prophesie will not generally be fulfilled till this time. Rev. 12: 9. . . .

As I was in a trance not long since, divers matters were present to my sight, which here must not be related. Likewise I heard these words, *Worke together. Eat bread together*; declare this all abroad. Likewise I heard these words. *Whosoever it is that labours in the earth, for any person or persons, that lifts up themselves as Lords & Rulers over others, and that doth not look upon themselves equal to others in the Creation, The*

*hand of the Lord shall be upon that labourer: I the Lord have spoke it and I will do it;*
Declare this all abroad.

After I was raised up, I was made to remember very fresh what I had seen and
heard, & did declare al things to them that were with me, and I was filled with
abundance of quiet peace and secret joy. And since that time those words have
been like very fruitfull seed, that have brought forth increase in my heart, which
I am much prest in spirit to declare all abroad.

The poor people by their labours in this time of the first *Adams* government,
have made the buyers and sellers of land, or rich men, to become tyrants and
oppressours over them.

But in the time of *Israels* restoration, now begining, when the King of Righteousnesse himself shall be Governor in every man; none then shall work for hire,
neither shal any give hire, but every one shal work in love: one with, and for
another; and eat bread together, as being members of one houshold; the Creation
in whom Reason rules King in perfect glory. Ier. 23: 5, 6.

He that cals any part of the Creation his own in particular, in this time of *Israel's*
return from the mistery of *Ægyptian* bondage, is a destroyer of the Creation, a lifter
up of the proud covetous flesh againe, a bringer in of the curse againe, and a mortal
enemy, to the Spirit. Act. 4: 32.

For upon *Israel's* returne from captivity, the Lord himself wil burn up the curse,
and restore the Creation, fire, water, earth and air from that slavery, and make the
earth to be a common treasury to them all; for they are but one house of Israel
still, though twelve Tribes; And they have but one King, one Law-giver, one teacher
amongst them all, even the Lord himself, who is Reason, The King of Righteousnesse; they are all filled with one spirit, and they shall all live comfortably upon
one earth; and so the whole earth is the Lords. Ier. 35: 38. Isa. 29: 20, 21. Rom.
8: 21. Ioh. 6: 45.

And this is the inward and outward liberty, which the Lord wil give to *Sion*.
And this work is begun, the foundation of this spiritual building is laid, and the
spreading of this one spirit in every sonne and daughter, and the lifting up the
earth to be a common treasury, wil make *Jerusalem a praise in the whole earth*, and
the glory of the earth indeed, and so the Father of all things shall be honoured in
the works of his own hands. Zech. 8: 3. Isa. 62: 17.

No man shal have any more land, then he can labour himself, or have others
to labour with him in love, working together, and eating bread together, as one of
the Tribes or families of Israel, neither giving hire, nor taking hire.

. . . talking of love is no love, it is acting of love in righteousnesse, which the Spirit
Reason, our Father delights in. And this is to relieve the oppressed, to let goe the
prisoner, to open bags and barns that the earth may be a common treasury to preserve all without complainings; for the earth was not made for a few to live at
ease upon, and to kil such as did not observe the Law of their own making, but
it was made for all to live comfortably upon, and the power of life and death is
reserved in the hand of the Spirit, not in the hand of flesh: None ought to kil,

but such as can make alive; therefore let every one walk righteously in the Creation, and trust the Spirit for protection. Mat. 7: 12. . . .

. . . Was the earth made for to preserve a few covetous, proud men, to live at ease, and for them to bag and barn up the treasures of the earth from others, that they might beg or starve in a fruitful Land, or was it made to preserve all her children, Let Reason, and the Prophets and Apostles writings be Judge, the earth is the Lords, it is not to be confined to particular interest.

None can say, Their right is taken from them; for let the rich work alone by themselves, and let the poor work together by themselves; the rich in their inclosures, saying, *This is mine*; The poor upon their Commons, saying *This is ours*, the earth and fruits are common.

And who can be offended at the poor for doing this? None but covetous, proud, lazy, pamper'd flesh, that would have the poor stil to work for that devil (particular interest) to maintain his greatnesse, that he may live at ease.

What doe we get by our labour in the earth, but that we may eat bread and live together in love and community of righteousnesse, *This shall be the blessing of Israel*. Isa. 62: 8.

But as *Esau* hath setled his Kingdome, they that work live in straits; *They that live idle surfet with fulnesse, and makes all places stink with unrighteous envious oppression.*

Wel, when the Lord cals forth Israel to live in tents, which I believe wil be within a short time, he wil protect them; This Trumpet is stil sounding in me, *Work together, Eat bread together, declare this all abroad*. Ier. 25: 37, 38.

Surely the Lord hath not revealed this in vain; for I shal see the fruit of righteousnesse follow after it, which wil be the beginning of the great day of veangence to the Oppessour, that hath held the earth under the bondage of civil propriety: ruling a Tyrant over others: forcing the poor to work for hire: But in the day of restoration of *Israel* is not to eat the bread of a hireling in no kind; he is neither to give hire, nor take hire.

Did the light of Reason make the earth for some men to ingrosse up into bags and barns, that others might be opprest with poverty? Did the light of Reason make this law, that if one man have not such abundance of the earth as to give to others he borrowed of; that he that did lend should imprison the other, and starve his body in a close room? Did the light of Reason make this law, that some part of man kinde should kil and hang another part of man-kinde, that could not walk in their steps?

Surely Reason was not the God that made that law; for this is to make one part of the Creation alwaies to be quarrelling against another part; which is mighty dishonour to our Maker.

But covetousnesse, that murdering God of the world, was that Lawmaker, And that is the God, or ruling power, which all men that claim a particular interest in the earth, do worship. 2 Cor. 4: 4.

For the Earth is the Lords; that is, the spreading power of righteousnes, not the Inheritance of covetous, proud flesh that dies. If any man can say that he makes Corn or Cattle, he may say, That is mine: But if the Lord make these for the use of his Creation, surely then the earth was made by the Lord, to be a common Treasury for all, not a particular Treasury for some. . . .

. . . the Clergy, the Universities are the standing ponds of stinking waters, . . . the curse of ignorance, confusion and bondage spreads from hence all the Nations over.

The paying of tythes, the greatest sin of oppression, is upheld by them; pride, covetousnesse, idlenesse, bitternesse of spirit, despising and treading all under-foot; in whom the spirit of the Lamb appears, is upheld by them; these are the standing enemies against Christ.

Their Churches are the successours of the *Jews* Synagogues, and are houses of bondage; their Universities are successours of the *Scribes* and *Pharisees* houses of learning. And though they persecuted Christ and the Apostles, and would own none of their Doctrines; yet when they found that Christs Doctrines began to fill the earth, and to make the way of the Law odious, and their trade began to fail,

Then did those houses of learning begin to take in and own the writings of the Apostles, and to own that doctrine, prevailing with the Magistracy through the deceit of their subtilety, to establish tythes in their hands still for their maintainance (though Christs doctrine threw down that oppression). And then from legall Sacrificers, they became hearsay-Preachers of the Gospel, not from any testimony of light within themselves, but from the writings of the Apostles, which they professe great love to, and keep charily, for their tythes sake; and by the one they deceive the souls of people, for they preach the letter for the Spirit, and by the other they pick their purses.

And this is very manifest by their carriage; for though those writings which they live by, were not writings that proceeded from any Schollars, according to humane art, but from Fishermen, Shepherds, Husbandmen, and the Carpenters son, who spake and writ as the Spirit gave them utterance, from an inward testimony.

Yet now these learned schollars have got the writings of these inferior men of the world so called, do now slight, despise and trample them under feet, pressing upon the powers of the earth, to make laws to hold them under bondage, and that lay-people, trades-men, and such as are not bred in schools, may have no liberty to speak or write of the Spirit.

And why so? Because out of these despised ones, doth the spirit rise up more and more to clearer light, making them to speak from experience; and every fresh discovery of the Father, shines more glorious then the old, till at last the creature is made to see the Father face to face in his own light.

But now the learned schollars having no inward testimony of their own to uphold their trade by a customary practice, they hold fast the old letter, getting their living by telling the people the meanings of those trades-mens words and writings; but alas, they mightily corrupt their meaning, by their multitude of false expositions and interpretations; for no man knows the meaning of the spirit, but he that hath the spirit.

And if the Father send forth any of these tradesmen, to declare the testimony which is in them: as in these dayes he sends forth many. And these true labourers shall encrease, let the Universitie men do the worst they can; yet the Schollars seek to suppresse them, calling them new-lights, factious, erroneous, blasphemers, and the like.

And why do they all this? Because the light of truth that springs up out of this earth, which the schollars tread under feet, will shine so clear, as it will put out the candle of those wicked learned deceivers.


## The True Levellers Standard Advanced (April 1649)

A DECLARATION TO THE POWERS OF ENGLAND, AND TO ALL THE POWERS OF THE WORLD, shewing the cause why the common people of England have begun, and gives consent to digge up, manure, and sowe corn upon George-Hill in Surrey; by those that have subscribed, and thousands more that gives consent

In the beginning of Time, the great Creator Reason, made the Earth to be a Common Treasury, to preserve Beasts, Birds, Fishes, and Man, the lord that was to govern this Creation; for Man had Domination given to him, over the Beasts, Birds, and Fishes; but not one word was spoken in the beginning, That one branch of mankind should rule over another.

And the Reason is this, Every single man, Male and Female, is a perfect Creature of himself; and the same Spirit that made the Globe, dwels in man to govern the Globe; so that the flesh of man being subject to Reason, his Maker, hath him to be his Teacher and Ruler within himself, therefore needs not run abroad after any Teacher and Ruler without him, for he needs not that any man should teach him, for the same Anoynting that ruled in the Son of man, teacheth him all things.

But since humane flesh (that king of Beasts) began to delight himself in the objects of the Creation, more then in the Spirit Reason and Righteousness, who manifests himself to be the indweller in the Five Sences, of Hearing, Seeing, Tasting, Smelling, Feeling; then he fell into blindness of mind and weakness of heart, and runs abroad for a Teacher and Ruler: And so selfish imagination taking possession of the Five Sences, and ruling as King in the room of Reason therein, and working with Covetousnesse, did set up one man to teach and rule over another; and thereby the Spirit was killed, and man was brought into bondage, and became a greater Slave to such of his own kind, then the Beasts of the field were to him.

And hereupon, The Earth (which was made to be a Common Treasury of relief for all, both Beasts and Men) was hedged in to In-closures by the teachers and rulers, and the others were made Servants and Slaves: And that Earth that is within this Creation, made a Common Store-house for all, is bought and sold, and kept in the hands of a few, whereby the great Creator is mightily dishonored, as if he were a respector of persons, delighting in the comfortable Livelihood of some, and rejoycing in the miserable povertie and straits of others. From the beginning it was not so. . . .

. . . But for the present state of the old World that is running up like parchment in the fire, and wearing away, we see proud Imaginary flesh, which is the wise Serpent, rises up in flesh and gets dominion in some to rule over others, and so forces one part of the Creation man, to be a slave to another; and thereby the Spirit is killed in both. The one looks upon himself as a teacher and ruler, and so is lifted up in pride over his fellow Creature: The other looks upon himself as imperfect, and so is dejected in his Spirit, and looks upon his fellow Creature of his own Image, as a Lord above him.

And thus *Esau*, the man of flesh, which is Covetousness and Pride, hath killed *Jacob*, the Spirit of meeknesse, and righteous government in the light of Reason, and rules over him: And so the Earth that was made a common Treasury for all to live comfortably upon, is become through mans unrighteous actions one over another, to be a place, wherein one torments another. . . .

But when once the Earth becomes a Common Treasury again, as it must, for all the Prophesies of Scriptures and Reason are Circled here in this Community, and mankind must have the Law of Righteousnesse once more writ in his heart, and all must be made of one heart, and one mind.

Then this Enmity in all Lands will cease, for none shall dare to seek a Dominion over others, neither shall any dare to kill another, nor desire more of the Earth then another; for he that will rule over, imprison, oppresse, and kill his fellow Creatures, under what pretence soever, is a destroyer of the Creation, and an actor of the Curse, and walks contrary to the rule of righteousnesse: (*Do, as you would have others do to you; and love your Enemies, not in words, but in actions*). . . .

The Work we are going about is this, To dig up *Georges-Hill* and the waste Ground thereabouts, and to Sow Corn, and to eat our bread together by the sweat of our brows.

And the First Reason is this, That we may work in righteousness, and lay the Foundation of making the Earth a Common Treasury for All, both Rich and Poor, That every one that is born in the Land, may be fed by the Earth his Mother that brought him forth, according to the Reason that rules in the Creation. Not Inclosing any part into any particular hand, but all as one man, working together, and feeding together as Sons of one Father, members of one Family; not one Lording over another, but all looking upon each other, as equals in the Creation; so that our Maker may be glorified in the work of his own hands, and that every one may see, he is no respecter of Persons, but equally loves his whole Creation, and hates nothing but the Serpent, which is Covetousness, branching forth into selvish Imagination, Pride, Envie, Hypocrisie, Uncleanness; all seeking the ease and honor of flesh, and fighting against the Spirit Reason that made the Creation; for that is the Corruption, the Curse, the Devil, the Father of Lies; Death and Bondage that Serpent and Dragon that the Creation is to be delivered from.

And we are moved hereunto for that Reason, and others which hath been shewed us, both by Vision, Voyce, and Revelation.

For it is shewed us, That so long as we, or any other, doth own the Earth to be the peculier Interest of Lords and Landlords, and not common to others as well as them, we own the Curse, and hold the Creation under bondage; and so long as we or any other doth own Landlords and Tennants, for one to call the Land his, or another to hire it of him, or for one to give hire, and for another to work for hire; this is to dishonour the work of Creation; as if the righteous Creator should have respect to persons, and therefore made the Earth for some, and not for all: And so long as we, or any other, maintain this Civil Propriety, we consent still to hold the Creation down under that bondage it groans under, and so we should hinder the work of Restoration, and sin against Light, that is given into us, and so through the fear of the flesh man, lose our peace.

And that this Civil Propriety is the Curse, is manifest thus, Those that Buy and Sell Land, and are landlords, have got it either by Oppression, or Murther, or Theft; and all landlords live in the breach of the Seventh and Eighth Commandements, *Thou shalt not steal, nor kill.* . . .

Take notice, That *England* is not a Free People, till the Poor that have no Land, have a free allowance to dig and labour the Commons, and so live as Comfortably as the Landlords that live in their Inclosures. For the People have not laid out their Monies, and shed their Bloud, that their Landlords, the *Norman* power, should still have its liberty and freedom to rule in Tyranny in his Lords, landlords, Judges, Justices, Bayliffs, and State Servants; but that the Oppressed might be set Free, Prison doors opened, and the Poor peoples hearts comforted by an universal Consent of making the Earth a Common Treasury, that they may live together as one House of Israel, united in brotherly love into one Spirit; and having a comfortable livelihood in the Community of one Earth their Mother.

If you look through the Earth, you shall see, That the landlords, Teachers and Rulers, are Oppressors, Murtherers, and Theeves in this manner; But it was not thus from the Beginning. And this is one Reason of our digging and labouring the Earth one with another, That we might work in righteousness, and lift up the Creation from bondage: For so long as we own Landlords in this Corrupt Settlement, we cannot work in righteousness; for we should still lift up the Curse, and tread down the Creation, dishonour the Spirit of universal Liberty, and hinder the work of Restauration.

Secondly, In that we begin to Digge upon *George-Hill*, to eate our Bread together by righteous labour, and sweat of our browes; It was shewed us by Vision in Dreams, and out of Dreams, That that should be the Place we should begin upon; And though that Earth in view of Flesh, be very barren, yet we should trust the Spirit for a blessing. And that not only this Common, or Heath should be taken in and Manured by the People, but all the Commons and waste Ground in *England*, and in the whole World, shall be taken in by the People in righteousness, not owning any Propriety; but taking the Earth to be a Common Treasury, as it was first made for all.

Thirdly, It is shewed us, That all the Prophecies, Visions, and Revelations of Scriptures, of Prophets, and Apostles, concerning the calling of the Jews, the Restauration of Israel; and making of that People, the Inheritors of the whole Earth; doth all seat themselves in this Work of making the Earth a Common Treasury . . .

Fourthly, This work to make the Earth a Common Treasury, was shewed us by Voice in Trance, and out of Trance, which words were these,

*Work together, Eate Bread together, Declare this all abroad.*

Which Voice, was heard Three times: And in Obedience to the Spirit, Wee have Declared this by Word of mouth, as occasion was offered. Secondly, We have declared it by writing, which others may reade. Thirdly, We have now begun to declare it by Action, in Diging up the Common Land, and casting in Seed, that we may eat our Bread together in righteousness. And every one that comes to work, shall eate the Fruit of their own labours, one having as much Freedom in the Fruit of the Earth as another. Another Voice that was heard was this,

*Israel shall neither take Hire, nor give Hire.*

And if so, then certainly none shall say, This is my Land, work for me, and I'le give you Wages: For, The Earth is the Lords, that is, Mans, who is Lord of the Creation, in every branch of mankind; for as divers members of our human bodies, make but one body perfect; so every particular man is but a member or branch of mankind; and mankind living in the light and obedience to Reason, the King of righteousness, is thereby made a fit and compleat Lord of the Creation. And the whole Earth is this Lords Man, subject to the Spirit. And not the Inheritance of covetous proud Flesh, that is selvish, and enmity to the Spirit. . . .

This Declares likewise to all Laborers, or such as are called Poor people, that they shall not dare to work for Hire, for any Landlord, or for any that is lifted up above others; for by their labours, they have lifted up Tyrants and Tyranny; and by denying to labor for Hire, they shall pull them down again. He that works for another, either for Wages, or to pay him Rent, works unrighteously, and still lifts up the Curse; but they that are resolved to work and eat together, making the Earth a Common Treasury, doth joyn hands with Christ, to lift up the Creation from Bondage, and restores all things from the Curse.

Fifthly, That which does incourage us to go on in this work, is this; We find the streaming out of Love in our hearts towards all; to enemies as well as friends; we would have none live in Beggery, Poverty, or Sorrow, but that every one might enjoy the benefit of his creation: we have peace in our hearts, and quiet rejoycing in our work, and filled with sweet content, though we have but a dish of roots and bread for our food.

## *A Watch-Word to the City of London and the Armie* (August 1649)

### *TO THE CITY OF LONDON, FREEDOME AND PEACE DESIRED*

Thou City of London, I am one of thy sons by freedome, and I do truly love thy peace; while I had an estate in thee, I was free to offer my Mite into thy publike Treasury Guild-hall, for a preservation to thee, and the whole Land; but by thy cheating sons in the theeving art of buying and selling, and by the burdens of, and for the Souldiery in the beginning of the war, I was beaten out both of estate and trade, and forced to accept of the good will of friends crediting of me, to live a Countrey-life, and there likewise by the burthen of Taxes and much Free-quarter, my weak back found the burthen heavier then I could bear; yet in all the passages of these eight yeers troubles I have been willing to lay out what my Talent was, to procure Englands peace inward and outward, and yet all along I have found such as in words have professed the same cause, to be enemies to me. Not a full yeere since, being quiet at my work, my heart was filled with sweet thoughts, and many things were revealed to me which I never read in books, nor heard from the mouth of any flesh, and when I began to speak of them, some people could not bear my words, and amongst those revelations this was one, *That the earth shall be made a common Treasury of livelihood to whole mankind, without respect of persons*; and I had a voice within me bad me declare it all abroad, which I did obey, for I declared it by word of mouth wheresoever I came, then I was made to write a little book called, *The new Law of righteousnesse*, and therein I declared it; yet my mind was not at rest, because nothing was acted, and thoughts run in me, that words and writings were all nothing, and must die, for action is the life of all, and if thou dost not act, thou dost nothing. Within a little time I was made obedient to the word in that particular likewise; for I tooke my spade and went and broke the ground upon *George-hill* in Surrey, thereby declaring freedome to the Creation, and that the earth must be set free from intanglements of Lords and Landlords, and that it shall become a common Treasury to all, as it was first made and given to the sonnes of men . . . all men have stood for freedom, thou hast kept fasting daies, and prayed in morning exercises for freedom; thou hast given thanks for victories, because hopes of freedome; plentie of Petitions and promises thereupon have been made for freedome, and now the common enemy is gone, you are all like men in a mist, seeking for freedom, and know not where, nor what it is: and those of the richer sort of you that see it, are ashamed and afraid to owne it, because it comes clothed in a clownish garment, and open to the best language that scoffing *Ishmael* can afford, or that railing *Rabsheka* can speak, or furious *Pharaoh* can act against him; for freedom is the man that will turn the world upside downe, therefore no wonder he hath enemies.

## A New-yeers Gift for the Parliament and Armie (January 1650)

. . . True Religion, and undefiled, is this, To make restitution of the Earth, which hath been taken and held from the Common people, by the power of Conquests formerly, and so *set the oppressed free*. Do not All strive to enjoy the Land? The Gentry strive for Land, the Clergie strive for Land, the Common people strive for Land; and Buying and Selling is an Art, whereby people endeavour to cheat one another of the Land. Now if any can prove, from the Law of Righteousness, that the Land was made peculiar to him and his successively, shutting others out, he shall enjoy it freely, for my part: But I affirm, It was made for all; and true Religion is, To let every one enjoy it. Therefore, you Rulers of *England*, make restitution of the Lands which the Kingly power holds from us: *Set the oppressed free*; and come in, and honour Christ, who is the Restoring Power, and you shall finde rest.

## Fire in the Bush (March 1650)

[T]here is a foure-fold power, much Idolized, and doted upon by covetous flesh, which must be shaken to pieces; And woe, woe, woe, to the Inhabitants of the Earth, to those that live in, or are the upholders of those powers.

The first is the Imaginary, teaching power, called hear-say, booke-studying, University, Divinity, which indeed, is *Iudas* Ministry, for this cries *hayle Master*, to the Spirit, and seemes to kisse him in Love, in outward shew, by preaching of him, and by long prayers to him; But betrayes him into the hand of the selfish power. . . .

Then secondly, The Imaginary Kingly power, who by the power of the sword, and successive conquests doe set up one part of Mankinde, to rule over another; pretending to keep the Creation in peace, but yet proves a selfe-upholder; By murder and theft, treading others under foot; this power takes ease, honour, fulnesse of the Earth to himselfe by the sword, and rules over the labours and bodies of others at his will and prerogative. . . .

Thirdly, the imaginary Judicature, called the Law of Justice; which indeed is but the declarative will of Conquerours, how they will have their Subjects be ruled; And this pretends to keep all in peace, and yet it is the very support of Envie, hardnesse of heart, and unrighteous covetousnesse; . . .

Fourthly, buying and selling of the Earth, with the fruits of the Earth; This is an Imaginary Art, to fetch in content from without, and breeds discontent, and divides the creation, and makes mankinde to imprison, enslave, and destroy one another. . . .

These foure powers are the foure Beasts, which *Daniel* saw rise up out of the Sea. *Dan.* 7: 3, &c. And this Sea is the bulke and body of mankinde, . . . for out of Mankinde arises all that darknesse and Tyranny that oppresses it selfe; . . .

The first Beast which *Daniell* saw rise up out of the deceived heart of mankinde, was like a Lion; and had Eagles wings: And this is Kingly power, which takes the Sword, and makes way to rule over others thereby, dividing the Creation, one part from another; setting up the Conqueror to rule, making the conquered a slave; giving the Earth to some, denying the Earth to others; . . .

The second Beast was like a Beare; And this is the power of the selfish Lawes, which is full of covetousnesse, . . . the power of Prisons, . . . the power of whiping, banishment, and confiscation of goods, whereby he kills . . . , the power of hanging, pressing, burning, martering; . . . take these three ribs out of the mouth of the Law, or Innes of Court trade, and that Beast hath no power, but dies.

The third Beast was like a Leopard, . . . this is the thieving Art of buying and selling the Earth with her fruits one to another. . . . this Beast had foure wings; Policy, Hypocrisie, Self-Love, and hardnesse of Heart; for this Beast is a true self-Lover, to get the Earth to himself, to lock it up in Chests and barnes, though others starve for want. . . .

The fourth Beast is the Imaginary Clergy-Power, which indeed is *Iudas*; and this is more terrible and dreadful then the rest; . . . All these Beasts, they differ in shape, and yet they agree all in one oppressing power, supporting one another; one cannot live without another; and yet they seeme to persecute one another; and if one truly die, all dies. . . .

The Creation will never be in quiet, peace, till these foure Beasts, with all their heads and hornes, the variety of their branching powers doe run into the Sea againe, and be swallowed up in those waters; that is, into Mankinde, who shall be abundantly inlightned; . . .

This worke Christ will bring to passe, at his more glorious appearance, . . . their returne back into the Sea, will be the rising up of Love, who is the Sonne of righteousnesse, . . .

When Christ the Anoynting spirit rises up, and inlightens mankind, then in his light, they shall see the deceit and falshood of this Beast, that hath deceived all the world; and shall fall off from him, and leave him naked and bare; and if he will teach and rule, let him shew his power over the Beasts; for the people will all looke up to God, to be taught and governed by him. . . .

If you would finde true Majestie indeed, goe among the poore despised ones of the Earth; for there Christ dwells, and there you shall see Light and Love shine in Majestie indeed, rising up to unite the Creation indeed, into the unitie of spirit, and band of peace; the blessing of the Lord is amongst the poore, and the covetous, scoffing, covenant-breaking, thieves and murderers, that croud themselves under the name Magistracie, shall be sent emptie away.

These great ones are too stately houses for Christ to dwell in; he takes up his abode in a manger, Inne, and amongst the poore in spirit, and despised ones of the Earth. . . .

For when Christ sent out his Disciples to preach, he saith, that which you have heard and seen, goe preach; and saith *Paul*, we cannot but speake the things which we have heard and seen from the Father; But the Universitie publick Ministrie runs before he be sent; they take up another mans message, and carries abroad other mens words, or studies or imagines a meaning; and this is their ministrie; This is not to preach the truth, as it was in Jesus, purely and experimentally, as they received it of the Father, but as they receive it from man, and by man.

### *The Law of Freedom in a Platform* (1652)

Wherefore are you so covetous after the World, in buying and selling? counting your self a happy man, if you be rich, and a miserable man if you be poor. And though you say, *Heaven after death is a place of glory, where you shall enjoy God face to face*, yet you are loth to leave the Earth to go thither.

Do not your Ministers preach for to enjoy the Earth? Do not professing Lawyers, as well as others, buy and sell the Conquerors Justice, that they may enjoy the Earth? Do not professing Soldiers fight for the Earth, and seat themselves in that Land, which is the Birth-Right of others, as well as theirs, shutting others out? Do not all professors strive to get Earth, that they may live in plenty by other mens labors?

Do you not make the Earth your very Rest? Doth not the enjoying of the Earth please the spirit in you? and then you say, God is pleased with your ways, and blesseth you. If you want Earth, and become poor, do you not say, God is angry with you, and crosseth you?

Why do you heap up riches? why do you eat and drink, and wear clothes? why do you take a woman, and lie with her to beget children? Are not all these carnal and low things of the Earth? and do you not live in them, and covet them as much as any? nay more then many which you call men of the world?

And it being thus with you, what other spiritual or heavenly things do you seek after more then others? And what is in you more then in others? If you say, there is; then surely you ought to let these earthly things alone to the men of the world, as you call them, whose portions these are, and keep you within the compass of your own sphere, that others seeing you live a life above the world in peace and freedom, neither working your self, nor deceiving, nor compelling others to work for you, they may be drawn to embrace the same spiritual life by your single-hearted conversation. Well, I have done here.

*Let us now examine your Divinity,*

Which you call heavenly, and spiritual things, for herein speeches are made not to advance knowledge, but to destroy the true knowledge of God; for Divinity does not speak the truth, as it is hid in every body, but it leaves the motional knowledge of a thing as it is, And imagins, studies, or thinks what may be, and so runs the hazzard true or false: And this Divinity is always speaking words to deceive the simple, that he may make them work for him, and maintain him, but he never comes to action himself to do as he would be done by; for he is a monster who is all tongue and no hand.

This divining Doctrine, which you call spiritual and heavenly things, is the thief and the robber; he comes to spoile the Vinyard of a mans peace, and does not enter in at the door, but he climbes up another way: . . .

★ ★ ★

## A *Declaration* of the Grounds and Reasons, Why We the Poor Inhabitants of the

*Parrish of* Iver *in* Buckinghamshire*, have begun to digge and mannure the common and wast Land belonging to the aforesaid Inhabitants, and there are many more that gives consent*

The word of God hath witnessed unto us, that the Lord created the earth with all that is therein for whole Mankind, equall to one as to another, and for every one to live free upon to get an ample Livelihood therein, and therefore those who have by an unrighteous power made merchandize of the earth, giving all to some, and none to others, declares themselves tyranicall and usurping Lords over Gods heritage, and we affirm that they have no righteous power to sell or give away the earth, unless they could make the earth likewise, which none can do but God the eternall Spirit.

2. We are very sensible that although Mankind was by the will of his Maker, constituted in all his branches, a supream Lord over all Creatures of other kinds, yet we see that no creature is so much deprived of a Being and subsistance as mankind is; and though those who are become Lords and Masters over their fellow

Creatures, do challenge a larger circuit of earth to be given of God, more particularly to them then to others; we say that this is false, unlesse they mean their God
covetousnesse, the God of this world, who hath blinded their eyes, and hardned
their hearts, and this God is an unequall and impartial divider, and therefore he
must be destroyed.

   We know that *Cain* is still alive in all the great Landlords, and such like Earth-
mongers who are continually crucifying their poor Brethren by oppression, cheating and robbery: therefore you Lords of Mannors especially, the Lord hath set *Cains*
mark upon you, because he will surely find you out, if you do not repent and give
over, lye down therefore and submit (and why not) that your Iniquities may be
no more in remembrance, and that the cry of your cruelty may be heard no more
in the Land.

   3.   Then thirdly, there is a promise in Scripture (which God hath made) to
free us from that bondage wherein you have involved us, and that pride and oppression shall be heard of no more in the Land, and that the Lord will restore the
whole Creation into the glorious liberty of the Sonnes of God, which is no other
liberty then that which Christ himself by his spirit hath invested us withall, and
that is equality, community and fellowship with our own kind; for the first shall
be last, and the last shall be first, as he that sitteth, and he that serveth.

   4.   We are urged to go forth and Act in this righteous work, because of our
present necessity, and want of the comfort which belongs to our Creation, that the
earth being inclosed into the hands of a few, whereby time, custome and usurping Lawes have made particular Interests for some, and not for all: so that these
great Taskmasters will allow us none of the earth whilst we are alive, but onely
when we are dead, they will afford us just as much as will make the length of our
graves, because they cannot then keep it from us, and that then we should be equall
with them; but why may we not whilst we are alive with them, have as much of
the earth as themselves? yes truly, remove but covetousnesse, and kill that cursed
power, and then those men would not keep all to themselves, but would willingly
suffer their fellow Creatures to enjoy the Birthright of their creation; for whiles
the great ones like Ratts and Mice drawe all the treasures and fruits of the earth
into their nests and holes after them, resolving rather to spoile these good things,
then to suffer the common sort to have part with: and therefore they have now
got a custome to dyet the Markets, and make a dearth in time of plenty, and though
the Lord be pleased to give us joyfull and fruitfull seasons, yet we see that this
helpeth us nothing: we must be starved neverthelesse, and why? because the rich
will have it so, no other reason can be rendred: Therefore you of the poorer sort,
understand this, that nothing but the manuring of the common Land, will reduce
you into a comfortable condition; and likewise we declare, that though we keep
our selves close to our hard labours, breaking our due and necessary rest which
should refresh us, whereby our lives are become a burthen to us, and yet our care-
full and diligent labour, will afford us no other then a distracted, languishing and
miserable life, for how can it be otherwise? seeing we cannot enjoy the benefit of
our labors our selves but for the maintenance of idle persons, slow bellies who
raigne and ride over the common people in every Parrish, as Gods and Kings: And

therefore if this be that freedom which we have for these nine years striven for: then we pray you to exchange this freedom for our old bondage, and to set us down in that kennel where you did first lift us out.

5. And further we declare before God and the whole World, that the inhumane cruelty of our Taskmasters is, and hath ever been the just cause of all our miseries, and of the whole Nation into this sad condition, and that we see no hope, comfort, or redresse to be had from any that are in Authority in our Parrish, who say they will do nothing but what they are forc'd to do: therefore from their own words we may gather, that their full intent is to make us absolute slaves and vassalls to their wills.

6. We have great encouragement from this present *Parliament*, by making of those two excellent Lawes, the one to cast out *Kingly Power*, and the other to make us all a free people, which we understand, is to break the neck of the *Norman Power* which was brought in upon us by the *Norman Bastard*, continued and encreased ever since within this Nation, by every King who was his Successor.

7. This act of ours endeavouring to make the wast Land fruitfull, is an Act full of Honour, Righteousnesse, Justice and Peace, and consequently agreeing with the Law of God and the Law of reason; for the Scripture saith, *The meek shall inherite the earth* [Mt. 5:5] this work therefore of ours is not to be carried on by force of Armes, it is a thing which we much abhorre, but in love onely and meeknesse, and this power onely shall at last conquer, and bring in the *Kings* and *Princes* of the earth: therefore all you that are prepared to act freedom and love, come forth and break your Swords into Plough shares, and leavie Warre no more [Is. 2:4, Micah 4:3].

8. There is a principle of Reason that teacheth every man to do as he would be done by, that is to live in love, and be at peace with all men, and to do as we would be done by, is to allow the same liberty to others, that we our selves are willing to enjoy, which is food and rayment, freely without being a slave to any of our fellow Creatures: We desire all those that are free to act with us in this work, that they would come forth and set their hands to remove this bondage which we have lain under this 600. yeares: And further we desire, that those who cannot come forth as yet in person, that they would lend us their assistance and encouragement to supply our necessities whilst our labours lies buried in the earth untill the fruit comes up; our condition being but poor at the beginning, that so this righteous work may not fall off and perish, to give the Adversarie cause to perceive that we are again brought back into bondage.

10. [sic] And lastly, we do not intend to proceed upon this work in any other power, but that which is before exprest, which is the Lords own way, even peace and love, stedfastly resolving not to meddle with any mans propriety, but what is known to be common Land, and these are the essentiall grounds and reasons of us the poor Inhabitants of *Iver* in *Buckinghamshire* . . .

# Chapter 22

# Abiezer Coppe (1619–1672)

A Fiery Flying Roll **(1649)**

Coppe studied at Oxford, but when civil war broke out he became chaplain to a garrison of the New Model Army. Though once a Baptist, he is most famously associated with the Ranter movement which emerged around 1649, the year he published his main works, *Some Sweet Sips of Some Spirituall Wine* and *A Fiery Flying Roll*. The Ranters' worldview was informed by a blend of antinomianism, mysticism, and pantheism which manifested itself in displays of drinking, swearing, lewdness and mockeries of religious worship, including the eucharist. Since God was to be found in all creation, no object or person could be sinful, and heaven and hell existed only in people's consciences. Ranters' potential to shock was considerable, and Bunyan, Cromwell, Fox, and Winstanley are only the better known of their many contemporaries who denounced them for their beliefs and practices.

   *A Fiery Flying Roll* appeared originally in two volumes, and is written in a prose style unlike anything else which has survived from the seventeenth century. Like many radicals, Coppe acknowledged no source for his ideas, claiming that his message came from "my most excellent majesty and eternal glory (in me) ..." In his reading of Scripture, Coppe finds both an ethic of non-violence and justification for his bitter condemnations of the rich, and although his fury at the hypocrisy of the well-fed godly shines forth from every page, he explicitly disavowed 'digging levelling.' In 1650 the *Roll* was condemned by Parliament for containing 'many horrid blasphemies,' and both volumes were ordered to be publicly burnt. Coppe himself was committed to Newgate Prison and released shortly afterwards following a partial recantation. He continued to preach during the 1650s, but after the Restoration he changed his name and practised as a physician in Surrey.

Source

Norman Cohn, *The Pursuit of the Millennium*, London, 1957, pp. 321–5, 330.

## Further reading

Andrew Hopton, ed., *Abiezer Coppe: Selected Writings*, London, 1987.
A. L. Morton, *The World of the Ranters*, London, 1970.
Christopher Hill, *The World Turned Upside Down*, London, 1972.
J. F. McGregor and B Reay, eds., *Radical Religion in the English Revolution*, Oxford, 1986.
Nigel Smith, *A Collection of Ranter Writings from the 17th Century*, London, 1983.

## *A Fiery Flying Roll* (1649)

Thus saith the Lord, *I inform you, that I overturn, overturn, overturn.* And as the Bishops, *Charles,* and the Lords, have had their turn, overturn, so your turn shall be next (ye surviving great ones) by what Name or Title soever dignified or distinguished, who ever you are, that oppose me, the Eternall God, who am UNIVERSALL Love, and whose service is perfect freedome, and pure Libertinisme . . .

And now thus saith the Lord:

Though you can as little endure the word LEVELLING, as could the late slaine or dead *Charles* (your forerunner, who is gone before you – ) and had as live heare the Devill named, as heare of the Levellers (Men-Levellers) which is, and who (indeed) are but shadowes of most terrible, yet great and glorious good things to come.

Behold, behold, behold, I the eternall God, the Lord of Hosts, who am that mighty Leveller, am comming (yea even at the doores) to Levell in good earnest, to Levell to some purpose, to Levell with a witnesse, to Levell the Hills with the Valleyes, and to lay the Mountaines low.

High Mountaines! lofty Cedars! its high time for you to enter into the Rocks, and to hide you in the dust, for feare of the Lord, and for the glory of his Majesty. For the lofty looks of man shall be humbled, and the haughtinesse of men shall be bowed downe, and the Lord ALONE shall be exalted in that day . . .

Hills! Mountains! Cedars! Mighty men! Your breath is in your nostrils.

Those that have admired, adored, idolized, magnified, set you up, fought for you, ventured goods, and good name; limbe and life for you, shall cease from you.

You shall not (at all) be accounted of (not one of you) ye sturdy Oake[s] who bowe not downe before eternall Majesty: Universall Love, whose service is perfect freedome, and who hath put down the mighty (remember, remember, your forerunner) and who is putting down the mighty from their seats; and exalting them of low degree . . .

And the Prime levelling, is laying low the Mountaines, and levelling the Hils in man.

But this is not all.

*For lo I come (saith the Lord) with a vengeance, to levell also your Honour, Riches, &c to staine the pride of all your glory, and to bring into contempt all the Honourable (both persons and things) upon the earth,* Isa. 23.9.

For this Honour, Nobility, Gentility, Propriety, Superfluity, &c. hath (without contradiction) been the Father of hellish horrid pride, arrogance, haughtinesse, loftinesse, murder, malice, of all manner of wickednesse and impiety; yea the cause of all the blood that ever hath been shed, from the blood of the righteous *Abell*, to the blood of the last Levellers that were shot to death. *And now (as I live saith the Lord) I am come to make inquisition for blood; for murder and pride, &c.*

I see the root of it all. *The Axe is laid to the root of the Tree* (by the Eternall God, *My Self*, saith the Lord) *I will hew it down.* And as I live, I well plague your Honour, Pompe, Greatness, Superfluity, and confound it into parity, equality, community; that the neck of horrid pride, murder, malice, and tyranny, &c. may be chopt off at one blow. And that my selfe, the Eternall God, who am Universall Love, may fill the Earth with universall love, universall peace, and perfect freedome; which can never be by humane sword or strength accomplished . . .

### Chapter II

Thus saith the Lord: Be wise now therefore, O ye Rulers, &c. Be instructed, &c. Kisse the Sunne, &c. Yea, kisse Beggers, Prisoners, warme them, feed them, cloathe them, money them, relieve them, release them, take them into your houses, don't serve them as gods, without doore, &c.

Owne them, they are flesh of your flesh, youre owne brethren, your owne Sisters, every whit as good (and if I should stand in competition with you) in some degrees better then your selves.

Once more, I say, own them; they are your self, make them one with you, or else go howling into hell; howle for the miseries that are comming upon you, howle.

The very shadow of levelling, sword-levelling, man-levelling, frighted you, (and who, like your selves, can blame you, because it shook your Kingdome?) but now the substantiality of levelling is coming.

The Eternall God, the mighty Leveller is comming, yea come, even at the door; and what will you do in that day . . .

(Thus saith the Lord,)

I say (once more) deliver, deliver, my money which thou hast . . . to poor creeples, lazars, yea to rogues, thieves, whores, and cut-purses, who are flesh of thy flesh, and every whit as good as thy self in mine eye, who are ready to starve in plaguy Gaols, and nasty dungeons, or els by my selfe, saith the Lord, I will torment thee day and night, inwardly, or outwardly, or both waies, my little finger shall shortly be heavier on thee, especially on thee thou holy, righteous, religious *Appropriator*, then my loynes were on *Pharaoh* and the Egyptians in time of old; you shall weep and howl for the miseries that are suddenly coming upon you; for your riches are corrupted, &c. and whilst impropriated, appropriated the plague of God is in them.

The plague of God is in your purses, barns, houses, horses, murrain will take your hogs, (O ye fat swine of the earth) who shall shortly go to the knife, and be hung up i'th roof, except – blasting, mill-dew, locusts, caterpillars, yea fire your houses and goods, take your corn and fruit, the moth your garments, and the rot your sheep, did you not see my hand, this last year, stretched out?

You did not see.

My hand is stretched out still.

Your gold and silver, though you can't see it, is cankered, the rust of them is a witnesse against you, and suddainly, because by the eternall God, my self, its the dreadful day of Judgement, saith the Lord, shall eat your flesh as it were fire, *Jam.* 5.1 to 7.

The rust of your silver, I say, shall eat your flesh as it were fire . . .

. . . give, give, give, give up, give up your houses, horses, goods, gold, Lands, give up, account nothing your own, have ALL THINGS common, or els the plague of God will rot and consume all that you have.

By God, by my self, saith the Lord, its true.

*Come! give all to the poore and follow me, and you shall have treasure in heaven.*

## Chapter III

*A strange, yet most true story; under which is couched that Lion, whose roaring shall make all the beasts of the field tremble, and all the Kingdoms of the earth quake . . .*

Follow me, who, last Lords day Septem. 30. 1649. met him in open field, a most strange deformed man, clad with patcht clouts: who looking wishly on me, mine eye pittied him; and my heart, or the day of the Lord, which burned as an oven in me, set my tongue on flame to speak to him, as followeth.

How now friend, art thou poore?

He answered, yea Master very poore.

Whereupon my bowels trembled within me, and quivering fell upon the worm-eaten chest, (my corps I mean) that I could not hold a joynt still.

And my great love within me, (who is the great God within that chest, or corps) was burning hot toward him; and made the lock-hole of the chest, to wit, the mouth of the corps, again to open: Thus.

Art poor?

Yea, very poor, said he.

Whereupon the strange woman who flattereth with her lips, and is subtill of heart, said within me,

It's a poor wretch, give him two-pence.

But my EXCELLENCY and MAJESTY (in me) scorn'd her words, confounded her language; and kickt her out of his presence.

But immediately the WEL-FAVOURED HARLOT (whom I carried not upon my horse behind me) but who rose up in me, said:

'Its a poor wretch give him 6d. and that's enough for a Squire or Knight, to give to one poor body.

'Besides (saith the holy Scripturian Whore) hee's worse then an Infidell that provides not for his own Family.

'True love begins at home, &c.

'Thou, and thy Family are fed, as the young ravens strangely, though thou hast been a constant Preacher, yet thou hast abhorred both tythes and hire; and thou knowest not aforehand who will give thee the worth of a penny.

'Have a care of the main chance.'

And thus she flattereth with her lips, and her words being smoother then oile; and her lips dropping as the honey comb, I was fired to hasten my hand into my pocket; and pulling out a shilling, said to the poor wretch, give me six pence, heer's a shilling for thee.

He answered, I cannot, I have never a penny.

Whereupon I said, I would fain have given thee something if thou couldst have changed my money.

Then saith he, God blesse you.

Whereupon with much reluctancy, with much love, and with amazement (of the right stamp) I turned my horse head from him, riding away. But a while after I was turned back (being advised by my Demilance) to wish him cal for six pence, which I would leave at the next Town at ones house, which I thought he might know (*Saphira* like) keeping back part.

But (as God judged me) I, as she, was struck down dead.

And behold the plague of God fell into my pocket, and the rust of my silver rose up in judgement against me, and consumed my flesh as with fire: so that I, and my money perisht with me.

I being cast into that lake of fire and brimstone.

And all the money I had about me to a penny (though I thought through the instigation of my *quondam Mistris* to have reserved some, having rode about 8 miles, not eating one mouthfull of bread that day, and had drunk but one small draught of drink; and had between 8 or 9 miles more to ride, ere I came to my journeys end: my horse being lame, the waies dirty, it raining all the way, and I not knowing what extraordinary occasion I might have for money.) Yet (I say) the rust of my silver did so rise up in judgement against me, and burnt my flesh like fire: and the 5. of *James* thundered such an alarm in mine ears, that I was fain to cast all I had into the hands of him, whose visage was more marr'd then any mans that I ever saw.

This is a true story, most true in the history.

Its true also in the mystery.

And there are deep ones couch't under it, for its a shadow of various, glorious (though strange) good things to come.

Well! to return – after I had thrown my rusty canker'd money into the poor wretches hands, I rode away from him, being filled with trembling, joy, and amazement, feeling the sparkles of a great glory arising up from under these ashes.

After this, I was made (by that divine power which dwelleth in this Ark, or chest) to turn my horse head – whereupon I beheld this poor deformed wretch, looking earnestly after me: and upon that, was made to put off my hat, and bow to him seven times, and was (at that strange posture) filled with trembling and amazement, some sparkles of glory arising up also from under this; as also from under these ashes, yet I rode back once more to the poor wretch, saying, because I am a King, I have done this, but you need not tell any one.

*Chapter VI*

Again, thus saith the Lord, I in thee, who am eternall Majesty, bowed down thy form, to deformity.

And I in thee, who am durable riches, commanded thy perishable silver to the poore, &c.

Thus saith the Lord,

Kings, Princes, Lords, great ones, must bow to the poorest Peasants; rich men must stoop to poor rogues, or else they'l rue for it . . .

Well! we must all bow, and bow, &c. And MEUM must be converted. . . . It is but yet a very little while; and you shall not say that ought that you possesse is your own, &c. . . .

It's but yet a little while, and the strongest, yea, the seemingly purest propriety, which may mostly plead priviledge and Preorogative from Scripture, and carnall reason; shall be confounded and plagued into community and universality. And ther's a most glorious design in it: and equality, community, and universall love; shall be in request to the utter confounding of abominable pride, murther, hypocrisie, tyranny and oppression, &c. . . .

*Chapter VII*

. . . Howl, howl, ye nobles, howl honourable, howl ye rich men for the miseries that are coming upon you.

For our parts, we that hear the APOSTLE preach, will also have all things common; neither will we call any thing that we have our own.

Do you (if you please) till the plague of God rot and consume what you have.

We will not, wee'l eat our bread together in singlenesse of heart, wee'l break bread from house to house.

# Chapter 23

# Anna Trapnel (ca. 1654)

## The Cry of a Stone **(1654)**

Anna Trapnel was one of a large number of women visionaries and prophets in England in the seventeenth century, particularly among the Quakers, reflecting the important role that women played in that movement (see the survey in E. Hobby, *Virtue of Necessity: English Women's Writing 1649-88*, Ann Arbor: University of Michigan, 1988 and P. Crawford, *Women and Religion in England 1500–1720*, London: Routledge, 1993). Anna Trapnel was a Fifth Monarchist; that is, she looked forward to the Reign of God, the fifth empire, which would replace the kingdoms of this world, prophesied by Daniel 2 and 7. Anna's visionary trance in 1654 during which she prophesied, details of which are recorded in *The Cry of a Stone*, is evidence of the disillusionment which was felt among a segment of the population that the hoped for new age ushered in by the overthrow of monarchy, far from taking place, had seemingly been thwarted. Indeed, Anna sees the present state as the last empire of Daniel's prophecy. She was imprisoned for her political prophecy. Her prophecies were written down, some of them as she was in the middle of the visionary experience (a feature which has its parallels in the ancient apocalyptic texts like the Ascension of Isaiah, see H. F. D. Sparks, *The Apocryphal Old Testament*). In *Voice for the King of Saints* there is an explicit link between her visions and that of John of Patmos and a clear statement of the inclusion of women around the throne of God (see Hobby, 1988, p. 33). She sees her sufferings as a sign of the imminence of God's kingdom (a theme already well established in the apostle Paul's interpretations of his sufferings, Colossians 1:24).

In *The Cry of a Stone* there is a clear plea to Cromwell to recognize the dominion of Christ and accept a theocracy, and there is the harking back to the democratic aims of the army to enable the common people to have their proper stake in the divine commonwealth. There is in her prophecy, as in the more extensive prophetic political theology of Anna's contemporary, Gerrard Winstanley, a clear sense that an opportunity, a *kairos*, has been missed for the spirit of God to effect a change in human polity. All the marks of the old order (private property, a stratified social order and a familiar, albeit non-episcopal, church structure) had been implemented. The ferment of hope quickly led to disillusionment and the need for a different understanding of how the reign of perfection could be implemented under monarchy and established religion. The history of early Quakerism is an example of the rapid shifts in response to the changing political circumstances (see C. Hill, *The World Turned Upside Down*, London: Penguin 1972 and J. F. McGregor and B. Reay, *Radical Religion in the English Revolution*, Oxford: Oxford University Press, 1984). To those who looked to the reign of King Jesus this was apostasy. Anna Trapnel's prophecy not only offers an example of the kind of prophetic challenge which was made by many at the time but also indicates the important role that women played in the social movements of the day.

## Source

*http://chaucer.library.emory.edu/wwrp/index.html/*

## Further reading

E. Hobby, *Virtue of Necessity: English Women's Writing 1649–88*, Ann Arbor: University of Michigan 1988.
P. Crawford, *Women and Religion in England 1500–1720*, London: Routledge 1993.

## *The Cry of a Stone* (1654)

And the manner how she lay eleven days, and twelve nights in a Trance, without taking any sustenance, except a cup of small Beer once in 24 hours: during which time, she uttered many things herein mentioned, relating to the Governors, Churches, Ministry, Universities, and all the three Nations; full of Wonder and Admiration, for all that shall read and peruse the same.

> . . . she had many visions, and Revelations touching the Government of the Nation, the Parliamentary Army, and Ministry, and having fasted nine days, nothing coming within her lips, she had a most strange Vision of horns; she saw fair Horns, which were 4 Powers: the first was that of the Bishops, which first Horn she saw broken in two, and thrown aside: then appeared the second Horn, and joined to it an head, and although it seemed to bee more white then the first, yet it endeavouring to get

aloft it was suddenly pulled down and broken to pieces. The third Horn had many splinters joined to it like to the scales of a fish, and this was presented to a Parliament consisting of many men, having very fair and plausible pretences of love: yet this Horn she saw broken to pieces, and so scattered that not so much as one bit remained. Then she saw the 4. Horn, and that was very short, but very sharp, and full of variety of colours sparkling red and white, and it was said to her, that this last horn was different from the other three, because of great proud and swelling words, and great promises of kindness should go forth to it from all people, like unto that of Absolom, speaking good words to the people in the gate to draw their affections away from honest David. After this she had a Vision, wherein she saw many Oaks, with spreading branches full of leaves; and presently she saw a very goodly tree for stature and completeness every way, before which great Tree the rest of the Oaks crumbled to dust; which she perceiving, desired Scripture to make known to her the Vision: whereupon Reply was made in the first of Isaiah, – They shall be confounded in the Oaks which they have chosen.

Another Vision she had two nights before the Lord Protector was proclaimed; at which time she saw a glorious Throne with winged Angels flying before the throne, and crying, Holy, holy, holy, unto the Lord; the great one is coming down with terror to the enemies, and glory and deliverance to the sincere, and them that are upright in the earth. In another Vision she saw a great company of little children walking on the earth, and a light shining round about them, and a very glorious person in the midst of them, with a Crown on his head, speaking these words: These will I honour with my Reigning presence in the midst of them, and the Oppressor shall dye in the wilderness. . . .

. . . she brake forth, and sang praise, and the Lord said to her, Mark that Scripture, three horns shall arise, and a fourth shall come out different from the former, which shall be more terrible to the Saints then others that went before: though like a Lamb, as is spoken in the Revelations, in appearance a Lamb; but pushing with his horns, like a Beast: being not only one, but many, and much strength joined together . . .

. . . how can any go and cry out to King Jesus, if he have him not in his own bosom. But oh, he is a sealed One, then how beautiful will his Walks be; and if the Spirit of Christ reign in his soul, then he may reign for Christ. Otherwise not. Therefore, you doubting Christians, have a care that you have courage given  into your harts, before you go out to plead against Antichrist, the Devil and Wickedness, and come you Army-men, and acquaint your selves with the Lord Jehovah, for if you have not acquaintance with him, then all you have is nothing. Oh do justice, and do it for Justice-sake, and not for by ends or respects.

# Chapter 24

# Priscilla Cotton and Mary Cole

## To the Priests and People of England (1655)

Priscilla Cotton and Mary Cole were Quakers imprisoned for prophecy in Exeter goal from 1655 to 1666. Although women played an important and influential role in the early Quaker movement, in society at large, and notably in the church, they were considered and treated as inferior to men. Though some of the dissenting sects recognized the spiritual equality of men and women, and permitted both to preach, the Church employed St. Paul's injunction "Let your women keep silence in the churches," [1 Cor. 14:34] to ensure they had neither influence nor authority within its bounds.

The significance of Cotton and Cole's text, here reproduced in full, lies both in its engagement with the question of women speaking and its attempt to rewrite the terms of that debate; for not only do they argue, on the basis of other passages in St. Paul, a women's right to speak in church, they treat metaphorically, again by reference to Scripture, the terms "male" and "female" to show that their priestly oppressors are the ones in fact who should keep silence. In common with many of their radical contemporaries, Cotton and Cole also defend the right of the unlearned to interpret the Scriptures. A fuller treatment of the question of women speaking appeared in a tract by another leading Quaker, Margaret Fell, ten years later (*Women's Speaking Jusified*, 1667).

Cotton was married to a Plymouth merchant and had a daughter, and Cole husband's was a Plymouth shopkeeper. Little is known of the fate of either women after their incarceration, although Cotton produced a further tract in 1656 entitled *As I Was In the Prison-house*, and died in 1664.

Source

Hilary Hinds, *God's Englishwomen: Seventeenth-century radical sectarian writing and feminist criticism*, Manchester, 1996, pp. 222–6.

## Further reading

Phyllis Mack, *Visionary Woman: Ecstatic Prophecy in Seventeenth-century England*, Berkeley, 1992.
Elaine Hobby, *Virtue of Necessity: English Women's Writing 1649–88*, London, 1988.
Paul Salzman, ed., *Early Modern Women's Writing: An Anthology 1560–1700*, Oxford, 2000.
Suzanne Trill, Kate Chedgzoy and Melanie Osborne, eds., *Lay By Your Needles Ladies, Take the Pen: Writing Women in England, 1500–1700*, London and New York, 1997.
Charlotte F. Otten, ed., *English Women's Voices, 1540–1700*, Miami, 1992.
Stevie Davies, *Unbridled Spirits: Women of the English Revolution: 1640–1660*, London, 1998.

## To the Priests and People of England, We Discharge Our Consciences, and Give Them Warning

Friends,

We have no envy nor malice to any creature, priest or people, but are to mind you of your conditions, without any partiality or hypocrisy, and wish your eternal good: and what we contend against is your greatest enemy, and will be your everlasting woe and torment, if it be not destroyed in you. For know, there is the seed of the woman, and the seed of the serpent in the world [Genesis 3:15; Revelation 12:17], there is the generation of Cain and righteous Abel. Now it lieth upon you all to know what generation you are of: for little did the false prophets and that generation that put to death the true prophets of the Lord think they were of Cain's race; nor did the scribes and Pharisees, that with their priests put Christ to death, think they were of Cain's generation, for they garnished the sepulchres of the righteous, and said if they had been in the days of their fathers, they would not have slain them [Matthew 23:29–30]; yet Christ Jesus told them that all the blood spilt since righteous Abel, should be required of that generation [Matthew 23:35; Luke 11:51]; and that they were the children of them that murthered the prophets [Matthew 23:31]. Is it not strange, that the learned priests and scribes, and Pilate that had the Hebrew and Greek besides Latin, should not find out by all their high learning the original of the Scriptures of the prophets, concerning Christ Jesus, that he was the true Messiah: but that they that read the Gospel every Sabbath day, that spake of Christ, should murder and put him to death? Now Christ Jesus himself gives the reason, and thanks his Father, that he had hid it from the wise, and prudent, and revealed it to babes [Matthew 11:25], because it was the Father's good pleasure, and the Scriptures declare them to be ignorant, that had the Hebrew, Greek and Latin, for had they known it, they would not have crucified the Lord of life and glory [1 Corinthians 2:7–8].

Now people, this was the same generation of Cain in them after Christ's death, that persecuted the apostles and put them to death; and it was the same spirit in them that put the martyrs to death, and of that generation were the bishops that persecuted, and so it continueth still to this day in the world; for Cain's generation is now still envying, hating, and persecuting the righteous Abel. Now the persecuting Cainish generation would never acknowledge they were such, but in all ages persecuted the just under some false colour, as they of old said the true prophets were troublers of Israel [1 Chronicles 2:7]; and Amaziah the priest of Bethel said of Amos, that the land was not able to bear his words [Amos 7:10]; and Haman said that the laws of the people of God were contrary to the laws and customs of all nations [Esther 3:8]; and of Christ they said he was a deceiver [Matthew 27:63] and had a devil [John 7:20; 8:48, 52; 10:20]; and of Stephen, that he spake against the holy place and the law [Acts 6:13]; and, that Paul was a pestilent fellow, and a mover of sedition [Acts 24:5]. So that all along it was on a false account the just were persecuted: so in the days of the bishops, the martyrs were burnt and butchered under the name of heretics; so now the seed of the serpent is subtle, and will not persecute the truth, as it is the truth, but under some false pretence or other, else all would see their deceit. But the truth is, it's from the first rise, because their own works are evil, and their brothers' good: they hated Christ Jesus, because he testified that their works were evil. So now Cain's generation hates the just and pure seed of God, because it declares that their works are evil.

Objection: 'But do not the priests declare against evil works?'

Answer: Yes, they do so: the scribes and Pharisees spake good words, they spake of the Messiah, yet they killed the substance of what they spake: so the priests speak true words, good words, and yet kill, and persecute, pursue, and imprison the substance and life of what they speak, for he that departs from evil makes himself a prey to priest and people; and sometimes when the light in their consciences tells them, when they are persecuting the just seed, that they are innocent, yet they wilfully run on against the very light of their own consciences, as did Stephen's persecutors [Acts 7:57].

And is it not so? I speak to that in your consciences, that though the priests speak true words, yet priests and people that live in Cain's race do pursue and persecute even to the very death, the life and power of what they do preach. And know you of a truth, that all the blood since Abel shall be required of this generation [Luke 12:51]; for, as it groweth to the end, it heighteneth and ripeneth its malice and wickedness, and so shall its judgement be, for double plagues shall be poured out upon her.

Now to you all I speak, sin not against the light in your own consciences, be not wilfully blind, but hearken to the light of Jesus Christ in your consciences, that you may come to see what generation you are of, whether of Cain or Abel: and if you did abide in the light, you should come to witness the life and power of what you profess, and so come to that life that gave forth the Scriptures, and not wrest them to your own opinions and lusts [Psalms 56:5; 2 Peter 3:16], one saying 'Lo!' here in Presbytery; another 'Lo!' there in Independency; and another in Prelacy; and another in Baptism. But the Scriptures are not divided, they agree, and hold out one thing; but you divide them, because you live not in that life that gave them forth, yet you boast of your learning, that you have the Hebrew and Greek, and know the original: but you see Pilate and the Jews had the Hebrew, Greek and Latin, yet knew not the original, for had they known it, they would not have crucified the Lord of life and glory [1 Corinthians 2:8].

Therefore know you, that you may be, and are ignorant, though you think your-selves wise. Silly men and women may see more into the mystery of Christ Jesus, than you: for the apostles, that the scribes called illiterate, and Mary and Susanna (silly women [2 Timothy 3:6], as you would be ready to call them, if they were here now) these know more of the Messiah, than all the learned priests and rabbis; for it is the spirit that searcheth all things, yea, the deep things of God, you may know, and yet murther the just, and think you do God good service.

This I warn you in love, for I cannot but think that there are some among you that ponder on this day, and if you would hearken to the light of Jesus Christ in your consciences, it would lead you from your own wisdom, learning, and self-conceitedness, into the simplicity of Jesus Christ, which is a mystery of faith hid in a pure conscience [1 Timothy 3:9]: for your own wisdom must be denied, if ever you will come to witness the life and power of true wisdom, which the fear of the Lord is the beginning of; for so did they of old.

Paul and Apollos were very learned and eloquent, saith the Scriptures, yet Paul counted all his learning dung for the excellency of the knowledge of Christ [Philippians 3:8], let his second chapter of his first Epistle to the Corinthians be a full witness of this: and Apollos was willing to be instructed of his hearers Aquila and Priscilla that were tent-makers [Acts 18:26], and the learned that studied curious arts burnt their books that were of great price, when they came to the knowledge of Jesus Christ [Acts 19:19]. So you now, would you hearken to Jesus Christ, and obey his light in your consciences, you would come down to humil-ity and the fear of the Lord, to the true wisdom and understanding, that you would not need so many authors, and books, you would not need to rent your heads with studying, but you would come to see your teacher in you, which now is removed into a corner, you would come to live a preaching life, and witness that faith you talk of, to purify your hearts [James 4:8] from envy, pride and malice, and to get the victory over the world's glory and honour that is so highly esteemed by you; and coming to see yourselves in the light of Jesus Christ, you will not lord it over God's heritage [1 Peter 5:3], nor lift yourselves up above your brethren in pride [1 Timothy 3:6] and arrogancy, but be a servant to all in love.

Therefore, come now to the light, sin no longer against that in your conscience; for Antichrist must be destroyed by the brightness of his coming [2 Thessalonians 2:8], and God is gathering his people out from idol-shepherds [Zechariah 11:17] into his own fold, to make them one flock and to give them one shepherd [John 10:16], that they may serve him with one consent [Zephaniah 3:9], for he hath fulfilled this Scripture in thousands this day whom he hath gathered out of Antichrist's opinions to worship one God in one way, in spirit and truth, speak-ing all the same things: if you speak with ten thousand of them, they all agree, having one king, one law giver.

Now fret not at this, you that live at Babylon in confusion, in divisions: for the little stone cut out of the mountain without hands, shall break Babylon's idols.

Now consider, Friends and people, your conditions, for what good doth all your preaching and hearing do you? Break your sleep, rent your brains, and as it were, speak out your lungs, and alas who is bettered by it! Was there ever more pride, lightness, vanity, and wantonness, manifested in your assemblies, than now? You make it the place where you set forth your pride, and vanity to the utmost: was there ever the like injustice, violence, falsehood and deceit in any age, that scarce can a man tell what men mean by what they say any longer?

Men say in effect that God hath forsaken the earth by their wicked practices: the people cry out upon the priests, and say that their opinions have made them so wicked; and the priests cry out upon the people, and say that the fault is theirs: so that the Lord beheld, and instead of righteousness, equity and judgement [Proverbs 2:9], there is a cry. So your whole religion is but a noise, the life, power and substance is not in it.

Oh apostate England, what shall the God of mercies do for thee? What shall he do unto thee? He hath tried thee with mercies, and with the sword, and then with peace again, and yet thou repentest not; he hath given thee his witness, his just one to reprove thee, to convince thee of sin in thy conscience, but thou hast slain the witness, murthered and slain the just: he will not always strive with man, he will now roar from Sion, and the children of the west shall tremble [Hosea 11:10], those that worship their idols; he will redeem Sion with judgement, and he will tear his flock out of the mouth of the greedy devouring shepherds, that have made a prey upon them, and the idol-shepherds shall have their arm dried up, and their right eye darkened [Zechariah 11:17].

Come down thou therefore that hast built among the stars [Obadiah 4] by thy arts and learning; for it's thy pride and thy wisdom, that hath perverted thee; thou hast gone in the way of Cain, in envy and malice, and ran greedily after the reward of Balaam, in covetousness, and if thou repent not, shalt perish in the gainsaying of Kore [Jude 11]: for if a son or a daughter be moved from the Lord, to go into the assembly of the people, in a message from the Lord God, thou canst not endure to hear them speak sound doctrine [2 Timothy 4:3], having a guilty conscience, and fearing they would declare against thy wickedness, thou incensest the people, telling them that they are dangerous people, Quakers, so making the people afraid of us: and incensest the magistrates, telling them that they must lay hold on us, as troublers of the people, and disturbers of the peace, and so makes them thy drudges to act thy malice, that thy filthiness may not be discovered, and thy shame appear; but God will make them in one day to forsake thee, and leave and fly from thee, though for the present thou lordest it over magistrates, people, meeting-house, and all, as though all were thine: and thou sittest as a queen and lady over all, and wilt have the pre-eminence, and hast got into the seat of God, the consciences of the people, and what thou sayest must not be contradicted: if thou bid them fight and war, they obey it; if thou bid them persecute and imprison, they do it; so that they venture their bodies and souls to fulfil thy lusts of envy and pride, and in thy pride thou contemnest all others, thou tellest the people women must not speak in a church [1 Corinthians 14:34–5], whereas it is not spoke only of a female, for we are all one both male and female in Christ Jesus [Galatians 3:28], but it's weakness that is the woman by the Scriptures forbidden, for else thou puttest the Scriptures at a difference in themselves, as still it's thy practice out of thy ignorance; for the Scriptures do say that all the church may prophesy one by one [1 Corinthians

14:31], and that women were in the church, as well as men, do thou judge; and the Scripture saith that a woman may not prophesy with her head uncovered, lest she dishonour her head [1 Corinthians 11:5]: now thou wouldst know the meaning of that head, let the Scripture answer, 1 Corinthians 11:3, 'The head of every man is Christ'. Man in his best estate is altogether vanity [Psalms 39:5], weakness, a lie. If therefore any speak in the church, whether man or woman, and nothing appear in it but the wisdom of man [1 Corinthians 2:4–5, 13], and Christ, who is the true head, be not uncovered, do not fully appear, Christ the head is then dishonoured. Now the woman or weakness, that is man, which in his best estate or greatest wisdom is altogether vanity, that must be covered with the covering of the spirit, a garment of righteousness [Isaiah 61:10], that its nakedness may not appear, and dishonour thereby come. Here mayst thou see from the Scriptures, that the woman or weakness whether male or female, is forbidden to speak in the church. [1 Corinthians 14:34]; but it's very plain, Paul, nor Apollos, nor the true church of Christ, were not of that proud envious spirit that thou art of, for they owned Christ Jesus in man or woman; for Paul bid Timothy to help those women that laboured with him in the Gospel [Philippians 4:3], and Apollos hearkened to a woman, and was instructed by her [Acts 18:26], and Christ Jesus appeared to the women first, and sent them to preach the resurrection to the apostles [Matthew 28:9–10; John 20:14–18], and Philip had four virgins that did prophesy [Acts 21:9]. Now thou dost respect persons I know, and art partial in all things, and so judgest wickedly, but there is no respect of persons with God [Acts 10:34]. Indeed, you yourselves are the women, that are forbidden to speak in the church, that are become women; for two of your priests came to speak with us; and when they could not bear sound reproof and wholesome doctrine [2 Timothy 4:2–3], that did concern them, they railed on us with filthy speeches, as no other they can give to us, that deal plainly and singly with them, and so ran from us. So leaving you to the light in all your consciences to judge of what we have writ, we remain prisoners in Exeter gaol for the word of God.

Priscilla Cotton,
Mary Cole.

FINIS

# Chapter 25

# Anne Wentworth (ca. 1679)

### The Revelation of Jesus Christ (ca. 1679)

The apocalyptic prophecy of the Baptist Anne Wentworth is closely linked with persecution by her husband, who, emboldened by certain ecclesiastical colleagues has falsely accused Anne. An introduction to the text by a woman friend explains that she was thrown out of her home by her husband and suffered the opprobrium attached to such an eviction. She had been subjected to "cruel usage" as well as the "bitter words" of his "sharp tongue." The apocalyptic language of Babylon is here applied to this particular example of oppression. Anne is empowered in this situation by her conviction that Christ has spoken to her much as he did to John on Patmos. This is an extraordinary testimony to the rectitude of her experience of oppression and the way in which apocalyptic imagery has enabled this to be interpreted.

Wentworth explains that God sent an angel to tell her to write and publish the truth about her husband's treatment of her. Her husband's behavior is like the oppression of Zion by Babylon in the Bible: she, the abused wife, is Zion; Babylon is figured in the violent man. God's undertaking to free Zion and punish Babylon is therefore a promise made to all abused women, and the Lord is exasperated by the public's failure to understand this. The problem is that they will not go to the root of the matter, they cannot see the two conflicting Spirits at work: "That Spirit, which hath dictated the Verses in this Book; or that, which speaks all those evil Words and Defamations: For God cannot own both. It is the struggle between Zion and Babylon" (*Revelation*, p. 9). All current churches, including Baptists and Quakers, have lost sight of divine will, and lapsed into a formal religion that conceals from them the true interpretation of scripture. Anne Wentworth has divine assurance "that the man of earth shall oppress me no more; no more shall be under the hands of the hard-hearted persecutors, unless he become a new man, a changed man sensible of the wrong he has done me, with his fierce looks, bitter words, sharp tongue and cruel usage" (*Vindication* quoted in p. 5, Hobby 1988, p. 50). The spirit of the English Revolution could still, thirty years on, justify the dissolution of violent marriages and in this, the overthrow of Babylon.

The extract starts with an explanation by Anne's friend and ends with Anne's own explanation of her situation and her visionary empowerment. The extracts reflect typical passages of the apocalyptic tradition, including the image of Babylon at work as an oppressive force in England (derived from Revelation 17) and may be compared with the use made of the Apocalypse by one of her oppressors, probably Hanserd Knowlys (see Kenneth Newport, *Apocalypse and Millennium*, Cambridge: Cambridge University Press, 2000, pp. 27–35).

## Source

## Further reading

E. Hobby, *Virtue of Necessity: English Women's Writing 1649–1688,* London: Virago, 1988.
P. Crawford, *Women and Religion in England 1500–1720,* London: Routledge, 1993.

## The Revelation of Jesus Christ

Psal. 8: 2. Out of the mouths of babes and sucklings hast thou
    ordained strength, because of thine enemies, that thou mightest
    still the enemy and the avenger.
    I Cor. 1: 27, 28. God hath chosen the foolish things of the
    world to confound the wise; and God hath chosen the weak things of the world,
    to confound the things which are mighty: And base
    things of the world, and things which are despised, hath God
    chosen; yea, and things which are not, to bring to nought
    things that are: That no flesh should glory in his presence . . .
    Here are presented to thee [reader] a few Verses, written by
    the hand of Anne Wentworth, who thought not to have published
    any thing this way, till she had made ready her whole
    Testimony, given her by the Lord Jesus, to declare to the

world; but some of these Verses falling into the hand of one,
that was once an Enemy to her, they so wrought upon her, that
she resolved to have them Printed:

But Saints, do ye hear, for he for you will make room.
    To live, and rejoice, and praise his most holy Name,
    Who by his own Blood wrought for you the same.
    But the Hypocrites in Zion they will all mourn,
    All the wicked, proud in heart, that did so scorn,
    When they see the Battle of the Lord to be fought,
    And how it was the Lord alone, that me taught,
    And in his strength I was by Grace enabled to stand,
    Against all my Enemies, with his Battle-axe in my hand,
    To wound, kill, amaze, put to flight, and cut them down
    And when they are in their Graves, I shall wear a Crown.
    O this God! so great in power! wonderful is his Name!
    Who will exalt those of low degree, & give his Enemies shame,
    . . . .
    Come all Saints, come sing and rejoice with me,
    At Babylon's fall, and the glorious days, which ye shall see:
    When the great Battle is fought, the day past, and all done,
    Then all Honour, Glory and Praise to God must be sung.
    Rejoice, ye Heavens and Prophets, for God avengeth your
    Cause,
    That Babylon would have deprived you of by her unjust Laws.
    This is a great Mystery, who now can this read?
    And know it rightly, and in so narrow a path doth tread?
    Who is able to bear, to have whole Babylon come down?
    Who can endure to hear, that they are in Babylon?
    Who doth think, that in England is the painted Whore?
    Who did think, they should ever hear of me any more?
    When they sit as Queen, and say, they shall have no sorrow,
    I am raised up again, and freed from all their horror.
    When they thought, to put me in the Grave, & have me slain,
    I am raised up more strong, and brought to Life again.

Whereas the Lord has made way, to bring forth into the World
his Revelations sooner, than I expected or thought of, and
commanded me very earnestly, to add thereunto, what I have
suffered and suffer for being his Messenger, in bearing his
Testimony to the World: And I endeavoured, to put it by, for
shame's sake. There fear and trembling came upon me, that I
could not withstand it, but was forced to declare herewith
openly, how for obeying the Word of the Lord, and his
Commandments, I am reproached as a proud, wicked, deceived,
deluded, lying Woman; a mad, melancholy, crack-brained, self
willed, conceited Fool, and black Sinner, led by whimsies,
notions, and knif-knafs of my own head; one that speaks
blasphemy, not fit to take the Name of God in her mouth; an

Heathen and Publican, a Fortune-teller, an Enthusiast, and the like much more, whereof I appeal to God, to judge: And then let all slanderers challenge their own words . . .

And as concerning my Husbands Behaviour towards me in this Case of the Lords, He the Lord will also judge betwixt Him and Me, and make known, whether I am an impudent Hussy, a disobedient Wife to him, one that run away from her Husband, and the like. Or whether He is the Man, that will not suffer me to live with him, that will not receive me into his Habitation, unless I deny the Lord, and his Message, and avow to be deluded by a lying Spirit. And therefore he takes no care of me, nor once looks after me these almost two years. These things the Lord will judge and bring to light, that all People shall know, how He likes of their encouraging my Husband against me, in making me the Butt of their malice; but my Husband, they make the patient, meek Lamb, and strengthen him thus against the Lord. Therefore all that have done, and do so, shall feel the Rod of an angry God, as there is Hanserd Knowles with his Church, and Nehemiah Cocks, my Husbands Pastor, Thomas Hicks, William Dicks, Philip Barder, my Relations, and hundreds more, that have a hand in setting my Husband against me, so that he will not own me: And then they go on to blame and defame me, and say, that I am run away from him!

So far it is the will of God, that the World should know the true reason, why I must live alone and apart from my said Husband, which (as it will stand before God) is no other, but that I cannot deny the Testimony of Jesus, but keep the Commandments of God, being obedient to all his Wills. And this is the thing, the only thing, that makes my Husband and hundreds more, to be wroth with me, and endeavour to take away my good Name, in spreading abroad, that I keep Men company, and have my Rogues come to me, and live a scandalous life in an Alms-house. But as the Pharisees of old said of the Son of God, that he was a gluttonous man, a Wine-bibber, a Friend of Publicans and Sinners [Luke 7:34], and one that hath the Devil; and yet he bore it patiently: So shall I wait in patience, how the Lord Jesus doth love and like of their thus defaming me, which will be seen and known openly, for to be recorded to Generations to come.

# Chapter 26

# James Nayler (ca. 1617–1660)

**Behold You Rulers (1658)**

Having formerly served in the Parliamentary army, Nayler, a native of Wakefield, York-shire, was originally amongst the most influential Quaker leaders in the early years of the movement. However, some of his followers became so devoted to his inspirational teachings and Christ-like character, that they began to worship Nayler as Christ himself. The culmination of this devotion came when Nayler, entering Bristol on horse-back, was greeted by crowds in much the same fashion as the gospels tell us Christ had been welcomed on entering Jerusalem. All of this led to Nayler being tried and found guilty of blasphemy by parliament in 1656. He was sentenced to tortuous punishment and imprisoned. Although later released, his influence never fully regained its former level and his writings have been much neglected since. His many writings were shaped by his profound beliefs concerning the Quaker doctrine of the Inner Light and empha-size the practical nature of Christian teaching above all else.

Our extract was written in the time of Oliver Cromwell and addressed "to him, his rulers and teachers" (406 in *Collection*). It is both a warning and exhortation to the political powers of the time and can be viewed as an early tract in the political theology of governance. Nayler believed that social justice goes hand in hand with good governance and was steadfast in his belief that authority should never be blindly adhered to by those subject to rulers, for they take their lead from a higher power, the gospel of Jesus Christ.

Source

The text comes from the volume *Quaker Tracts, 1652–62*, which is kept in the Rare Books Room, Cambridge University Library (reference number: Syn 7.65.52). Original pamphlet: London, Printed for Thomas Simmons, 1658. See also: *A Collection of Sundry Books, Epis-tles and Papers written by James Nayler*, London, J. Sowle, 1716. A new edition of Nayler's *Works* is edited by Emlyn Warren, Oxford, 1995–6.

Further reading

Bittle, William G., *James Nayler, 1618–1660 – the Quaker Indicted by Parliament*, York, Sessions in association with Friends United Press, 1986.
Brailsford, Mabel Richmond, *A Quaker in Cromwell's Army – James Nayler*, London, Swarthmore Press, 1927.
Nimmo, Dorothy, *A Testimony to the Grace of God in the Life of James Nayler*, York: Sessions Book Trust, 1993.
Nuttall, Geoffrey F: *James Nayler – a Fresh Approach*, London: Friends' Historical Society, 1954.
Whitehead, George, *An Impartial Account of Some of the Most Remarkable Transactions Relating to James Nayler*, ed. Emlyn Warren, Oxford, 1995.

## *Behold You Rulers* (1658)

*Behold You Rulers, and hearken proud Men and Women, who have let in the Spirit of the World into your hearts, whereby you are lifted up in the Earth; hear what Truth saith.*

You have gained riches, and you seeke worldly glory, an evil covetousness to your selves; and these Idols being set up in your hearts to be worshipped, you rage and wonder why the Children of Light will not worship your gods you have set up, and fall down before the glory of this world in you; so you are angry: But why are you so blind, to think that such who have denied to bow to the same spirit and pride in themselves, and have (through the Cross) obtained power from above to cast out the same Idols out of their own hearts and can they bow to them in another? Nay, the Day is come, and the children of light have found the living God in worship, and there is none besides him to us. And now in vain is the Idols preached; we cannot worship with you, however you be tormented; it is of God to famish the world's Idols; and he alone will be worshipped who is mighty to save. What have we to do any more with idle vanity? Pride cannot save us, nor can the world's glory preserve in the hour of temptation, though we should bow thereto; we cannot trust in uncertain riches, nor may we take counsel at silver or gold, flocks or herds. We have proved your Idols and know what is in them; and have found Destroyers, and not Saviours: Whatever your glory promises you (who most seek it), we know in its right hand is a lye, flattery and falsehood, and all who loves it comes short of the glory of God. Humility is our glory, and he is our Saviour who saith, *Learn of me, for I am lowly, and ye shall find rest for your souls* [Mt. 11:29]. And this we have proved, and we find his words truth, and all loftiness a lye. So having found the Truth, the Truth hath made us free; free from pride, free from vain glory, free from that spirit that puts it on, and would have it worshipped, free from the Manners of the Gentiles, who exercise Lordship in that nature which is out of the Light and Doctrine of Christ.

So the Truth having made us free, in that Liberty we stand fast, and may not be entangled again with your yoke of bondage, nor the Manners of the gentiles, and then you say it's our pride and stubbornness, and many such accusations you cast on us: Alas! What darkness is this! And how you have lost your judgement! What is *Mordecai* become prouder than *Haman* with you? Is he proud who denies to worship pride, and he that would be worshipped free? Is not this to put light to darkness, and darkness for light? To condemn the innocent, to hide the offender? Come down to that of God in your consciences, and let that judge, and let pride be seen, and ashamed where it is. And then you plead scripture and say, *Let every soul be subject to the higher power; and be subject to every Ordinance of man for the Lord's sake, &c* [Rom. 13:1]. Now this we say also, and owns the Scriptures; But man's pride is not the higher power; in Humility we find a power above pride, higher then the oppression, higher then men's wills, higher then lusts of the eye, yea higher then all in man that would exalt against it: So we deny the lower that we may subject ourselves to that which excelleth, which is ordained of God. And to every ordinance of man we are subject for the Lord's sake; but should we bow to the spirit of pride, we should betray the Lord, and give his honor to another, and that is not for the Lord's sake: so what we see for the Lord, and of him in every Ordinance of man, we subject to for the Lord's sake; and what is aganist him, for his sake we deny, and with him suffer under it, as witnesses for him against it; so we give *Caesar* his due, and custom to whom it belongs; but all due glory and worship to God alone, to whom it is due.

But say you, *That worship we plead for, is civil, not religious.* But where do you read in scripture of civil Worship? We find *honor all men in the Lord*; and that which is in the Lord, is religious; and that which is not in the Lord, is idolatrous. Is there anything honourable in man but the image of God, which is spiritual; he that worships where that is not, worships the beast, or that which is worse, the devil; and if any bow to that of God in man, how comes it not be religious, and yet you say for conscience-sake, and not religious: so your distinctions will not gain Worship from them who knows God and his Image, and the beast and his image, in their several appearances; and by this they are known forever, He that's from above seeks not honor from man, but that honor which is of God alone; God's presence in him makes him honourable in the hearts of all that loves God; so God gives him grace and glory, and honor. But the other must have none from God, who abides not in that which is honourable, and so becomes as the beast, seeking honor by force from such as he hath power over, and rages if he cannot have it; and their Nature hath no right to it, though the false prophet join with him to plead for it, who must into the lake together; and all that worship the beast and his image, must drink of the Wine of the wrath of God, powered out without mixture, as saith the scripture.

So you that are in place to rule, and seeke for honor seek first that which is honourable, and none can hold you from honor; and know it is the gift of God only to such as honor him, and not themselves; seek that glory and honor that hath immortality and eternal life, which is obtained of God by continuance in well-doing: seek Humility, that goes before honor; exalt Justice, set up righteousness, and truth in judgement; hold forth God's sword to all people under you, and not your own wills, then you honor God and he will honor you. Seek first the Kingdom of God, that he may rule in your own hearts, over your pride, over your passion, over lust, over covetousness, over respect of persons, and over all unright-eousness; so shall you set up the Higher Power in you, for every soul to be subject to, which that of God in every conscience shall answer to; then you are ministers of God, and he shall add to you that honor which is of God, which is immortal, binding every conscience and soul in subjection to your Authority, which all that resist, receive damnation to themselves. And this is Religious and an Ordinance of God, and receives not its honor from man, but from God alone, who hath ever honourned holy men and women that ruled for God, with God, as you may read in the Scriptures, who never needed to seek it from men while they retained God: But *Saul* when God was departed from him, through covetousness and disobedi-ence, cried, *Honor me before the people*; who had lost the Kingdom of God, had lost his honor, had lost that which binds the conscience, and to which the soul is subject, who cryed, *Honor me before the people*, from whom God was departed, who had departed from God, who sought honor to himself without God, the Kingdom of God being rent from him, his honor departed.

So you that would have honor, seek God and retain him, exalt his kingdom in your hearts, and he will add honor thereto: but if you be disobedient, and your souls be not subject to the Higher Power, then another power rules, to which the righteous soul cannot subject for conscience sake; then gets up that's out of God's Kingdom and cries, Honor me before the people, and this is he that sought *David's* life, and seeks the life of his seed, who is disobedient, who is covetous, who is greedy of honor, who is a murderer, who keeps not the Word of God, nor abode in the truth, to keep down pride and vainglory; then the false Prophet cries, *worship this*; to such as be out of the faith of Christ, disobedient to the Law of God, and in respect of persons; such as be flatterers, lyars, scorners, fighters, suers, drunkards, swearers, and such as be out of the Kingdom of God, whose souls are not subject to the higher power for conscience sake; such bow and worship with putting off hats, and bowing of the knees to the person, but the soul of such is not subject to the power that is of God for conscience sake; yet such is the darkness of many Rulers, as to account this subjection to Authority, while such whose souls do truly bow to the power of Righteousness, Justice and Equity, where-ever it is, without flattering where it is not, are condemned for unmannerliness, disorder, and suffer as disobedient to Authority. But to that of God in every conscience do we appeal Whether such souls exalt the power which is of God, and seek his honor, or their own; and so as you honor God, with God shall you be honored; but seek it as eagerly as you will, without him it will flye from you, though flattery you may obtain, which will corrupt your judgement, and let in upon you everlasting dis-honor. Wherefore turn to the Lord with your whole hearts, and seek his glory alone, that he may put upon you his spirit of humility, and righteous Judgement that you may be covered therewith, as with a garment, so shall you freely have our souls' subjection, which now in secret mournes for you with prayers and tears before God, and openly suffers under you for a testimony against you. And now you that are not in place to rule, and seek to be worshipped of us, what is it you would have us bow to, in you, or upon you? Gladly would we see humility appear in you, and behold you covered with the spirit of God, that in our souls we might subject thereto, and so in the Lord honor you; but should we bow to your gold and silver Lace, your costly apparel, or earthly riches? To that of God in you we appeal, If we should not worship Idols, and break the Law of God, for which doing, how we should be excused before God at the day of account, let such as fear God more than man, judge.

# Chapter 27

# John Bunyan (1628–1688)

### The Pilgrim's Progress **(1678)**

Though he appears never to have joined any of the radical political groups he would have encountered during the civil wars and their aftermath, Bunyan shared their disdain for those who lorded it over the poor: his unsavoury characters are nearly always men or women of social standing, while his pilgrims are uneducated, humble and despised by the world. Bunyan himself came from lowly stock and received little formal education, yet the best known of his more than sixty books have enjoyed a status unparalleled by almost any other work except the Bible. A tinker by trade and preacher and pastor by calling, Bunyan spent more than twelve years in prison after the Restoration. *The Pilgrim's Progress* was almost certainly written in confinement, probably during his (shorter) second term which lasted from December 1676 to June 1677. His spiritual autobiography, *Grace Abounding to the Chief of Sinners* (1666), was also written in prison.

Like *Grace Abounding*, *The Pilgrim's Progress* is a compelling conversion narrative. It begins with the pilgrim, clothed in rags and with his sins in a burden on his back, setting out from the City of Destruction under the spiritual direction of Evangelist. After surviving the Slough of Despond he eventually loses his burden at the cross, after which, having exchanged his rags for new garments and assumed the name Christian, he continues his precarious journey to the Celestial City, across from the River of Death. Those he encounters along the way prove to be both good and bad influences, and this extract relates his dealings with one By-Ends, decidedly an uninspiring companion. Also in attendance is Hopeful, who has joined Christian as a consequence of witnessing his and Faithful's stand at Vanity Fair and the latter's martyrdom.

Christian's discourse with By-Ends displays not only Bunyan's skill as an allegorist to ridicule and satirize the complacent and self-important, but his concern to expose the shallowness and inauthenticity of a religion held only for outward show. For Bunyan's Pilgrim, as for Bunyan himself, true religion eschews compromise with the world, and treads a path far too hazardous for those shod only in silver slippers.

## Source

John Bunyan, *The Pilgrim's Progress*, London, 1928 edition, pp. 106–8.

## Further reading

Christopher Hill, *A Turbulent, Seditious and Factious People: John Bunyan and his Church*, Oxford, 1989.
G. Offor, ed., *The Works of John Bunyan*, 1860.
Vincent Newey, ed., *The Pilgrim's Progress: Critical and Historical Views*, Liverpool, 1980.
Roger Sharrock, ed., *The Pilgrim's Progress: A Casebook*, London, 1976.
Roger Sharrock, *John Bunyan*, London and New York, 1968.
John Brown (ed., Robert Backhouse), *John Bunyan, His Life, Times and Work*, London, 1994.

## From *The Pilgrim's Progress*

Now I saw in my dream, that Christian went not forth alone; for there was one whose name was Hopeful (being so made by the beholding of Christian and Faithful in their words and behaviour, in their sufferings at the fair), who joined himself unto him, and entering into a brotherly covenant, told him that he would be his companion. Thus one died to bear testimony to the truth, and another rises out of his ashes to be a companion with Christian in his pilgrimage. This Hopeful also told Christian, that there were many more of the men in the fair that would take their time and follow after.

So I saw, that quickly after they were got out of the fair they overtook one that was going before them, whose name was By-ends; so they said to him, What countryman, sir? and how far go you this way? He told them, that he came from the town of Fair-speech, and he was going to the Celestial City; but told them not his name.

From Fair-speech? said Christian; is there any good that lives there?

By. Yes, said By-ends, I hope.

Chr. Pray, sir, what may I call you? said Christian.

By. I am a stranger to you, and you to me: if you be going this way, I shall be glad of your company; if not, I must be content.

Chr. This town of Fair-speech, said Christian, I have heard of it; and, as I remember, they say it's a wealthy place.

By. Yes, I will assure you that it is; and I have very many rich kindred there.

Chr. Pray who are your kindred there, if a man may be so bold.

By. Almost the whole town; and in particular, my Lord Turn-about, my Lord Time-server, my Lord Fair-speech, from whose ancestors that town first took its name; also Mr Smooth-man, Mr Facing-both-ways, Mr Any-thing; and the parson of our parish, Mr Two-tongues, was my mother's own brother, by father's side; and, to tell you the truth, I am become a gentleman of good quality; yet my great-grandfather was but a water-man, looking one way and rowing another, and I got most of my estate by the same occupation.

Chr. Are you a married man?

By. Yes, and my wife is a very virtuous woman, the daughter of a virtuous woman; she was my Lady Feigning's daughter; therefore she came of a very honourable family, and is arrived to such a pitch of breeding, that she knows how to carry it to all, even to prince and peasant. 'Tis true, we somewhat differ in religion from those of the stricter sort, yet but in two small points: First, we never strive against wind and tide. Secondly, we are always most zealous when Religion goes in his silver slippers; we love much to walk with him in the street, if the sun shines, and the people applaud him.

Then Christian stepped a little aside to his fellow Hopeful, saying, It runs in my mind that this is one By-ends, of Fair-speech; and if it be he, we have as very a knave in our company as dwelleth in all these parts. Then said Hopeful, Ask him; methinks he should not be ashamed of his name. So Christian came up with him again, and said, Sir, you talk as if you knew something more than all the world doth; and, if I take not my mark amiss, I deem I have half a guess of you. Is not your name Mr By-ends, of Fair-speech?

By. This is not my name; but, indeed, it is a nickname that is given me by some that cannot abide me, and I must be content to bear it as a reproach, as other good men have borne theirs before me.

Chr. But did you never give an occasion to men to call you by this name?

By. Never, never! The worst that ever I did to give them an occasion to give me this name was, that I had always the luck to jump in my judgment with the present way of the times, whatever it was, and my chance was to get thereby; but if things are thus cast upon me, let me count them a blessing; but let not the malicious load me, therefore, with reproach.

Chr. I thought, indeed, that you were the man that I heard of; and to tell you what I think, I fear this name belongs to you more properly than you are willing we should think it doth.

By. Well, if you will thus imagine, I cannot help it; you shall find me a fair company-keeper, if you will still admit me your associate.

Chr. If you will go with us, you must go against wind and tide; the which, I perceive, is against your opinion: you must also own Religion in his rags, as well as when in his silver slippers; and stand by him, too, when bound in irons, as well as when he walketh the streets with applause.

By. You must not impose, nor lord it over my faith; leave me to my liberty, and let me go with you.

Chr. Not a step farther, unless you will do in what I propound as we.

Then said By-ends, I shall never desert my old principles, since they are harmless and profitable. If I may not go with you, I must do as I did before you overtook me, even go by myself, until some overtake me that will be glad of my company.

Now I saw in my dream, that Christian and Hopeful forsook him, and kept their distance before him . . .

# Chapter 28

# William Blake (1757–1827)

Songs of Innocence and Experience **(1794)**
Vala, or The Four Zoas **(ca. 1800)**
**Preface to** Milton **(1804)**

William Blake, prophet, visionary, poet, painter, and engraver stands at the heart of this collection. He came from an artisan background and was apprenticed to an engraver in London, a skill which he refined and perfected so that he evolved a way of producing the exercise of his own imagination. Thereby inspiration and execution came to be united in a way which is without parallel in the history of artistic production. His religious roots lie in the Bible, but he was open to the mystical currents of his day though he became disillusioned with some of the minority groups, as he discovered that in them the signs of embryonic hierarchy and control which Blake so much wanted to challenge (note the reference to "the priests in black gowns walking their rounds in "The Garden of Love"). Blake regarded himself as a prophet in the tradition of the biblical prophets. The sense of prophetic vocation and insight equips Blake to offer the meaning of contemporary events, as in the biblical prophecies against the nations or the visions of the beast and Babylon in the Book Revelation. Indeed, he recognizes the prophets of the Bible as kindred spirits (in *The Marriage of Heaven and Hell*, 12–13 he writes about dining with Isaiah and Ezekiel). His work epitomizes radical religion: its roots are in the Bible; it probes the roots of humanity's disaffection and alienation from God and from one another. There is a clearer recognition of the problematic nature of the radical challenge of the inadequacy of a mere appeal to that which is written; and, indeed, the recognition that it is often part of the problem. Blake found men and women using the Bible as a book of rules rather than as an inspiration for the imagination. He saw his contemporaries merely repeat texts, recalling that which was past rather than be guided by the present Spirit within, while he yearned for them to speak of God in their own way and for their own time. Because of the way the Bible seemed harnessed to an oppressive religion and morality, Blake evolved his own mythology, rooted in the symbols and images of the biblical prophecies and apocalypses, to challenge the domination of deference to the old words and phrases and to seek to enable the expression of a different, more humane, conception of human life. Blake realized that for Scripture to speak there had to be found ways of enabling its imagery to reborn by word, picture, and artistic ingenuity, so the Scripture and the spiritual experiences of previous generations could become present truth and words of life. In addition to preoccupation with the letter of the Scripture Blake inveighed against a theology which viewed God as a remote divine monarch and law-giver. One may imagine him seeing the Ten Commandments inscribed on wooden boards in the churches of his day and finding in this an affront to the way of Jesus. He saw the words "Thou shalt not" too often determining life rather than mutual forgiveness. Herein lies the problem of European religion, a forbidding and remote deity, too exalted to wipe tears from human eyes. As far as Blake is concerned, the worship of God is "Honouring his gifts in other men each according to his genius" . . . (*Marriage of Heaven and Hell*, 22).

The items in this book come from the deceptively simple "Songs of Innocence and Experience," in which Blake uses his perception of what he calls "minute particulars" to juxtapose the contrary situations of human life to provoke imaginative engagement with hope and injustice, lofty ideals and brute reality. In "The Little Black Boy" the importance of experience of God in life rather than in taught religion is stressed as the wisdom of the little black boy's mother keeps alive the value of what is learnt from the experience of life in what we would now call the Third World. In "The Divine Image" and its companion poem "The Human Abstract" the ideal is contrasted with the way in which theology can become mere abstraction, remote from human life when what is required is the recognition of the divine in the human. Also, even the exercise of those charitable instincts can become a way of buttressing injustice, however, if all we do is pity. In this the church with its religion of rules has constrained the desires and imagination of the divine spirit in men and women. In "London" the realities of contemporary life in the world around him are brought home as the poet as prophet, like Ezekiel or John of the Apocalypse, sees in London the marks of economic idolatry and oppression in his own city and the extent to which the prophet has to confront in "the mind-forg'd manacles," the pervasive ideologies of the day, much as Isaiah 6:9f had indicated.

The penultimate extract from Blake's long poem, Vala or "The Four Zoas" is a satirical comment on the behavior of the wealthy elite who seek to keep the poor in order. In the context of Blake's poem, however, it is the advice of the spiritual divinities inspiring the political conservatism of his day, whose effects Blake saw in the terrible conditions of the poor in south London in the 1790s as a Tory government imposed its harsh economics on an already impoverished people (see D. Erdman *Blake Prophet Against Empire*, p. 341). Blake saw greater forces at work than the sum of the actions of human individuals whose power to enslave humans, whether individually or socially, needed to be recognized before it could be addressed and liberation take place.

At the beginning of some versions of *Milton* we find the poem commonly known as "Jerusalem," in which he contrasts prophetic religion with the dominance of the classical tradition in Christianity, to the detriment of a truly radical theology. Blake condemns the domination of classical culture, which has quenched the vitality of biblical inspiration and by which Blake's hero, John Milton, was influenced and from which Blake's own poetic writing is a means of liberation. The New Jerusalem in the famous stanzas at the conclusion of the quotation is not something remote or far off but a possibility, something which may be built in England's green and pleasant land. In the opening stanzas the poet-prophet questions whether the lamb of God has already appeared in this green and pleasant land. The answer is an emphatic "no." "Mental Fight" is needed to challenge dominant patterns of thinking and behaving. The "mental fight" is the vocation of the prophet and above all else is the requirement of those who are going to be true to their humanity.

## Sources

All the following extracts have been transcribed from the facsimiles in *William Blake's Illuminated Books*, six volumes, General Editor David Bindman, Tate Gallery Publications/William Blake Trust, London, 1991–5; the extract from the Four Zoas is taken from *Blake: The Complete Writings*, edited by G. Keynes, Oxford: Oxford University Press, 1972.

## Further reading

*William Blake's Illuminated Books*, six volumes, General Editor David Bindman, Tate Gallery Publications/William Blake Trust, London, 1991–5.

D. Bindman, *William Blake. The Complete Illuminated Books*, London: Thames and Hudson, 2000.

*Blake: The Complete Writings*, edited by G. Keynes, Oxford: Oxford University Press, 1972.

M. Butlin, *The Paintings and Drawings of William Blake*, Newhaven: Yale University Press, 1981.

D. V. Erdman, *Blake: Prophet against Empire*, Princeton: Princeton University Press, 1977.

N. Frye, *Fearful Symmetry*, Princeton: Princeton University Press, 1947.

J. Mee, *Dangerous Enthusiasm*, Oxford: Oxford University Press, 1990.

## From *Songs of Innocence and Experience* (1794)

*The Little Black Boy*

> My mother bore me in the southern wild,
> And I am black, but O! my soul is white.
> White as an angel is the English child:
> But I am black as if bereav'd of light.

My mother taught me underneath a tree
And sitting down before the heat of day.
She took me on her lap and kissed me,
And pointing to the east began to say.

Look on the rising sun: there God does live
And gives his light, and gives his heat away.
And flowers and trees and beasts and men receive
Comfort in morning joy in the noon day.

And we are put on earth a little space..
That we may learn to bear the beams of love.
And these black bodies and this sunburnt face
Is but a cloud, and like a shady grove.

For when our souls have learn'd the heat to bear
The cloud will vanish we shall hear his voice.
Saying: come out from the grove my love & care.
And round my golden tent like lambs rejoice.

Thus did my mother say and kissed me.
And thus I say to little English boy.
When I from black and he from white cloud free,
And round the tent of God like lambs we joy:

Ill shade him from the heat till he can bear,
To lean in joy upon our fathers knee.
And then I'll stand and stroke his silver hair,
And be like him and he will then love me.

## The Divine Image

To Mercy Pity Peace and Love.
All pray in their distress:
And to these virtues of delight
Return their thankfulness.

For Mercy Pity Peace and Love,
Is God our father dear:
And Mercy Pity Peace and Love,
Is Man his child and care.

For Mercy has a human heart
Pity, a human face:
And Love, the human form divine,
And Peace, the human dress.

Then every man of every clime,
That prays in his distress,
Prays to the human form divine
Love Mercy Pity Peace,

## The Human Abstract

Pity would be no more,
If we did not make somebody Poor;
And Mercy no more could be.
If all were as happy as we;

And mutual fear brings peace;
Till the selfish loves increase.
Then Cruelty knits a snare,
And spreads his baits with care.

He sits down with holy fears.
And waters the ground with tears:
Then Humility takes its root
Underneath his foot.

Soon spreads the dismal shade
Of Mystery over his head;
And the Catterpiller and Fly.
Feed on the Mystery.

And all must love the human form.
In heathen, turk or jew,
Where Mercy, Love & Pity dwell,
There God is dwelling too.

And it bears the fruit of Deceit.
Ruddy and sweet to eat:
And the Raven his nest has made
In its thickest shade.

The Gods of the earth and sea,
Sought thro' Nature to find this Tree
But their search was all in vain:
There grows one in the Human Brain


## London

I wander thro' each charter'd street.
Near where the charter'd Thames does flow
And mark in every face I meet
Marks of weakness, marks of woe.

In every cry of every Man.
In every Infants cry of fear.
In every voice; in every ban,
The mind-forg'd manacles I hear

How the Chimney-sweepers cry
Every blackning Church appalls.
And the hapless Soldiers sigh
Runs in blood down Palace walls

But most thro' midnight streets I hear
How the youthful Harlots curse
Blasts the new-born Infants tear
And blights with plagues the Marriage hearse.


## The Garden of Love

I went to the Garden of Love.
And saw what I never had seen:
A Chapel was built in the midst,
Where I used to play on the green.

And the gates of this Chapel were shut,
And "Thou shalt not" writ over the door;
So I turn'd to the Garden of Love,
That so many sweet flowers bore,

And I saw it was filled with graves,
And tomb-stones where flowers should be:
And Priests in black gowns, were walking their rounds,
And binding with briars, my joys & desires.

## *Vala, or The Four Zoas,* **Night the Seventh 80, lines 9–20**

Compell the poor to live upon a Crust of bread, by soft mild arts.
Smile when they frown, frown when they smile; & when a man looks pale
With labour & abstinence, say he looks healthy & happy;
And when his children sicken, let them die; there are enough
Born, even too many, & our Earth will be overrun
Without these arts. If you would make the poor live with temper,
With pomp give every crust of bread you give; with gracious cunning
Magnify small gifts; reduce the man to want a gift & then give with pomp.
Say he smiles if you hear him sigh. If pale, say he is ruddy
Preach temperance: say he is overgorg'd & drowns his wit
In strong drink tho you know that bread & water are all
He can afford. Flatter his wife pity his children, till we can
Reduce all to our will, as spaniels are taught with art.

## Preface to *Milton*

The Stolen and Perverted Writings of Homer & Ovid: of Plato & Cicero, which all
Men ought to contemn: are set up by artifice against the Sublime of the Bible, but
when the New Age is at leisure to Pronounce; all will be set right: and those Grand
Works of the more ancient & consciously and professedly Inspired Men, will hold
their proper rank, & the Daughters of Memory shall become the Daughters of Inspiration. Shakespeare & Milton were both curbd by the general malady & infection
from the silly Greek & Latin slaves of the Sword.

Rouze up O Young Men of the New Age ! set your foreheads against the ignorant
Hirelings ! For we have Hirelings in the Camp, the Court & the University, who
would if they could forever depress Mental & prolong Corporeal War. Painters! on
you I call! Sculptors! Architects! Suffer not the fash[i]onable Fools to depress your
powers by the prices they pretend to give for contemptible works or the expensive
advertizing boasts they make of such works; believe Christ & his Apostles that there
is a Class of Men whose whole delight is in Destroying. We do not want either
Greek or Roman models if we are but just & true to our own Imaginations, those
Worlds of Eternity in which we shall live for ever; in Jesus our Lord

And did those feet in ancient time.
Walk upon Englands mountains' green :
And was the holy Lamb of God.
On England's pleasant pastures seen !

And did the Countenance Divine.
Shine forth upon our clouded hills ?
And was Jerusalem builded here,
Among these dark Satanic Mills ?

Bring me my Bow of burning gold :
Bring me my Arrows of desire :

Bring me my Spear : O Clouds unfold :
Bring me my Chariot of fire :

I will not cease from Mental Fight.
Nor shall my Sword sleep in my hand :
Till we have built Jerusalem,
In England's green & pleasant Land

Would to God that all the Lords people were Prophets Numbers xi. 29V.

Chapter 29

# John Woolman (1720–1772)

## Some Considerations on the Keeping of the Negroes (1754)

As with many Christian advocates of social reform, the Quaker, John Woolman, was also known as something of a mystic. His spiritual and social legacy go hand in hand. Born in New Jersey, he is primarily remembered for being amongst the first vociferous opponents of slavery in the USA, and his compassionate disposition also led him to champion the rights of North American Indians, the poor in general and, indeed, of all living beings. His fervent belief in pacifism led to his refusal to pay taxes in 1755, because they were levied to fund the conflict with the French and Indians (1754–63). Woolman believed materialism and the thirst for power helped bring about such conflicts and he chastised the rich Quaker rulers of Pennsylvania for deserting their pacifism in such conflicts. Woolman's passion for social justice must be understood as the natural correlate of the inner perfection which he advocated in his spiritual exhortations.

He worked first as a shop assistant, then as a tailor and was a Quaker minister from 1743 until his death. His profound sense of pastoral concern was evident in the countless visitations which he made ("traveling in the ministry"), both far and near, to aid the spiritual and physical well-being of his fellow human beings. From his observations in Virginia of the practice of "holding fellow men in property," he soon took every opportunity to campaign against slavery, even bringing the campaign to England prior to his death in York, from smallpox.

The extract comes from Woolman's most influential piece of writing on the subject of slavery, Some Considerations on the Keeping of the Negroes (1754). His arguments in the first part concerned opposing slavery on the grounds of the Quaker principles of universal fraternity and redemption and the Golden Rule of doing to others as one would have done to oneself. Woolman goes on to confront slave-owners with the moral implications of their practices. His great gift was his ability to persuade others to see the wrong-ness of their ways without angering or alienating them. Woolman cared as much for the sinner as the sinned against. His efforts helped persuade the Quakers first to advocate that its members free all their slaves and eventually to forbid any Friend from "owning" slaves altogether. He was ahead of his time in such practices as condemning those who profited from slavery and in abstaining from sugar because it was the product of slave labour.

## Source

*The Journal and Major Essays of John Woolman*, ed. Phillips P. Moulton, Oxford: Oxford University Press, 1971, pp. 203–4, 220–1, 237.

## Further reading

Cadbury, Henry J: *John Woolman in England, 1772 – a Documentary Supplement*, London, 1972.
Cady, Edwin, *John Woolman*, New York, 1965.
Dodson, Shirley, *John Woolman's Spirituality and Our Contemporary Witness*, Philadelphia, 1995.
Peare, Catherine Owens, *John Woolman – Child of Light: the Story of John Woolman and his friends*, New York, 1954.
Reynolds, Reginald, *The Wisdom of John Woolman*, London, 1977.
Shore, W. T., *John Woolman – His Life and Our Times*, London, 1913.
Moulton, Phillips P., *The Living Witness of John Woolman*, Wallingford, PA, 1973.
Sox, David, *John Woolman – Quintessential Quaker*, 1720–72, York: Sessions Book Trust, 1999.
Whitney, Janet, *John Woolman – Quaker*, London, 1943.

## *Some Considerations on the Keeping of the Negroes* (1754)

To humbly apply to God for wisdom, that we may thereby be enabled to see things as they are and ought to be, is very needful; hereby the hidden things of darkness may be brought to light and the judgment made clear. We shall then consider mankind as brethren. Though different degrees and a variety of qualifications and abilities, one dependent on another, be admitted, yet high thoughts will be laid aside, and all men treated as becometh the sons of one Father, agreeable to the doctrine of Christ Jesus.

> He hath laid down the best criterion by which mankind ought to judge of their own conduct, and others judge for them of theirs, one towards another – viz., "Whatsoever ye would that men should do unto you, do ye even so to them" [Mt. 7:12]. I take it that all men by nature are equally entitled to the equity of this rule and under the indispensable obligations of it. One man ought not to look upon another man or society of men as so far beneath him but that he should put himself in their place in all his actions towards them, and bring all to this test – viz., How should I approve of this conduct were I in their circumstance and they in mine? – Arscott's *Considerations*, Part III, Fol. 107.

This doctrine, being of a moral unchangeable nature, hath been likewise inculcated in the former dispensation: "If a stranger sojourn with thee in your land, ye shall not vex him; but the stranger that dwelleth with you shall be as one born amongst you, and thou shalt love him as thyself." Lev. 19:33, 34. Had these people come voluntarily and dwelt amongst us, to have called them strangers would be proper. And their being brought by force, with regret and a languishing mind, may well raise compassion in a heart rightly disposed. But there is nothing in such treatment which upon a wise and judicious consideration will any ways lessen their right of being treated as strangers. If the treatment which many of them meet with be rightly examined and compared with those precepts, "Thou shalt not vex him nor oppress him; he shall be as one born amongst you, and thou shalt love him as thyself" (Lev. 19:33; Deut. 27:19), there will appear an important difference betwixt them . . .

It is our happiness faithfully to serve the Divine Being who made us. His perfection makes our service reasonable; but so long as men are biased by narrow self-love, so long an absolute power over other men is unfit for them. Men taking on them the government of others may intend to govern reasonably and make their subjects more happy than they would be otherwise. But as absolute command belongs only to him who is perfect, where frail men in their own wills assume such command it hath a direct tendency to vitiate their minds and make them more unfit for government.

Placing on men the ignominious title SLAVE, dressing them in uncomely garments, keeping them to servile labour in which they are often dirty, tends gradually to fix a notion in the mind that they are a sort of people below us in nature, and leads us to consider them as such in all our conclusions about them. And, moreover, a person which in our esteem is mean and contemptible, if their language or behaviour toward us is unseemly or disrespectful, it excites wrath more powerfully than the like conduct in one we accounted our equal or superior, and where this happens to be the case it disqualifies for candid judgment; for it is unfit for a person to sit as judge in a case where his own personal resentments are stirred up, and as members of society in a well-framed government we are mutually dependent. Present interest incites to duty and makes each man attentive to the convenience of others; but he whose will is a law to others and can enforce obedience by punishment, he whose wants are supplied without feeling any obligation to make equal returns to his benefactor, his irregular appetites find an open field for motion, and he is in danger of growing hard and inattentive to their convenience who labour for his support, and so loses that disposition in which alone men are fit to govern.

The English government hath been commended by candid foreigners for the disuse of racks and tortures, so much practiced in some states; but this multiplying slaves now leads to it. For where people exact hard labour of others without a suitable reward and are resolved to continue in that way, severity to such who oppose them becomes the consequence; and several Negro criminals among the English in America have been executed in a lingering, painful way, very terrifying to others.

It is a happy case to set out right and persevere in the same way. A wrong beginning leads into many difficulties, for to support one evil, another becomes customary. Two produces more, and the further men proceed in this way the greater their dangers, their doubts and fears, and the more painful and perplexing are their circumstances, so that such who are true friends to the real and lasting interest of our country and candidly consider the tendency of things cannot but feel some concern on this account . . .

Negroes are our fellow creatures and their present condition amongst us requires our serious consideration. We know not the time when those scales in which mountains are weighed may turn. The parent of mankind is gracious. His care is over his smallest creatures, and a multitude of men escape not his notice; and though many of them are trodden down and despised, yet he remembers them. He seeth their affliction and looketh upon the spreading, increasing exaltation of the oppressor. He turns the channels of power, humbles the most haughty people, and gives deliverance to the oppressed at such periods as are consistent with his infinite justice and goodness. And wherever gain is preferred to equity, and wrong things publicly encouraged, to that degree that wickedness takes root and spreads wide amongst the inhabitants of a country, there is real cause for sorrow to all such whose love to mankind stands on a true principle and wisely consider the end and event of things.

# Chapter 30

# The Narrative of Sojourner Truth (ca. 1797–1883)

The Narrative of Sojourner Truth concerns a northern slave woman, Isabella or Sojourner Truth (ca. 1797–1883), and her role in the abolitionist movement. It is a story dictated to a friend and first published in the middle of the nineteenth century and extant in several versions. The passages included indicate the importance of listening to Scripture, the extraordinary courage and presence of mind and an example of the kind of song of liberty she sang.

## Source

Olive Gilbert, *Narrative of Sojourner Truth A Bondswoman of Olden Time, With a History of her Labours and Correspondence drawn from her "Book of Life,"* edited with and introduction and notes by Nell Irvin Painter, Harmondsworth: Penguin, 1998, especially pp. 74, 91–3, 94–5, 208–9.

## Further reading

O. Equiano, *The Interesting Narrative and Other Writings*, Penguin: Harmondsworth, 1995.

D. Hopkins and G. Cummings, *Cut Loose Your Stammering Tongues. Black Theology in the Slave Narratives*, Maryknoll: Orbis, 1991.

J. M. Washington *Conversations with God. Two Centuries of Prayers by African-Americans*, San Francisco: HarperTrade, 1995.

T. Fulop and A. Raboteau, *African American Religion: Interpretive Essays in History and Culture*, London: Routledge, 1997.

# The Narrative of Sojourner Truth (ca. 1797–1883)

*Silver, Lake, Kosciusko Co., Ind.,*
*October 1, 1858.*

FRIEND W. L. GARRISON. – Sojourner Truth, an elderly colored woman, well known throughout the Eastern States, is now holding a series of anti-slavery meetings in Northern Indiana. Sojourner comes well recommended by H. B. Stowe, yourself, and others, and was gladly received and welcomed by the friends of the slave in this locality. Her progress in knowledge, truth, and righteousness is very remarkable, especially when we consider her former low estate as a slave. The border-ruffian Democracy of Indiana, however, appear to be jealous and suspicious of every anti-slavery movement. A rumor was immediately circulated that Sojourner was an impostor; that she was, indeed, a man disguised in women's clothing. It appears, too, from what has since transpired, that they suspected her to be a mercenary hireling of the Republican party.

At her third appointed meeting in this vicinity, which was held in the meeting-house of the United Brethren, a large number of democrats and other pro-slavery persons were present. At the close of the meeting, Dr. T. W. Strain, the mouth-piece of the slave Democracy, requested the large congregation to 'hold on,' and stated that a doubt existed in the minds of many persons present respecting the sex of the speaker, and that it was his impression that a majority of them believed the speaker to be a man. The doctor also affirmed (which was not believed by the friends of the slave) that it was for the speaker's special benefit that he now demanded that Sojourner submit her breast to the inspection of some of the ladies present, that the doubt might be removed by their testimony. There were a large number of ladies present, who appeared to be ashamed and indignant at such a proposition. Sojourner's friends, some of whom had not heard the rumor, were surprised and indignant at such ruffianly surmises and treatment.

Confusion and uproar ensued, which was soon suppressed by Sojourner, who, immediately rising, asked them why they suspected her to be a man. The Democracy answered, 'Your voice is not the voice of a woman, it is the voice of a man, and we believe you are a man.' Dr. Strain called for a vote, and a boisterous 'Aye,' was the result. A negative vote was not called for. Sojourner told them that her breasts had suckled many a white babe, to the exclusion of her own offspring; that some of those white babies had grown to man's estate; that, although they had sucked her colored breasts, they were, in her estimation, far more manly than they (her persecutors) appeared to be; and she quietly asked them, as she disrobed her bosom, if they, too, wished to suck! In vindication of her truthfulness, she told them that she would show her breast to the whole congregation; that it was not to her shame that she uncovered her breast before them, but to their shame. Two young men (A. Badgely and J. Horner) stepped forward while Sojourner exposed her naked breast to the audience. I heard a democrat say, as we were returning home from meeting, that Dr. Strain had, previous to the examination, offered to bet forty dollars that Sojourner was a man! So much for the physiological acumen of a western physician.

As 'agitation of thought is the beginning of wisdom,' we hope that Indiana will yet be redeemed.

Yours, truly, for the slave,
WILLIAM HAYWARD.

*Meeting in New Lisbon*

Sojourner Truth interested an audience in New Lisbon, Ohio, at the Methodist Episcopal Church, for nearly an hour, talking of slavery in this country, and the suffering and injustice inseparable from it. If earnestness is eloquence, she has a just claim to that appellation; for she makes some powerful appeals, which cannot but strike a chord of sympathy in every human heart.

She sang the following original song at the close of the meeting: –

> I am pleading for my people –
> A poor, down-trodden race,
> Who dwell in freedom's boasted land,
> With no abiding place.
>
> I am pleading that my people
> May have their rights astored [restored];
> For they have long been toiling,
> And yet had no reward.
>
> They are forced the crops to culture,
> But not for them they yield,
> Although both late and early
> They labor in the field.
>
> Whilst I bear upon my body
> The scars of many a gash,
> I am pleading for my people
> Who groan beneath the lash.
>
> I am pleading for the mothers
> Who gaze in wild despair
> Upon the hated auction-block,
> And see their children there.
>
> I feel for those in bondage –
> Well may I feel for them;
> I know how fiendish hearts can be
> That sell their fellow-men.
>
> Yet those oppressors steeped in guilt –
> I still would have them live;
> For I have learned of Jesus
> To suffer and forgive.
>
> I want no carnal weapons,
> No enginery of death;
> For I love not to hear the sound
> Of war's tempestuous breath.

I do not ask you to engage
In death and bloody strife,
I do not dare insult my God
By asking for their life.

But while your kindest sympathies
To foreign lands do roam,
I would ask you to remember
Your own oppressed at home.

I plead with you to sympathize
With sighs and groans and scars,
And note how base the tyranny
Beneath the stripes and stars.

I had forgotten to mention, in its proper place, a very important fact, that when she was examining the Scriptures, she wished to hear them without comment; but if she employed adult persons to read them to her, and she asked them to read a passage over again, they invariably commenced to explain, by giving her their version of it; and in this way, they tried her feelings exceedingly. In consequence of this, she ceased to ask adult persons to read the Bible to her, and substituted children in their stead. Children, as soon as they could read distinctly, would re-read the same sentence to her, as often as she wished, and without comment; and in that way she was enabled to see what her own mind could make out of the record, and that, she said, was what she wanted, and not what others thought it to mean. She wished to compare the teachings of the Bible with the witness within her; and she came to the conclusion, that the spirit of truth spoke in those records, but that the recorders of those truths had intermingled with them ideas and suppositions of their own. This is one among the many proofs of her energy and independence of character.

# Chapter 31

# Elizabeth Cady Stanton (1815–1902)

**Address to the First Women's-Rights Convention (1848)**
The Woman's Bible **(1895–8)**

Elizabeth Cady Stanton was a leading campaigner for antislavery and women's rights in the United States. The mother of seven children, she was the prime mover behind the first USA Women's Rights Convention, the women's rights newspaper, *Revolution*, and the National Women's Suffrage Association. Her campaigning led to changes in the law governing married women's property rights and, though not effected until after her death, women's suffrage. She played a leading role in the production of the *Woman's Bible*, which she described as an attempt to "revise only those biblical texts and chapters directly referring to women, and those also in which women are made prominent by exclusion."

The two writings included here convey something of their author's passion for justice: women have a right to the vote on account of their humanity, Stanton argues, and thus what they are not required to do is appeal to men to make a magnanimous gesture. The point about revising the Bible, she argued, was that the "chief obstacle in the way of women's elevation" was the "degrading position" assigned to her by religion: hence *The Woman's Bible* was an attempt to offer fresh interpretations of all the biblical texts which are used to oppress, silence, or marginalize women. The book's reception at the time was mixed, and it largely disappeared from view until the early 1990s. Its influence on contemporary feminist theology has, however, been acknowledged.

Source

http://www. libertynet.org/edcivic/stanton.html

Rosemary Skinner Keller and Rosemary Radford Ruether, eds., *In Our Own Voices: Four Centuries of American Women's Religious Writings*, San Francisco: Harper, pp. 274–6.

Further reading

Ann Loades, ed., *Feminist Theology: A Reader*, London: SPCK, 1990.
M. Fortune and J. Haugerud, A *Study Guide to the Woman's Bible*, 1975.
M. D. Pellauer, *Toward a Tradition of Feminist Theology*, 1991.

## Address to the First Women's-Rights Convention (1848)

We have met here today to discuss our rights and wrongs, civil and political, and not, as some have supposed, to go into the detail of social life alone. We do not propose to petition the legislature to make our husbands just, generous, and courteous, to seat every man at the head of a cradle, and to clothe every woman in male attire. None of these points, however important they may be considered by leading men, will be touched in this convention. As to their costume, the gentlemen need feel no fear of our imitating that, for we think it in violation of every principle of taste, beauty, and dignity; notwithstanding all the contempt cast upon our loose, flowing garments, we still admire the graceful folds, and consider our costume far more artistic than theirs. Many of the nobler sex seem to agree with us in this opinion, for the bishops, priests, judges, barristers, and lord mayors of the first nation on the globe, and the Pope of Rome, with his cardinals, too, all wear the loose flowing robes, thus tacity acknowledging that the male attire is neither dignified nor imposing. No, we shall not molest you in your philosophical experiments with stocks, pants, high-heeled boots, and Russian belts. Yours be the glory to discover, by personal experience, how long the kneepan can resist the terrible strapping down which you impose, in how short time the well-developed muscles of the throat can be reduced to mere threads by the constant pressure of the stock, how high the heel of a boot must be to make a short man tall, and how tight the Russian belt may be drawn and yet have wind enough left to sustain life.

But we are assembled to protest against a form of government existing without the consent of the governed – to declare our right to be free as man is free, to be represented in the government which we are taxed to support, to have such disgraceful laws as give man the power to chastise and imprison his wife, to take the wages which she earns, the property which she inherits, and, in case of separation, the children of her love; laws which make her the mere dependent on his bounty. It is to protest against such unjust laws as these that we are assembled today, and to have them, if possible, forever erased from our statute books, deeming them a shame and a disgrace to a Christian republic in the nineteenth century. We have met

To uplift woman's fallen divinity
Upon an even pedestal with man's.

And, strange as it may seem to many, we now demand our right to vote according to the declaration of the government under which we live. This right no one pretends to deny. We need not prove ourselves equal to Daniel Webster to enjoy this privilege, for the ignorant Irishman in the ditch has all the civil rights he has. We need not prove our muscular power equal to this same Irishman to enjoy this privilege, for the most tiny, weak, ill-shaped stripling of twenty-one has all the civil rights of the Irishman. We have no objection to discuss the question of equality, for we feel that the weight of argument lies wholly with us, but we wish the question of equality kept distinct from the question of rights, for the proof of the one does not determine the truth of the other. All white men in this country have the same rights, however they may differ in mind, body, or estate.

The right is ours. The question now is: how shall we get possession of what rightfully belongs to us? We should not feel so sorely grieved if no man who had not attained the full stature of a Webster, Clay, Van Buren, or Gerrit Smith could claim the right of the elective franchise. But to have drunkards, idiots, horse-racing, rum-selling rowdies, ignorant foreigners, and silly boys fully recognized, while we ourselves are thrust out from all the rights that belong to citizens, it is too grossly insulting to the dignity of woman to be longer quietly submitted to. The right is ours. Have it, we must. Use it, we will. The pens, the tongues, the fortunes, the indomitable wills of many women are already pledged to secure this right. The great truth that no just government can be formed without the consent of the governed we shall echo and re-echo in the ears of the unjust judge, until by continual coming we shall weary him.

There seems now to be a kind of moral stagnation in our midst. Philanthropists have done their utmost to rouse the nation to a sense of its sins. War, slavery, drunkenness, licentiousness, gluttony, have been dragged naked before the people, and all their abominations and deformities fully brought to light, yet with idiotic laugh we hug those monsters to our breasts and rush on to destruction. Our churches are multiplying on all sides, our missionary societies, Sunday schools, and prayer meetings and innumerable charitable and reform organizations are all in operation, but still the tide of vice is swelling, and threatens the destruction of everything, and the battlements of righteousness are weak against the raging elements of sin and death. Verily, the world waits the coming of some new element, some purifying power, some spirit of mercy and love. The voice of woman has been silenced in the state, the church, and the home, but man cannot fulfill his destiny alone, he cannot redeem his race unaided. There are deep and tender chords of sympathy and love in the hearts of the downfallen and oppressed that woman can touch more skillfully than man.

The world has never yet seen a truly great and virtuous nation, because in the degradation of woman the very fountains of life are poisoned at their source. It is vain to look for silver and gold from mines of copper and lead. It is the wise mother that has the wise son. So long as your women are slaves you may throw your colleges and churches to the winds. You can't have scholars and saints so long as your mothers are ground to powder between the upper and nether millstone of tyranny and lust. How seldom, now, is a father's pride gratified, his fond hopes realized, in the budding genius of his son! The wife is degraded, made the mere creature of caprice, and the foolish son is heaviness to his heart. Truly are the sins of the fathers visited upon the children to the third and fourth generation. God, in His wisdom, has so linked the whole human family together that any violence done at one end of the chain is felt throughout its length, and here, too, is the law of restoration, as in woman all have fallen, so in her elevation shall the race be recreated.

"Voices" were the visitors and advisers of Joan of Arc. Do not "voices" come to us daily from the haunts of poverty, sorrow, degradation, and despair, already too long unheeded. Now is the time for the women of this country, if they would save our free institutions, to defend the right, to buckle on the armor that can best resist the keenest weapons of the enemy – contempt and ridicule. The same religious enthusiasm that nerved Joan of Arc to her work nerves us to ours. In every generation God calls some men and women for the utterance of truth, a heroic action, and our work today is the fulfilling of what has long since been foretold by the Prophet – Joel 2:28: "And it shall come to pass afterward, that I will pour out my spirit upon all flesh; and your sons and your daughters shall prophesy." We do not expect our path will be strewn with the flowers of popular applause, but over the thorns of bigotry and prejudice will be our way, and on our banners will beat the dark storm clouds of opposition from those who have entrenched themselves behind the stormy bulwarks of custom and authority, and who have fortified their position by every means, holy and unholy. But we will steadfastly abide the result. Unmoved we will bear it aloft. Undauntedly we will unfurl it to the gale, for we know that the storm cannot rend from it a shred, that the electric flash will but more clearly show to us the glorious words inscribed upon it, "Equality of Rights".

## The Woman's Bible (1895–8)

From the inauguration of the movement for woman's emancipation the Bible has been used to hold her in the "divinely ordained sphere," prescribed in the Old and New Testaments.

The canon and civil law; church and state; priests and legislators; all political parties and religious denominations have alike taught that woman was made after man, of man, and for man, an inferior being, subject to man. Creeds, codes, Scriptures and statutes, are all based on this idea. The fashions, forms, ceremonies and customs of society, church ordinances and discipline all grow out of this idea. . . .

The Bible teaches that woman brought sin and death into the world, that she precipitated the fall of the race, that she was arraigned before the judgment seat of Heaven, tried, condemned and sentenced. Marriage for her was to be a condition of bondage, maternity a period of suffering and anguish, and in silence and subjection, she was to play the role of a dependent on man's bounty for all her material wants, and for all the information she might desire on the vital questions of the hour, she was commanded to ask her husband at home. Here is the Bible position of woman briefly summed up. . . .

These familiar texts are quoted by clergymen in their pulpits, by statesmen in the halls of legislation, by lawyers in the courts, and are echoed by the press of all civilized nations, and accepted by woman herself as "The Word of God." So perverted is the religious element in her nature, that with faith and works she is the chief support of the church and clergy; the very powers that make her emancipation impossible. When, in the early part of the Nineteenth Century, women began to protest against their civil and political degradation, they were referred to the Bible for an answer. When they protested against their unequal position in the church, they were referred to the Bible for an answer.

This led to a general and critical study of the Scriptures. Some, having made a fetish of these books and believing them to be the veritable "Word of God," with liberal translations, interpretations, allegories and symbols, glossed over the most objectionable features of the various books and clung to them as divinely inspired. Others, seeing the family resemblance between the Mosaic code, the canon law, and the old English common law, came to the conclusion that all alike emanated from the same source; wholly human in their origin and inspired by the natural love of domination in the historians. Others, bewildered with their doubts and fears, came to no conclusion. While their clergymen told them, on the one hand, that they owed all the blessings and freedom they enjoyed to the Bible, on the other, they said it clearly marked out their circumscribed sphere of action: that the demands for political and civil rights were irreligious, dangerous to the stability of the home, the state and the church. Clerical appeals were circulated from time to time conjuring members of their churches to take no part in the anti-slavery or woman suffrage movements, as they were infidel in their tendencies, undermining the very foundations of society. No wonder the majority of women stood still, and with bowed heads, accepted the situation. . . .

How can woman's position be changed from that of a subordinate to an equal, without opposition, without the broadest discussion of all the questions involved in her present degradation? For so far-reaching and momentous a reform as her complete independence, an entire revolution in all existing institutions is inevitable.

Let us remember that all reforms are interdependent, and that whatever is done to establish one principle on a solid basis, strengthens all. Reformers who are always compromising, have not yet grasped the idea that truth is the only safe ground to stand upon. The object of an individual life is not to carry one fragmentary measure in human progress, but to utter the highest truth clearly seen in all directions, and thus to round out and perfect a well balanced character.

There are some who write us that our work is a useless expenditure of force over a book that has lost its hold on the human mind. Most intelligent women, they say, regard it simply as the history of a rude people in a barbarous age, and have no more reverence for the Scriptures than any other work. So long as tens of thousands of Bibles are printed every year, and circulated over the whole habitable globe, and the masses in all English-speaking nations revere it as the word of God, it is vain to belittle its influence. The sentimental feelings we all have for those things we were educated to believe sacred do not readily yield to pure reason. I distinctly remember the shudder that passed over me on seeing a mother take our family Bible to make a high seat for her child at table. It seemed such a desecration. I was tempted to protest against its use for such a purpose, and this, too, long after my reason had repudiated its divine authority.

To women still believing in the plenary inspiration of the Scriptures, we say give us by all means your exegesis in the light of the higher criticism learned men are now making, and illumine the Woman's Bible, with your inspiration. . . .

The only points in which I differ from all ecclesiastical teaching is that I do not believe that any man ever saw or talked with God, I do not believe that God inspired the Mosaic code, or told the historians what they say he did about woman, for all the religions on the face of the earth degrade her, and so long as woman accepts the position that they assign her, her emancipation is impossible. Whatever the Bible may be made to do in Hebrew or Greek, in plain English it does not exalt and dignify woman.

# Chapter 32

# Charles Haddon Spurgeon (1834–1892)

**Disestablishment (1877)**

Spurgeon was the most celebrated preacher of his day, and a nationally-known figure in Victorian England. An established Baptist minister in London while still only a teenager, he preached regularly for nearly 40 years to congregations of several thousand, the 6,000-capacity Metropolitan Tabernacle at the Elephant and Castle being built for him when he was 26. Printed versions of his sermons sold up to 350,000 copies per week, and his Sunday messages were cabled every Monday to New York for inclusion in the large-circulation newspapers in the United States. He was also a prolific author of books, pamphlets, tracts and other writings, and an activist in the fields of social concern and education, founding children's homes, a pastors' college, and other charitable institutions.

Spurgeon was noted for his plain speaking and firm views: "People come to me for one thing," he once remarked, "I preach to them a Calvinist creed and a Puritan morality. That is what they want and that is what they get." Yet though conservative in theology and morality, he was noted for his support of the Liberal cause, and not infrequently went against the grain of Victorian society by denouncing war, empire and all forms of racial discrimination. He was also a convinced dissenter and passionate opponent of the privileged position of the established Church, and this extract, taken from a speech delivered at the Annual Meeting of the Liberation Society in 1877, demonstrates his strength of feeling on the issue as well as his skill as a rhetorician. The tone is one more of sorrow than of anger, but it is representative of the views of many nonconformists of the Victorian age. Spurgeon left the Liberation Society, which existed primarily to fight for disestablishment, the year before his death.

Source

Charles Haddon Spurgeon, *Speeches at Home and Abroad*, Pasadena, Texas: Pilgrim Publishers, 1974, pp. 139–41.

## Further reading

C. H. Spurgeon, *Autobiography*, 2 vols., Edinburgh and Carlisle, and Pennsylvania, 1962.
Patricia Stallings Kruppa, *Charles Haddon Spurgeon: A Preacher's Progress*, New York and London, 1982.
Tim Curnow, et al., *A Marvellous Ministry*, Ligonier, PA, 1993.
Mark T. E. Hopkins, "Baptists, Congregationalists and Theological Change: Some late 19th-century leaders and controversies," D.Phil. Thesis, University of Oxford, 1988.
Helmut Thielicke, *Encounter With Spurgeon*, London, 1964.
David Bebbington, *The Nonconformist Conscience*, London, 1982.
D. M. Thompson, *Nonconformity in the Nineteenth Century*, London, 1972.
Clyde Binfield, *So Down to Prayers*, London, 1977.

## From Disestablishment

We wish to see the Church separated from the State for these reasons. First, we hold that the establishment of one peculiar form of Christianity, and the leaving out of other Christians, is a clear wrong and injustice. We feel that, if we were the patronized sect, we should find it difficult with the light we possess to defend our position. We should be half ashamed to meet our episcopal brethren who were unendowed if we Baptists and Congregationalists were endowed; we should always feel as if we owed them an apology, and we should say to them, "We cannot help it; somehow or other we have got to be endowed; pray forgive us and bear with us, for ours is an anomalous position; we feel that we are doing an injustice to you, and we are sorry for it." That is how we should feel; and because our denominations are inferior in number, taken one by one, to the Church of England, I think it all the more unjust. There is an island of the Turks out yonder in the sea which contains a certain number of white persons who all go to church, a number of brown persons who are all Wesleyans, and a larger number of black persons who are all Baptists. As far as my observation goes, it is very much the same thing here. The white people, the very respectable ones, go to church; the next grade, to the Wesleyans; and the very black people belong to the Baptists. Now, it would seem to me to be an injustice that there should be an endowment in Turk's Island for the support of the religion of the whites, who are those who have the most money, and, therefore, could support their own religion, while the black man and the brown man receive nothing from the national treasury. If you endow any people, let the weaker brethren have it. Surely, if there were any justice in it there would be a kind of chivalry about the matter; but for a sect that numbers nearly all the lords and the great people of the land to come to the treasury to take gold out of it − ah! where can be the justice of this?

And because we do not want our nation to go on perpetrating what is certainly a grievous bodily wrong − the denial of religious equality to us all − therefore we must lift up our voices. If we were quietly to endure it, we should be accomplices in the wrong; we must speak and continue to speak until that wrong is redressed. The union of the Church with the State causes, before all the world, a misrepresentation of what the Church is. It always must be so. I dare say the Church of England is as fair a representation of the Church of Christ as could very well be produced under the circumstances. But look at its membership. Who are members of the Church? I am one. We are all members of it. I have been informed that I am a non-attending member, an outside member. All Englishmen are said to be members of the National Church, and they are treated as such. Did Christ ever mean to set forth to the world that his Church really was everybody born within a certain district? I had thought there were some hedges for his fields; that there was a sort of division between his spiritual kingdoms and the kingdoms of this world. But where is discipline? Is discipline possible? Let it be attempted. It has been attempted bravely here and there, if not wisely; but it cannot be carried out. How can it be? You are brought and made members of Christ, children of God, while you are yet unconscious of it. You take those solemn vows upon your-selves at certain periods, and you are all of you, whatever your character may be, members of this great National Church. I say that is a misrepresentation altogether of the church of Christ. To me one of the most sorrowful things is, that in this Church Jesus Christ is practically dethroned. First, by name; for who – it is no fault of hers, God bless her! – who is the head of the English Church? Who is declared to be so?

Then to whom do we refer if we want to know whether this practice is right to not? What is the statute book of the Church? Is it the Bible? No, sirs; it is a book that was made by human, uninspired hands. Ay, and above that, is the Parliament of Great Britain and Ireland, made up of a great many sorts of people, "all honourable men." It seems to me that to ask Parliament what I am to do, if I am Christ's servant, is to be disloyal at once to my Lord. He has given me his statute book, and if I do not understand it I must seek his enlightening spirit by prayer. But to go down to the House of Commons to ask those gentlemen about it! I would ask them about a great many things, but certainly not about religion. . . . The Church must be free, and Christ must be her sole Master, cost what it may, in England, Scotland, and everywhere else.

# Chapter 33

# Joseph Arch (1826–1919)

## Autobiography (1898)

Joseph Arch was a leading figure in the British trade union movement during its for-
mative years. An itinerant laborer for the first forty years of his working life, he came
increasingly to the view that workers could only improve their conditions through com-
bining, and in 1872 delivered a speech to a group of laborers which led to the forma-
tion of the National Agricultural Labourers' Union. Arch then played a leading role in
this union, at one time one of the most influential in the country, but later devoted more
of his energies to politics and served twice as a Liberal Member of Parliament.

   Like some of the Tolpuddle labourers and other pioneers of the trade union movement, Arch was a lay preacher of the Primitive Methodist Connexion, with little sympathy for established religion. The first extract graphically describes how this attitude
developed while he was still young, though the hostility of some Anglican bishops
toward his union in its early days would have done little to improve his temper
toward their Church in his later life (though he did receive very public support from
the Roman Catholic Archbishop of Westminster, Cardinal Manning). The second
extract is Arch's account of the events of that day in February 1872 when, like a
latter-day Moses, he prepared to lead his oppressed comrades out from their Egypt.

## Source

Joseph Arch (ed. John Gerard O'Leary), *The Autobiography of Joseph Arch*, London:
MacGibbon & Kee, 1966, pp. 25–6, 42–4.

## Further reading

R. Palmer, *The Painful Plough: Portrait of the Agricultural Labourer in the Nineteenth Century
   from Folksongs, Ballards and Contemporary Accounts*, Cambridge: Cambridge University
   Press, 1972.

P. Horn, *Joseph Arch (1826–1919): the Farmworkers' Leader*, Kineton: Roundwood, 1971.
Bob Scarth, *Well All Be Union Men: the Story of Joseph Arch and his Union*, Coventry: Industrial Pioneer Publications, 1998.

## From *Autobiography*

With bowed head and bended knee the poor learned to receive from the rich what was only their due, had they but known it. Years of poverty had ground the spirit of independence right out of them; these wives and mothers were tamed by poverty, they were cowed by it, as their parents had been before them in many cases, and the spirit of servitude was bred in their very bones. And the worst of it was the mischief did not stop at the women – it never does. They set an example of spiritless submission, which their children were only too inclined to follow. Follow it too many of them did, and they and their children are reaping the consequences and paying the price of it today.

I can remember when the squire and the other local magnates used to sit in state in the centre of the aisle. They did not, if you please, like the look of the agricultural labourers. Hodge sat too near them, and even in his Sunday best he was an offence to their eyes. They also objected to Hodge looking at them, so they had curtains put up to hide them from the vulgar gaze. And yet, while all this was going on, while the poor had to bear with such high-handed dealings, people wondered why the Church had lost its hold, and continued to lose its hold, on the labourers in the country districts! It never had any hold on me – in that, I was my mother's son also. I never took the Communion in the parish church in my life. When I was seven years old I saw something which prevented me once for all. One Sunday my father was going to stop to take the Communion, and I, being a boy, had of course to go out before it began. I may here mention that the church door opened then in a direct line with the chancel and the main aisle, so that anybody looking through the keyhole could easily see what was going on inside. The door is now more to the side of the church, and out of direct line with the chancel. I was a little bit of a fellow, and curious. I said to myself, 'What does father stop behind for? What is it they do? I'll see.' So I went out of church, closed the door, placed by eye at the keyhole and peeped through, and what I saw will be engraved on my mind until the last day of my life. That sight caused a wound which has never been healed. My proud little spirit smarted and burned when I saw what happened at that Communion service.

First, up walked the squire to the communion rails; the farmers went up next; then up went the tradesmen, the shopkeepers, the wheelwright, and the blacksmith; and then, the very last of all, went the poor agricultural labourers in their smock frocks. They walked up by themselves; nobody else knelt with them; it was as if they were unclean – and at that sight the iron entered straight into my poor little heart and remained fast embedded there. I said to myself, 'If that's what goes on – never for me!' I ran home and told my mother what I had seen, and I wanted to know why my father was not as good in the eyes of God as the squire, and why the poor should be forced to come up last of all to the table of the Lord. My mother gloried in my spirit . . .

The day was 7th February, 1872. It was a very wet morning, and I was busy at home on a carpentering job; I was making a box. My wife came in to me and said, 'Joe, here's three men come to see you. What for, I don't know.' But I knew fast enough. In walked the three; they turned out to be labourers from over Wellesbourne way. I stopped work, and we had a talk. They said they had come to ask me to hold a meeting at Wellesbourne that evening. They wanted to get the men together, and start a Union directly. I told them that, if they did form a Union, they would have to fight hard for it, and they would have to suffer a great deal; both they and their families. They said the labourers were prepared both to fight and suffer. Things could not be worse; wages were so low, and provisions were so dear, that nothing but downright starvation lay before them unless the farmers could be made to raise their wages. Asking was of no use; it was nothing but waste of breath; so they must join together and strike, and hold out till the employers gave in. When I saw that the men were in dead earnest, and had counted the cost and were determined to stand shoulder to shoulder till they could squeeze a living wage out of their employers, and that they were the spokesmen of others likeminded with themselves, I said I would address the meeting that evening at 7 o'clock. I told them that I had left nine shillings a week behind me years ago, and as I had got out of the ditch myself, I was ready and willing to help them out too. I said, 'If you are ready to combine, I will run all risk and come over and help you.'

I remember that evening, as if it were but yesterday. When I set out I was dressed in a pair of cord trousers, and cord vest, and an old flannel-jacket. I have that jacket at home now, and I put a high value on it. As I tramped along the wet, muddy road to Wellesbourne my heart was stirred within me, and questions passed through my mind and troubled me. Was it a false start, a sort of hole-and-corner movement, which would come to nothing, and do more harm to the men than good? If a Union were fairly set afoot, would the farmers prove too strong for it?

When I reached Wellesbourne, lo, and behold, it was as lively as a swarm of bees in June. We settled that I should address the meeting under the old chestnut tree; and I expected to find some thirty or forty of the principal men there. What then was my surprise to see not a few tens but many hundreds of labourers assembled; there were nearly two thousand of them. The news that I was going to speak that night had been spread about; and so the men had come in from all the villages round within a radius of ten miles. Not a circular had been sent out nor a handbill printed, but from cottage to cottage, and from farm to farm, the word had been passed on; and here were the labourers gathered together in their hundreds. Wellesbourne village was there, every man in it; and they had come from Moreton and Locksley and Charlecote and Hampton Lucy, and from Barford, to hear what I had to say to them. By this time the night had fallen pitch dark; but the men got bean poles and hung lanterns on them, and we could see well enough. It was an extraordinary sight, and I shall never forget it, not to my dying day. I mounted an old pig-stool, and in the flickering light of the lanterns I saw the earnest upturned faces of these poor brothers of mine – faces gaunt with hunger and pinched with want – all looking towards me and ready to listen to the words, that would fall from my lips. These white slaves of England stood there with the darkness all about them, like the Children of Israel waiting for someone to lead them out of the land of Egypt. I determined that, if they made a mistake and took the wrong turning, it would not be my fault, so I stood on my pig-stool and spoke out straight and strong for Union. My speech lasted about an hour, I believe, but I was not measuring minutes then. By the end of it the men were properly roused, and they pressed in and crowded up asking questions; they regularly pelted me with them; it was a perfect hailstorm. We passed a resolution to form a Union then and there, and the names of the men could not be taken down fast enough; we enrolled between two and three hundred members that night. It was a brave start, and before we parted it was arranged that there should be another meeting at the same place in a fortnight's time. I knew now that a fire had been kindled which would catch on, and spread, and run abroad like sparks in stubble; and I felt certain that this night we had set light to a beacon, which would prove a rallying point for the agricultural labourers throughout the country.

# Chapter 34

# Henry Scott Holland (1847–1918)

## Our Neighbours **(1911)**

Scott Holland is a leading figure in the Christian socialist tradition in Britain. Heavily influenced by Ruskin, he developed an interest in social questions while a don at Oxford in the 1870s, and formed the Christian Social Union in 1889. From a privileged background, Holland worked in inner city parishes in London and developed a passionate concern for the poor. Though contemporary critics – and some of its leading members – saw the CSU as less "socialist" than "social," Holland wrote of Socialism as an ideal to be worked towards, and advocated a role for the state in helping to bring about a more caring society.

In *Our Neighbours: A Handbook for the CSU*, Holland emphasizes the Christian duty of neighborliness, redefining "our neighbors" as those in society who enable us to live, work, and eat. In the final chapter, from which this extract is taken, he considers two kinds of poverty, that "of spirit," which he views in wholly positive terms, and the material poverty found in unjust societies. This latter is an insult to God and an obstacle to the coming of Kingdom.

## Source

Henry Scott Holland, *Our Neighbours: A Handbook for the C.S.U.*, London and Oxford, 1911.

## Further reading

Alan Wilkinson, *Christian Socialism: From Scott Holland to Tony Blair*, London, 1998.
Chris Bryant, *Possible Dreams*, London, 1996.

## From *Our Neighbours*

And then we turn, more sick and weary of heart than ever, to remember the other Poverty, which is so bitterly familiar to us – the Poverty which our Lord never saw – the Poverty which we, with our advanced civilisation, with our unlimited abundance, with our wicked wealth, have, in these last days, created to be our terror and our shame. The Poverty of a London or a Birmingham Slum! Does that form the best preparation for the Kingdom of Heaven? Is that the soil in which the soul finds its finest freedom and its growth? Is that the condition in which our noblest manhood ripens into flower? Is it there that man comes to his full strength, and wins his supreme nobility, and discloses a secret fount of moral dignity and austere grace?

We are not going to deny the miracles which grace can work in spite of all that we can do to hinder it. Jesus can find His own, can heal and save, anywhere and everywhere – even in these disastrous streets of ours. But these miracles are not to disguise from us the real nature of the facts which they defy. We have, in our Slum Cities, manufactured a Poverty which, instead of bracing and disciplining our manhood into higher service, tends only to maim and stunt and discredit and degrade it. Here are Poor who, far from discovering their true selves through the pressure of their poverty, find in it a cloud which for ever hides them from themselves. It loads them down. It overrides. It oppresses. It drains them of their native force. It lowers their vitality. It impoverishes the blood. It allows them no room to breathe, to grow, to expand. It gives no time for spiritual interests. It chokes back the religious instincts. It offers no opportunities for the play of the higher energies. They are too tired to think, or to read, or to pray.

And, then, their life, far from being plain and simple, is hopelessly insecure. It can never anticipate what will happen on the morrow. It is casual, shifting, feckless, disorganised, by sheer necessity. It is charged with alarm lest it find itself workless and penniless, it cannot tell when or why. It has no hold whatever over the forces with which it labours to co-operate. It cannot tell, from moment to moment, what they will do; whether they will still allow its chance of winning a daily pittance; or whether they will mysteriously retire, and leave it impotent, and broken, and miserable. It cannot look before or after; and, therefore, cannot exercise the distinctive privilege of manhood. It lives permanently below the level at which human life begins. Everything about it proclaims to it its own worthlessness. It does not count in men's eyes. For, indeed, it has no value. It contributes no particular skill. It is hopelessly overcrowded. Its market is overstocked. It has no position; no reputation. No one cares what it does, or how it fares. The enormous city labours on at its task, without any regard for it. If it dropped out, no one would mind or notice. So our Poor live. There are acres upon acres of our cities filled with such as these.

And do we suppose that Jesus Christ has laid His Blessing on this unholy Poverty? Do we really imagine that this is what He had in His eye, as He pronounced the Benediction? Nay! This is the Poverty which blights and curses. This is the Poverty which God hates. This is the Poverty which is an outrage on man, and an insult to God. Far from accepting it as a preparation for the Kingdom of Heaven, we have, in the name of that Kingdom, to demand that it be swept off the face of the earth and be never again seen. For, indeed, it wars against the coming of that Kingdom. It robs men and women, who fall under its degradation, of the power or leisure to exercise the faculties by which the Kingdom can be recognised. It forbids them the opportunity of responding to its call. It keeps them down below the level of that spiritual growth, which would feel after the Kingdom, and would foretell its arrival. It preoccupies the soul with the burden of physical necessities, and with the terror of their failing. It means, so far as it can work its evil will, spiritual impotence; death.

And, therefore, we have but one duty towards it – to learn, by steady patient study, how best to do away with it – to cancel its right to exist – to sweep its place clean. It is a type of Poverty which cannot be justified or tolerated, by a Society that names the name of Jesus Christ. For it wrecks the body, and lowers the life, and kills the soul. We may not rest, until we have found out how to heal and end it.

After all, Jesus did not intend to perpetuate even the Poverty that He blessed. He did not say 'Blessed are the Poor! [Luke 6:20] – therefore keep them poor,' any more than He said, 'Blessed are the hungry; therefore let them remain hungry.' Nay! Let their hunger cease; let them be filled! That is their blessing. Hunger is only blessed because it leads to being filled. Mourning is only blessed, because it is on the way to be comforted. The best of Poverties, the blessed Poverty, is to find its blessing in the riches of the Kingdom of Heaven.

How much more, then, is that evil Poverty, that wicked Poverty, that fatal Poverty, which withholds from the Kingdom – to cease and disappear? Herein lies our task, the special task of Social Reform. You are asked, in the name of Him who loved the Poor, to commit yourselves to an internecine war against that Poverty which mercilessly caricatures those whom He loved – that Poverty which soils and discredits the Cause which He made sacred – that Poverty which curses those whom He blessed.

# Chapter 35

# Padraig Pearse (1879–1916)

The Fool
The Rebel

Padraig Henry Pearse was the founder of the Irish Citizen Army and the leader of the Easter Rising who read the proclamation of the Republic outside the General Post Office on Easter Monday, 1916. He passionately believed in a righteous revolution to free Ireland. Pearse formulated a doctrine built upon the Gaelic legends and history. He enunciated the ideas of new "resurrection" in Ireland from his nationalistic faith. He was the first leader of the Rising to be executed, and was shot in the early hours of May 3. To succeed by failure was Pearse's way of imitating his Christ.

Pearse was socialist in principle, if not party membership. The 1916 proclamation reflects all his main concerns, with some given a more leftward slant by James Connolly, a Christian Marxist who should be mentioned alongside Pearse. In *Labour, Nationality and Religion* Connolly cites the advocacy of common ownership in the patristic writings and argues that economic oppression of the Jewish people in the first century CE accounted for their prayers for the promised liberator, with whose experience and that of the early Christian communities the Irish people shared many parallel experiences.

Sources

Pádraic H. Pearse, *Collected Works – Plays, Stories and Poems*, Dublin, 1917.

Further reading

James Connolly, *Labour, Nationality and Religion*, Dublin: The Harp Library, 1910.
Martin F. X. (ed.), *Leaders and Men of the Easter Rising – Dublin 1916*, London, 1967.

Moran, Seán Farrell: *Patrick Pearse and the Politics of Redemption: the Mind of the Easter Rising, 1916*, Washington, D.C.: Catholic University of America Press, 1994.

Murphy, Brian P., *Patrick Pearse and the Lost Republican Ideal*, Dublin: James Duffy, 1991.

Morgan, Austen, *James Connolly – a Political Biography*, Manchester: Manchester University Press, 1989.

## The Fool

SINCE the wise men have not spoken, I speak that am only a fool;
A fool that hath loved his folly,
Yea, more than the wise men their books or their counting houses or their quiet homes,
Or their fame in men's mouths;
A fool that in all his days hath done never a prudent thing,
Never hath counted the cost nor recked if another reaped
The fruit of his mighty sowing, content to scatter the seed;
A fool that is unrepentant, and that soon at the end of all
Shall laugh in his lonely heart as the ripe ears fall to the reaping hooks
And the poor are filled that were empty
Tho' he go hungry.

I have squandered the splendid years that the Lord God gave to my youth
In attempting impossible things, deeming them alone worthy the toil.
Was it folly or grace? Not men shall judge me, but God.
I have squandered the splendid years:
Lord, if I had the years I would squander them over again,
Aye, fling them from me!
For this I have heard in my heart, that a man shall scatter, not hoard,
Shall do the deed of today, nor take thought of tomorrow's teen,
Shall not bargain nor huxter with God; or was it a jest of Christ's
And is this my sin before men, to have taken Him at his word?
The lawyers have sat in council, the men with the keen long faces,
    said, "This man is a fool," and others have said, "He blasphemeth;"
And the wise have pitied the fool that hath striven to give a life
In the world of time and space amongst the bulks of actual things,
To a dream that was dreamed in the heart, and that only the heart could hold.

O wise men, riddle me this: what if the dream come true?
What if the dream come true? And if millions unborn shall dwell
In the house that I shaped in my heart, the noble house of my thought?
Lord, I have staked my soul, I have staked the lives of my kin
On the truth of Thy dreadful word. Do not remember my failures,
But remember this my faith.

## The Rebel

I am come of the seed of the people, the people that sorrow,
That have no treasure but hope,
No riches laid up but a memory
Of an Ancient glory.
My mother bore me in bondage, in bondage my mother was born,
I am of the blood of serfs;
The children with whom I have played, the men and women with whom I have
    eaten,
Have had masters over them, have been under the lash of masters,
And, though gentle, have served churls;
The hands that have touched mine, the dear hands whose touch is familiar to me,
Have worn shameful manacles, have been bitten at the wrist by manacles,
Have grown hard with the manacles and the task-work of strangers,
I am flesh of the flesh of these lowly, I am bone of their bone,
I that have never submitted;
I that have a soul greater than the souls of my people's masters,
I that have vision and prophecy and the gift of fiery speech,
I that have spoken with God on the top of His holy hill.

And because I am of the people, I understand the people,
I am sorrowful with their sorrow, I am hungry with their desire:
My heart has been heavy with the grief of mothers,
My eyes have been wet with the tears of children,
I have yearned with old wistful men,
And laughed or cursed with young men;
Their shame is my shame, and I have reddened for it,
Reddened for that they have served, they who should be free,
Reddened for that they have gone in want, while others have been full,
Reddened for that they have walked in fear of lawyers and of their jailors
With their writs of summons and their handcuffs,
Men mean and cruel!
I could have borne stripes on my body rather than this shame of my people.

And now I speak, being full of vision;
I speak to my people, and I speak in my people's name to the masters of my people.
I say to my people that they are holy, that they are august, despite their chains,
That they are greater than those that hold them, and stronger and purer,
That they have but need of courage, and to call on the name of their God,
God the unforgetting, the dear God that loves the peoples
For whom He died naked, suffering shame.
And I say to my people's masters: Beware,
Beware of the thing that is coming, beware of the risen people,
Who shall take what ye would not give. Did ye think to conquer the people,
Or that Law is stronger than life and than men's desire to be free?
We will try it out with you, ye that have harried and held,
Ye that have bullied and bribed, tyrants, hypocrites, liars!

# Chapter 36

# Frank Weston (1871–1924)

**Address to the Second Anglo-Catholic Congress (1923)**

The 1920s saw the Anglo-Catholic movement very much in the ascendancy in the Church of England, and its second congress, held in London in July 1923, attracted some 16,000 participants. Weston, who had been Bishop of Zanzibar since 1908, chaired all the sessions and gave the closing address, of which this is an extract. The themes of the Congress were "God above us," "God with us" and "God in us," and Weston considered what his hearers should do in response to this formulation of the faith. This extract appears during a reflection on the presence of Christ in the Blessed Sacrament and the need for devotion to Christ in the tabernacle.

Weston's sermon is characteristic of the concern for social and economic justice at the heart of the Anglo-Catholic tradition (cf. Kenneth Leech in this volume, p. 327). Many leading figures in the Christian Socialist movement were drawn from this tradition, and words similar to Weston's appear in the sermons of, for instance, Archbishop William Temple. Weston was to die the year following the Congress, but one offshoot of his challenge to "look for Jesus in the ragged and naked" was the Anglo-Catholic Summer Schools of Sociology, which explored the Christian doctrine of society.

Source

H. Maynard Smith, *Frank, Bishop of Zanzibar: the life of Frank Weston*, London: SPCK, 1928, p. 302.

Further reading

Adrian Hastings, *A History of English Christianity 1920–2000*, London, 2001.
Alec Vidler, *Scenes From A Clerical Life*, London, 1977.

## From the Address to the Second Anglo-Catholic Congress (1923)

But I say to you, and I say it with all the earnestness that I have, if you are pre-pared to fight for the right of adoring Jesus in His Blessed Sacrament, then, when you come out from before your tabernacles, you must walk with Christ, mystically present in you, through the streets of this country, and find the same Christ in the peoples of your cities and villages. You cannot claim to worship Jesus in the taber-nacle if you do not pity Jesus in the slum. . . . It is folly, it is madness, to suppose that you can worship Jesus in the Sacrament and Jesus on the throne of glory, when you are sweating Him in the bodies and souls of His children. . . . You have your Mass, you have your altars, you have begun to get your tabernacles. Now go out into the highways and hedges, and look for Jesus in the ragged and the naked, in the oppressed and the sweated, in those who have lost hope, and in those who are struggling to make good. Look for Jesus in them; and, when you have found Him, gird yourself with His towel of fellowship and wash His feet in the person of His brethren.

# Chapter 37

# *The Barmen Declaration* (1934)

This was drawn up, much influenced by Karl Barth, at the synod of the Confessing Church at Barmen in 1934 to define the doctrine of the church in the face of the compromises with the Third Reich. The Confessing Church resisted the tendency of the "German Christians" to allow the church to become an instrument of the policy of the Third Reich.

## Source

http://www.medg.lcs.mit.edu/doyle/personal/enters/hermann/declaration.html

## Further reading

Arthur C. Cochrane, *The Church's Confession Under Hitler*, Philadelphia: Westminster Press, 1962, pp. 237–42.
P. Matheson, *The Third Reich and the Christian Churches*, Edinburgh: T&T Clark, 1981.
K. Scholder, *The Churches and the Third Reich*, London: SCM Press, 1977–8.
T. Gorringe, *Karl Barth: Against Hegemony*, Oxford: Oxford University Press, 1999.

### *The Barmen Declaration* (1934)

IN VIEW OF THE ERRORS of the "German Christians" and of the present Reich Church Administration, which are ravaging the Church and at the same time also shattering the unity of the German Evangelical Church, we confess the following evangelical truths:

1.  "I am the Way and the Truth and the Life; no one comes to the Father except through me." John 14:6

"Very truly, I tell you, anyone who does not enter the sheepfold through the gate but climbs in by another way is a thief and a bandit. I am the gate. Whoever enters by me will be saved." John 10:1, 9

Jesus Christ, as he is attested to us in Holy Scripture, is the one Word of God whom we have to hear, and whom we have to trust and obey in life and in death.

We reject the false doctrine that the Church could and should recognize as a source of its proclamation, beyond and besides this one Word of God, yet other events, powers, historic figures and truths as God's revelation.

2.   "Jesus Christ has been made wisdom and righteousness and sanctification and redemption for us by God." 1 Cor. 1:30

As Jesus Christ is God's comforting pronouncement of the forgiveness of all our sins, so, with equal seriousness, he is also God's vigorous announcement of his claim upon our whole life. Through him there comes to us joyful liberation from the godless ties of this world for free, grateful service to his creatures.

We reject the false doctrine that there could be areas of our life in which we would not belong to Jesus Christ but to other lords, areas in which we would not need justification and sanctification through him.

3.   "Let us, however, speak the truth in love, and in every respect grow into him who is the head, into Christ, from whom the whole body is joined together." Eph. 4:15–16

The Christian Church is the community of brethren in which, in Word and sacrament, through the Holy Spirit, Jesus Christ acts in the present as Lord. With both its faith and its obedience, with both its message and its order, it has to testify in the midst of the sinful world, as the Church of pardoned sinners, that it belongs to him alone and lives and may live by his comfort and under his direction alone, in expectation of his appearing.

We reject the false doctrine that the Church could have permission to hand over the form of its message and of its order to whatever it itself might wish or to the vicissitudes of the prevailing ideological and political convictions of the day.

4.   "You know that the rulers of the Gentiles lord it over them, and their great ones are tyrants over them. It will not be so among you; but whoever wishes to have authority over you must be your servant." Matt. 20:25–26

The various offices in the Church do not provide a basis for some to exercise authority over others but for the ministry [lit., "service"] with which the whole community has been entrusted and charged to be carried out.

We reject the false doctrine that, apart from this ministry, the Church could, and could have permission to, give itself or allow itself to be given special leaders [Führer] vested with ruling authority.

5.   "Fear God. Honor the Emperor." 1 Pet. 2:17

Scripture tells us that by divine appointment the State, in this still unredeemed world in which also the Church is situated, has the task of maintaining justice and peace, so far as human discernment and human ability make this possible, by means of the threat and use of force. The Church acknowledges with gratitude and reverence toward God the benefit of this, his appointment. It draws attention to God's Dominion [Reich], God's commandment and justice, and with these the responsibility of those who rule and those who are ruled. It trusts and obeys the power of the Word, by which God upholds all things.

We reject the false doctrine that beyond its special commission the State should and could become the sole and total order of human life and so fulfil the vocation of the Church as well.

We reject the false doctrine that beyond its special commission the Church should and could take on the nature, tasks and dignity which belong to the State and thus become itself an organ of the State.

6.   "See, I am with you always, to the end of the age." Matt. 28:20 "God's Word is not fettered." 2 Tim. 2:9

The Church's commission, which is the foundation of its freedom, consists in this: in Christ's stead, and so in the service of his own Word and work, to deliver all people, through preaching and sacrament, the message of the free grace of God.

We reject the false doctrine that with human vainglory the Church could place the Word and work of the Lord in the service of self-chosen desires, purposes and plans.

The Confessing Synod of the German Evangelical Church declares that it sees in the acknowledgment of these truths and in the rejection of these errors the indispensable theological basis of the German Evangelical Church as a confederation of Confessing Churches. It calls upon all who can stand in solidarity with its Declaration to be mindful of these theological findings in all their decisions concerning Church and State. It appeals to all concerned to return to unity in faith, hope and love.

> Verbum Dei manet in aeternum.
> The Word of God lasts for ever.

# Chapter 38

# Dorothy Day (1897–1980)

## The Long Loneliness and other writings by Dorothy Day and Peter Maurin

Dorothy Day was the founder, along with Peter Maurin of the Catholic Worker movement. This movement, which began in 1933 first with the launch of the *Catholic
Worker* newspaper and then with the opening of a house of hospitality, has as its aims
living out the radical social implications of the gospel. Dorothy Day and her coworkers
took an option for the poor, living out their faith in voluntary poverty and community
among the forgotten people of New York society. Dorothy Day was committed not just
to charitable work but to solidarity with the weak, oppressed and marginalized, which
involved challenging the actions and attitudes of the principalities and powers. Her traditional theology, radical social engagement, and pacifist stand were rooted in the
gospel, and in Jesus who was to be found in the person of the poor and the outcast,
as Matthew 25:31ff indicates. Today there are more than a hundred Catholic Worker
communities mainly in North America but also in Europe and Australia.

## Sources

D. Day, *The Long Loneliness*, New York: HarperCollins, 1952.

D. Day, *By Little and By Little. The Selected Writings of Dorothy Day*, edited by Robert
Ellsberg, A. Knopf, 1983, pp. 293–5.

P. Maurin, *Easy Essays*, Franciscan Press, 1977, pp. 9–10.

Editorials of *The Catholic Worker*, February 1940, June 1946.

## Further reading

James Wm. McClendon Jr., *Systematic Theology. Ethics*, Nashville, Abingdon, 1986, especially
   pp. 278–99.

## From *The Long Loneliness* and other writings, by Dorothy Day and Peter Maurin

Dorothy Day wrote in her autobiography *The Long Loneliness* of the beginnings of the Catholic Worker movement of which she and Peter Maurin were co-founders:

> We were just sitting there when Peter Maurin came in.
> We were just sitting there when lines of people began to form, saying, "We need bread." We could not say, "Go, be thou filled." If there were six small loaves and a few fishes, we had to divide them. There was always bread.
> We were just sitting there talking and people moved in on us. Let those who can take it, take it. Some moved out and that made room for more. And somehow the walls expanded.
> We were just sitting there and someone said, "Let's all go live on a farm."
> It was as casual as that, I often think. It just came about. It just happened . . .
> It all happened while we sat there talking, and it is still going on.

The following two extracts are taken from editorials of *The Catholic Worker*, the paper of the New York Catholic Worker house. The paper was first sold on May Day 1933 on Union Square during a Communist Party rally for a penny a copy. The price is still the same today!

Dorothy Day writes of the "Aims and Purposes" of the Catholic Worker movement (February 1940):

> The vision is this. We are working for "a new heaven and a new *earth*, wherein justice dwelleth." We are trying to say with action, "Thy will be done on *earth* as it is in heaven." We are working for a Christian social order.
> We believe in the brotherhood of man and the Fatherhood of God. This teaching, the doctrine of the Mystical Body of Christ, involves today the issue of unions (where men call each other brothers); it involves the racial question; it involves cooperatives, credit unions, crafts; it involves Houses of Hospitality and farming communes. It is with all these means that we can live as though we believed indeed that we are all members one of another, knowing that when "the health of one member suffers, the health of the whole body is lowered."
> This work of ours toward a new heaven and a new earth shows a correlation between the material and the spiritual, and, of course, recognizes the primacy of the spiritual. Food for the body is not enough. There must be food for the soul. Hence the leaders of the work, and as many as we can induce to join us, must go daily to Mass, to receive food for the soul. And as our perceptions are quickened, and as we pray that our faith be increased, we will see Christ in each other, and we will not lose faith in those around us, no matter how stumbling their progress is. It is easier to have faith that God will support each House of Hospitality and farming commune and supply our needs in the way of food and money to pay bills, than it is to keep a strong, hearty, living faith in each individual around us – to see Christ in him. If we lose faith, if we stop the work of indoctrinating, we are in a way denying Christ again.
> We must practice the presence of God. He said that when two or three are gathered together, there He is in the midst of them. He is with us in our kitchens, at

our tables, on our breadlines, with our visitors, on our farms. When we pray for our material needs, it brings us close to His humanity. He, too, needed food and shelter, He, too, warmed His hands at a fire and lay down in a boat to sleep.

When we have spiritual reading at meals, when we have the rosary at night, when we have study groups, forums, when we go out to distribute literature at meetings, or sell it on street corners, Christ is there with us. What we do is very little. But it is like the little boy with a few loaves and fishes. Christ took that little and increased it. He will do the rest. What we do is so little we may seem to be constantly failing. But so did He fail. He met with apparent failure on the Cross. But unless the seed fall into the earth and die, there is no harvest.

And why must we see results? Our work is to sow. Another generation will be reaping the harvest.

Under the heading "Love is the Measure" Dorothy Day writes (June 1946):

What we would like to do is change the world – make it a little simpler for people to feed, clothe, and shelter themselves as God intended them to do. And to a certain extent, by fighting for better conditions, by crying out unceasingly for the rights of the workers, of the poor, of the destitute – the rights of the worthy and the unworthy poor, in other words – we can to a certain extent change the world; we can work for the oasis, the little cell of joy and peace in a harried world. We can throw our pebble in the pond and be confident that its ever-widening circle will reach around the world.

We repeat, there is nothing that we can do but love, and dear God – please enlarge our hearts to love each other, to love our neighbor, to love our enemy as well as our friend.

## This Money Is Not Ours

A principle, Dorothy believed, remains abstract until it costs us something. In 1961, she welcomed the opportunity to test the value of one of her convictions in a gesture of disarming originality. The cost was $3,579.39.

For years *The Catholic Worker* had repeated Peter Maurin's defense of the medieval ban on usury. The acceptance of the belief that value resides in currency rather than labor, he believed, was a turning point in the transition from a functional to an acquisitive society. The Catholic Worker could not single-handedly reverse this process, but it could at least issue a solitary protest, and make what Peter would call a "point."

*The Catholic Worker*
*39 Spring Street*
*New York 12, N.Y.*
*July 1960*

*Treasurer*
*City of New York*

Dear sir:

We are returning to you a check for $3,579.39 which represents interest on the $68,700 which we were awarded by the city as payment for the property at 223

Chrystie Street which we owned and lived in for almost ten years, and used as a community for the poor. We did not voluntarily give up the property – it was taken from us by right of eminent domain for the extension of the subway which the city deemed necessary. We had to wait almost a year and a half for the money owed us, although the city permitted us to receive two-thirds of the assessed valuation of the property in advance so that we could relocate. Property owning having been made impossible for us by city regulations, we are now renting and continuing our work.

We are returning the interest on the money we have recently received because we do not believe in "money lending" at interest. As Catholics we are acquainted with the early teaching of the Church. All the early councils forbade it, declaring it reprehensible to make money by lending it out at interest. Canon law of the Middle Ages forbade it and in various decrees ordered that profit so obtained was to be restored. In the Christian emphasis on the duty of charity, we are commanded to lend gratuitously, to give freely, even in the case of confiscation, as in our own case – not to resist but to accept cheerfully.

We do not believe in the profit system, and so we cannot take profit or interest on our money. People who take a materialistic view of human service wish to make a profit but we are trying to do our duty by our service without wages to our brothers as Jesus commanded in the Gospel (Matthew 25). Loaning money at interest is deemed by one Franciscan as the principal scourge of civilization. Eric Gill, the English artist and writer, calls usury and war the two great problems of our time.

Since we have dealt with these problems in every issue of *The Catholic Worker* since 1933 – man's freedom, war and peace, man and the state, man and his work – and since Scripture says that the love of money is the root of all evil, we are taking this opportunity to live in practice of this belief, and make a gesture of overcoming that love of money by returning to you the interest.

Insofar as our money paid for services for the common good, and aid to the poor, we should be very happy to allow you to use not only our money without interest, but also our work, the Works of Mercy which we all perform here at the headquarters of *The Catholic Worker* without other salary or recompense than our daily food and lodging, clothes, and incidental expenses.

Insofar as the use of our money paid for the time being for salaries for judges who have condemned us and others to jail, and for the politicians who appointed them, and for prisons, and the execution chamber at Sing Sing, and for the executioner's salary, we can only protest the use of our money and turn with utter horror from taking interest on it.

Please also be assured that we are not judging individuals, but are trying to make a judgment on *the system* under which we live and with which we admit that we ourselves compromise daily in many small ways, but which we try and wish to withdraw from as much as possible.

Sincerely yours,
Dorothy Day, Editor

*September 1960*

## From Easy Essays, by Peter Maurin

*WHAT THE CATHOLIC WORKER BELIEVES*

> The Catholic Worker believes
> in the gentle personalism
> of traditional Catholicism.
> The Catholic Worker believes
> in the personal obligation
> of looking after
> the needs of our brother.
> The Catholic Worker believes
> in the daily practice
> of the Works of Mercy.
> The Catholic Worker believes
> in Houses of Hospitality
> for the immediate relief
> of those who are in need.
> The Catholic Worker believes
> in the establishment
> of Farming Communes
> where each one works
> according to his ability
> and gets
> according to his need.
> The Catholic Worker believes
> in creating a new society
> within the shell of the old
> with the philosophy of the new,
> which is not a new philosophy
> but a very old philosophy,
> a philosophy so old
> that it looks like new.

# Chapter 39

# The Worker–Priests

**Henri Perrin,** Priest and Worker **(1948)**
**John Rowe,** Wage-Workers in industry as an expression of
faith **(1965)**

In the annals of Christian history and mission, the stories of the original French and Belgium prêtres ouvriers (1944–54) remain among the most extraordinary accounts of Christian radicalism and politicization in the twentieth century.

During the Second World War, the Nazis refused to allow French priests to accompany workers deported to Germany as forced labour. A number of priests, however, some inspired by Fr Jacques Loew in Marseilles, who had donned overalls and gone to work in the docks, by the Abbé Godin's call to action in *France, pays de Mission?* and by other movements, went disguised as workers into the factories of the Third Reich. Those fortunate enough to survive the war (the less fortunate were caught and sent to concentration camps) returned, resolved to continue as worker-priests in factories, docks, and workshops all over France. Their intention was to live a life of complete solidarity with the workers, earning their own living and expressing the Christian gospel, as they saw it, through their human presence.

By 1949 the Holy Office had already grown concerned at what was happening. Despite a decree forbidding Catholics to have dealings with Communists many worker-priests were already deeply involved in the Communist-led Confédération Générale du Travail (CGT) union and in 1951 one priest actually became the full-time secretary of the metalworkers in Paris. Worker-priests also took part in the nationwide strikes in 1947 and again in 1950. Eventually, the Holy See, fearing that the true nature of priesthood was being compromised, forbade the practice to continue and the movement was officially brought to an end in March 1954 when religious were told to return to their orders and the clergy to parish work. Many simply refused to do so and carried on against the orders of their superiors even when the ban was reiterated in 1959.

Revived under Paul VI after Vatican II, many more joined the ranks in the mid-1960s. French and Belgium worker-priest have been credited with helping to bring

The editors are grateful to John Mantle for providing the material in this section.

about Vatican II and with being the precursors of later Latin-American radicalized clergy (Oscar Arnal, 1986). Beyond 2000 they recruit few into their ranks though this reflects the downturn in European vocations generally. The majority, now retired, continue their vocation working in local communities and are involved in a variety of social and political actions.

Henri Perrin, originally in training as a Jesuit, was one of the first to go to Germany in 1944; he was caught and returned to France where he later went to work in a Paris factory in the prints arrondissement XIII. In 1948 he wrote to friends:

> After a month spent getting my bearings, my factory life has been a slow and progressive revolt against the capitalist world. This began with the inhuman attitude of the manager, who inspects the workers as if they were a roomful of machines, and developed over questions of wages and production, women's work, and the union struggle – and the whole factory atmosphere in which workers have been bullied and exploited for a century. Over and above my personal reactions, I had those of the man on the ruling machine who has had forty years of working life. He is a fine type of skilled worker, conscientious, the sort of man I love and admire every bit as much as a scientist or a statesman. His conversation, which was infrequent, almost always embodied the revolt that has slowly accumulated in the heart of the working class. Whether because of the trivial fact that he has no 'right' to a snack between 7 in the morning and midday, or because his time and the organization of his production are controlled, the worker has become alienated in his work. He is not a man working with an engineer or a manager, but a productive ability that has been hired and has to be exploited to the maximum degree; he is not a man responsible for what he produces, but a hand who is valued only for his output. One of the most painful proofs of this lies in the habitual of raising the targets of production without a comparable increase in pay. To this must be added the intransigent attitude of the employers towards the workers organization, and the torpedoing of the worker committees, at which the workers' delegates are fobbed off with tales about hygiene, while they are denied any say in the management. Add to this the fact that the firm, far from being a community of men working together, is not even guided by a human sense of production, but by a shameless desire for profit and money . . . (Henri Perrin, *Priest and Worker*, London: Catholic Book Club, 1964, pp. 110–11).

Later, Perrin went to work at the construction site for the Isère-Arc dam, situated at the egress of the Pont-Seran Gorges at Notre-Dame-de-Briançon in Savoy. From there in May 1952 he wrote:

> life goes on the same at Isère-Arc. I'm always in the workshops doing hack jobs, which makes life tiring at times . . . I've managed to get union collectors and representatives appointed . . . (ibid., p. 195)

> On the whole, the work is going well, the rock is of good quality, the tunnel is progressing, the bonuses are fairly high. But there are daily rows about all kinds of things – taking men on, dismissing them, claims and so forth . . . (ibid., p. 195)

At the moment we are very disturbed by Government policy. For the first time, perhaps, we here are feeling direct repercussions of the policy pursued in Paris: unemployment, which is going to become serious in the coming months (the dams alone are going to release some thousands of workers in the region); the freezing of wages which might be revised in Savoy without formal orders from the Government to the prefects; the cessation of public works resulting from the fact that the national economy is bled white by war and rearmament; difficulties over foreigners' work permits, with the object of expelling them and thus camouflaging unemployment; the terrible problem of unemployed North Africans, who live clandestinely in the 'township' and queue up every day to be taken on and every day are turned away. This is not a question of party politics; we are up against serious human problems with deep influence on the lives of individuals. What is a Christian to think about a world which has ceased to even guarantee the right to work? Moreover, all the echoes that reach us here from outside make us feel we are in full 'reaction'. How shall we get out of it? (ibid., pp. 195–7)

Yet over and above the anguish of the general political situation and the demands made by life in the union, I am meeting men, with their difficulties and, as I discover every day, with their richness, their delicacy, their good will – and often crushed by a thousand circumstances for which God alone knows how responsible they are. Some day I would like to write a novel called the Children of God – of course I never shall! But the further I go and the more contact I make with men, the more sympathy I feel for them, and the more I discover possibilities which for most people would seem small indeed, but which are yet a manifestation of the Father's love. (ibid., pp. 110 and 196f)

Following demands that the worker-priests should stop work, Perrin, obviously distressed, sought a resolution to his own situation. In October 1954 however, on his way to an electrician's training course which his bishop had allowed him to start, he was killed, thrown from his motorcycle in an unexplained accident. Only twelve months earlier, on the news that the Papal Nuncio would intervene in the conference of French Bishops in Paris on 23 September 1953, the worker-priests of Paris drew up – in haste – a *Green Paper* (so-called simply because of its cover) which sought to clarify why they had become workers.

If today we are both priests and workers, unalterably and inseparably, it is to begin with because of a problem confronting the Church and our own priesthood. We set out for the factories with the encouragement, indeed the commission, of the Church, by way of answer to the absence of Christ from the millions of the proletariat, by way of answer to the rejections by the present forms of the Church of a whole world, the simplest and least endowed of all. It must not be forgotten that, whether or not of working-class origin, we have become workers, or returned to being workers, out of deep loyalty to this sacred appeal. To it we have given our entire life. . . .

... In fact the Church refuses to acknowledge this new working-class consciousness which we represent within her own midst, and refuses to allow us
to be what we are. . . .

Of course religious reasons are invoked for refusing to permit us to be what
we are . . . We are rejected-as working class is rejected by the established
system – because of our active participation in the workers struggle. Because
the Church – as respects the greater part of her members and her institutions
– is defending a system against which we in the company with the working
class, are struggling with all our might, because it is oppressive and unjust.
   We must be quite clear about this. The Church supports this system. Because
of her own conditions of existence, and because, in her institutions, she is mate-
rially bound to it, even in her most cherished endeavours.
   The condemnation of capitalism is only a matter of theory in the Church.
In practice the Church accepts capitalism thoroughly, and co-operates with it.
For a worker there is no doubt whatever about this. And for us, as for the
workers, acceptance of the system means support for it, even if, in words, one
takes up sides against the exploitation it represents. Class solidarity makes
demands like these. And we are not speaking of the support afforded by much
of the teaching, many of the political stands taken, many even of the silences
maintained by religious authorities . . . Is not the priest naturally inclined to
such things by his training, imbued as it is with bourgeois culture?
   We are told that we must accept the system as something relative, because
the church is incarnate, and lives now in the capitalist world just as she formerly
lived in the feudal world. But when people say that, they know full well – with,
by the way some little anxiety – that half of mankind has in practice rejected the
system, and that is already a grave defect in the Church universal to be restricted
to the dimensions of a minority system, a system on the way out, the more so
because even within the capitalist countries the vast mass of the proletariat has
already rejected in spirit this system whose victims they are.
   Feeling herself rejected along with the system, the church has taken fright
at the working class and the advent of the proletariat, with all the changes
which that would bring in institutions in the way of life and in the consciences
of men – more precisely because of the fear of Communism, which inspires this
upsurge of the proletariat and gives it its revolutionary force and its prospects
for the future.
   These, we think, are the essential reasons. But there are others. We fully understand that authority first of all invokes religious grounds for suppressing us. It is
authorities right and its duty. And it is hard to see, even if these religious grounds
are mixed, what others authority could put forward without stepping outside its
proper field. However that may be, there would, we are to suppose, be grave
dangers for the Church, for the faith, for our own priesthood, if we were left where
we are as we are . . .

There is fear lest we suffer 'Marxist contamination'. Now as one of us points out,
'The worker-priests are diocesan clergy or members of religious Orders. All have
had a training in philosophy, like all priests who go to the seminary. What then

are we to say to all those Christians the sum of whose training consists of learning the catechism for their first communion? Can we judge that for each of these workers the question of the faith arises is a less serious form, or is decided less important so far as concerns the salvation of the individual?'

We should, moreover, be gravely underrating the workers if we believed the conditions and the struggle of the working class to be incompatible with the faith and even with the priesthood. We should be underrating the nobility of labour and skill, and the magnitude of the injustices and sufferings borne by the working class, the grandeur of its revolts and its aspirations ... (John Petrie, *The Worker-Priests*, Routledge & Kegan Paul, 1956, pp. 159–64.)

In Britain there were only a handful of worker-priests in the 1950s and 60s and later non-stipendiary ministries in middle-class occupations which emerged in the Church of England, had more to do with resolving the problems of manpower shortage and keeping the parochial system going. Original worker-priests in the Church of England, together with their wives and lay friends formed the **Worker Church Group**. This welcomed into its ranks clergy and laity who laboured on the shop floor and, from time to time, met up with French and Belgium worker-priests. When Ted Wickham Bishop of Middleton and former leader of the Sheffield industrial mission up to the mid-sixties argued for industrial chaplains rather than worker-priests though he respected the latter, John Rowe, priest and electrician, working in the east-end of London, replied in a Rejoinder (published in 1965) that class divisions in England were nevertheless very real.

That the vocation in question implies a class analysis of British society is not to be denied. This in itself may show the 'worker-churchmen' to have a significance far beyond that of anything which they themselves can ever hope to build or accomplish. For in saying, by their action, that British society is radically and deeply class divided, they are swimming against the tide of ideological assumptions in Britain today. They demand that Christians should not delude themselves with the comfortable notion that prosperity and technology have done away with fundamental cleavages of interest in society. The control of the country's industrial wealth and productive capacity is not in more but in fewer hands than previously. . . .

The parson is himself a kind of crux of the problem. His education identifies him culturally with an upper class, yet, as the Bishop says, a sensible and forthright minister can before long talk man to man with a worker and break down the immediate prickly barriers ... But talking is not the point! ... When you have worked a while in a factory and seen the unconscious arrogance of authority, even in good men; when you have experienced the situation of being under command day after day, knowing that it will always be so; when you have clocked your card late and taken a quarter-of-an-hour's pay less, next pay day; when you have seen what that pay means in terms of housing and necessities and comforts, and learned the lessons of overtime; and when you have looked out from the circle of your workmates and seen with their eyes the manner of life of the socially superior, including the clergy, a realization is surely borne in upon you with unmistakable force . . .

Here is a class of men and women marked out by the nature of their work, the wage status and their style of life as belonging at the bottom level of an economic and social complex which accords the more privileges the higher you go . . . Is it not an absolutely genuine gospel reaction to desire to share the conditions which straiten and limit life at that level? Not just to sympathize with them, and to try and correct the characteristic misconceptions and psychological reactions of that status, but to share the conditions because sharing is so basically Christian a motive' . . . (John Rowe, *Priests and Workers, a Rejoinder*, London: Darton Longman and Todd, 1965, p. 16f.)

In February 1959 the British worker-priests with wives and lay friends produced a STATEMENT setting out the reasons for their chosen way of life. Rowe quotes it in full as an Appendix in the Rejoinder.

It is now widely recognized that there is a serious and deep-rooted estrangement between the Church and the industrial wage-earners of this country . . . Committees, missions and projects of all kinds are springing up to tackle the problem.

Most of these efforts are addressed to the workers from conventional footholds in the Church – chaplaincies, parishes, and formal missions. The Church may be expected to gain much from these, providing they are inspired with humility and patience and willingness to re-examine traditional assumptions.

We ourselves, however, feel called to answer this challenge at another level, by binding up our own salvation with that of the industrial workers. This, we feel, can only be done by working as they work and living upon the earnings of our labour as they do. Substantially, therefore we speak as a group of men and women, with their families, all committed by this decision to a certain form of life, addressing the working people primarily by involvement rather than by propaganda. What we espouse is not primarily a 'technique of evangelism' but a form of obedience . . .

We may further clarify our position as follows:

*The Way of Incarnation*

The Church is out of contact with the lives of most working-class people. It is not a natural growth within their kind of life but stands without. Speaking generally it does not understand them and their problems and they have little confidence in its representatives. This separation is primarily regarded in the Church as a technical rather than a spiritual problem. We think it should be clearly recognised that for the Church to be out of contact with people is sin. Technique is no answer to sin.

It seems to us that the answer to this situation is for the Church to enter with humility and sympathy into the life of the working people and build up the church from within-that is, by Christians who are called to it to becoming or remaining workers. Even on the human level this seems the obvious way to grow in under-standing of the workers and to win their confidence. But beyond this, it is surely right for a faith founded on the Incarnation. The Christian minister or missionary must be, and must be felt and known to be, one with his people. 'It is not enough for the Church to speak out of its security. Following our incarnate and crucified Lord, we must live in such identification with man, with his sin, his hopes and fears, his misery and needs, that we become his brother and can witness from his place and condition to God's love for him. Those outside the Church make little distinction between faith and works' (World Council of Churches, Evanston Report, Section II). Work is for us not an opportunity for propaganda, but the means whereby we become one with the working people.

This is not a wasteful use of the Church's manpower. This is a proper exer-cise in faith. In the midst of a world which believes in salvation through money, technique and force, Christians believe in the power of the 'foolishness of the cross'. . . . ['STATEMENT of a Group of Churchmen, priests and lay, who have chosen to be wage-workers in industry as an expression of their faith.' Appen-dix A in John Rowe, *Priests and Workers, A Rejoinder*, p. 65f.]

The British Worker-Church Group lasted till 1982 when newcomers, a number from Scotland joined-up. It became the Shop Floor Association. But a more radical shift took place and towards the beginning of the nineties it too came to an end. Former members of these two groups, however, like French and Belgium worker-priests today, continue to live in some of the areas where they began and again like the French and Belgium though mainly retired, still often engage with those who are socially excluded.

## Sources

Henri Perrin, *Priest and Worker*, London: Catholic Book Club, 1964, pp. 110 and 196f.

John Petrie, *The Worker-Priests*, London: Routledge & Kegan Paul, 1956, p. 159f.

John Rowe, *Priests and Workers, A Rejoinder*, London: DLT, 1965, pp. 65f.

## Further reading

Oscar L. Arnal, *Priests in Working-Class Blue*, Mahwah: Paulist Press, 1986.
John Mantle, *Britain's First Worker-Priests*, London: SCM, 2000.
John Petrie, *The Worker Priests*, London: Routledge & Kegan Paul, 1956.
Gregor Siefer, *The Church and Industrial Society: a survey of the worker-priest movement and its implications for the Christian mission*, London: Darton, Longman and Todd, 1964.
Stanley Windass, *The Chronicle of the Worker Priests*, Merlin Press, 1966.

# Chapter 40

# Jacques Ellul (1912–1994)

### The Presence of the Kingdom **(1951)**

Jacques Ellul, the French lawyer, sociologist, and lay theologian is probably best known for his sociological studies of modern society. These explained why he believed that if Marx were analyzing the twentieth century he would see that Technique not Capital was now the driving force in the contemporary world. Ellul's theological works reflect his French Reformed background and the influence of Barth and Kierkegaard. Through his own personal engagement with church and society such as his ground-breaking work with young delinquents in the 1950s, organization of local groups opposing centralized state development of his region on ecological grounds, his teaching of law and politics at Bordeaux University, and work for education reform in church and society, he embodied the link between theory and practice.

The extract which follows is taken from one of his earliest books – *The Presence of the Kingdom*. In it he sought to explore how Christians should be present in the post-war world. Ellul's writing continues to provide the church with an account of radical Christian non-conformity and an analysis of the structure of our present age.

### Source

J. Ellul, *The Presence of the Kingdom*, London: SCM Press, pp. 39–44.

### Further reading

D. J. Fasching, *The Thought of Jacques Ellul*, Lewiston: Edwin Mellen, 1981.
A. J. Goddard, *The Life and Thought of Jacques Ellul*, Oxford D.Phil., 1995.

**From** *The Presence of the Kingdom* **(1951)**

This, then, is the revolutionary situation: to be revolutionary is to judge the world by its present state, by actual facts, in the name of a truth which does not yet exist (but which is coming) – and it is to do so because we believe this truth to be more genuine and more real than the reality which surrounds us. Consequently it means bringing the future into the present as an explosive force. It means believing that future events are more important and more true than present events; it means understanding the present in the light of the future, dominating it by the future, in the same way as the historian dominates the past. Henceforth the revolutionary act forms part of history: it is going to create history, by inflecting it toward this future, and this notion of revolution is valid for all revolutions which have taken place in the course of history, whether they were successful or not. It is still true for the Communist movement, but, as we have seen, the latter has abandoned its revolutionary line in order to follow the main trend of historical development. Indeed, to direct this action toward a future which seems most likely to be realized, and is the logical outcome of present conditions, is certainly *not* the way to achieve a revolution!

The Christian, on the contrary, even if he does not make a great show politically, or a great demonstration of revolutionary power, but if he really lives by the power of Christ – if, by hope, he makes the coming of the Kingdom actual – is a true revolutionary. He judges the present time in virtue of a meta-historical fact, and the incursion of this event into the present is the only force capable of throwing off the dead weight of social and political institutions which are gradually crushing the life out of our present civilization. Here, again, it is not a question of "keeping an open mind" – of choosing to do this or that, as though there were various possibilities – it is the only possible attitude that faith can adopt. To abandon this position would mean ceasing to believe that we have been saved, for we are saved by hope, through faith (Rom. 8:24), and hope is precisely this eschatological force in the present world.

Thus we have before us the two fundamental theological facts which make the Christian life necessarily revolutionary, truths which have not been created by the will of each individual but by the situation which God creates for his children; and we ought to be convinced that if we do not live in accordance with this vision we have no idea of what the Christian life really is. Now we must draw conclusions from this fact.

One of the first series of conclusions will doubtless appear very abstract and difficult! It consists in the fact that the Christian cannot judge, or act, or live according to "principles," but according to the reality, lived here and now, of the *eschaton* – the very opposite of an ethic.

We must be convinced that there are no such things as "Christian principles." There is the person of Christ, who is the principle of everything. But if we wish to be faithful to him, we cannot dream of reducing Christianity to a certain number of principles (though this is often done), the consequences of which can be logically deduced. This tendency to transform the work of the living God into a philosophical doctrine is the constant temptation of theologians, and also of the faithful, and their greatest disloyalty when they transform the action of the Spirit which brings forth fruit in themselves into an ethic, a new law, into "principles" which only have to be "applied." The Christian life does not spring from a "cause," but it moves toward an "end"; it is this which completely changes the outlook for humanity, and renders the Christian life different from every other life.

What is true in the individual sphere is also true in the social sphere. There are no Christian political and social principles, defined in an absolute way. What God reveals to us in this sphere by the Scriptures is not a doctrine or principles – it is judgment and action, wholly directed toward the accomplishment of the work of God. We never see a logical causal process, any more than we see the establishment of a static or a permanent order, but the action of God always appears as a power in movement, like a torrent which crosses and recrosses history, which changes its course, rolls along in great floods, and stirs up all the elements of creation. The Bible shows us a God at work in political and civil history, using the works of men and bringing them into his action for his promised Kingdom.

From what the Scripture reveals to us about this action we can draw similar analogies, we can conceive the essential direction which our action should take. We can have a glimpse of a contemporary order with a changing shape, but not of a system, or of political principles. Whenever we have to transcribe the action of God in the world, in an incomplete manner, intelligible to humanity, there can be no question of any dogmatism, which is the very contrary of this action. Thus, the first consequence of this revolutionary function of the Christian is that he ought to be open to all human action, that he ought to welcome it as giving him valuable direction. We are never called to set aside a political or a social attempt on account of "principles" which are supposed to be "Christian." Everything that seems to be a step in this right direction (in the sense in which this was defined above) should be most carefully examined.

On the other hand, it is evident that the Christian can never be tied to the past or to a principle. In the political world he must apply the rule of Ecclesiastes (chapter 3): "To everything there is a season, a time to every purpose under the heaven. . . . He hath made everything beautiful in its time." Thus there is not a Christian attitude which can be applied to all times; but, according to different times, attitudes which appear to be contradictory may be equally good, to the extent in which they make their mark on history as fidelity to the purpose of God.

Thus it is not necessary to be loyal to an idea, to a doctrine, or to a political movement. What is called fidelity in the language of the world is too often only habit or obstinacy. The Christian may belong to the Right or to the Left, he may be a Liberal or a Socialist, according to the times in which he lives, and according as the position of the one or the other seems to him more in harmony with the will of God at the particular time. These attitudes are contradictory from the human point of view, it is true, but their unity consists in the search for the coming

Kingdom. It is in the light of this Kingdom that the Christian is called to judge present circumstances, and these circumstances cannot be judged according to their moral content or their individual political outlook – nor according to their relation to a human doctrine, or to their attachment to the past – but simply according to their relation, which always exists, to the *Parousia*. There is no doubt that this is a difficult attitude, full of snares and dangers, but it is also the only attitude which seems to be in line with the Christian life; we were never told that this would be either easy or secure.

The fact that almost all Christian political attitudes have been either wrong or disastrous (that of the Jesuits as well as that of Constantine, for instance) is due to the fact that judgment has been diverted from the Kingdom of God into a line governed by an ethical doctrine, and that people have always tried to construct a political system deduced from the gospel!

But, you will say, "What do we know about this Kingdom of God?" In reality, we must take care that we do not make the Kingdom of God into an ethical system, by trying to outline the form in which it should be reproduced upon earth!

The central point which we can already know, and which is already real, is the lordship of Jesus Christ, and all Christian realism ought to be based upon this lordship. This lordship is the objective element in the revolutionary Christian situation, as hope is its subjective element, and this alone permits us to take our stand in our different political positions, in our successive judgments on the concrete problems of politics and economics.

A thing is never good or bad in itself, not even by the use man makes of it. A thing is only good or bad in its own time, according to its situation in the light of the Kingdom of God, according to its conformity to the work of God for the coming of the Kingdom, and, finally, according to its possible use for the glory of God, or vice versa. These are the three criteria, which are very precise and concrete, once we have abandoned our obsession with ethical formulae or political doctrines. It is in the daily application of these three criteria to social facts that the action of the Christian is revolutionary, by "actualizing the *eschaton*."

But we can see, quite easily, that this attitude goes far beyond all current systems of idealism and realism. The constant presence of the Kingdom in the Christian life is a demand which urges one continually to go further, to look at situations in their depth, and to make still greater claims, for no revolution can fully satisfy, and in the same way every achievement, however humble it may be, is worthy of being preserved. Thus we need to take account of all the facts, and to transcend them – not, however, in a spirit of intellectual arrogance or in the name of some abstract dogma. The vitality of this realism is due to the fact that it judges nothing by "effecting" a success; its only criterion is the lordship of Christ. Thus the Christian is called to "judge all things," an order which St. Paul gives in an absolute manner. That is to say, it concerns the whole of life, and not only "moral values" or the "spiritual life." We ought also to emphasize the point that in the text this injunction appears in a passage between an exhortation about prophecy and the reminder that the whole of the Christian life has only one aim – to be preserved unto the coming of our Lord Jesus Christ; and, in consequence, that this Pauline sequence of ideas is at the very heart of all that we have been able to write here about the revolutionary position of the Christian.

This judgment (which is not derived from human rules or customs), which has to be ever new, and ever renewed, is the very heart of the realist position of the Christian. I am quite aware of the possible criticisms which may be raised – how this may seem to denote a lack of unity, of continuity, of fidelity, and the like – but I believe that all this is due to a wrong Christian attitude, adapted far too much to the pagan idea of what this attitude ought to be. Nothing is more irritating than the way in which non-Christians use biblical phrases, which they do not understand, in order to criticize the attitude of Christians. The value of their criticism of Christians does not come from their knowledge of Scripture but from their way of living. Non-Christians are an example when they live differently from, and better than, Christians, on any particular point, but Christians have not to follow the intellectual or moral lessons or doctrines which the non-Christians may want to give them (Luke 16:8). Now this equation of Christian thought and Christian ethics, which has been an obvious fact for the last two hundred years, is the secularization of Christianity – by Christians themselves, with their lack of daring and of fidelity; and on this particular point the criticisms addressed to Christian realism are a manifestation of this attitude.

# Chapter 41

# Alan Ecclestone (1904–1992)

**The Parish Meeting at Work (1953)**

Alan Ecclestone was for many years parish priest of Darnall in inner city Sheffield. He left an academic career for parochial ministry and pioneered a form of community church which in many ways anticipated the Basic Ecclesial Communities of Latin American liberation theology, which were to emerge in the wake of Vatican II some twenty or more years later. His major writings, which were completed after his retirement, give little impression of the controversial ministry and his membership of the Communist Party. Those of us who got to know him in the last years of his life could still glimpse some of that radical fire and the extraordinary insight into contemporary affairs which owed as much to an intimate knowledge of English literature (he read Shakespeare's plays regularly and was devoted to Blake) and the writings of Karl Marx as to the Christian theological tradition, about which he had mixed feelings. He hung a copy of Padraic Pearse's poem "The Fool" on the wall of his church in Darnall and included part of it in his "book of days" for 3 May, the date of Pearse's execution in 1916 after the Easter Uprising. The piece that follows gives an insight into the rationale and practice of the parish meeting, which was a constitutive feature of parish life in Darnall throughout his ministry there.

Source

A. Ecclestone, "The Parish Meeting at Work," *Firing the Clay. Articles and Addresses*, compiled by Jim Cotter, Sheffield: Cairns, 1999, pp. 85–121.

Further reading

T. Gorringe, *Alan Ecclestone Priest as Revolutionary*, Sheffield: Cairns, 1994.
A. Ecclestone, *Gather the Fragments. A Book of Days*, Sheffield: Cairns, 1993.

## From *The Parish Meeting at Work*

### *What It Is and How To Begin*

The Parish Meeting is the assembling of the local church, the church in the parish, in order that it may realize and work out its essential life. It is a meeting whose character is implied in the New Testament word 'fellowship'. It is a meeting, the agenda or business of which is the whole life and work of the Christian Community in the world. It can be described on the one hand with the utmost simplicity: that week by week the members of the church in the parish meet together to talk over, plan, execute, and report upon the work of the Christian Church in whose life they share. It much be recognized on the other hand that in this matter we are making the most tremendous claims: that this meeting is nothing less than the representation of the Body of Christ, which in the very power and commission of Pentecost is setting about its work and revealing its life. We are not talking about an organization devised by a parish priest and enjoyed by some parishioners. We are not talking about a study group, a prayer meeting, a business meeting, a consultative committee, a social. We are not thinking in terms of Chairman, Secretary, minutes, correspondence, and agenda. We are talking about the Church, whose primary business is to be the Church. The Parish Meeting is to be thought of in these overwhelming terms or it is better left alone.

How then do we arrive at this? In every parish church, Sunday by Sunday, a number of Christian people come together to take part in an act of worship. When this is concluded, they disperse. They have 'been to church'. Very many of them do not meet or see each other again until they repeat this 'going to church'. Some of them belong to and take part in various social functions arranged by various organizations, for boys and girls, men and women. From each of these things they derive much that is important, delightful, and valuable.

A few people, however, have possibly felt that there is something missing from this weekly round as the expression of the corporate life of the Christian Church. The services may well have been offered to God with all sincerity and earnestness, with beauty and devotion; the social and moral witness afforded by one or more of the organizations may have been diligently and courageously performed. But is this the whole of Christian life? Is this all that the membership of Christ's Body means? Is there not something else, presupposed alike by the services and the personal witness, something else out of which the services and the personal witness may be said to issue, which is unfortunately scarcely visible and hardly known, to which could be given a name like 'the Body' or 'the Fellowship'? Is there not something else, more conscious of itself and its work than the congregation in the pews can often claim to be, more active, disciplined, purposeful, informed, and spiritually alert than the meetings of the organizations that we know? . . .

### *The Conduct of the Meeting*

Where shall we hold the Meeting? The question is not unimportant, because our intention is to try to get as far as we can from the usual atmosphere of meetings.

We are thinking in terms of a family coming together and it is in the setting of a home that we should most naturally desire to meet. How can we get this? It is far better to be crowded in the Vicarage than to be spaciously accommodated in the Parish Hall or the School. That does not mean that we must rule out either of these, but that we must always take trouble to see that the impression given by the surroundings is friendly, informal, unofficial, and capable of making people feel at ease with each other.

The force of this applies specially to the actual conduct of the Meeting. What is the job of the parish priest in this respect? From the beginning it should be understood that his position here is vastly different from that of the preacher in the pulpit, the chairman in the chair, the lecturer on the platform, simply because the Meeting itself is different from any other kind of gathering. The people here are not assembled to hear an address but to talk together, to communicate with each other, and therefore the chief thing is to enable that activity to become as valuable as we can make it. On the other hand the conversation is not aimless and it requires steering. The parish priest is possibly the best person for the job, but this should not be taken for granted, and it is important that the Meeting should not become totally dependent upon his being there. While the very nature of the Meeting as we have described it makes it clear that normally he will be there, the Meeting must certainly go on when he is absent. It must be possible to call on others to take his place as a result of the experience they have gained from being familiar with the way in which it is done. Nor should it be taken for granted that the parish priest knows immediately how to perform this difficult task. He is there in the position of a learner like everyone else, and is just as likely to make mistakes. Indeed, a good deal of his background and training makes the position particularly difficult for him, accustomed as he is to preaching – the very last thing that is needed at the Meeting.

The steering of the Meeting is, even so, a different matter from the art of competent chairmanship, because the people have not come together primarily to transact business. They are gathered together as fellow-Christians, and the primary job of the Meeting is two-fold like this title. It must bring out as clearly as possible what being 'fellows' means and what this relationship implies. In this sense, the job of the Meeting is to enable Christians to discover something more of the truth about themselves, to find a more real meaning and a deeper content in the phrases that they have heard so often. That is why each Meeting, however confused it may become, has something Pentecostal about it. The biblical foundation should never be forgotten. 'Then they that feared the Lord spake often one to another, and the Lord hearkened and heard it.'

There can be no question then of allowing a contemptuous dismissal of the Meeting as 'just talk', because it does not set out to follow the usual lines of a business meeting, or to carry decisions by votes, or to draw up its conclusions in a series of neat 'findings'. There may be something much more honest and edifying in arriving at a confession of ignorance, bafflement, and something like humiliation, felt by all those present, and not least by the parish priest himself. Put very simply, his job is to get people to talk, to overcome those barriers of shyness and reserve, to be natural and honest and unaffected with each other. In talking of almost anything connected with religion this is far more difficult for most people than it sounds. Here apparently more than anywhere else we are determined to 'keep up appearances' and to talk vaguely and as generally as possible lest we should give ourselves away. The fact that someone with a good deal of courage shows us how it can be done and bravely goes ahead in an honest declaration does not by any means win the unqualified approval of others. It has indeed been known that such honesty has been taken as something like a personal affront. But difficult though it may be to attain this ideal, we must go on believing that it is worth seeking.

Simply to get people to talk is plainly not enough, for we must do our talking with a difference. It is not enough to remember that everyone must be kept in mind; our talking must also have direction. It must be talking, not to a fixed point known to the parish priest beforehand, as would be the case with a teacher and a junior class, but to a point in the unknown. The Meeting is a meeting of disciples, assembled to learn what is the mind of the Spirit, a 'not knowing whither he went'. Such ventures have obvious disadvantages, so that it is not at all surprising that many priests and people with some slight experience of what happens hastily return to the beaten tracks and the more familiar landmarks. Equally it is not surprising to hear from others that they had sleepless nights after the Meeting thinking over what had been said. This last remark, which points to real excitement of mind and spirit, is not so trivial as it sounds. A spark has been kindled into a flame.

What happens if people will not talk? What do you do if one person tends to monopolize the talking? In the first place we must recognize that we are doing something novel to the majority of our churchgoing people today. We have only to face this fact to realize what an indictment of our methods and what a formidable handicap to our work it is. Even today, after years of Summer Schools, Parochial Conventions, Missions, and the like, the majority of the people in our congregations are not accustomed to talk naturally about the Christian faith. It is true that there are arguments in the works, in the railway carriages, in the office, on religious matters, but it is noticeable that, apart from the intervention of some enthusiast, the discussion is carried on on an impersonal level. What nobody wants is the unpleasantness of getting 'personal'.

Consequently we must recognize that the awkward silence while so frequently overtakes a Parish Meeting in its earliest years is an indication both of our lack of training and of our ignorance. There is no easy answer to the problem. One parish priest who endeavoured to correct this by announcing that instead of a sermon there would be a discussion in church the following Sunday night, found the church empty, and later overheard the remark that 'he was paid to preach'. Others have struggled with the most difficult art of coaxing into life the beginnings of discussion over many months, and found that in spite of everything they tried a stodgy silence descended.

It is at this point that many have recourse to the practice of having a speaker. It is not unknown that some parish priests have worked out for a year ahead a rota of speakers and have printed a card to indicate their subjects. For many this plan has the obvious advantage of giving discussions a foundation of information and something to talk about. But the advantages are likely to be bought at too great a price. Valuable as it may be to stimulate discussion, and important as it is that we should hear the views of worthwhile speakers, it is likely to be disastrous if this becomes the usual procedure of the Parish Meeting. It is not too much to say that speakers should be asked to come in proportion to our strength and not our weakness in discussion. For it is true of both priest and people that when we are listening to a speaker, we are, with the exception of a few experienced listeners, more passive than we should otherwise be. To put it crudely, speakers are popular because they make it easier. We tend to sit back where otherwise we should be called upon to be wrestling.

In the long run therefore, whatever the immediate advantages of listening to a speaker, our job is something that we cannot leave to anyone else. Speakers can help us with information, with the stimulus of personal contact, with the honesty of their approach to their subjects, but our job remains when they have come and gone. Our growing together in common understanding and common acceptance of responsibility still turns upon our willingness to disclose our minds to each other in sincerity and truth. It is for this reason that hours spent in saying and listening to the most commonplace remarks and the most trite observations are never wasted, provided that we do not let them pass unexamined and provided that we wrestle with them. It is the job of the parish priest to ensure that this wrestling goes on. It will not happen if, in the earlier stages, he shows signs of impatience with those who seem able only to contribute platitudes. What matters is that he should be able and ready to sift the grain and chaff, taking infinite trouble to do so, and to see that the grain is examined and re-examined by those present at the Meeting. He may read more into what is volunteered by someone than they dreamt of. Nevertheless it is his job to encourage the timid and reserved to make their contribution, and himself to realize that nothing is so encouraging as the knowledge that our halting contribution, so diffidently offered, was genuinely welcomed and used. A personal knowledge of the people who attend the Meeting must be the guide in deciding whether the encouragement of some particular person shall take the form of a direct question: 'What do you think about that, Jack?' or whether we throw out the questions generally and catch the first reply.

Still more will turn upon the attitude of the parish priest as leader. In view of what has been said of the character of the Meeting, it is plainly not his function to give the impression that he thinks he knows all the answers, or that this is a glorious opportunity for delivering a lecture. His steering, his interrogation, and his sifting must all be done as by a member of the Body and not as by one set over it. The atmosphere of the family and the completely informal approach to the whole business of the Meeting must go hand-in-hand with an obvious desire to learn and a willingness to act upon what is agreed.

This last point is mentioned here because it has a great bearing upon the question of the survival and growth of the Parish Meeting. It raises the whole problem of what participation in the Meeting is going to mean. We are asking people to regard it with the utmost seriousness and to come into it as wholeheartedly as possible; to drop a good many of the usual barriers of social small-talk, and to speak honestly of the things that concern them most. Seriousness does not mean severity and gloom, but it does mean a recognition of the fact that we are not talking for talking's sake. Quite quickly the people present will ask themselves whether the parish priest who has called the meeting as an assembly of the Church, the Body of Christ, the Temple of the Spirit, does really mean what he said about it. Does he, for example, take seriously what is said there, does he think over it, as he expects the parishioners to think over what he himself has said? Does he intend that the Church should act upon what is decided, or does he go his own way when all has been said? The complaint has been made already many times: 'He says that he wants to hear what we think, but he never acts upon it; we might just as well have held our tongues.' Actually the outcome of this kind of thing is even worse. People rightly resent being called upon to do something which is costly to the sensitive-minded unless they can be assured that it is rightly valued. They are quick to detect a note of superficiality and humbug.

> Why didst thou promise such a beauteous day
> And make me travel forth without my cloak?
>> Sonnet 34

It is not too much to say that the position of the parish priest in this respect is vital to the right understanding of what the Parish Meeting stands for. Humanly speaking, everything turns upon his integrity and sensitiveness. He can help the Meeting to go forward to hitherto quite undreamt-of levels of understanding, spiritual insight, and adventurous courage, changing the whole outlook and will of the Church, or he can fritter away the time, the resources, and the confidence of his people. One of the earliest signs of what is happening will be found in the way in which people respond to this opportunity to speak. There is a world of difference between the silence of those who are thinking and the silence of those who are merely waiting for someone to say something . . .

*What place has Bible Study in the Parish Meeting?*
The question can best be answered by drawing as fully as we can from actual experience. One evening we faced the matter in this way. 'Why do we do our Bible-study so badly? Why do we so often find that a large number of people at once relapse into silence?' For the plain fact was that a slight feeling of unreality appeared to descend upon the Meeting.

Some explanation may be given by going back to what was said earlier about reading books aloud in the Meeting. Even the most ordinary reading-matter sets up a kind of barrier, and introduces a break in the conversation. How much more then, when what is read in the Bible language, when a traditional text-employing mode of usage has bedevilled the approach, and when there is a certain feeling that this is all remote from our world.

All these things are far greater difficulties than most clergymen ever suppose. Their own education and training have been so largely literary and biblical that they find it difficult to imagine just how the man in the pews thinks of the Bible. They can be more natural in reading it and talking about it than the layman. They can read it with some of the necessary historical transposition and theological understanding that surmounts so many difficulties.

But the literal approach which so quickly shows itself in the Parish Meeting at once reveals the difficulties. We are studying, for example, the Sermon on the Mount. We encounter the remarks on our attitude to borrowers, and at this point one of two things is likely to happen. Either the difficult words are read and passed over without a remark, as if implying that of course we all know how to apply them to an importunate borrower of our acquaintance, or else some person, possibly the parish priest, breaks in and exclaims that this is not quite as acceptable to any of us as our silence suggests. In other words we are not really facing the difficulties. Because this book is the Bible we are passing over remarks of which we should certainly be more critical if we met them elsewhere. To make matters worse, it is common to find that, if we are challenged to say how we think that so many of these difficult things are to be faced, phrases like 'We must have faith' promptly make their appearance. As statements they may be unexceptionable, but they are often to cover up the most awkward gaps in our thinking. The result is that we tend to emerge from our time of Bible-study with a new note of unreality in our discussion.

To overcome this, it would appear to be more profitable to do our Bible-study in very close relation to the actual problems of the day, drawing upon the Bible as we go along for comment, rather than reading ahead chapter by chapter. It is useful, for example, to study a subject with Bible references, or to build up a vivid picture of the Ministry of our Lord, or even to work out the meanings we attach to phrases like the Kingdom of God. All this really requires great preparation on the part of the parish priest, not simply in order that he may know the text to be studied but much more that he may himself be faced with the difficulties it presents. When we spoke earlier on of wrestling, it was with the implication that this wrestling was a reality for everyone. The unreality which creeps into so much of our Bible-study is due as much as anything to the fact that while we have to work out the problems of daily life, the difficulties of the Bible are for so many of us academic and not vital to our lives.

The force of this is very clearly emphasized when we turn to a different problem, that of politics. 'Do politics come into the discussion at the Parish Meeting?' Since we began by insisting that all matters which enter our daily life are the proper concern of the Meeting, we can hardly avoid the wide range of subjects which have their roots in politics. To do so would be at once to excise from our programme matters of great concern to our social and personal life. The difficulties are very real, and we can appreciate the attitude which so often finds expression in forbidding 'Religion and Politics' from discussion because both these subjects produce a deeply controversial note. We have heard of one Parish Meeting which decided to do Bible-study because current topics were too controversial. Certainly it would be easier if we could avoid the tensions which politics set up, but nothing is really gained by running away.

What we have to learn is the much more difficult task of declaring and maintaining our differences in politics and investigating the roots of them, within the acknowledged unity of the Church. Something is terribly wrong if the Church is any one Party at prayer to the exclusion of the others. Common sense must obviously be our guide. We must neither run away from nor run madly into the turmoil which the political scene presents. There are times when it is inexpedient to press the political issues further; when it is much more advisable to turn to matters where common ground is more easily discovered, from which indeed we hope to return to the difficult patches with second wind.

# Chapter 42

# Martin Luther King, Jr. (1929–1968)

### Letter from Birmingham Jail (1963)

Martin Luther King first came to prominence in 1955 when, while pastor of a Baptist church in Montgomery, Alabama, he led a bus boycott in the city in protest against enforced racial segregation in public transport. The boycott achieved its goal after a year, but during that time King was arrested and jailed, received threats on his life, and had his home bombed. His non-violent protest did earn him the respect of his peers, however, and when black clergymen in the South formed the Southern Christian Leadership conference, King became its first president. In 1960 King moved to Atlanta in order to participate more effectively in the national leadership of the burgeoning civil rights movement, and in 1963 he led the historic March on Washington and delivered his "I Have a Dream" speech. On April 3, 1968 King spoke of having "been to the mountain top and seen the Promised Land," but like Moses he was not to see it, an assassin's bullet ending his life the next day. Profoundly inspired by M. K. Gandhi, King remained faithful to the principle of non-violent action throughout his life.

In 1963 King led a massive civil rights campaign in Birmingham, Alabama, as a consequence of which he was briefly imprisoned. While in jail he had occasion to see a statement by local clergy questioning the wisdom of his action, and the letter reproduced here is his response. In it he defends his policy of direct, non-violent action in the cause of racial justice, and takes his critics to task for their apparent lack of commitment to the civil rights cause. He also expresses concern at their failure to look deeply at the contemporary situation, particularly with respect to the "justness" of the laws they accuse him of breaking. King's letter has many similarities to the Kairos Document.

### Source

Martin Luther King, Jr., "Letter from Birmingham Jail" in *The Christian Century*, June 12, 1963, pp. 767–73.

Further reading

Martin Luther King, *Strength To Love*, London, 1964.
Martin Luther King, *Chaos or Community?*, London, 1967.
David J. Garrow, *Bearing the Cross: Martin Luther King Jr and the Southern Christian Leadership Conference*, London, 1988.

## From *Letter from Birmingham Jail*

*A vigorous, eloquent reply to criticism expressed by a group of eight clergymen*

MY DEAR FELLOW CLERGYMEN:

... I am in Birmingham because injustice exists here. Just as the prophets of the eighth century B.C. left their villages and carried their "thus saith the Lord" far afield and just as the Apostle Paul left his village of Tarsus and carried the gospel of Jesus Christ to the far corners of the Greco-Roman world, so am I compelled to carry the gospel of freedom beyond my own home town. Like Paul, I must constantly respond to the Macedonian call for aid.

Moreover, I am cognizant of the interrelatedness of all communities and states. I cannot sit idly by in Atlanta and not be concerned about what happens in Birmingham. Injustice anywhere is a threat to justice everywhere. We are caught in an inescapable network of mutuality, tied in a single garment of destiny. Whatever affects one directly affects all indirectly. Never again can we afford to live with the narrow, provincial "outside agitator" idea. Anyone who lives inside the United States can never be considered an outsider anywhere within its bounds.

You deplore the demonstrations taking place in Birmingham. But your statement, I am sorry to say, fails to express a similar concern for the conditions that brought about the demonstrations. I am sure that none of you would want to rest content with the superficial kind of social analysis that deals merely with effects and does not grapple with underlying causes. It is unfortunate that demonstrations are taking place in Birmingham, but it is even more unfortunate that the city's white power structure left the Negro community with no alternative. ...

... We have waited for more than 340 years for our constitutional and God-given rights. The nations of Asia and Africa are moving with jet-like speed toward gaining political independence, but we still creep at horse-and-buggy pace toward gaining a cup of coffee at a lunch counter. Perhaps it is easy for those who have never felt the stinging darts of segregation to say "Wait." But when you have seen vicious mobs lynch your mothers and fathers at will and drown your sisters and brothers at whim; when you have seen hate-filled policemen curse, kick and even kill your black brothers and sisters with impunity; when you see the vast majority of your 20 million Negro brothers smothering in an air-tight cage of poverty in the midst of an affluent society; when you suddenly find your tongue twisted as you seek to explain to your six-year-old daughter why she can't go to the public amusement park that has just been advertised on television, and see tears welling up when she is told that Funtown is closed to colored children, and see ominous clouds of inferiority beginning to form in her little mental sky, and see her beginning to distort her personality by unconsciously developing a bitterness toward white people; when you have to concoct an answer for a five-year-old son asking, "Daddy, why do white people treat colored people so mean?"; when you take a cross-country drive and find it necessary to sleep night after night in the uncomfortable corners of your automobile because no motel will accept you; when you are humiliated day in and day out by nagging signs reading "white" and "colored"; when your first name becomes "nigger," your middle name becomes "boy" (however old you are) and your last name becomes "John," and your wife and mother are never given the respected title "Mrs."; when you are harried by day and haunted by night by the fact that you are a Negro, never quite knowing what to expect next, and are plagued with inner fears and outer resentments; when you are forever fighting a degenerating sense of 'nobodiness" – then you will understand why we find it difficult to wait. There comes a time when the cup of endurance runs over, and men are no longer willing to be plunged into an abyss of injustice where they experience the bleakness of corroding despair. I hope, sirs, you can understand our legitimate and unavoidable impatience.

You express a great deal of anxiety over our willingness to break laws. This is certainly a legitimate concern. Since we so diligently urge people to obey the Supreme Court's decision of 1954 outlawing segregation in the public schools, at first glance it may seem rather paradoxical for us consciously to break laws. One may well ask, "How can you advocate breaking some laws and obeying others?" The answer lies in the fact that there are two types of laws: just and unjust. I agree with St. Augustine that "an unjust law is no law at all."

Now what is the difference between the two? How does one determine whether a law is just or unjust? A just law is a man-made code that squares with the moral law or the law of God. An unjust law is a code that is out of harmony with the moral law. To put it in the terms of St. Thomas Aquinas, an unjust law is a human law that is not rooted in eternal law and natural law. Any law that uplifts human personality is just. Any law that degrades human personality is unjust. All segregation statutes are unjust because segregation distorts the soul and damages the personality. It gives the segregator a false sense of superiority and the segregated a false sense of inferiority. Segregation, to use the terminology of the Jewish philosopher Martin Buber, substitutes an "I-it" relationship for an "I-thou" relationship and ends up relegating persons to the status of things. Hence segregation is not only politically, economically and sociologically unsound, it is sinful. Paul Tillich has said that sin is separation. Is not segregation an existential expression of man's tragic separation, his awful estrangement, his terrible sinfulness? Thus it is that I can urge men to disobey segregation ordinances, for such ordinances are morally wrong. . . .

Of course, there is nothing new about this kind of civil disobedience. It was evidence sublimely in the refusal of Shadrach. Meshach and Abednego to obey the laws of Nebuchadnezzar, on the ground that a higher moral law was at stake. It was practiced superbly by the early Christians who were willing to face hungry lions rather than submit to certain unjust laws of the Roman empire. To a degree, academic freedom is a reality today because Socrates practiced civil disobedience. We should never forget that everything Adolf Hitler did in Germany was "legal" and everything the Hungarian freedom fighters did in Hungary was "illegal." It was "illegal" to aid and comfort a Jew in Hitler's Germany. Even so, I am sure that had I lived in Germany at the time I would have aided and comforted my Jewish brothers. If today I lived in a communist country where certain principles dear to the Christian faith are suppressed, I would openly advocate disobeying that country's antireligious laws. . . .

. . . though I was initially disappointed at being categorized as an extremist, as I continued to think about the matter I gradually gained a measure of satisfaction from the label. Was not Jesus an extremist for love: "Love your enemies, bless them that curse you, do good to them that hate you, and pray for them which despitefully use you, and persecute you." Was not Amos an extremist for justice: "Let justice roll down like waters and righteousness like an everflowing stream." Was not Paul an extremist for the Christian gospel: "I bear in my body the marks of the Lord Jesus." Was not Martin Luther an extremist: "Here I stand; I can do no other so help me God." And John Bunyan: "I will stay in jail to the end of my days before I make a butchery of my conscience." And Abraham Lincoln: "This nation cannot survive half slave and half free." And Thomas Jefferson: "We hold these truths to be self-evident, that all men are created equal . . ." So the question is not whether we will be extremists but what kind of extremists we will be. Will we be extremists for hate or for love? Will we be extremists for the preservation of injustice or for the extension of justice? Perhaps the south, the nation and the world are in dire need of creative extremists. . . .

. . . Let me take note of my other major disappointment. Though there are some notable exceptions. I have also been disappointed with the white church and its leadership. I do not say this as one of those negative critics who can always find something wrong with the church. I say this as a minister of the gospel, who loves the church; who was nurtured in its bosom; who has been sustained by its spiritual blessings and who will remain true to it as long as the cord of life shall lengthen.

When I was suddenly catapulted into the leadership of the bus protest in Montgomery, Alabama, a few years ago I felt we would be supported by the white church. I felt that the white ministers, priests and rabbis of the south would be among our strongest allies. Instead, some have been outright opponents, refusing to understand the freedom movement and misrepresenting its leaders; all too many others have been more cautious than courageous and have remained silent and secure behind stained-glass windows.

In spite of my shattered dreams I came to Birmingham with the hope that the white religious leadership of this community would see the justice of our cause and with deep moral concern would serve as the channel through which our just grievances could reach the power structure. But again I have been disappointed.

I have heard numerous southern religious leaders admonish their worshipers to comply with a desegregation decision because it is the *law*, but I have longed to hear white ministers declare, "Follow this decree because integration is morally *right* and because the Negro is your brother." In the midst of blatant injustices inflicted upon the Negro I have watched white churchmen stand on the sideline and mouth pious irrelevancies and sanctimonious trivialities. In the midst of a mighty struggle to rid our nation of racial and economic injustice I have heard many ministers say, "Those are social issues with which the gospel has no real concern," and I have watched many churches commit themselves to a completely otherworldly religion which makes a strange, unbiblical distinction between body and soul, between the sacred and the secular.

We are moving toward the close of the 20th century with a religious community largely adjusted to the status quo – a taillight behind other community agencies rather than a headlight leading men to higher levels of justice.

I have traveled the length and breadth of Alabama, Mississippi and all the other southern states. On sweltering summer days and crisp autumn mornings I have looked at the south's beautiful churches with their lofty spires pointing heavenward, and at her impressive religious education buildings. Over and over I have found myself asking: "What kind of people worship here? Who is their God? Where were their voices when the lips of Governor Barnett dripped with words of interposition and nullification? Where were they when Governor Wallace gave a clarion call for defiance and hatred? Where were their voices of support when bruised and weary Negro men and women decided to rise from the dark dungeons of complacency to the bright hills of creative protest?"

Yes, these questions are still in my mind. In deep disappointment I have wept over the laxity of the church. But be assured that my tears have been tears of love. There can be no deep disappointment where there is not deep love. Yes, I love the church. How could I do otherwise? I am in the rather unique position of being the son, the grandson and the great-grandson of preachers. Yes, I see the church as the body of Christ. But, oh! How we have blemished and scarred that body through social neglect and through fear of being nonconformists.

There was a time when the church was very powerful – in the time when the early Christians rejoiced at being deemed worthy to suffer for what they believed. In those days the church was not merely a thermometer that recorded the ideas and principles of popular opinion; it was a thermostat that transformed the mores of society. Whenever the early Christians entered a town the power structure immediately sought to convict them for being "disturbers of the peace" and "outside agitators." But the Christians pressed on, in the conviction that they were "a colony of heaven," called to obey God rather than man. Small in number, they were big in commitment. By their effort and example they brought an end to such ancient evils as infanticide and gladiatorial contest.

Things are different now. So often the contemporary church is a weak, ineffectual voice with an uncertain sound. So often it is an archdefender of the status quo. Far from being disturbed by the presence of the church, the power structure of the average community is consoled by the church's silent – and often even vocal – sanction of things as they are.

But the judgment of God is upon the church as never before. If today's church does not recapture the sacrificial spirit of the early church, it will lose its authenticity, forfeit the loyalty of millions, and be dismissed as an irrelevant social club with no meaning for the 20th century. Every day I meet young people whose disappointment with the church has turned into outright disgust.

Perhaps I have once again been too optimistic. Is organized religion too inextricably bound to the status quo to save our nation and the world? Perhaps I must turn my faith to the inner spiritual church, the church within the church, as the true *ecclesia* and the hope of the world. But again I am thankful to God that some noble souls from the ranks of organized religion have broken loose from the paralyzing chains of conformity and joined us as active partners in the struggle for freedom. They have left their secure congregations and walked the streets of Albany, Georgia, with us. They have gone down the highways of the south on torturous rides for freedom. Yes, they have gone to jail with us. Some have been kicked out of their churches, have lost the support of their bishops and fellow ministers. But they have acted in the faith that right defeated is stronger than evil triumphant. Their witness has been the spiritual salt that has preserved the true meaning of the gospel in these troubled times. They have carved a tunnel of hope through the dark mountain of disappointment.

I hope the church as a whole will meet the challenge of this decisive hour. But even if the church does not come to the aid of justice, I have no despair about the future. I have no fear about the outcome of our struggle in Birmingham, even if our motives are at present misunderstood. We will reach the goal of freedom in Birmingham and all over the nation, because the goal of America is freedom. Abused and scorned though we may be, our destiny is tied up with America's destiny. Before the pilgrims landed at Plymouth we were here. Before the pen of Jefferson etched across the pages of history the mighty words of the Declaration of Independence, we were here. For more than two centuries our forebears labored in this country without wages; they made cotton king; they built the homes of their masters while suffering gross injustice and shameful humiliation – and yet out of a bottomless vitality they continued to thrive and develop. If the inexpressible cruelties of slavery could not stop us, the opposition we now face will surely fail. We will win our freedom because the sacred heritage of our nation and the eternal will of God are embodied in our echoing demands.

# Chapter 43

# Camilo Torres (1929–1966)

## Love and Revolution (ca. 1965)

Like some later liberation theologians, Torres understood faith primarily as praxis and argued that, for "love of neighbor" to be effective in oppressive situations, structural transformation must be countenanced. Torres argued that charity such as the church traditionally practised could have no impact in societies structurally biased against the poor, and therefore revolution was a Christian imperative. "The Catholic who is not a revolutionary is living in mortal sin," he was once reported to have said, and he himself eventually joined the revolutionary guerrilla movement in his native Colombia. In this he has not been an inspiration to later Latin American theologians, though his writings and example did have considerable influence among church-people and political activists long after his death, at the hands of an army patrol, in February 1966.

This essay summarizes Torres' revolutionary Christianity and the biblical principles he believed underpinned it. Although undated, it is almost certainly one of the numerous articles and letters he wrote explaining his position, and exhorting others to follow him, in the months before his "disappearance" to join the National Liberation Army in October 1965.

## Source

John Gerassi, ed., *Revolutionary Priest: The Complete Writings and Messages of Camilo Torres*, London: Jonathan Cape, 1971, pp. 327–32.

## Further reading

Walter J. Broderick, *Camilo Torres: A Biography of the Priest-Guerrillero*, New York, 1975.
Germán Guzmán, *Camilo Torres*, New York, 1969.

John Alvarez Garcia and Christian Restrepo Calle, eds., *Camilo Torres: Priest and Revolution-ary*, London, 1968.

Paul Lehmann, *The Transfiguration of Politics*, London, 1975.

J. G. Davies, *Christians, Politics and Violent Revolution*, London, 1976.

## From *Love and Revolution* (ca. 1965)

. . . we Latin-Americans love each other, but not always in a rational or construc-tive way. Among the common people there is love, cooperation, hospitality, and a spirit of service. The upper class is different. At the risk of generalizing unduly, I can say that those who make the greatest fuss about their faith and their support for the clergy are those who love their fellow man least and that those who serve their brothers most are many times those who do not take part in the external rites of the church. All those who are, are not in; and all those who are in, are not. A real Christian can be identified by the love he demonstrates. When the people speak of Catholics, they refer to external observances. The church seems to be made up of a majority of persons who fulfill their external obligations and do not understand the Christian faith; they practice it only externally. Can either of these be said to be Christian? If they have bad faith, certainly not. Those who love, even if they are fetishists or believe they are atheists, are Christians. These people belong in spirit to the church, and if they are baptized they belong to the church in body as well.

The situation seems totally abnormal. Those who love do not have faith, and those who have faith – at least as faith is externally defined – do not love. ". . . he who loves his neighbor has fulfilled the Law," says Saint Paul (Romans 13:8). "Love and you may do what you please," says Saint Augustine. The surest proof of predestination is love for our fellow man.

Saint John tells us: "If anyone says, 'I love God,' and hates his brother, he is a liar. For how can he who does not love his brother, whom he sees, love God, whom he does not see?" (I John 4:20).

However, this love for fellow man must be effective. We will not be judged by our good intentions alone but principally by our actions serving Christ, Who is represented in each of our fellow men: "For I was hungry, and you did not give me to eat; I was thirsty and you gave me no drink" (Matthew 25:42).

In Latin America, in the conditions that exist here today, we see that it is not possible to feed, provide clothing for, or house the majority of our people. Those who are in power constitute that economic minority which dominates through its control over those who hold political power, cultural power, military power, and – unfortunately – even ecclesiastical power in countries in which the church has temporal goods. This minority will not make decisions against its own interests. Therefore, governmental decisions are not made in favor of the majorities. To give them food, drink, and clothing requires basic decisions that can only come from the government. We already have the technical solutions – or we will have them.

But who decides whether to apply them? The minority, against its own interests? A group acting against its own interests would be a sociological absurdity.

Then the seizure of power by the majorities must be preached. The majority must take over the government to change the structures through economic, social, and political reforms that favor the majority. This is called revolution. If it is necessary in order for men to love each other, the Christian must be revolutionary. How difficult it is for those who believe themselves Catholics to understand this! But how easy it is to understand it if we reflect on what we have just said about the church!

Christians, Catholics, seem to be stoical spectators at the collapse of a world that seems not to be their concern. They do not commit themselves to the struggle. In reading the phrase "My kingdom is not of this world" (John 18:36), they take "world" to mean "present life," not "sinful life," which is its real meaning. They forget Christ's prayer to His Father: "I do not pray that thou take them out of the world, but that thou keep them from evil" (John 17:15).

Many times, men leave the world but are not kept from evil. If the members of the community love each other, the priest offers the Eucharist more genuinely. This is not an individual but rather a collective offering. An offering should be made to God only if those who offer it love one another.

Hence, if the laity is not committed to the fight for well-being of their brothers, the priesthood tends to become ritualistic, individualistic, and superficial. The priest has the obligation to take the place of the laity in its temporal commitment if the love of fellow man so demands. When this love seems no longer to be considered exclusive patrimony of the church, it is necessary to testify that the communal spirit of the church is love. Unfortunately, the public does not recognize the testimony of the laity as the testimony of the church. The priest, in this case, should give the testimony of the church until the public is educated to understand that the testimony of every baptized person is a testimony of the church.

To see a priest involved in political struggles, abandoning the external practices of his priesthood, is something repugnant to our traditional mentality. However, let us consider for a while that his priestly testimony and love for fellow man may impel him to this commitment to be true to his own conscience and, hence, to be true to God.

When Christians live fundamentally motivated by love and teach others to love, when faith is manifest in life and especially in divine life, in the life of Jesus and the church, then the external rites will be the true expressions of love within the Christian community; then we will be able to say that the church is strong, not in economic or political power but in love. If a priest's temporal commitment in political struggles contributes to this end, his sacrifice would appear to be justified.

# Chapter 44

# Dorothee Soelle (1929– )

**Credo from** Political Evensong **(1968)**
Mary and Martha **(1990)**

Dorothee Soelle is a leading practitioner of political theology, a praxis-centered theology which attempts to recapture the "public" or "political" dimension of the Christian message. At its heart is a conviction that the "eschatological promises of the biblical tradition: liberty, peace, justice, reconciliation" do not admit of solely individual and spiritual interpretation, but present a profound challenge to society. Hence theology, to use Metz's term, has to be "deprivatized," and the relationship between faith and politics determined anew. In her writing, teaching, and campaigning for justice Soelle has emphasized this unity of faith and action, prayer and politics, and concluded that "theological reflection without political consequences [is] tantamount to blasphemy."

The first of these extracts is drawn from a liturgy composed by Soelle and others in 1967–8. At that time a lecturer at the University of Cologne, Soelle had been campaigning vigorously against the Vietnam War and staging church-based actions in support of this protest. Her liturgy was first used in St Anthony's Church, Essen, in 1968, within the context of a late-night prayer service organized by her group. The second piece is a later writing in which, reflecting upon the New Testament accounts of Mary and Martha, Soelle argues that contemplation and action are not "either/ors" for the Christian.

## Sources

Dorothee Soelle, *Against the Wind: Memoir of a Radical Christian* (trans. Barbara and Martin Rumscheidt), Minneapolis: Augsberg Fortress, 1999, pp. 39–40.

Dorothee Soelle, *The Window of Vulnerability: A Political Spirituality*, Minneapolis: Fortress Press, 1990, pp. 93–6.

## Further reading

Dorothee Soelle, *Political Theology*, New York, 1974.
Dorothee Soelle, *Thinking About God*, Philadelphia and London, 1990.
Dorothee Soelle and Fulbert Steffensky, *Not Just Yes and Amen*, Minneapolis, 1985.
Johannes B. Metz, *Theology of the World*, New York, 1969.
Jürgen Moltmann, *Theology of Hope*, London and New York, 1967.

## Credo

I believe in God
who created the world not ready-made
like a thing that must forever stay what it is,
who does not govern according to eternal laws
that have perpetual validity,
nor according to natural orders
of poor and rich,
experts and ignoramuses,
people who dominate and people subjected.
I believe in God
who desires the counter-arguments of the living
and the alteration of every condition
through our work
through our politics.

I believe in Jesus Christ
who was right when he
"as an individual who can't do anything"
just like us
worked to alter every condition
and came to grief in so doing.
Looking to him I discern
how our intelligence is crippled,
our imagination suffocates,
and our exertion is in vain,
because we do not live as he did.

Every day I am afraid
that he died for nothing
because he is buried in our churches,
because we have betrayed his revolution
in our obedience to and fear
of the authorities.
I believe in Jesus Christ
who is resurrected into our life
so that we shall be free
from prejudice and presumptuousness,
from fear and hate

and push his revolution onward
and toward his reign.

I believe in the Spirit
who came into the world with Jesus,
in the communion of all peoples
and our responsibility for
what will become of our earth:
a valley of tears, hunger, and violence
or the city of God.
I believe in the just peace
that can be created,
in the possibility of meaningful life
for all humankind,
in the future of this world of God.
Amen.

## Mary and Martha

### The Unity of Action and Dreams

As I was rereading the story of Mary and Martha, I remembered my childhood. In our Lutheran church in a suburb of Cologne there was a stained-glass window with the legend: "Only one thing is needful!" There sat Mary at Jesus' feet, tender, delicate of limb, humble of mien. Leaning on the table, feet apart, a mixing-bowl in her hand, stood Martha, her other hand lifted in reproach. "Lord, do you not care that my sister has left me to serve alone?" (Luke 10:40). I remember that I could not stand that story.

The Western tradition has seen these two women as prototypes of the contemplative and the active life. But meditation and efficiency, the quiet hearing of the Word and the restless concern for the daily needs of the body, the *vita contemplativa* and the *vita activa*, were not simply contrasted with one another. They were placed in an order of rank derived more from Aristotle than from Jewish thought. The contemplative life was the higher, more spiritual, and more essential; the active, practical life is necessary but inferior. Mary has "chosen the better part" (10:42). Martha is regarded in this tradition as useful but somewhat narrow and restricted. It is one of the basic principles of Western thought to regard "pure" theory as superior to mere practice; they are related to one another as headwork to handwork. It is true that the Reformation suppressed the cloisters of contemplative sisters in favor of practical, bourgeois life, but it further devalued the figure of Martha, the active, realistic woman. Luther said: "Martha, your work must be punished and regarded as worthless. . . . I want no work but that of Mary, which is faith."

It was not the Reformation, but a very different movement that spoke up against the dominance of this spiritualizing and anti-Jewish tradition of interpretation in favor of Mary and against Martha – namely, the mystics. In a radical new interpretation, Meister Eckhart, in his Sermon 28, set the still immature Mary at the beginning of the spiritual life and assigned to the mature Martha, on the basis of her experience, a greater nearness to that which is really necessary. Martha "feared that Mary would remain in this feeling of pleasure and make no further progress." She wants Mary to be like her. Eckhart continues in a brilliant new Christian (not clerical) reading (*relecture*) that reflects the spirit of the growing women's movement of the late Middle Ages: "Then Christ replied to her . . . 'Be reassured, Martha, she has chosen the best part, which will lose itself in her. The highest thing that can happen to a creature will happen to her. She will be as happy as you!'"

Women today who deliberately get involved with the Christian tradition are in the process of learning how to distinguish between the oppressive, woman-hating features of that tradition and the liberating ones. For our story, that means taking two steps. I call the first one "rediscovering Martha," and the second "receiving Mary and Martha together." We not only have to understand Martha, we have to revalue her, accept her strength, make her energy our own. We must see her not with Luke's eyes, but bringing in John 11, the story of the raising of Lazarus. In this story Martha is the actor who strives with Jesus as Job strove with God. She is the realistic, active person who knows that her brother, after four days in the grave, is already putrid, and she is the theological thinker who confesses Christ: "Yes, Lord, I believe that you are the Christ, the Son of God who has come into the world" (11:27) – a profession otherwise spoken only by Peter.

Discovering this Christian woman, as Elisabeth Moltmann-Wendel has done in exemplary fashion, helps us to deflate the hierarchy, even the one that has taken root inside us. Hierarchy as warranted domination that has no need to justify itself, that dispenses superiority and privilege, has always been directed against the deepest interests of women even when, as in the Mary-Martha model, it crops up among women themselves. Hierarchical thinking always undergirds contempt for women, making them comic or trivial. I think I sensed that, even as a little girl. I felt sorry for Martha, and she was an embarrassment. It was painful and distressing that women could be like the Martha cliché I had inherited.

Rediscovering Martha, learning to love the strong, self-confident, sober, clear-headed woman, helps me. In the Lazarus story we also see how differently the two sisters react to the death of their brother. Mary throws herself weeping at Jesus' feet; Martha reproaches him because he was so close by and could have come sooner without any difficulty! She is brash and does not give in. It is she, a female Peter, who speaks the truth. It is no accident that she was later depicted as a dragon-killer.

The other necessary step in interpretation that is of the utmost importance for women *and* men today is also connected to the rediscovery of this Martha who had been made so ugly for us. We have to learn that we need not choose between contemplation and action. No one has the right to compel us to this choice. We need not divide the world into doers and dreamers, into gentle, listening, self-surrendering Marys on the one side and pragmatic, busy Marthas on the other. We need both Mary and Martha, for in fact we ourselves are both sisters. Teresa of Avila, who followed the mystical tradition of interpretation and condemned a contemplation that is closed in on itself, said: "Believe me, Martha and Mary must be together in order to give lodging to the Lord and have him always with them. Otherwise he would be badly served and remain unfed. How could Mary, who was always sitting at his feet, have given him anything to eat if her sister had not come to help her? But his food is that we gather souls in every possible way, so that they may be saved and may praise him forever." It is only the two sisters together who can "give lodging to" Christ so that he has a place in the world.

Nowadays in the rich world there is a great longing for spirituality, for immersion, for contemplation and mysticism. Mary can symbolize this half-developed, still immature spirituality. Many young people despair of the possibilities of action in our world; they see the trees dying and the children of the poor starving, and they retreat into an inwardness about which the mystics warned us. Eckhart says of Mary that at that time, while she was sitting at the feet of Christ, "she was still not the true Mary. . . . For she sat still in a feeling of pleasure and sweetness, was received into the school, and learned how to live. But Martha remained quite real there."

I always think of this distinction when I see the strong women of my generation who act unflinchingly and struggle against the dragon that controls us. They have broken openly and unequivocally with the racists in South Africa; they stand in front of the big stores and they talk with the people in the little shops on the corner; they call on the bank directors; they say loudly and unambiguously what they think. In these groups of women who for years have been organizing the boycott, "Don't buy the fruits of apartheid," I see a lot of Marthas together, just as in the women who put a girdle around the other big dragon who lives in the Pentagon and began to act against it. That is the Martha whom Meister Eckhart saw, the one the people of southern France pictured as a dragon-slayer, who, according to a folk legend, crossed the sea with her sister Mary in order to teach and to preach. If one day our churches would "give lodging to" Christ and feed him, such women would be the bishops and teachers of the church. The Martha in me ought not to repress the Mary. In every woman, the young girl she once was should be visible. But the best women I know are no longer willing to accept the either-or.

When I was a little girl, the youngest after three brothers, I sometimes had to hide my Indian books and pretend to be doing my homework in order to escape the "snares of mediocrity," as Kierkegaard so exactly described it. Most women know the problem of having to make a place for themselves where they have the freedom to grow and not to be kept artificially small. It is clear that Mary and Martha in the Bible also express a mother-daughter problem. But the Bible transforms mothers and daughters into sisters, and the legend allows them both to cross the sea with Jesus' disciples and to teach and preach, so that they have both action and dreams, doing justice and praying, *lutte et contemplation*, in their lives – and the world becomes a more sisterly place.

# Chapter 45

# The Solentiname Community (1966–1977)

## Nicaraguan Peasant Mass (1970s)

The "Misa Campensina," or "Peasant Mass," emerged from the base community founded in the 1960s by Ernesto Cardenal on the island of Solentiname in Lake Nicaragua. Famous for its participative bible studies, which have been transcribed and published, and art, poetry and handicrafts, Solentiname played an active role in the popular struggle to overthrow the Somoza dictatorship in Nicaragua, suffering destruction at the hands of government forces two years before the struggle triumphed. Solentiname was one of thousands of base communities which appeared in Latin America in the decade following Vatican II, many playing a significant role in the development of liberation theology. Ernesto Cardenal, a priest, poet and some- time pupil of Thomas Merton, became Minister of Culture in the Sandinista admin- istration following the downfall of Somoza.

The Misa Campesina, set to music by the Nicaraguan composer Carlos Mejía Godoy, is a lively adaptation of the traditional Catholic Mass using the language of the people. In each of its main sections – Entry, Kyrie, Gloria, Credo, Offering, Meditation, Sanctus, Communion Song, and Farewell Song – it attempts to "demys- tify" the Christ of more conventional liturgies, and portray him, without stooping to irreverence, as one of the people, a *compañero* in the struggle to forge the new society. It can be compared to the Panamanian Mass and the African "Misa Luba."

## Source

Sylvia Mullally and Tony Ryan, "Misa Campesina" in *Nicaraguan Perspectives*; translation by Mullally and Ryan based on *Misa Campesina Nicaragüense*, published by the Minsitry of Culture, Managua, Nicaragua, 1981.

## Further reading

Ernesto Cardenal, *Love in Practice: The Gospel in Solentiname*, London, 1977.
Philip and Sally Scharper, eds., *The Gospel in Art by the Peasants of Solentiname*, Maryknoll, NY and Dublin, 1984.
Teofilo Cabestrero, ed., *Ministers of God, Ministers of the People: Testimonies of Faith from Nicaragua*, New York and London, 1983.
Phillip Berryman, *The Religious Roots of Rebellion*, London, 1984.
Andrew Bradstock, *Saints and Sandinistas*, London, 1987.

# From the *Nicaraguan Peasant Mass* (1970s)

*Entrance Song*

You are the God of the poor
the human and simple God
the God that sweats in the street
the God with the weathered face
that is why I speak to you
like my people speak
because you are the laborer God
the worker Christ

*Stanza 1*

Hand in hand you walk with my people
you struggle in the fields and the city
you stand in line at the camp
in order to be paid your day's wages
you eat there in the park
with Eusebio, Pancho and Juan José
and you even complain about the syrup
when there's not enough honey in it.

*Stanza 2*

I have seen you at the corner store
parked on a bench
I have seen you selling lottery tickets
without being ashamed of that role
I have seen you in the gas stations
changing the tires on a truck
and even working on the highways
with leather gloves in the sizzling sun.

*Credo*

*Stanza 1*

I firmly believe, Lord
that from your fertile thought
this whole world was born;
that from your artist's hand,
like a primativist painter,
all beauty flourished:
the stars and the moon
the little houses, lagoons,
the little boats floating
down the river to the sea,
the immense coffee plantations,
the white cotton fields
and the forests mutilated
by the criminal axe.

*Chorus*

I believe in you
architect, engineer,
artisan, carpenter,
bricklayer and shipbuilder
I believe in you
creator of thought
of music and the winds
of peace and love

*Stanza 2*

I believe in you, worker Christ
light of light and true
only begotten son of God
who became flesh
in Mary's humble and pure womb
to save the world.
I believe that you were beaten
with jeers, tortured,
martyred on the cross
when Pontius Pilate,
the hideous and soulless
Roman imperialist
tried to erase the mistake
by washing his hands of all blame

*Stanza 3*

I believe in you, *Compañero*
human Christ, worker Christ

conqueror of death
by your immense sacrifice
you have begotten the new human
who is destined for liberation
You are alive in every arm
that raises itself to defend the people
because you are alive in the ranch
in the factory, in the school
I believe in your struggle without truce
I believe in your resurrection.

# Chapter 46

# Steve Biko (1946–1977)

Black Consciousness and the Quest for a True Humanity **(1973)**

Biko first came to prominence in the late 1960s as a co-founder of the South African Students Organisation and the Black Community Programs. By the early 1970s he was a forceful advocate of Black Consciousness, which held that "the black man must reject all value systems that seek to make him a foreigner in the country of his birth and reduce his basic dignity." Biko rejected "racial integration" on the grounds that, once achieved, white values would continue to dominate, and argued instead that, if whites wanted to sit around the same table in Africa with blacks, this had to be on the blacks' terms. As this extract demonstrates, Biko saw a role for Christianity in the development of Black Consciousness, once it was stripped of all the extras with which the white missionaries had overlaid it.

During the 1970s Biko was subjected to banning orders, house arrests, and periods of imprisonment. On September 6, 1977 he was arrested, taken to jail, and tortured by white security police officers. He died six days later, the official cause of death being "hunger strike." The hated apartheid system in South Africa came to an end in the early 1990s.

Source

Basil Moore, ed., *Black Theology: A South African Voice*, London, 1973, pp. 41–3.

Further reading

Donald Woods, *Biko*, London, 1979.

## From *Black Consciousness and the Quest for a True Humanity*

Black Consciousness is an attitude of mind and a way of life, the most positive call to emanate from the black world for a long time. Its essence is the realisation by the black man of the need to rally together with his brothers around the cause of their oppression – the blackness of their skin – and to operate as a group to rid themselves of the shackles that bind them to perpetual servitude. It is based on a self-examination which has ultimately led them to believe that by seeking to run away from themselves and emulate the white man, they are insulting the intelligence of whoever created them black. The philosophy of Black Consciousness therefore expresses group pride and the determination of the black to rise and attain the envisaged self. Freedom is the ability to define oneself with one's possibilities held back not by the power of other people over one but only by one's relationship to God and to natural surroundings. On his own, therefore, the Black Man wishes to explore his surroundings and test his possibilities – in other words to make his freedom real by whatever means he deems fit. At the heart of this kind of thinking is the realisation by blacks that the most potent weapon in the hands of the oppressor is the mind of the oppressed. If one is free at heart, no man-made chains can bind one to servitude but if one's mind is so manipulated and controlled by the oppressor as to make the oppressed believe that he is a liability to the white man, then there will be nothing the oppressed can do to scare his powerful masters. Hence thinking along lines of Black Consciousness makes the black man see himself as a being complete in himself. It makes him less dependent and more free to express his manhood. At the end of it all he cannot tolerate attempts by anybody to dwarf the significance of his manhood.

In order that Black Consciousness can be used to advantage as a philosophy to apply to people in a position like ours, a number of points have to be observed. As people existing in a continuous struggle for truth, we have to examine and question old concepts, values and systems. Having found the right answers we shall then work for consciousness among all people to make it possible for us to proceed towards putting these answers into effect. In this process, we have to evolve our own schemes, forms and strategies to suit the need and situation, always keeping in mind our fundamental beliefs and values.

In all aspects of the black-white relationship, now and in the past, we see a constant tendency by whites to depict blacks as of an inferior status. Our culture, our history and indeed all aspects of the black man's life have been battered nearly out of shape in the great collision between the indigenous values and the Anglo-Boer culture.

The first people to come and relate to blacks in a human way in South Africa were the missionaries. They were in the vanguard of the colonisation movement to 'civilise and educate' the savages and introduce the Christian message to them. The religion they brought was quite foreign to the black indigenous people. African religion in its essence was not radically different from Christianity. We also believed in one God, we had our own community of saints through whom we related to our God, and we did not find it compatible with our way of life to worship God in isolation from the various aspects of our lives. Hence worship was not a specialised function that found expression once a week in a secluded building, but rather it featured in our wars, our beer-drinking, our dances and our customs in general. Whenever Africans drank they would first relate to God by giving a portion of their beer away as a token of thanks. When anything went wrong at home they would offer sacrifice to God to appease him and atone for their sins. There was no hell in our religion. We believed in the inherent goodness of man – hence we took it for granted that all people at death joined the community of saints and therefore merited our respect.

It was the missionaries who confused the people with their new religion. They scared our people with stories of hell. They painted their God as a demanding God who wanted worship 'or else'. People had to discard their clothes and their customs in order to be accepted in this new religion. Knowing how religious the African people were, the missionaries stepped up their terror campaign on the emotions of the people with their detailed accounts of eternal burning, tearing of hair and gnashing of teeth. By some strange and twisted logic, they argued that theirs was a scientific religion and ours a superstition – all this in spite of the biological discrepancy which is at the base of their religion. This cold and cruel religion was strange to the indigenous people and caused frequent strife between the converted and the 'pagans', for the former, having imbibed the false values from white society, were taught to ridicule and despise those who defended the truth of their indigenous religion. With the ultimate acceptance of the western religion down went our cultural values!

While I do not wish to question the basic truth at the heart of the Christian message, there is a strong case for a re-examination of Christianity. It has proved a very adaptable religion which does not seek to supplement existing orders but – like any universal truth – to find application within a particular situation. More than anyone else, the missionaries knew that not all they did was essential to the spread of the message. But the basic intention went much further than merely spreading the word. Their arrogance and their monopoly on truth, beauty and moral judgment taught them to despise native customs and traditions and to seek to infuse their own new values into these societies.

Here then we have the case for Black Theology. While not wishing to discuss Black Theology at length, let it suffice to say that it seeks to relate God and Christ once more to the black man and his daily problems. It wants to describe Christ as a fighting god, not a passive god who allows a lie to rest unchallenged. It grapples with existential problems and does not claim to be a theology of absolutes. It seeks to bring back God to the black man and to the truth and reality of his situation. This is an important aspect of Black Consciousness, for quite a large proportion of black people in South Africa are Christians still swimming in a mire of confusion – the aftermath of the missionary approach. It is the duty therefore of all black priests and ministers of religion to save Christianity by adopting Black Theology's approach and thereby once more uniting the black man with his God.

# Chapter 47

# Stanley Hauerwas on John Howard Yoder (1927–1997)

**Stanley Hauerwas,** Messianic Pacifism **(1973)**

For centuries the sixteenth-century anabaptist movement had been defined negatively. John Yoder was among those who have rehabilitated the anabaptist vision
and made it a significant force in late twentieth century theology. During his distinguished academic career Yoder wrote a tremendous amount. *The Politics of Jesus*,
however, is the book that has been so influential. Jim Wallis, editor of *Sojourners*
magazine, says that "John Yoder inspired a whole generation of Christians to follow
the way of Jesus into social action and peacemaking" and Stanley Hauerwas
said that "when Christians look back on this century of theology in America *The
Politics of Jesus* will be seen as a new beginning." In this article Yoder's friend Hauerwas expounds John Yoder's vision of Christian pacifism.

## Source

S. Hauerwas "Messianic Pacifism. Non-resistance as a defense of a good and just social order,"
*Worldview* 16 (6) June 1973, pp. 29–33.

## Further reading

J. H. Yoder. *The Christian Witness to the State*, North Newton, KS: Faith & Life Press,
  1962/1977 (Reprinted: Eugene, OR: Wipf & Stock, 1997).
J. H. Yoder *The Politics of Jesus*, 2nd edn. Grand Rapids, MI: Wm. B. Eerdmans, 1994.
S. Hauerwas, "The Nonresistant Church: The Theological Ethics of John Howard Yoder," *Vision
  and Virtue*, Notre Dame, IN: University of Notre Dame Press, 1981.
S. Hauerwas, C. K. Huebner, H. J. Huebner, and M. Thiessen-Nation, eds., *The Wisdom of
  the Cross: Essays in Honor of John Howard Yoder*, Grand Rapids, MI: Wm. B. Eerdmans,
  1999.
M. Thiessen-Nation, "A Comprehensive Bibliography of the Writings of John Howard Yoder,"
  *The Mennonite Quarterly Review* LXXI (January 1997): 93–145.

# From *Messianic Pacifism*

### *Non-resistance as a defense of a good and just social order*

Yoder critically analyzes the variety of pacifist positions. This is an extremely helpful book for nonpacifists, who may often assume that all pacifists' positions are cut from the same cloth. Of course Yoder prefers any pacifist position to one that legitimates violence, but often his critiques of pacifism are as trenchant as Niebuhr's. He is particularly doubtful of that pacifism – which some, perhaps mistakenly, associate with Gandhi and King – that claims political and social effectiveness as its warrant. Not only does this pacifism too often betray a naive faith in the good will of men, it accepts the assumption of power politicians that the good is that which works – a far more dangerous attitude than naiveté. For to admit a pragmatic test is to open the door to the justification of violence, since for short-term political goals it can be shown to work much more effectively than pacifism.

Moreover, such pacifism tends to be morally caught in an inner contradiction, as it absolutizes life as a good in itself. The pacifist, if he accepts this kind of position, seems committed to argue that there is nothing in his life worth dying for or having others die for. Contrary to this, Yoder's own position assumes that there is much worth dying for, and the Christian's willingness to die is exactly the element that makes his pacifism viable.

Yoder's rejection of any pacifism based on consequential reasoning does not commit him, however, to a pacifism of absolute principle (biblical fundamentalism), conscience (many C.O.'s) or moral ideal (Quaker and liberal Protestantism). Pacifism based on such principles not only tends to be legalistic and self-righteous but fails to notice that the meaning of absolute commands or ideals, even if divinely sanctioned, are not unequivocal. The pacifism of absolute principle fails to account for the conflict of principle that often occurs in complex situations where violence often seems an appropriate response to defend the innocent. Moreover, since the principles of absolute pacifism are often negatively formulated, they are too easily transformed into a search for moral purity rather than into an expression of love of the neighbor. It is possible, therefore, to be very scrupulous about not taking life, but to fail to undertake the positive forms of action that genuine respect for the same life entails.

In contrast to pragmatic or absolute pacifism Yoder describes his pacifism as that of the Messianic community where the "person of Jesus is indispensable" for the meaning and concrete form of nonviolence. Yoder is aware that this Christological center will appear to many as a decisive objection to his position. Yet he argues that Christian social ethics cannot, and should not, be written for or from the point of view of all men of good will. It is, of course, possible that men of other convictions will find themselves in sympathy with some aspects of the Christian's stance, but this cannot, or need not, be the Christian's first concern. The way of Christ is a calling for every man, be he Christian or not, but the responsibility of the Christian ethicist is to write to those who have accepted that call and its obligations.

Since Yoder's pacifism is but a correlate of his Christology, an understanding of how he views the person and work of Christ is crucial. He is extremely critical of pacifism that is based on individual teachings or acts of Jesus. It is not what Jesus taught that obligates the Christian to nonresistance but the person and work of Christ that finds its clearest expression in the cross, where God decisively dealt with evil, not by responding in kind, but through self-giving, nonresistant love. The Christian refusal to use violence is not therefore based on a legalistic abhorrence to violence or to an absolute commitment to life as an end in itself but "by the Lord it seeks to reflect. Christian nonresistance can be no more interested in 'success' or in 'effectiveness' than He." Nonresistance is right, not because it works, but because it anticipates the triumph of the Lamb that was slain.

Niebuhr and Realism generally have had some respect for this kind of pacifism as long as it was willing consistently to take the consequences; realists claimed such a position entailed the withdrawal from any attempt to work toward a less evil social order. The integrity of such a position could be admitted, though such integrity was bought at the great price of responsible action in the world – i.e., sectarian withdrawal.

Yoder, however, refuses to accept "prophetic" or "vocational" as an accurate interpretation of his position, since this interpretation can only lead to the illusion that it is possible to live "apolitically"; he believes that there is no way to avoid participation in the economic, educational and professional life of modern society. Moreover, such "prophetic" pacifism tends to be conservative, as it accepts the world of violence as normative beyond the bounds of the minority community. To accept such a dualistic position of the Christian relation to the world is to spiritualize the gospel and deny the social reality of the cross. Christ's ministry is not to provide men with the means to avoid political options but rather to incarnate and call men to "one particular social-political-ethical option." The theologians of revolution are right to claim that Jesus was a political figure, but the formal character of their claim in this respect is too easily ideologically perverted to justify political alternatives contrary to the form of Christ's Kingdom. For Yoder this is not possible, because Jesus did not bring an admonition to be concerned with the political; rather Jesus brought a definite form of politics by calling men to participation in the nonresistant community.

Yoder thus rejects the widespread assumption that the gospel contains no sufficient basis for the development of a social ethic. He has no use for social ethics based on the "natural," whether they be natural law (Catholic), orders of creation (Lutheran) or claims of "responsible" political activity (Protestant Realism). Each of these in its own way bases its social ethics on a reality other than the redemption wrought in Christ. The problem is not that there is no basis for a social ethic in the gospel but that we choose to ignore it because of the radical demand it places on us.

Yoder rejects just as strongly the social gospel attempts of Protestant pietists to spiritualize and individualize the gospel. Christ's cross is not primarily for *my* justification, whether such justification is interpreted in crass pietistic terms or in the existential transformation of the self-understanding; it is the first mark of the creation of a new social reality. The cross of Christ was not a difficult family situation or the frustration of personal fulfillment but the political and legally expected results of a moral clash with the powers ruling society. Jesus could not help calling into question the prevailing social order because it ruled through violence. Believers must also expect the cross as the price of social nonconformity occasioned by participation in the reality of the Kingdom to come in an unwilling world.

The gospel Jesus brings is a call for men voluntarily to take part in this new social order in which the only condition of membership is the willingness to become a disciple of nonresistant love. This society provides a new way for men to live together, where wrongdoers are not to be punished but forgiven and violence is to be dealt with through innocent suffering. This new community thus gives a new way to deal with a corrupt society; it builds a new order rather than smashing the old.

As the bringer and embodiment of such a Kingdom Jesus is often mistaken as an adherent of the righteous violence of the revolutionary. He used their language, he took the side of the poor with them, he condemned the same evils, he created a disciplined community of followers prepared to die for the divine cause. Yet he rejected the path of the zealots, not because the zealot changes too much, but because he changes too little. What is wrong with the revolutionary is not that he often fails or that in succeeding he is corrupted by the temptation to assume the complete righteousness of his cause to justify the violence used to win. What is wrong with the order produced by the zealot is that it is still the order produced by the *sword*. It continues to subordinate person to causes, preserves unbroken the self-righteousness of the mighty *and* denies the suffering servanthood through which God has chosen as his tool to remake the world.

The Christian cannot consistently force upon others the new way of life brought by Christ, because God wills to rule his kingdom only through voluntary obedience. The mark of the Church is that of a voluntary society of those who freely accept subordination as a sign that they represent not simply an alternative to present experience but rather a renewed way of living with the present. They can do this in the confidence that God has declared irrevocably in Christ that the cross and not the sword, suffering and not brute power, will determine the meaning of history. The cross is not a ritually prescribed instrument of propitiation but stands as a political alternative to both insurrection and quietism. The cross provides the basis for the refusal to resist evil with more evil, but also an alternative refusal to acquiesce to evil, since we are not condemned to participate in the social order as given.

Yoder's pacifism, like Niebuhr's Realism, is thus based on a substantive understanding of history. If this were not the case then pacifism would be but a subtle technique to obtain everything you really wanted without killing; the rejection of violence would become a less dangerous or more shrewd way to impose one's will upon someone else in the name of love. What Jesus renounced, however, is not first of all violence but rather the compulsiveness of purpose that leads men to violate the dignity of others. "The point is not that one can attain all of one's legitimate ends without using violent means. It is rather that our readiness to renounce our legitimate ends whenever they cannot be attained by legitimate means itself constitutes our participation in the triumphant suffering of the Lamb."

The way of the cross, the way of suffering servanthood and innocent suffering, is not a peculiarly efficacious technique for getting one's way. The key to the triumph of the good is not any calculation at all but simply obedience that reflects the character of the love of God. Christian pacifism rests on a deeper basis than the question of whether we should or should not use violence, for it calls into question the more substantial assumption that it is the Christian's duty to be in conformity with history or to make it move in the right direction. Pacifism is but a correlative dispositional stance of the claim that the cross is the meaning of history. The Christian's duty is to follow Christ with the full assurance that what appears to the world as the way of weakness is the triumph of God's kingdom. For the Christian the calculating link between our obedience and ultimate efficacy is broken, since the triumph of God comes through resurrection and not through effective sovereignty or assured survival.

Yoder is not recommending suffering as an end in itself or martyrdom as a value to be sought after. He is sensitive to the subtle forms of masochism that too often invite aggression rather than provide for conditions of peace. Christians do not seek their minority status in the interest of being different but because the world does not share the loyalties that form their distinctive way of life.

The tension between Church and world is not something God imposes upon the world by prior metaphysical distinctions between orders of creation and redemption or predetermined levels of righteousness. Rather, the distinction between Church and world is the difference between agents, between the basic posture of men, some of whom confess and others who do not confess that Jesus is Lord. Thus the "world" is not for Yoder a sphere of inherent evil with which the Christian can have nothing to do, but rather it is all of that in creation that has not yet taken the freedom to believe. As such, the potential of action in the world of unbelief is limited, since it does not share the convictions of Christ's redemption.

There can therefore be no "withdrawal" ethic, since the gospel the Church embodies is inherently a message about the good ordering of society. The first task of the Church, however, as a community of nonresistance, is simply to be a sign that Christ has established a sphere of liberation from the powers of this world. Thus the Church's strength is in her "otherness," a distinctiveness constituted by the justice and mercy that characterize a common life where social differences have lost their power to divide. From this "otherness" the Church reaches out and acts in society by providing the institutional space and rest necessary for social discernment. Such discernment includes not only help not provided by society with its limited presuppositions of care but also the ability to unmask the pretensions of those who have gone mad trying to control the world through violence. Without such a society there is never any place to stand outside the system, as without such a community we have no living symbolic speech or stories immune from social degradation.

# Chapter 48

# William Stringfellow (1928–1985)

## An Ethic for Christians and Other Aliens in a Strange Land (1973)

William Stringfellow is an obscure figure on the North American theological scene. Heralded by Karl Barth as the theologian to whom America should listen, his interests and range were eclectic and far reaching: early civil rights activist and protestor against the war in Vietnam; local politician; lawyer; connoisseur of the circus; advocate of the marginalized in the church and outside of it, in both law and theology; international speaker; one of the first to call for Nixon's impeachment; critic of both the church and state; advocate of God's kingdom. To the annoyance of the legal establishment Stringfellow turned his back on this, and headed to the margins that were New York's notoriously poor East Harlem where he lived and worked for many years amongst the poor. And it was here he discovered and recovered in a concrete way the biblical theology of the "principalities and powers" and their contemporary social reality – a recovery that was to provide significant for many, especially Walter Wink. He set about writing a Christian social ethic for contemporary America. He had an unswerving commitment to the importance and centrality of politics *and* faith to the Christian life and gave a central place to the Bible. "America," he said, "is a demonic principality, in which death is the reigning idol," and resistance to the power of death is the only way to live humanly.

The extract, from *An Ethic for Christians and Other Aliens in a Strange Land*, articulates how one is to live amidst the consequences of the Fall. "My concern," he writes, "is to understand America biblically . . . to treat the nation within the tradition of biblical politics – to understand America biblically – *not* the other way round." In so doing he asserts the authority of the Book of Revelation for determining that ethic. He elaborates the apocalyptic vision for perceiving the fullness of the spiritual and moral reality in which we live. Written against the backdrop of the Vietnam war, and the widespread resistance to it throughout America, this book speaks of the relevance of the images of Babylon and Jerusalem to his own age (much as Blake had done one hundred and fifty years before), and the necessity of confronting the reign of the power of death. In other words, Vietnam bespeaks the horror not only of military war, but of the moral and spiritual war being raged in creation, and in America in particular: America, in short, is in the throws of a demonic war, of which Vietnam is but one terrible symptom. It is a possession with political consequences.

## Source

William Stringfellow, *An Ethic for Christians and Other Aliens in a Strange Land*, Waco: Word, 1973, pp. 48–64.

## Further reading

C. Heyward. "Requiem for a Theologian, Advocate, Friend," *The Witness* 68 (4) (1985), 4–5 (who writes of Stringfellow's solidarity during the struggle for women's ordination to the priesthood).
A. McThenia, *Radical Christian and Exemplary Lawyer*, Grand Rapids: Eerdmans, 1995.
W. Stringfellow, *My People is the Enemy: An Autobiographical Polemic*, New York: Holt, Rinehart and Winston, 1964
——, *Dissenter in a Great Society*, New York: Holt, Rinehart and Winston, 1966.
——, *Conscience and Obedience*, Waco: Word, 1977.
——, *A Simplicity of Faith: My Experience in Mourning*, Nashville: Abingdon, 1982.
——, *Suspect Tenderness*, New York: Holt, Rinehart and Winston, 1971.
Bill Wylie-Kellermann, *A Keeper of the Word: Selected Writings of William Stringfellow*, Grand Rapids: Eerdmans, 1994.

## From *An Ethic for Christians and Other Aliens in a Strange Land* (1973)

*Babylon and Jerusalem as Events*

It is in connection with this peculiarity of biblical faith, this unique comprehension of time and history in this world, as distinguished from the myths, ideals, or hypotheses of religion or ideology or philosophy, that the two societies of the Bible – Babylon and Jerusalem – have specific significance.

To speak of the relevance of the Babylon passages in the Book of Revelation as a parable for America in the seventies or for Nazi Germany in the thirties – or, for that matter, for any nation in any decade – recognizes the biblical Word as an event in an esoteric sense. Babylon in Revelation is a disclosure and description of an estate or condition which corresponds to the empirical reality of each and every city – of all societies – in history. The Babylon of Revelation is archetypical of all nations.

The biblical witness in the Babylon episode is not a morbid hindsight into the decline and disintegration of a certain ancient city in Central Mesopotamia. *That* Babylon had long since vanished from the earth by the time the Book of

Revelation was uttered, and the visible "Babylon" contemporaneous with the Book was not the Babylonia of Mesopotamia but the Roman Empire under Domitian's reign. Thus the Word in Revelation is an event in an immediate way. But the Word also becomes event more than transiently, for more than the tenure of Domitian's regime, in that the essential character and authority of the Roman State at that particular time verifies the essential character and actual authority upon which any nation, and any regime in any nation, relies at any time in history.

By the same token, the Babylon of Revelation does not represent a predestinarian forecast, inevitably and automatically to be played out in due course like some cosmic horoscope, in violence to the creaturehood of both nations and humans and in travesty of the reputation of God as made known otherwise and elsewhere in the biblical testimony. To view the Babylon material in Revelation as mechanistic prophecy – or to treat any part of the Bible in such a fashion – is an extreme distortion of the prophetic ministry. It is in fact a contradiction of prophetic insight because it refutes the eventful predilection of the biblical Word. A construction of Revelation as foreordination denies in its full implication that either principalities or persons are living beings with identities of their own and with capabilities of decision and movement respected by God. And, in the end, such superstitions demean the vocation which the Gospels attribute to Jesus Christ, rendering him a quaint automaton, rather than the Son, of God.

This does not mean that the Babylon story in Revelation is of poetic status alone. This Babylon is allegorical of the condition of death reigning in each and every nation or similar principality. The fallenness of this same Babylon is empirically evident and, indeed, enacted everywhere, everyday, in the experience of specific nations. Thus the Word in the Babylon reference in Revelation is not abstract, but the Word is an event in that it concretely exposes and truthfully describes both the essential character and the particular situation of a nation, and of all principalities in the world within the era of time. Babylon is the parable of the nation beheld in the manifold dimensions of the nation's actual, fallen existence in history. Babylon is – to put it most succinctly – the parable of the nation in the fullness of its apocalyptic reality.

*The Word is event* – in an esoteric or a discreet sense. That is, of course, the mark which distinguishes the whole biblical literature as contrasted with Greek thought or Marxist dogmatics or Buddhist introspections or with assorted sectarian or churchly disfigurements of the Bible. Do not mistake my appreciation for the empirical vitality of the biblical Word as literalism, however. Any literalistic interpretations of the Bible are a false pretense – a substitute for, rather than a type of exegesis – which violates by their verbatim mechanics the Bible's generic virtue as a living testament. They devalue the humanity of the reader or listener by assigning the person a narrow and passive role depleted of the dignity of participation in encounter with the biblical Word which the vitality of that Word itself at once invites and teaches.

The relevance of Babylon as a parable of the fallen nation in the maturity of its apocalyptic destiny stands in counterpoint to the significance of the other biblical nation, Jerusalem. What Babylon means theologically and, hence, existentially for all nations or other principalities in the dimensions of fallenness, doom, and death, Jerusalem means to each nation or power in the terms of holiness, redemption, and life. Babylon describes the apocalyptic while Jerusalem embodies the eschatological as these two realities become recognizable in the present, common history of the world.

I am not implying that there is a neat parallelism in the manner in which Babylon on the one hand and Jerusalem on the other relate to the nations and institutions or to the practical situation of any particular principality. The interplay of Babylon and Jerusalem is dynamic and ironic and poignant, and it is specific as to each and every nation and power. Any description is inevitably too simplified, any analytical statement is insufficient. But, at least for now, it is enlightening to notice the paradoxical and the dialectical aspect of this interplay. The elementary truth of Babylon's apocalyptic situation is Babylon's radical confusion concerning her own identity and, in turn, her relationship to Jerusalem. The awful ambiguity of Babylon's fallenness is expressed consummately in Babylon's delusion that she is, or is becoming, Jerusalem. This is the same moral confusion which all principalities suffer in one way or another; this is the vocational crisis, really, which every nation in history endures. This is the vanity of every principality – and notably for a nation – that the principality is sovereign in history; which is to say, that it presumes it is the power in relation to which the moral significance of everything and everyone else is determined. Babylon's famous wantonness, Babylon's decadence, Babylon's profligacy has only most superficially to do with materialism, lust, or the decline of moral values, and Babylon's fall is not particularly a punishment for her greed or vice or aggrandizement, despite what some preachers allege. Babylon's futility is her idolatry – her boast of justifying significance or moral ultimacy in her destiny, her reputation, her capabilities, her authority, her glory as a nation. The moral pretenses of Imperial Rome, the millennial claims of Nazism, the arrogance of Marxist dogma, the anxious insistence that America be "number one" among nations are all versions of Babylon's idolatry. All share in this grandiose view of the nation by which the principality assumes the place of God in the world. In the doom of Babylon by the judgment of God this view is confounded and exposed, exhausted and extinguished. A magnificent celebration in heaven extols the triumph of God's sovereignty over principalities as well as human beings (Rev. 18:20; 19:1–2).

As every nation incarnates Babylon and imitates her idolatry, so each nation strives, vainly, to be or become Jerusalem. But, refuting and undoing that aim of nations, the reality of Jerusalem is *not* embodied in any nation or other power. Jerusalem is the holy nation; Jerusalem is a separate nation. In the biblical image of Jerusalem and in the historic manifestations of Jerusalem as the priest of nations, Jerusalem lives within and outside the nations, alongside and over against the nations, coincident with but set apart from the nations. The emphatic tone in the Revelation passages in which the call "Come out [of Babylon], my people" is recited again and again points to this peculiar posture of simultaneous involvement and disassociation (Rev. 18:4–5). It is pertinent to remember the prominence of this matter elsewhere in the New Testament. It was an issue, remember, which caused grave misunderstandings between Jesus and his disciples throughout his ministry. That is evidenced in their persistent bemusement at his parables, by their misapprehension of the Palm Sunday events, by their conduct at his arrest, by their mourning after the Crucifixion, by their surprise and consternation at Easter (i.e., Matt. 13; Mark 14:50; Luke 8:9–15, 19:28–44, 24:1–11; John 18:2–22). Only when Pentecost happens – where Israel is restored as a visible, viable, historic community and institution, as the holy nation – do the disciples and the others called into this new estate of humanity as society begin to comprehend the whereabouts of Jerusalem and Jerusalem's vocation among the nations (Acts 2:5–11, 36–47).

Babylon is concretely exemplified in the nations and the various other principalities – as in the Roman Empire, as in the U.S.A. – but Jerusalem is the parable for the Church of Jesus Christ, for the new or renewed Israel, for the priestly nation living both within and apart from the nations and powers of this world. Jerusalem is visibly exemplified as an embassy among the principalities – sometimes secretly, sometimes openly – or as a pioneer community – sometimes latently, sometimes notoriously – or as a prophetic society – sometimes discreetly, sometimes audaciously. And the life of Jerusalem, institutionalized in Christ's Church (which is never to be uncritically equated with ecclesiastical structures professing the name of the Church) is marvelously dynamic. Constantly changing in her appearances and forms, she is incessantly being rendered new, spontaneous, transcendent, paradoxical, improvised, radical, ecumenical, free.

In beholding some specific society or nation in history – like America – we must recognize the symbolic juxtaposition of the two biblical societies, Babylon and Jerusalem. Their contiguity signifies the convergence or confrontation or, indeed, collision of the apocalyptic and the eschatological events through which the past is consummated and the future is apprehended within the immediate scope and experience of that particular nation. It is in relation to these impending apocalyptic omens and imminent eschatological signs, in a time and in a place, that the body of the Church – and the person who is a Christian – decides and acts . . .

Again, how does the biblical juxtaposition of Babylon and Jerusalem set a precedent for and inform the life-style and witness of the Church of Christ in America now? What do the ethics of biblical politics have to do concretely with the politics of the principalities and powers in America now?

To all such queries, biblical politics *categorically* furnish no answers.

The ethics of biblical politics offer no basis for divining specific, unambiguous, narrow, or ordained solutions for any social issue. Biblical theology does not deduce "the will of God" for political involvement or social action. The Bible – if it is esteemed for its own genius – does not yield "right" or "good" or "true" or "ultimate" answers. The Bible does not do that in seemingly private or personal matters; even less can it be said to do so in politics or institutional life . . .

A Christian lives politically within time, on the scene of the Fall, as an alien in Babylon, in the midst of apocalyptic reality. Coincidentally, a biblical person lives politically, on the identical scene, as member and surrogate of Christ's Church, as a citizen of Jerusalem, the holy nation which is already and which is vouchsafed, during the eschatological event.

In ethical decision and in political action, in this world, a Christian is always, as it were, saying *no* and *yes* simultaneously.

A Christian says *no* to the power of death but in the same breath he bespeaks the authority of life freed from bondage to death. He exposes the reign of death in Babylon while affirming the aspiration for new life intuitive in all human beings and inherent in all principalities. He confounds the wiles and stratagems of death by insistently, defiantly, resiliently living as no less and none other than a human being; he enjoins the works of death by living in human fulfillment now. He warns of the autonomy of God's judgment while rejoicing in the finality of God's mercy. He suffers whatever death can do as he celebrates the resurrection from death here and now.

One marvelous example of the biblical genius in discerning the ethical as the sacramental has, of course, been rendered at the outset of this book, in citing the jubilation of the heavenly chorus at Babylon's doom. The ethical question *what is to be done when the great city dies?* is answered in a sacramental way – *sing praise of the sovereignty of God over all nations*. In the event, the *no* which issues against death *is* at once the *yes* which celebrates life as a gift.

# Chapter 49

# Ian M. Fraser

## Christian Grassroots Communities in Europe **(1980)**

Christian Base Communities flourished in Latin America in the 1960s and '70s. Essentially groups of poor Christians from the same neighborhood or workplace who met together to worship, pray and reflect on their experience, these communities came into their own as liberation theology began to take root and laypeople were encouraged to read the Scriptures themselves. Their orientation toward "liberation" led to their being perceived as subversive by some political authorities (as in the case of the Solentiname community, see p. 243), and they also fell foul of the institutional Catholic church which held them to be rejecting the authority of their bishops and establishing a "parallel magisterium." The communities themselves spoke of wanting to encourage the Church to become less hierarchical and one in which the gifts of the whole people of God could be acknowledged and utilized, but they have been unable to make much headway and, since the 1980s, have adopted a much lower profile.

While the base community movement in Latin America has been well-documented, those in the first world have received rather less attention. In this extract, from a paper read at a Latin America/UK Theological Consultation in Birmingham in 1980, Ian Fraser examines the main features of the Christian Grassroots Communities found in Europe in the 1970s. Fraser is a Church of Scotland minister and former Dean and Head of the Department of Mission at the Selly Oak Colleges, Birmingham. His books include *Reinventing Theology as the People's Work*.

## Source

Ian M. Fraser, "Christian Grassroots Communities in Europe" in Derek Winter, ed., *Putting Theology to Work*, London: CFWM, 1980, pp. 50–8.

## Further reading

Leonardo Boff, *Ecclesiogenesis: The Base Communities Reinvent the Church*, New York, 1986.
Leonardo Boff, *Church, Charism and Power*, London, 1981.
Margaret Hebblethwaithe, *Base Communities: An Introduction*, London, 1993.
Andrew Dawson, *Church in Transition*, Bethesda, 1999.
Guillermo Cook, *The Expectation of the Poor*, New York, 1985.

## From *Christian Grassroots Communities in Europe* (1980)

One can call the appearance of Christian Grassroots Communities after the for-
mation of the World Council of Churches and especially after Vatican II (since the
phenomenon is very substantially Roman Catholic, although it is essentially ecumenical in nature) a *movement*, quite distinctively. It has developed all over the
world – it would appear by the direct action of the Spirit. It is as if water fell on
land which had been desert for fifty years – and things took root and sprang up
with fresh life all over the place! I have come across Communities behind mountain ranges which cut them off substantially from the main life of their own
country, who were fully aware that they were part of a great world movement,
though nobody had said what was happening elsewhere and I might have been
the first messenger to give flesh and bones to what they instinctively knew existed
(instinctively probably means 'by prayer and humble self-offering, getting a sense
of what God was doing'). Recently, in the USA, Bishop Ting from China described
what followed the Maoist Cultural Revolution, when Christians were driven to
meet in small groups, in houses, in separation from one another. The separation
itself encouraged the growth of certain distortions and heretical tendencies. It did
not have a 'movement character' – especially it lacked awareness that concentration on the immediate situation must not extract one from the large community
of faith but rather contribute concretely to its life through mutual sharing and
support. A base for critical reflection and broader perspectives on the particular
work engaged in derived from this solidarity.

These communities are not para-churches. The word 'para' seems at times to be
used to give a cloak-and-dagger flavour to some novel and daring enterprises. The
use of the word may provide authorities with an excuse for marginalising and
denouncing something they can label a bit off-centre, to be suspected, 'to the side
of' the real thing. When a broad stream of Christian faith develops a head of water
which bursts the institutional banks which have contained it for so long so that
areas which were previously desert are irrigated, the new life which results is plainly
and simply 'church'.

Christian Grassroots Communities, wherever found, know themselves to be part
of a movement that is world-wide and is a sign of the new church. Although there
is an enormous diversity in the way in which groups operate, there are features
which can be said to be, by and large, hallmarks, distinguishing this kind of community from such as religious orders, house churches, communes and so on. I hold
the following marks to be basic:

1.   A rejection of the 'church of power' – the church which has position and clout in society, which is wealthy through investments in land and property, which is heavily institutionalised, with power in the hands of people at the top rather than exercised from the base. Instead, an option is declared for a church which is exposed and vulnerable, with no power place to lay its head.

2.   There is an affirmation of the ecumenical movement in both senses of the word

(a)   as the movement of the whole household of mankind (the oikumene) in its groaning and travailing and reaching out towards the promise of God – a new heaven and a new earth, and

(b)   as a movement of Christians from different traditions joining together in new companies of venturing so that, through fresh commitment to the mission of God in our time, they realise a sisterhood/brotherhood which spills beyond denominations . . .

3.   As has been suggested above, the Bible and the situation in which people find themselves are taken seriously and together. This is what Jaap Swart, co-ordinator of Christian Grassroots Communities in Holland, called 'walking on two legs'. Christians have a responsibility of making, together, a thorough analysis of the situation which faces them so that they may know the terms on which they can take creative action in favour of the Kingdom of God. They have a responsibility for continually digging into the scripture and sharing and checking their discoveries with one another. But these must be seen as two legs in constant interplay if the body of Christ is to move forward . . .

4.   The development of Christian Grassroots Communities could be interpreted as a decision for maturity. There is some kind of dawning confidence among ordinary Christians that they were not brought to new life to trail behind the decisions of church hierarchs and bureaucrats, but to grow up into Him in all things who is the head, even Christ. They are determined to 'be no more children'. Together, they take the responsibilities of adult Christians, leaving behind them the 'milk' stage of development . . .

5.   The life of the Christian Grassroots Communities is a kind of reaffirmation of the wholeness or catholicity of the church:

(a)   Prayer, politics, worship, work, reflection, commitment, evangelism, service, all belong together in the life of the Community. There are not some people who pray and others who are politically involved, some who specialise in worship and some in work – but a whole community who are growing up together into Christ with all these marks characterising the common life.

(b)   Neglected classes, sexes, ages are reinherited. The Isolotto Community in Florence is working-class, distinctively, in its approach. Many Communities in Belgium, connected with Christians for Socialism, have strong proletarian roots. The classes which have been encouraged to believe that the church is not for them in Britain have place and significance in the Christian Grassroots Communities in the rest of Europe.

Women do not need to be given a special place simply because they are as much in the leadership as men are. Real partnership is being re-established. . . .

(c)   Theology is being done by the Community as a whole. This means that insights and cross-checking which come from a great variety of experiences are put to work to produce something which is biblically convincing, soundly based in reality and relevant for action.

The insistence of the Christian Grassroots Communities that they live lives which are fruit-bearing rather than which fit in with existing ecclesiastical systems, itself produces situations which make it imperative to do theology. As Jaap Swart said in an interview 'Once you do things out of conviction which do not fit in with the usual pattern, you find the theological questions get raised' . . .

6.   The relationship of movement and institution are highlighted. A major question is whether the church as institution will give space for Christian Grass-roots Communities to develop in their own characteristic way instead of either cutting them off and trying to get rid of them or seeking to assimilate them to the existing organisation. The signs are not all hopeful . . .

7.   Among dangers which have been identified in the development of Chris-tian Grassroots Communities have been the following:

(a)   'Doing one's own thing' in a determination guided by the desire for self-expression rather than for obedience.

(b)   There can be what Georges Casalis called 'an extreme form of congrega-tionalism'. He instanced a French Christian Grassroots Community which believed that freedom to the group was assured only if at any point it could do what it wanted – for instance deciding one hour beforehand not to take part after all in a consultation of Communities in the area to which they had agreed and which they helped to set up. If they did take part, they would insist that every member contributed from her or his own particular angle, considering it a form of oppression if a contribution from the group as a whole were asked for.

(c)   There may be, in some cases, reluctance to face the demands proper to sustain institutions and required to hold life together and continue it signifi-cantly in complex societies.

(d)   Jaap Swart pointed out to me that, in Holland, the strains of living in a highly mobile society made it attractive to middle-class people to work in groups which dealt with a compassable area of life in which face-to-face rela-tionships could be established.

# Chapter 50

# Carter Heyward

## Liberating the Body **(1980)**

Isabel Carter Heyward was one of the "Philadelphia Eleven," a group of women "irregularly" ordained priests at Philadelphia in 1974, before the Episcopal Church of the United States officially accepted women's ordination. William Stringfellow officiated at the ceremony. Unable to secure a position within the Church, Heyward accepted a chair at the Episcopal Divinity School (EDS) in Cambridge, Massachusetts, where she still is. EDS is considered the most radical Episcopal seminary in the US, and is particularly attentive to the needs of the marginalized, and strong on issues of gender, race, and sexuality. Heyward has played a leading role in moving the institution in this direction, and been influential in campaigns for women's ordination within the Episcopal Church and for gay and lesbian rights.

Heyward is an original and challenging writer, always on the "edge" pushing into new and sometimes uncomfortable territory. Some of her most influential work has involved reconceptualizing the divinity, leaving behind a God who stands over-against us and embracing instead God the source of relational power, God who works among us to create right relationships. In this extract, taken from an address delivered at a Unitarian Church in Boston in 1980 and reproduced in *Our Passion for Justice*, she reflects on the sanctity and value of the human body – the "ground of all holiness" – and on "passion," which "will always characterize inspiration."

## Source

Carter Heyward, *Our Passion for Justice: Images of Power, Sexuality and Liberation*, New York: The Pilgrim Press, 1984, pp. 140–5.

Further reading

Carter Heyward, *The Redemption of God: A Theology of Mutual Relation*, Washington DC, 1982.
Carter Heyward, *A Priest Forever*, New York, 1976.
Mary Grey, *Redeeming the Dream*, London, 1989.

## From *Liberating the Body* (1980)

The grass-roots theology springing up in Latin American countries today, rising out of the struggle of the poor for food and survival, instructs us that the body is to be taken with ultimate seriousness. There is nothing higher, nothing more holy. It is nonsense, it is wrong, to contrast God with the body. Be it the individual human body, or the body of humanity itself, or indeed, the body of all that was created: the creation. My body is not a shell into which and out of which God moves, leaving me either godly or ungodly. The body of humanity is not a network of flesh and blood and bones that is either visited by or not visited by God, leaving humanity itself either godly or ungodly. If God is worth our bother and if the life of our brother Jesus means anything worth our knowing, it is that the body is godly, the body is holy, without qualification. Our hands are God's hands in the world. Our hearts are God's heart in the world. God pulsating. God beating. God yearning and open and growing in history. Our suffering and our tears are God's pain and trauma in history. Our laughter and our pleasure are God's own joy in history. Our work and our commitments are God's activity in this world. Our sexualities, our expressions of sexuality, our lovemaking in this world, is God's own expressiveness, God's own lovemaking, in history. When a human being reaches out to comfort, to touch, to bridge the gap separating each of us from everyone else, God comes to life in that act of reaching, of touching, of bridging. The act is love and God is love. And when we love, we god. And I use the word god here intentionally as a verb. If we are as fully human as we are able to be, and Jesus suggested we *are* able to be, then we are godders, we god – human beings/created bodies bringing God to life again, and again. Serving God in the act of serving humanity. Loving God in the act of loving humanity and one another. To point to a spiritual realm "up there" and a physical world "down here" is blasphemy, a destructive assault against both humanity and divinity. Because God is here to be fed, healed, encouraged, given shelter, befriended, accepted in the person of the neighbor or not at all.

Granted, we encounter a puzzling confusion between the holy value of who each of us is as a body on one hand, each of us needing badly to realize and celebrate the wonder that she or he is, and a preoccupation with the self on the other. Therapy, spirituality, charismatic religion, women's and gay/lesbian movements have heightened our capacities to claim our worth and power. This can be, and usually is, a very good thing. Its positive effects are often self-evident. Women and men are able to cast off sex-role expectations and other false expectations that prevent our knowledge of ourselves. We are meant and called to be more creative, more honest, more joyful, and more caring human beings when we do this than when we see ourselves largely through the eyes of others – parents, employers, doctors, lovers, gurus, those to whom we give social and ecclesiastical authority. Yes, there is a moral imperative to love ourselves, to be tender with ourselves, to comfort and enjoy ourselves, our bodies – to grow in self-esteem, to take pleasure in who we are, delighted to realize that our bodies are members of God's body in the world. And in tending our own needs and yearnings, we are tending God's.

But this same self-centeredness/centeredness of self that is vital to our constructive faith can be perverted. And this happens in the very instant we forget that *all* bodies are holy and as important as our own. And that, therefore, *you* must be as holy to me as *I* am to myself. Constructive faith is grounded in relation between a God who is good, a God who is love, a God who is justice, and the people of God who bring this God to life on earth. God does not stand alone beyond relation.

Unitarians may well look upon the doctrine of the Trinity with deep bemusement. If so, it is a confusion shared by most Trinitarian Christians, if we are honest. The Trinity is a much overworked, underthought and often glib doctrine. But I am coming, through my own Trinitarian roots, to believe that there is an important impulse behind the doctrine. An important dimension of human intuition. An intuition of ultimacy in relation. An intuition of a God who is "internally" relational. The Trinity is a patriarchal and sexist image about which, I must hasten to add, something will have to be done if self-affirming women are to continue as members of any traditional Christian body. For those who do not know, the Trinity is a homophilial/homoerotic image of relations between *males* (father/son). But my point is not right now the unequivocally sexist imagery. The point is the love relation, the intimate friendship, as that which is ultimate, most valuable, as that which is God. God is imaged as in the relation between those who speak, touch, reach, walk, weep, and act. God is nothing except in relation. Behind this badly reified, stagnant doctrine is the intuition that nothing has been, nothing is, and nothing will ever be unrelated.

And in the image of God so too are humanity and creation in relation. We, no one of us, are important in and of ourselves. Life cannot be lived in front of a mirror unless it is to be lived in a distorted, ultimately evil way. No one of us can live creatively or responsibly apart from the needs of the rest of the human body. Each of us as a body is a member of a larger body – the human body, human family, humanity itself – alongside and with other creatures, the "four-leggeds" and the "wingeds" who join us, the "two-leggeds," at the banquet of life. My body is significant not because I have unique or special needs, desires, or goals. My body is valuable because this flesh and blood and mind and heart and spirit represent the flesh and blood and dreams of every woman and man that has ever lived on this earth. Everybody is as valuable to the creation and to the creator as any other body has ever been.

Granted, we are not taught to believe this, and we must realize the extent to which we are not taught to accept it. Presidents seem more valuable than peasants. Generals seem more valuable than foot soldiers. Chairmen of the board seem more important than welfare mothers. The rich seem more valuable than the poor. Episcopal bishops seem more valuable and more important than gay/lesbian seminarians.

But constructive faith corrects this distorted vision by driving us toward the realization of a God who was active among a two-bit bunch of first-century nobodies. God was potent in the lives of these folks, Jesus and the others. Jesus and his friends, other outcasts, lived and taught a very simple life of faith, of expectation, and of love of neighbor and self. They bore witness to the power of love as the only necessary common ground among people who desire to experience themselves as valuable and worthwhile. These Jesus-people seemed to realize the value of the human body, the whole human body, as the cornerstone of constructive faith. They were/we are called to live for the body, in the body, as one of its member bodies, to stand and act as centered selves, cultivated in appreciation of our value, our power and glory in solidarity with all others whose power and glory and dignity and worth we are willing to struggle for.

We do not live above others. If we love others, we cannot hand things down to them, expecting that they will choose what we will choose, or live the way we will live. Rather, our commitment is that all persons can discover and attain whatever they need and want to live and grow in relation to still others. One of the reasons lesbians and gay men seem to pose such a threat when we acknowledge who we are is that the very word sexual implies body – and not just our own bodies, those of us who are gay or lesbian, but also the bodies of those who fear and despise homosexuality/sexuality itself. These are people who, like us all, have learned well to denigrate and renounce our bodies in embarrassment and trivialization and shame. Those of us who are gay and lesbian will learn better how to cope with homophobia, how to defeat it, when we realize that it is not simply something that others have toward us, but rather that homophobia is rooted in a fear of the body – the individual body and the collective body. A body that we share, a fear that we share.

How many folks do not fear the body's changes, the mysteries of our cells and pulses, the fleetingness of bodily pleasure, the unpredictability of bodily pain, accident, loss, and death? How many of us do not fear losing control over our own bodies, or being introduced to new and seemingly alien feelings, functions, fantasies in our bodies? How many of us do not fear bodies that seem to be quite unlike us? Bodies maddened, bodies starved, bodies stretched in strange-looking ways? Bodies speaking goals and dreams and languages that sound to us like babble? Angry bodies, bleeding bodies, bodies yearning for justice? Iranian bodies, Guatemalan bodies, Palestinian bodies, Salvadoran bodies, Ugandan bodies, Native American bodies, and Appalachian bodies? Bodies that we neither understand nor appreciate well as members of our own human body? How many of us do not fear bodies we must distance from our own in order to feel that we are in control of at least one body in this world?

The moment we see ourselves in others and realize that, in reaching for and touching some bodies, we ourselves are reached and touched, we encounter the ultimate meaning, the divinity, if you will, of being human, of being *some body*. We love, we god, we let go of our need to control any body, including ourselves. Our control gives way to the movement of God. And our fear is increasingly swallowed up in our faith.

Now, passion. This characteristic of faith, and it would seem today especially of born-again faith and right-wing religions, merits a few words. Listen to what the author of Isaiah 55 (1, 12–13) says.

> Ho, every one who thirsts,
> come to the waters;
> and [the one] who has no money,
> come, buy and eat! . . .
> You shall go out in joy,
>    and be led forth in peace;
> the mountains and the hills before you
>    shall break forth into singing,
>    and all the trees of the field shall
>       clap their hands.
> Instead of the thorn shall come up the cypress;
>    instead of the brier shall come up the myrtle;
> and it shall be to the Lord for a memorial,
>    for an everlasting sign which shall not be
>       cut off.

Why is it that liberal religious people do not insist that yes, indeed, by God and for the sake of humanity, we have seen an everlasting sign which shall not be cut off? Either we have not seen the sign, in which case we should ask ourselves what, if anything, it really does mean to be people of God. Or we have seen signs somewhere, hidden however deeply in the recesses of what we dare admit. And we are so often reluctant to say so with passion – to insist, to stake our reputation, our interests, our possessions, and maybe even our lives upon what we have seen: the value, the power, the centrality, the holiness, indeed, the divinity of the human body, the whole body with its many members, breathing, pulsating, yearning, speaking – the body of humanity. We have seen each and all of us as God's hands and heart and spirit on earth.

We have seen signs which shall not be cut off. The branches shall not be cut off from the vine. Our power will not be diminished or rendered ineffective. The sacrament of life shall not be withheld – the body, the blood, the sensuality of God's presence on earth. God is here/now. She is no absent deity, no God away in God's heaven, but rather the power of *actual* love among us. This is our God incarnate. Our God in flesh. Our God with us, among us, between us. God our sister. God our mother. God our father. God our brother. God our friend. God our lover. The sign is the power of human love. God's own lovemaking in history. That which strives for justice. That which strives toward mutuality. The creation of relations and governments in which no body is denied. No body betrayed. No body put down. No body cast out. No body crucified on the basis of greed, fear, or malice.

Either we have seen this sign – the power of human love for human bodies – or we have not. If we have not, it is because we do not want to. It is because we choose to deny ourselves the power of God. It is because we choose to grovel in the restlessness of our own failures rather than to look and see what is right before our eyes: bodies of people, indeed the body of creation, groaning in search of family, in search of relationships in which bodies can rest, in which bodies are at home.

In 1980, I attended the Theology of the Americas Conference in Detroit. This gathering of six hundred North Americans, Latin Americans, Africans, Asians, and a few Europeans wrestled for six days with what it means to do a theology of liberation. This was, on the whole, not a gathering of liberal Christians who pass resolutions on world hunger, sexuality, and peace. This gathering, I know, would have scandalized the Episcopal Church, just as it would have scandalized the various conventions of fundamentalist activists. But I left Detroit realizing that it probably would have scandalized the fundamentalists *less* than it would have scandalized the Episcopalians. Because, like the fundamentalists, the liberation theologians gathered in Detroit were filled with zeal, commitment to values that were spiritual and political. Like the fundamentalists, many of whom had been gathered in Detroit two weeks earlier at the GOP convention, we shared our dismay about the state of the world and about United States society in particular. Like the fundamentalists, we deplored the ineffectual liberalism of many of the major denominations we ourselves represent and need to accept responsibility for. Like the fundamentalists, we stated a corporate belief that the economic, sexual, racial, and other social and political problems besetting our society are basic theological problems, basic religious issues – and that it is most certainly the business of faith to do something in society about whatever we believe.

It is precisely, primarily, and specifically the business of the church to act on its faith. There is no other reason for the church. To pretend that there is, to belabor images of a spiritual realm that is worth more attention than the present world, is to blaspheme against both God and humanity. Racism is a spiritual and a theological problem. Sexism is a spiritual, theological problem. Classism and ageism and homophobia are spiritual, theological problems. And none of these problems will be solved unless people of faith commit ourselves unconditionally and absolutely to the undoing of injustice within and without the church. There can be no greater priority for us, it seems to me, than an uncompromising allegiance to the re-creation of a church, a society, and a world in which black, brown, yellow, red, and white women and men stand on common ground, holding all things in common, encouraged to make love/make justice in relationships where there is commitment to mutual well-being, growth, and choice; a world in which color, gender, sexual preference, nationality, and age are simply not issues in terms of human worth and value; a world built not on the bodies of the poor, but a common-wealth in the most literal, nonimperialistic sense of what that word might mean. Holding our wealth in common. The common-wealth of God.

Finally, acknowledging, as I believe we must, and bowing, as I believe we must, before the mystery and the wonder of all that is created, we go, aware of our own limitations and boundaries, beginning with those of our own skins. We go with one another, according ourselves and one another a tenderness and a compassion that will become a resource of our courage and our power. We go, comforted/strengthened by God, who is nothing other than the power of love in history, the power for right-relation in history, the power of justice in this world. We go, believing that either we will re-create the world, or we will destroy it. We go now, responsible for what happens in this world. We move as a body seeking a commonwealth that we will break down with our indifference or build up with our lives.

# Chapter 51

# Herbert McCabe (1926–2001)

## The Class Struggle and Christian Love (1980)

While institutionally the Christian church has denounced Marxism as an atheistic and dehumanizing creed, theologians and other church-people have from time to time dialogued with members of Marxist parties and movements to explore common themes and concerns. Aspects of Marxist thought may be discerned in the emergence and development of political and liberation theologies, and in regions of the Third World Christians and Marxists have found a common commitment to overcoming oppression drawing them onto the same side in revolutionary struggles.

The essay from which this extract is taken was one of many writings produced in the 1960s, '70s and '80s by Christians arguing that the scriptural imperative to do justice, practise love of neighbor, and represent the values of the kingdom of God compels Christians to join with Marxists in their opposition to capitalism and commitment to its overthrow. Whereas capitalism is predicated on human antagonism, McCabe argues, Christianity announces the possibility that people might live together in peace. McCabe was a leading Dominican with British and Irish nationality, who wrote and lectured widely on theology, philosophy, and politics. In 1967 he was briefly suspended from the priesthood by Rome.

### Source

Herbert McCabe, "The Class Struggle and Christian Love" in Rex Ambler and David Haslam, eds., *Agenda for Prophets: Towards a Political Theology for Britain*, London: Bowerdean, 1980, pp. 163–7.

### Further reading

Peter Hebblethwaite, *The Christian–Marxist Dialogue and Beyond*, London, 1977.
Denys Turner, *Marxism and Christianity*, Oxford, 1983.

José Míguez Bonino, *Christians and Marxists*, London, 1976.
David McLellan, *Marxism and Religion*, London, 1987.
J. Andrew Kirk, *Theology Encounters Revolution*, Leicester, 1980.
John Marsden, *Marxian and Christian Utopianism*, New York, 1991.
Tim Gorringe, *Capital and the Kingdom: Theological ethics and economic order*, Maryknoll, New York: Orbis, 1994.

## From *The Class Struggle And Christian Love* (1980)

The struggle of the working class is not . . . simply a struggle within capitalism, as though it were a matter of reversing positions and 'putting the workers on top' (as in the game of parliamentary elections); it is a struggle within capitalism which, insofar as it is successful, leads beyond capitalism. As Marx puts it:

> An oppressed class is a vital ingredient of every society based on class antagonism. The emancipation of the oppressed class therefore necessarily involves the creation of a new society . . . Does this mean the downfall of the old society will be followed by a new class domination expressing itself in a new political power? No, the condition for the emancipation of the working class is the abolition of all classes.

. . . there are certain things we can say:

1.   The class struggle is not a product of the envy of the poor for the rich; it is not about establishing some ideal equality between people's incomes.

2.   The class struggle is not something we are in a position to *start*; it is a condition of the process called capitalism within which we find ourselves. If anybody could be said to have 'started' the class struggle it was, I suppose, those enterprising medieval men who found ways to get round or break out of the stifling customs and traditions of feudalism and thus found ways to make products available more cheaply and more profitably.

3.   The class struggle is not something we are in a position to refrain from. It is just there; we are either on one side or the other. What looks like neutrality is simply a collusion with the class in power.

Now of course everything would be so much simpler if the class struggle were altogether perspicuous, but it is not; it comes in a variety of disguises. In the first place the simple division into two classes won't do. The basic antagonism that lies at the root of society produces a whole series of mutually hostile groupings engaged in shifting alliances and confrontations. It is almost never a simple matter to decide in the case of any particular dispute which side is to be supported in the furtherance of the emancipation of the working class and the consequent abolition of all class antagonisms. Very familiar instances of these difficulties occur with national liberation movements which are always a confusion of different elements struggling for different and sometimes incompatible aims.

Nothing in Karl Marx that I know of and certainly nothing in the New Testament provides you with a simple key to what to do in such cases. Marx said:

'All the struggles within the State, the struggle between democracy, aristocracy and monarchy, the struggle for the franchise, etc, are merely the illusory forms in which the real struggles of the different classes with each other are fought out.' No doubt, but getting through the illusions to the reality is a difficult and delicate business.

What is wrong with capitalism, then, is not that it involves some people being richer than I am. I cannot see the slightest objection to other people being richer than I am; I have no urge to be as rich as everybody else, and no Christian (and indeed no grown-up person) could possibly devote his life to trying to be as rich or richer than others. There are indeed people, very large numbers of people, who are obscenely poor, starving, diseased, illiterate, and it is quite obviously unjust and unreasonable that they should be left in this state while other people or other nations live in luxury; but this has nothing specially to do with capitalism, even though we will never now be able to alter that situation until capitalism has been abolished. You find exactly the same conditions in, say, slave societies and, more-over, capitalism, during its prosperous boom phases, is quite capable of relieving distress at least in fully industrialised societies – this is what the 'Welfare State' is all about. What is wrong with capitalism is simply that it is based on human antag-onism, and it is precisely here that it comes in conflict with Christianity. Capital-ism is a state of war, but not just a state of war between equivalent forces; it involves a war between those who believe in and prosecute war as a way of life, as an economy, and those who do not. . . .

Christianity is deeply subversive of capitalism precisely because it announces the improbable possibility that men might live together without war; neither by domination nor by antagonism but by unity in love. It announces this, of course, primarily as a future and nearly miraculous possibility and certainly not as an estab-lished fact; Christians are not under the illusion that mankind is sinless or that sin is easily overcome, but they believe that it will be overcome. It was for this reason that Jesus was executed – as a political threat. Not because he was a political activist; he was not. Although amongst his disciples he attracted some of the Jewish nationalist Zealots, the Provos of the time, they did not attract him. Certainly Jesus was not any kind of socialist – how could anyone be a socialist before capitalism had come into existence? But he was nonetheless executed as a political threat because the gospel he preached – that the Father loves us and therefore, in spite of all the evidence to the contrary, we are able to love one another and stake the meaning of our lives on this – cut at the root of the antagonistic society in which he still lives.

Christianity is not an ideal theory, it is a praxis, a particular kind of practical challenge to the world. Christians, therefore, do not, or should not, stand around saying 'What a pity there is capitalism and the class war'. They say, or should say, 'How are we going to change this?' It might have been nice if we had never had capitalism; who can tell what might have happened? Only the most naive mech-anist supposes that history has inevitable patterns so that you could predict every stage of it. It is at least theoretically possible that there might never have been cap-italism and that *might* have been nice, though it is hard to see how we could have gone through the enormous strides towards human liberation that were in fact made under and through capitalism. The point is that all that is useless speculation; we do have capitalism, we do have class war; and the Christian job is to deal with these facts about our world. . . .

The Christian who looks for peace and for an end to antagonism has no option but to throw himself wholeheartedly into the struggle against the class enemy; he must be unequivocally on one side and not on the other. As I have said, it is not always perfectly simple to sort out which side is which in the various protean disguises that the class struggle takes, but given that they are sorted out there should be no question but that the Christian is on one side with no hankering after the other. The other side is the enemy. If you doubt this, watch how he behaves: he will seek either to buy you or crush you. The world, as John has Jesus saying, will hate you.

Now *how* will you carry on the fight? There are various pieces of advice that might be given, but I would like here to reiterate some traditional ones. In the first place be meek. Blessed are the meek for they shall inherit the earth; pray for those that persecute you; be a peacemaker; do not insult your enemy or be angry with him. Who, after all, wants a comrade in the struggle who is an arrogant, loud-mouthed, aggressive bully? The kind of person who jumps on the revolutionary bandwagon in order to work off his or her bad temper or envy or unresolved conflict with parents does not make a good and reliable comrade. Whatever happened to all those 'revolutionary' students of 1968? What the revolution needs is grown-up people who have caught on to themselves, who have recognised their own infantilisms and to some extent dealt with them – people in fact who have listened to the Sermon on the Mount.

It is a simple piece of right-wing lying that those who carry on the struggle are motivated by pride and greed, envy and aggression. Real revolutionaries are loving, kind, gentle, calm, unprovoked to anger; they don't hit back when someone strikes them, they do not insist on their own way, they endure all things; they are extremely dangerous. It is not the revolution but the capitalist competitive process that is explicitly and unashamedly powered by greed and aggression. The Christian demand for love and peace is precisely what motivates us to take part in the class struggle: but more than that, the gospel of love, and in particular the Sermon on the Mount, provides us with the appropriate revolutionary discipline for effective action.

We still need though to face the question of revolutionary violence. How could that be compatible with the Sermon on the Mount? Well, first of all, in this matter we should not lose our sense of humour. There is something especially ludicrous about Christian churchmen coming round to the belief that violence is wrong. There is probably no sound on earth so bizarre as the noise of clergymen bleating about terrorism and revolutionary violence while their cathedrals are stuffed with regimental flags and monuments to colonial wars. The Christian Church, with minor exceptions, has been solidly on the side of violence for centuries, but normally it has only been the violence of soldiers and policemen. It is only when the poor catch on to violence that it suddenly turns out to be against the gospel.

But despite all this, the Church, since it is after all the Christian Church, has never simply professed itself in favour of the violence of the ruling classes, the violence of the status quo. What it has done is to profess itself on the side of justice and to note, quite rightly, that in our fallen world justice sometimes demands violence. This seems to me to make perfect sense – my only quarrel is with the way that justice has so often turned out to coincide with the interests of the rich. Justice and love can involve coercion and violence because the objects of justice and love are not just individual people but can be whole societies. It is an error (and a bourgeois liberal error at that) to restrict love to the individual I–Thou relationship. There is no warrant for this in the New Testament – it is simply a framework that our society has imposed on our reading of the gospels. If we have love for people not simply in their individuality but also in their involvement in the social structures, if we wish to protect the structures that make human life possible, then we sometimes, in fact quite often, find it necessary to coerce an individual for the sake of the good of the whole. The individual who seeks his or her own apparent interests at the expense of the whole community may have to be stopped, and may have to be stopped quickly. To use violence in such a case is admittedly not a perspicuous manifestation of love (if we were trying to teach someone the meaning of the word 'love' we would hardly point to such examples), but that does not mean that it is a manifestation of lack of love. In our world, before the full coming of the kingdom, love cannot always be perspicuous and obvious. We must not hastily suppose that just because an action would hardly do as a paradigm case of loving that it is therefore opposed to love.

# Chapter 52

# Oscar Romero (1917–1980)

The Political Dimension of the Faith from the Perspective of the Poor **(1980)**

Considered to be a conservative at the time of his appointment as archbishop of San Salvador in 1977, Romero became radicalized against the background of the heightening tension in El Salvador in the late 1970s. Increasingly vocal on the rights of the poor and the immorality of military repression, he came to be seen by his opponents as a threat to the status quo; and it is hardly doubted that his assassination on March 24, 1980 was prompted by his denunciations of the violence and terror of the authorities. Indeed, the day preceding his death he had made a direct appeal to members of the police and army to disobey orders to shoot their fellow citizens, on the grounds that such orders were immoral and counter to the law of God.

This extract is taken from an address Romero gave two months before his death at a ceremony at Louvain University, Belgium, to confer on him an honorary doctorate. In the opening sections he highlighted the call of Vatican II for the church to be of service to the world, and the mission of Jesus to bring good news to the poor, and noted that, in his own experience, the church had now begun to make the poor "the special beneficiaries of its mission."

Source

Alfred T. Hennelly, *Liberation Theology: A Documentary History*, Maryknoll, NY, 1990, pp. 296–302.

Further reading

Marie Dennis, *Oscar Romero*, Maryknoll, NY, 2000.
James Brockman, *Romero – A Life*, Maryknoll, NY, 1989.

Oscar Romero, *The Voice of the Voiceless: The Four Pastoral Letters and Other Statements*, Maryknoll, NY, 1985.

Oscar Romero, *A Shepherd's Diary*, London, 1993.

Philip Berryman, *The Religious Roots of Rebellion*, London, 1984.

Michael A. Hayes and David Tombs, eds. *Truth and Memory: the Church and Human Rights in El Salvador and Guatemala*, Leominster: Gracewing, 2001.

María López Vigil, *Oscar Romero: memories in mosaic*, London: Darton, Longman Todd, 2000.

Jon Sobrino, *Romero: Martyr for Liberation*, London: CIIR, 1982.

Jon Sobrino, *Companions of Jesus: the murder and martyrdom of the Salvadorean Jesuits*, London: CIIR, 1990.

## From *The Political Dimension of the Faith from the Perspective of the Poor* (1980)

*Commitment to the Defense of the Poor*

The church has not only incarnated itself in the world of the poor, giving them hope; it has also firmly committed itself to their defense. The majority of the poor in our country are oppressed and repressed daily by economic and political structures. The terrible words spoken by the prophets of Israel continue to be verified among us. Among us there are those who sell others for money, who sell a poor person for a pair of sandals; those who, in their mansions, pile up violence and plunder; those who crush the poor; those who make the kingdom of violence come closer as they lie upon their beds of ivory; those who join house to house, and field to field, until they occupy the whole land, and are the only ones there.

Amos and Isaiah are not just voices from distant centuries; their writings are not merely texts that we reverently read in the liturgy. They are everyday realities. Day by day we live out the cruelty and ferocity they excoriate. We live them out when there come to us the mothers and the wives of those who have been arrested or who have disappeared, when mutilated bodies turn up in secret cemeteries, when those who fight for justice and peace are assassinated. Daily we live out in our archdiocese what Puebla so vigorously denounced: "There are the anxieties based on systematic or selective repression; it is accompanied by accusations, violations of privacy, improper pressures, tortures, and exiles. There are the anxieties produced in many families by the disappearance of their loved ones, about whom they cannot get any news. There is the total insecurity bound up with arrest and detention without judicial consent. There are the anxieties, felt in the face of a system of justice that has been suborned or cowed."

In this situation of conflict and antagonism, in which just a few persons control economic and political power, the church has placed itself at the side of the poor and has undertaken their defense. The church cannot do otherwise, for it remembers that Jesus had pity on the multitude. But by defending the poor it has entered into serious conflict with the powerful who belong to the monied oligarchies and with the political and military authorities of the state.

*Persecuted for Serving the Poor*

This defense of the poor in a world deep in conflict has occasioned something new in the recent history of our church: persecution. You know the more important facts. In less than three years over fifty priests have been attacked, threatened, calumniated. Six are already martyrs – they were murdered. Some have been tortured and others expelled. Nuns have also been persecuted. The archdiocesan radio station and educational institutions that are Catholic or of a Christian inspiration have been attacked, threatened, intimidated, even bombed. Several parish communities have been raided.

If all this has happened to persons who are the most evident representatives of the church, you can guess what has happened to ordinary Christians, to the campesinos, catechists, lay ministers, and to the ecclesial base communities. There have been threats, arrests, tortures, murders, numbering in the hundreds and thousands. As always, even in persecution, it has been the poor among the Christians who have suffered most.

It is, then, an indisputable fact that, over the last three years, our church has been persecuted. But it is important to note why it has been persecuted. Not any and every priest has been persecuted, not any and every institution has been attacked. That part of the church has been attacked and persecuted that put itself on the side of the people and went to the people's defense.

Here again we find the same key to understanding the persecution of the church: the poor. Once again it is the poor who bring us to understand what has really happened. That is why the church has understood the persecution from the perspective of the poor. Persecution has been occasioned by the defense of the poor. It amounts to nothing other than the church's taking upon itself the lot of the poor.

Real persecution has been directed against the poor, the body of Christ in history today. They, like Jesus, are the crucified, the persecuted servant of Yahweh. They are the ones who make up in their own bodies that which is lacking in the passion of Christ. And for that reason when the church has organized and united itself around the hopes and the anxieties of the poor, it has incurred the same fate as that of Jesus and of the poor: persecution.

# Chapter 53

# John Vincent (1929–    )

## OK. Let's be Methodists **(1984)**

Since 1970, John Vincent has founded and worked in the Sheffield Inner City Ecumenical Mission, the Urban Theology Unit, and the Ashram Community, where he developed churches in shops and a pub, community houses, alternative congregations, and a Study Year for people seeking vocations. He is also an Honorary Lecturer in Biblical Studies at Sheffield University, where he supervises a doctoral program in contextual, urban, and liberation theologies. His writings come out of this dual commitment as theologian and as missioner, and indicate four dominant related concerns – the contemporising of the figure of Jesus; investigating Discipleship in the Gospels; the development of an Urban Theology; and the pioneering of Base Ecclesial Communities. He was President of the Methodist Conference in 1989–90. In the present piece, Vincent evokes John Wesley as a model for a contemporary Jesus-centred Radical Discipleship, which he characterizes in the "alternative journeys" of asceticism, down-sizing, economic sharing, community living, incarnation, and non-conformism.

## Source

J. Vincent, *OK Let's be Methodists*, London: Epworth 1984, pp. 15–21.

## Further reading

G. Nuttall, *The Holy Spirit in Puritan Faith and Experience*, Oxford: Blackwell, 1946.
J. Vincent, *Into the City*, London: Epworth, 1982.
J. Vincent, *Hope from the City*, London: Epworth, 2000.
D. L. Watson, *The Early Methodist Class Meeting*, Nashville: Abingdon, 1985.

# From *OK. Let's be Methodists* (1984)

*Rising of the Poor*

*A movement of common people*

It is natural to assume that Wesley *was* Methodism; that he created, defined, controlled it. Certainly without him, without his very strong and distinctive style and conviction, there would be no Methodism as we know it. But it is quite clear that there was a strong religious movement that Wesley did not start. There was already a widespread popular movement arising, indeed functioning in several parts of the country. Not only was there a great readiness among the hearers for the kind of powerful faith and intimate societies that proliferated with Wesley, but the work was already springing up in certain parts of England around a surprising number of individual preachers, prior to and quite separate from Wesley.

The main centres of Wesley's work were London (from 1738), Bristol (from 1739) and Newcastle (from 1742). One reason for this is that other evangelists were already at work in other places. John Bennet developed a wide circuit of societies and preaching places in Lancashire, Cheshire and Derbyshire. Selina, Countess of Huntingdon, built a vast connection across the North of England, mainly and exceptionally for the upper classes! In the North, too, Thomas Lee created societies out of his work place, the worsted trade. John Haime worked in a similar way within the expeditionary army, as did John Nelson in the West Riding. These and many others, in varying degrees, created new Christian work out of a people who clearly everywhere were ready for it. Some of these made links with Wesley, or even joined him, with relief and enthusiasm. Others never connected with his movement. What is crucial and significant is that they were there both before Wesley and independently of him.

One important characteristic of Wesley's movement arises from the fact of this existing mass, popular awakening. The preachers and the members of his societies were, almost without exception, from the ordinary working people, from the bottom of society. A list of Bristol preachers in 1741 includes '2 hoopers, 2 weavers, 2 master-mariners, 2 braziers, a house carpenter, a serge maker, a cork cutter' . . . and so on.

Not only were his preachers simple, working people, but Wesley 'sat at their feet'. They were often condemned as 'a few, raw, young, unlettered men' (*Journal*, 16 June 1755). But Wesley's sole criterion was whether a potential preacher had a spiritual power and a conviction to declare. He neither demanded education, nor offered it to his preachers. The 'travelling bookshop' in their saddle-bags was mainly religious biography. And he gave them enormous freedom to function as they were called. He trusted their call and learned from them. He believed God was at work and trusted him to continue it. Sometimes he was criticized for too easily giving a recommended person a licence to travel. But he was facilitating the work of God, not controlling it. Of course, control would in practice have been very difficult. He could not visit often and his only means of communication was the horse! But neither did he wish it.

Wesley received a great degree of acceptance and affection from the common people. He became ultimately more uncomfortable with the upper class, Oxford or London society, than with his Kingswood colliers. The massive awakening and response to his work was among such people. They affirmed the rightness of his work. Wesley might well have gained his decisive assurance, not from the Aldersgate Street 'heartwarming', but from seeing the New Testament church come alive among the common people. He then knew, assuredly, that he and his work were acceptable to God.

A recent unpublished essay by Bernard Hall on 'New Model Church' points out many of these elements and shows how, in fact, this artisan, grassroots, unordained, and untrained leadership was decisive for the whole of Wesley's lifetime and immediately afterwards. Indeed, Wesley's special places, London and Bristol, preserved an ordained ministry style – Charles came to London when John had to be away! – which was totally unique. Bernard Hall observes how the itinerant preachers who died before 1800 were rarely from London or Bristol (only 9) and even Wesley's Newcastle produced only 8, whereas 26 were from Yorkshire, 12 from adjacent counties, 18 were from Ireland, 11 from Cornwall, and 16 from elsewhere. The conclusion is plain: Bennet, Grimshaw, Darney and Nelson produced far more preachers than Wesley! Perhaps Sarah Crosby illustrates this most strongly. In London she was but a class leader. Moving to Derby, where there were no Methodists, she soon found a building and a congregation, and she became a preacher and leader.

Bernard Hall also sees the widespread popular religious movement in Wesley's time as a continuation of the Puritan tradition in the previous century which had been repressed by the law under the Restoration with the Act of Toleration of 1688.

*An alternative to revolution?*
The movement in which Wesley participated was thus a 'rising of the poor' in the sense that it was a movement of poor people, claiming for themselves a place within the religion of the time, which they had been otherwise denied, and creating for themselves societies and associations to support and extend their new-found consciousness.

But the movement was also a 'rising of the poor' in a more literal sense. The poor cried out from dire distress, and sought real change. In his sermon on 'National Sins and Miseries' in 1775, Wesley says:

> That the people suffer, none can deny . . . thousands of people in the west of England, throughout Cornwall in particular, in the north, and even in the midland counties, are totally unemployed . . . I have seen not a few of these wretched creatures . . . standing in the streets, with pale looks, hollow eyes, and meagre limbs; or creeping up and down like walking shadows. I have known families, who a few years ago lived in an easy, genteel manner, reduced to just as much raiment as they had on, and as much food as they could gather in the field. To this one or other of them repaired once a day, to pick up the turnips which the cattle had left; which

they boiled, if they could get a few sticks, or, otherwise, ate them raw. (*Works*, vii, p. 402)

It was this situation that produced a 'rising of the poor' for which the early Methodist societies provided a salutary place for at least a new self-consciousness and the exercise of charity.

Whether early Methodism provided anything more has been hotly debated. Elie Halevy argued that Methodism not only saved England from a French revolution, but also diverted into religious channels energies that could have secured social, economic and political reform. The argument has been hotly debated. Recently, Bernard Semmel, in *The Methodist Revolution* argues thet Methodism was in fact the British form of the Democratic Revolution. He says:

> I am persuaded by historians who see the period between 1760 and 1815 as an '*Age of the Democratic Revolution*' in the West, a time when the traditional, hierarchical society which had characterized Europe for many centuries was eroding and a recognizable modern society was taking its place. This was a time when the entire Atlantic world, moved by the desire for greater personal autonomy and roused by the slogans of liberty and equality, rose to overturn the privileged, governing classes, bringing the long-suppressed, inarticulate lower classes, onto the stage of events. (p. 7)

Thus, Methodism may have helped to block a violent English counterpart to the French Revolution by preempting the critical appeal and objective of that Revolution, and providing a counter to revolutionary violence.

The 'rising of the poor', then, at least in Wesley's day, and in the century which followed, did not produce the necessary social and economic reforms. Indeed, Methodism soon developed a more 'establishment' face, in line with Wesley's own innate Toryism. Thus, it would be possible for our Sheffield radical poet, Ebenezer Elliott, to write in his 'Open-Air Sermon' of 1833:

> Ask ye if I, of Wesley's followers one,
> Adjure the house where Wesleyans bend the knee?
> I do – because the *Spirit* thence is gone;
> And truth, and faith, and grace, are not, with me,
> The Hundred Popes of England's Jesuitry.
> What are the *deeds* of men called Christian, now?
> They roll themselves in dust before the great;
> Wherever Mammon builds a shrine, they bow,
> And would nail Jesus to their cross of hate,
> Should he again appear in *mean* estate . . .
> Pious they are, cool, circumspect, severe;
> And while they feel for woes beyond the wave,
> They laud the tyrants who starve millions here:
> The famish'd Briton *must* be fool or knave,
> But wrongs are precious in a foreign slave.
> Their Bibles for the heathen load our fleets;

Lo! gloating eastward, they inquire, 'What news?'
'We die,' we answer, 'foodless, in the streets,'
And what reply your men of Gospel-views?
Oh, 'they are sending bacon to the Jews!'
Their lofty souls have telescopic eyes,
Which see the smallest speck of distant pain,
While, at their feet, a world of agonies,
Unseen, unheard, unheeded, writhes in vain.

Thus did Wesley's successors desert the poor. And the poor had to look else-where for their revolution. The question that fascinates me, however, is whether there is not a revolution attainable by incarnation. Wesley became incarnate among the poor, the labouring artisans, the powerless people. He completely believed in their worth, so that his highest praise was to say that someone was like one of the Kingswood colliers. 'O that our London brethren would come to school at Kingswood,' he once wrote. The poor grew to love him, too. He fitted into their world. So much was this true that he no longer felt at ease among the Oxford and London upper classes where he began.

His style of living reflected his real incarnation into the world of working people. He kept a very simple 'cell' in London, Bristol and Newcastle. When else-where, he stayed with his preachers. He lived on £28 a year and gave away the rest to the poor. He urged and practised a diligent frugality. He saw to it that all the giving of his people went to the poor. Only in later Methodism was most of it deflected into buildings and ministerial salaries, with only a token 'Poor Fund' left at an infrequent sacrament. So fundamental was his rooting among the poor that several of his successors as President, after his death, were from the artisan, or even less skilled groups.

In a leaflet addressed to his fellow clergy, Wesley says: 'The rich, the honorable, the great, we are thoroughly willing to leave to you. Only let us alone with the poor, the vulgar, the base, the outcasts of men.' And to George II he declared: 'We are inconsiderable people, a people scattered afield and trodden underfoot. Silver and gold have we none.'

Wesley had joined a movement of the common people, and that is the first stage of a true revolution. Only when we are there can we ask, What does 'mission alongside the poor' mean?

# Chapter 54

# *The Kairos Document* (1985)

The Kairos Document is described as a Christian, biblical, and theological comment on the political crisis in South Africa. It was the result of meetings and discussions by a large number of concerned ministers and theologians. The Kairos Document starts with the words of Jesus at the opening of his ministry according to Mark 1:15, "the time (*kairos*) has come." Its tripartite arrangement with its critique of state and church and the advocacy of a prophetic theology articulates positions widely held in the radical political theology of the late twentieth century. The Kairos Document rejects reformism and the gradualist approach as being demonstrably ineffective. It also rejects non-violence as an absolute principle and exposes the violence perpetrated by the security forces as being as much, if not more, part of the problem of violence in South Africa. It affirms the just war theory that there are circumstances in which limited violence may be legitimately used. Prophetic theology involves exposing the interests of those maintaining the present system and the exploitation of those whose labor keeps in affluence the privileged minority. The document challenges the churches to take action, first of all by taking sides with "God who is always on the side of the oppressed" and to participate in the struggle (campaigns and consumer boycotts are offered as examples). Churches are told that they cannot collaborate with tyranny, and civil disobedience is suggested in order to avoid giving any moral legitimacy to the apartheid regime. The churches are urged to identify with popular organizations and not be a "third force" between oppressor and oppressed. The church of Jesus Christ is not called to be a bastion of caution and moderation but must preach its message not only in words and sermons and statements but also through its actions, programmes, campaigns and divine services.

Source

*Challenge to the Church. A Theological Comment on the Political Crisis in South Africa. The Kairos Document*, London: CIIR, 1985.

## Further reading

Charles Villa-Vicencio, *Between Christ and Caesar: Classic and Contemporary Texts on Church and State*, Grand Rapids: Eerdmans, 1986.

R. McAfee Brown, *Kairos. Three Prophetic Challenges to the Church*, Grand Rapids: Eerdmans 1990.

A. Nolan, *God in South Africa. The challenge of the gospel*, London: CIIR, 1988.

J. de Gruchy, *The Church Struggle in South Africa*, 2nd edition, London: Collins, 1986.

Trevor Huddleston, *Naught for Your Comfort*, London, 1956.

## *The Kairos Document* (1985)

### *The Moment of Truth*

The time has come. The moment of truth has arrived. South Africa has been plunged into a crisis that is shaking the foundations and there is every indication that the crisis has only just begun and that it will deepen and become even more threatening in the months to come. It is the KAIROS or moment of truth not only for apartheid but also for the Church.

We as a group of theologians have been trying to understand the theological significance of this moment in our history. It is serious, very serious. For very many Christians in South Africa this is the KAIROS, the moment of grace and opportunity, the favourable time in which God issues a challenge to decisive action. It is a dangerous time because, if this opportunity is missed, and allowed to pass by, the loss for the Church, for the Gospel and for all the people of South Africa will be immeasurable. Jesus wept over Jerusalem. He wept over the tragedy of the destruction of the city and the massacre of the people that was imminent, "and all because you did not recognise your opportunity (KAIROS) when God offered it" (Lk. 19: 44).

A crisis is a judgment that brings out the best in some people and the worst in others. A crisis is a moment of truth that shows us up for what we really are. There will be no place to hide and no way of pretending to be what we are not in fact. At this moment in South Africa the Church is about to be shown up for what it really is and no cover-up will be possible.

What the present crisis shows up, although many of us have known it all along, is that *the Church is divided*. More and more people are now saying that there are in fact two Churches in South Africa – a White Church and a Black Church. Even within the same denomination there are in fact two Churches. In the life and death conflict between different social forces that has come to a head in South Africa today, there are Christians (or at least people who profess to be Christians) on both sides of the conflict – and some who are trying to sit on the fence!

Does this prove that Christian faith has no real meaning or relevance for our times? Does it show that the Bible can be used for any purpose at all? Such problems would be critical enough for the Church in any circumstances but when we also come to see that the conflict in South Africa is between the oppressor and the oppressed, the crisis for the Church as an institution becomes much more acute. Both oppressor and oppressed claim loyalty to the same Church. They are both baptised in the same baptism and participate together in the breaking of the same bread, the same body and blood of Christ. There we sit in the same Church while outside Christian policemen and soldiers are beating up and killing Christian children or torturing Christian prisoners to death while yet other Christians stand by and weakly plead for peace.

The Church is divided and its day of judgment has come.

The moment of truth has compelled us to analyse more carefully the different theologies in our Churches and to speak out more clearly and boldly about the real significance of these theologies. We have been able to isolate three theologies and we have chosen to call them 'State Theology', 'Church Theology' and 'Prophetic Theology'. In our thoroughgoing criticism of the first and second theologies we do not wish to mince our words. The situation is too critical for that.

## Critique of State Theology

The South African apartheid State has a theology of its own and we have chosen to call it 'State Theology'. 'State Theology' is simply the theological justification of the status quo with its racism, capitalism and totalitarianism. It blesses injustice, canonises the will of the powerful and reduces the poor to passivity, obedience and apathy.

How does 'State Theology' do this? It does it by misusing theological concepts and biblical texts for its own political purposes. In this document we would like to draw your attention to four key examples of how this is done in South Africa. The first would be the use of Romans 13: 1–7 to give an absolute and 'divine' authority to the State. The second would be the use of the idea of 'Law and Order' to determine and control what the people may be permitted to regard as just and unjust. The third would be the use of the word 'communist' to brand anyone who rejects 'State Theology'. And finally there is the use that is made of the name of God.

### Romans 13: 1–7

The misuse of this famous text is not confined to the present government in South Africa. Throughout the history of Christianity totalitarian regimes have tried to legitimise an attitude of blind obedience and absolute servility towards the state by quoting this text. The well-known theologian Oscar Cullman, pointed this out thirty years ago:

> As soon as Christians, out of loyalty to the gospel of Jesus, offer resistance to a State's totalitarian claim, the representatives of the State or their collaborationist theological advisers are accustomed to appeal to this saying of Paul, as if Christians are here commended to endorse and thus to abet all the crimes of a totalitarian State. (*The State in the New Testament*, SCM, 1957, p. 56)

But what then is the meaning of Rom. 13: 1–7 and why is the use made of it by 'State Theology' unjustifiable from a biblical point of view?

'State Theology' assumes that in this text Paul is presenting us with the absolute and definitive Christian doctrine about the State, in other words an absolute and universal principle that is equally valid for all times and in all circumstances. The falseness of this assumption has been pointed out by numerous biblical scholars (see, for example, E. Käsemann, *Commentary on Romans*, SCM, pp. 354–7; O. Cullmann, *The State in the New Testament*, SCM, pp. 55–7).

What has been overlooked here is one of the most fundamental of all principles of biblical interpretation: every text must be interpreted *in its context*. To abstract a text from its context and to interpret it in the abstract is to distort the meaning of God's Word. Moreover the context here is not only the chapters and verses that precede and succeed this particular text nor is it even limited to the total context of the Bible. The context includes also the *circumstances* in which Paul's statement was made. Paul was writing to a particular Christian community in Rome, a community that had its own particular problems in relation to the State at that time and in those circumstances. That is part of the context of our text.

Many authors have drawn attention to the fact that in the rest of the Bible God does not demand obedience to oppressive rulers. Examples can be given ranging from Pharaoh to Pilate and through into Apostolic times. The Jews and later the Christians did not believe that their imperial overlords, the Egyptians, the Babylonians, the Greeks or the Romans, had some kind of divine right to rule them and oppress them. These empires were the beasts described in the Book of Daniel and the Book of Revelations. God *allowed* them to rule for a while but he did not *approve* of what they did. It was not God's will. His will was the freedom and liberation of Israel. Rom. 13: 1–7 cannot be contradicting all of this.

But most revealing of all is the circumstances of the Roman Christians to whom Paul was writing. They were not revolutionaries. They were not trying to overthrow the State. They were not calling for a change of government. They were, what has been called, 'antinomians' or 'enthusiasts' and their belief was that Christians, and only Christians, were exonerated from obeying any State at all, any government or political authority at all, *because* Jesus alone was their Lord and King. This is of course heretical and Paul is compelled to point out to these Christians that before the second coming of Christ there will always be some kind of State, some kind of secular government and that Christians are not exonerated from subjection to some kind of political authority.

Paul is simply not addressing the issue of a just or unjust State or the need to change one government for another. He is simply establishing the fact that there will be some kind of secular authority and that Christians as such are not exonerated from subjection to secular laws and authorities. He does not say anything at all about what they should do when the State becomes unjust and oppressive. That is another question.

Consequently those who try to find answers to the very different questions and problems of our time in the text of Rom. 13: 1–7 are doing a great disservice to Paul. The use that 'State Theology' makes of this text tells us more about the political options of those who construct this theology than it does about the meaning of God's Word in this text. As one biblical scholar puts it: "The primary concern is to justify the interests of the State and the text is pressed into its service without respect for the context and the intention of Paul".

If we wish to search the Bible for guidance in a situation where the State that is supposed to be "the servant of God" (Romans 13: 16) betrays that calling and begins to serve Satan instead, then we can study chapter 13 of the Book of Revelations. Here the Roman State becomes the servant of the dragon (the devil) and takes on the appearance of a horrible beast. Its days are numbered because God will not permit his unfaithful servant to reign forever.

## Law and Order

The State makes use of the concept of law and order to maintain the status quo which it depicts as 'normal'. But this *law* is the unjust and discriminatory laws of apartheid and this *order* is the organised and institutionalised disorder of oppression. Anyone who wishes to change this law and this order is made to feel that they are lawless and disorderly. In other words they are made to feel guilty of sin.

It is indeed the duty of the State to maintain law and order, but it has not divine mandate to maintain any kind of law and order. Something does not become moral and just simply because the State has declared it to be a law and the organisation of a society is not a just and right order simply because it has been instituted by the State. We cannot accept any kind of law and any kind of order. The concern of Christians is that we should have in our country a just law and a right order.

In the present crisis and especially during the State of Emergency, 'State Theology' has tried to re-establish the status quo of orderly discrimination, exploitation and oppression by appealing to the consciences of its citizens in the name of law and order. It tries to make those who reject this law and this order feel that they are ungodly. The State here is not only usurping the right of the Church to make judgments about what would be right and just in our circumstances; it is going even further than that and demanding of us, in the name of law and order, an obedience that must be reserved for God alone. The South African State recognises no authority beyond itself and therefore it will not allow anyone to question what it has chosen to define as 'law and order'. However, there are millions of Christians in South Africa today who are saying with Peter: "We must obey God rather than man (human beings)" (Acts 5: 29).

## The Threat of Communism

We all know how the South African State makes use of the label 'communist'. Anything that threatens the status quo is labelled 'communist'. Anyone who opposes the State and especially anyone who rejects its theology is simply dismissed as a 'communist'. No account is taken of what communism really means. No thought is given to why some people have indeed opted for communism or for some form of socialism. Even people who have not rejected capitalism are called 'communists' when they reject 'State Theology'. The State uses the label 'communist' in an uncritical and unexamined way as its symbol of evil.

'State Theology' like every other theology needs to have its own concrete symbol of evil. It must be able to symbolise what it regards as godless behaviour and what ideas must be regarded as atheistic. It must have its own version of hell. And so it has invented, or rather taken over, the myth of communism. All evil is communistic and all communist or socialist ideas are atheistic and godless. Threats about hell-fire and eternal damnation are replaced by threats and warnings about the horrors of a tyrannical, totalitarian, atheistic and terrorist communist regime – a kind of hell-on-earth. This is a very convenient way of frightening some people into accepting any kind of domination and exploitation by a capitalist minority.

The South African State has its own heretical theology and according to that theology millions of Christians in South Africa (not to mention the rest of the world) are to be regarded as 'atheists'. It is significant that in earlier times when Christians rejected the gods of the Roman Empire they were branded as 'atheists' – by the State.

### The God of the State

The State in its oppression of the people makes use again and again of the name of God. Military chaplains use it to encourage the South African Defence Force, police chaplains use it to strengthen policemen and cabinet ministers use it in their propaganda speeches. But perhaps the most revealing of all is the blasphemous use of God's holy name in the preamble to the new apartheid constitution.

> In humble submission to Almighty God, who controls the destinies of nations and the history of peoples; who gathered our forebears together from many lands and gave them this their own; who has guided them from generation to generation; who has wondrously delivered them from the dangers that beset them.

This god is an idol. It is as mischievous, sinister and evil as any of the idols that the prophets of Israel had to contend with. Here we have a god who is historically on the side of the white settlers, who dispossesses black people of their land and who gives the major part of the land to his "chosen people".

It is the god of superior weapons who conquered those who were armed with nothing but spears. It is the god of the casspirs and hippos, the god of teargas, rubber bullets, sjamboks, prison cells and death sentences. Here is a god who exalts the proud and humbles the poor – the very opposite of the God of the Bible who "scatters the proud of heart, pulls down the mighty from their thrones and exalts the humble" (Lk. 1: 51–52). From a theological point of view the opposite of the God of the Bible is the devil, Satan. The god of the South African State is not merely an idol or false god, it is the devil disguised as Almighty God – the antichrist.

The oppressive South African regime will always be particularly abhorrent to Christians precisely because it makes use of Christianity to justify its evil ways. As Christians we simply cannot tolerate this blasphemous use of God's name and God's Word. 'State Theology' is not only heretical, it is blasphemous. Christians who are trying to remain faithful to the God of the Bible are even more horrified when they see that there are Churches, like the White Dutch Reformed Churches and other groups of Christians, who actually subscribe to this heretical theology. 'State Theology' needs its own prophets and it manages to find them from the ranks of those who profess to be ministers of God's Word in some of our Churches. What is particularly tragic for a Christian is to see the number of people who are fooled and confused by these false prophets and their heretical theology.

## Critique of 'Church Theology'

We have analysed the statements that are made from time-to-time by the so-called 'English-speaking' Churches. We have looked at what Church leaders tend to say in their speeches and press statements about the apartheid regime and the present crisis. What we found running through all these pronouncements is a series of inter-related theological assumptions. These we have chosen to call 'Church Theology'. We are well aware of the fact that this theology does *not* express the faith of the majority of Christians in South Africa today who form the greater part of most of our Churches. Nevertheless the opinions expressed by Church leaders are regarded in the media and generally in our society as the official opinions of the Churches. We have therefore chosen to call these opinions 'Church Theology'. The crisis in which we find ourselves today compels us to question this theology, to question its assumptions, its implications and its practicality.

In a limited, guarded and cautious way this theology is critical of apartheid. Its criticism, however, is superficial and counter-productive because instead of engaging in an in-depth analysis of the signs of our times, it relies upon a few stock ideas derived from Christian tradition and then uncritically and repeatedly applies them to our situation. The stock ideas used by almost all these Church leaders that we would like to examine here are: reconciliation (or peace), justice and non-violence.

## Reconciliation

'Church Theology' takes 'reconciliation' as the key to problem resolution. It talks about the need for reconciliation between white and black, or between all South Africans. 'Church Theology' often describes the Christian stance in the following way: "We must be fair. We must listen to both sides of the story. If the two sides can only meet to talk and negotiate they will sort out their differences and misunderstandings, and the conflict will be resolved". On the face of it this may sound very Christian. But is it?

The fallacy here is that 'Reconciliation' has been made into an absolute principle that must be applied in all cases of conflict or dissension. But not all cases of conflict are the same. We can imagine a private quarrel between two people or two groups whose differences are based upon misunderstandings. In such cases it would be appropriate to talk and negotiate to sort out the misunderstandings and to reconcile the two sides. But there are other conflicts in which one side is right and the other wrong. There are conflicts where one side is a fully armed and violent oppressor while the other side is defenceless and oppressed. There are conflicts that can only be described as the struggle between justice and injustice, good and evil, God and the devil. To speak of reconciling these two is not only a mistaken application of the Christian idea of reconciliation, it is a total betrayal of all that Christian faith has ever meant. Nowhere in the Bible or in Christian tradition has it ever been suggested that we ought to try to reconcile good and evil, God and the devil. We are supposed to do away with evil, injustice, oppression and sin – not come to terms with it. We are supposed to oppose, confront and reject the devil and not try to sup with the devil.

In our situation in South Africa today it would be totally unChristian to plead for reconciliation and peace before the present injustices have been removed. Any such plea plays into the hands of the oppressor by trying to persuade those of us who are oppressed to accept our oppression and to become reconciled to the intolerable crimes that are committed against us. That is not Christian reconciliation, it is sin. It is asking us to become accomplices in our own oppression, to become servants of the devil. No reconciliation is possible in South Africa *without justice*.

What this means in practice is that no reconciliation, no forgiveness and no negotiations are possible *without repentance*. The Biblical teaching on reconciliation and forgiveness makes it quite clear that nobody can be forgiven and reconciled with God unless he or she repents of their sins. Nor are *we* expected to forgive the unrepentant sinner. When he or she repents we must be willing to forgive seventy times seven times but before that, we are expected to preach repentance to those who sin against us or against anyone. Reconciliation, forgiveness and negotiations will become our Christian duty in South Africa only when the apartheid regime shows signs of genuine repentance. The recent speech of P. W. Botha in Durban, the continued military repression of the people in the townships and the jailing of all its opponents is clear proof of the total lack of repentance on the part of the present regime.

There is nothing that we want more than true reconciliation and genuine peace – the peace that God wants and not the peace the world wants (Jn. 14: 27). The peace that God wants is based upon truth, repentance, justice and love. The peace that the world offers us is a unity that compromises the truth, covers over injustice and oppression and is totally motivated by selfishness. At this stage, like Jesus, we must expose this false peace, confront our oppressors and sow dissension. As Christians we must say with Jesus: "Do you suppose that I am here to bring peace on earth. No, I tell you, but rather dissension" (Lk. 12: 51). There can be no real peace without justice and repentance.

It would be quite wrong to try to preserve 'peace' and 'unity' at all costs, even at the cost of truth and justice and, worse still, at the cost of thousands of young lives. As disciples of Jesus we should rather promote truth and justice and life at all costs, even at the cost of creating conflict, disunity and dissension along the way. To be truly biblical our Church leaders must adopt a theology that millions of Christians have already adopted – a biblical theology of direct confrontation with the forces of evil rather than a theology of reconciliation with sin and the devil.

*Justice*

It would be quite wrong to give the impression that 'Church Theology' in South Africa is not particularly concerned about the need for justice. There have been some very strong and very sincere demands for justice. But the question we need to ask here, the very serious theological question is: What kind of justice? An examination of Church statements and pronouncements gives the distinct impression that the justice that is envisaged is *the justice of reform*, that is to say, a justice that is determined by the oppressor, by the white minority and that is offered to the people as a kind of concession. It does not appear to be the more radical justice that comes from below and is determined by the people of South Africa.

One of our main reasons for drawing this conclusion is the simple fact that almost all Church statements and appeals are made to the State or to the white community. The assumption seems to be that changes must come from whites or at least from people who are at the top of the pile. The general idea appears to be that one must simply appeal to the conscience and the goodwill of those who are responsible for injustice in our land and that once they have repented of their sins and after some consultation with others they will introduce the necessary reforms to the system. Why else would Church leaders be having talks with P. W. Botha, if this is not the vision of a just and peaceful solution to our problems?

At the heart of this approach is the reliance upon 'individual conversions' in response to 'moralising demands' to change the structures of a society. It has not worked and it never will work. The present crisis with all its cruelty, brutality and callousness is ample proof of the ineffectiveness of years and years of Christian 'moralising' about the need for love. The problem that we are dealing with here in South Africa is not merely a problem of personal guilt, it is a problem of structural injustice. People are suffering, people are being maimed and killed and tortured every day. We cannot just sit back and wait for the oppressor to see the light so that the oppressed can put out their hands and beg for the crumbs of some small reforms. That in itself would be degrading and oppressive.

There have been reforms and, no doubt, there will be further reforms in the near future. And it may well be that the Church's appeal to the consciences of whites has contributed marginally to the introduction of some of these reforms. But can such reforms ever be regarded as real change, as the introduction of a true and lasting justice. Reforms that come from the top are never satisfactory. They seldom do more than make the oppression more effective and more acceptable. If the oppressor does ever introduce reforms that might lead to real change this will come about because of strong pressure from those who are oppressed. True justice, God's justice, demands a radical change of structures. This can only come from below, from the oppressed themselves. God will bring about change through the oppressed as he did through the oppressed Hebrew slaves in Egypt. God does not bring his justice through reforms introduced by the Pharaoh's of this world.

Why then does 'Church Theology' appeal to the top rather than to the people who are suffering? Why does this theology not demand that the oppressed stand up for their rights and wage a struggle against their oppressors? Why does it not tell them that it is *their* duty to work for justice and to change the unjust structures? Perhaps the answer to these questions is that appeals from the 'top' in the Church tend very easily to be appeals to the 'top' in society. An appeal to the conscience of those who perpetuate the system of injustice must be made. But real change and true justice can only come from below, from the people – most of whom are Christians.

### Non-Violence

The stance of 'Church Theology' on non-violence, expressed as a blanket condemnation of all that is *called* violence, has not only been unable to curb the violence of our situation, it has actually, although unwittingly, been a major contributing factor in the recent escalation of State violence. Here again non-violence has been made into an absolute principle that applies to anything anyone *calls* violence without regard for who is using it, which side they are on or what purpose they may have in mind. In our situation, this is simply counterproductive.

The problem for the Church here is the way the word violence is being used in the propaganda of the State. The State and the media have chosen to call violence what some people do in the townships as they struggle for their liberation i.e. throwing stones, burning cars and buildings and sometimes killing collaborators. But this *excludes* the structural, institutional and unrepentant violence of the State and especially the oppressive and naked violence of the police and the army. These things are not counted as violence. And even when they are acknowledged to be 'excessive', they are called 'misconduct' or even 'atrocities' but never violence. Thus the phrase 'violence in the townships' comes to mean what the young people are doing and not what the police are doing or what apartheid in general is doing to people. If one calls for non-violence in such circumstances one appears to be criticising the resistance of the people while justifying or at least overlooking the violence of the police and the State. That is how it is understood not only by the State and its supporters but also by the people who are struggling for their freedom. Violence, especially in our cimcumstances, is a loaded word.

It is true that Church statements and pronouncements do also condemn the violence of the police. They do say that they condemn *all violence*. But is it legitimate, especially in our circumstances, to use the same word violence in a blanket condemnation to cover the ruthless and repressive activities of the State and the desperate attempts of the people to defend themselves? Do such abstractions and generalisations not confuse the issue? How can acts of oppression, injustice and domination be equated with acts of resistance and self-defence? Would it be legitimate to describe both the physical force used by a rapist and the physical force used by a woman trying to resist the rapist as violence?

Moreover there is nothing in the Bible or in our Christian tradition that would permit us to make such generalisations. Throughout the Bible the word violence is used to describe everything that is done by a wicked oppressor (e.g. Ps. 72: 12–14; Is. 59: 1–8; Jer. 22: 13–17; Amos 3: 9–10; 6: 3; Mic. 2: 2; 3: 1–3; 6: 12). It is never used to describe the activities of Israel's armies in attempting to liberate themselves or to resist aggression. When Jesus says that we should turn the other cheek he is telling us that we must not take revenge; he is not saying that we should never defend ourselves or others. There is a long and consistent Christian tradition about the use of physical force to defend oneself against aggressors and tyrants. In other words there are circumstances when physical force may be used. They are very restrictive circumstances, only as the very last resort and only as the lesser of two evils, or, as Bonhoeffer put it, "the lesser of two guilts". But it is simply not true to say that every possible use of physical force is violence and that no matter what the circumstances may be it is never permissible.

This is not to say that any use of force at any time by people who are oppressed is permissible simply because they are struggling for their liberation. There have been cases of killing and maiming that no Christian would want to approve of. But then our disapproval is based upon a concern for genuine liberation and a conviction that such acts are unnecessary, counter-productive and unjustifiable and not because they fall under a blanket condemnation of any use of physical force in any circumstances.

And finally what makes the professed non-violence of 'Church Theology' extremely suspect in the eyes of very many people, including ourselves, is the tacit support that many Church leaders give to the growing *militarisation* of the South African State. How can one condemn all violence and then appoint chaplains to a very violent and oppressive army? How can one condemn all violence and then allow young white males to accept their conscription into the armed forces? Is it because the activities of the armed forces and the police are counted as defensive? That raises very serious questions about whose side such Church leaders might be on. Why are the activities of young blacks in the townships not regarded as defensive?

In practice what one calls 'violence' and what one calls 'self-defence' seems to depend upon which side one is on. To call all physical force 'violence' is to try to be neutral and to refuse to make a judgment about who is right and who is wrong. The attempt to remain neutral in this kind of conflict is futile. Neutrality enables the status quo of oppression (and therefore violence) to continue. It is a way of giving tacit support to the oppressor.

*The Fundamental Problem*

It is not enough to criticise 'Church Theology' we must also try to account for it. What is behind the mistakes and misunderstandings and inadequacies of this theology?

In the first place we can point to a lack of *social analysis*. We have seen how 'Church Theology' tends to make use of absolute principles like reconciliation, negotiation, non-violence and peaceful solutions and applies them indiscriminatedly and uncritically to all situations. Very little attempt is made to analyse what is actually happening in our society and why it is happening. It is not possible to make valid moral judgments about a society without first understanding that society. The analysis of apartheid that underpins 'Church Theology' is simply inadequate. The present crisis has now made it very clear that the efforts of Church leaders to promote effective and practical ways of changing our society have failed. This failure is due in no small measure to the fact that 'Church Theology' has not developed a social analysis that would enable it to understand the mechanics of injustice and oppression.

Closely linked to this, is the lack in 'Church Theology' of an adequate understanding of *politics and political strategy*. Changing the structures of a society is fundamentally a matter of politics. It requires a political strategy based upon a clear social or political analysis. The Church has to address itself to these strategies and to the analysis upon which they are based. It is into this political situation that the Church has to bring the gospel. Not as an alternative solution to our problems as if the gospel provided us with a non-political solution to political problems. There is no specifically Christian solution. There will be a Christian way of approaching the political solutions, a Christian spirit and motivation and attitude. But there is no way of bypassing politics and political strategies.

But we have still not pinpointed the fundamental problem. Why has 'Church Theology' not developed a social analysis? Why does it have an inadequate understanding of the need for political strategies? And why does it make a virtue of neutrality and sitting on the sidelines?

The answer must be sought in the *type of faith and spirituality* that has dominated Church life for centuries. As we all know, spirituality has tended to be an other-worldly affair that has very little, if anything at all, to do with the affairs of this world. Social and political matters were seen as worldly affairs that have nothing to do with the spiritual concerns of the Church. Moreover, spirituality has also been understood to be purely private and individualistic. Public affairs and social problems were thought to be beyond the sphere of spirituality. And finally the spirituality we inherit tends to rely upon God to intervene in his own good time to put right what is wrong in the world. That leaves very little for human beings to do except to pray for God's intervention.

It is precisely this kind of spirituality that, when faced with the present crisis in South Africa, leaves so many Christians and Church leaders in a state of near paralysis.

It hardly needs saying that this kind of faith and this type of spirituality has no biblical foundation. The Bible does not separate the human person from the world in which he or she lives; it does not separate the individual from the social or one's private life from one's public life. God redeems the whole person as part of his whole creation (Rom. 8: 18–24). A truly biblical spirituality would penetrate into every aspect of human existence and would exclude nothing from God's redemptive will. Biblical faith is prophetically relevant to everything that happens in the world.

*Towards a Prophetic Theology*

Our present KAIROS calls for a response from Christians that is biblical, spirtual, pastoral and, above all, prophetic. It is not enough in these circumstances to repeat generalised Christian principles. We need a bold and incisive response that is prophetic because it speaks to the particular circumstances of this crisis, a response that does not give the impression of sitting on the fence but is clearly and unambiguously taking a stand.

## Social Analysis

The first task of a prophetic theology for our times would be an attempt at social analysis or what Jesus would call "reading the signs of the times" (Mt. 16: 3) or "interpreting this KAIROS" (Lk. 12: 56). It is not possible to do this in any detail in this document but we must start with at least the broad outlines of an analysis of the conflict in which we find ourselves.

It would be quite wrong to see the present conflict as simply a racial war. The racial component is there but we are not dealing with two equal races or nations each with their own selfish group interests. The situation we are dealing with here is one of oppression. The conflict is between an oppressor and the oppressed. The conflict is between two irreconcilable *causes* or *interests* in which the one is just and the other is unjust.

On the one hand we have the interests of those who benefit from the status quo and who are determined to maintain it at any cost, even at the cost of millions of lives. It is in their interests to introduce a number of reforms in order to ensure that the system is not radically changed and that they can continue to benefit from it as they have done in the past. They benefit from the system because it favours them and enables them to accumulate a great deal of wealth and to maintain an exceptionally high standard of living. And they want to make sure that it stays that way even if some adjustments are needed.

On the other hand we have those who do not benefit in any way from the system the way it is now. They are treated as mere labour units, paid starvation wages, separated from their families by migratory labour, moved about like cattle and dumped in homelands to starve – and all for the benefit of a privileged minority. They have no say in the system and are supposed to be grateful for the concessions that are offered to them like crumbs. It is not in their interests to allow this system to continue even in some 'reformed' or 'revised' form. They are no longer prepared to be crushed, oppressed and exploited. They are determined to change the system radically so that it no longer benefits only the privileged few. And they are willing to do this even at the cost of their own lives. What they want is justice for all.

This is our situation of civil war or revolution. The one side is committed to maintaining the system at all costs and the other side is committed to changing it at all costs. There are two conflicting projects here and no compromise is possible. Either we have full and equal justice for all or we don't.

The Bible has a great deal to say about this kind of conflict, about a world that is divided into oppressors and oppressed.

## Oppression in the Bible

When we search the Bible for a message about oppression we discover, as others throughout the world are discovering, that oppression is a central theme that runs right through the Old and New Testaments. The biblical scholars who have taken the trouble to study the theme of oppression in the Bible have discovered that there are no less than twenty different root words in Hebrew to describe oppression. As one author says, oppression is "a basic structural category of biblical theology" (T. D. Hanks, *God So Loved the Third World*, Orbis, 1983, p. 4).

Moreover the description of oppression in the Bible is concrete and vivid. The Bible describes oppression as the experience of being crushed, degraded, humiliated, exploited, impoverished, defrauded, deceived and enslaved. And the oppressors are described as cruel, ruthless, arrogant, greedy, violent and tyrannical and as the enemy. Such descriptions could only have been written originally by people who had had a long and painful experience of what it means to be oppressed. And indeed nearly 90 percent of the history of the Jewish and later the Christian people whose story is told in the Bible, is a history of domestic or international oppression. Israel as a nation was built upon the painful experience of oppression and repression as slaves in Egypt. But what made all the difference for this particular group of oppressed people was the revelation of Yahweh. God revealed himself as Yahweh, the one who has compassion on those who suffer and who liberates them from their oppressors.

> I have seen the miserable state of my people in Egypt. I have heard their appeal to be free of their slave-drivers. I mean to deliver them out of the hands of the Egyptians. . . .
>
> The cry of the sons of Israel has come to me, and I have witnessed the way in which the Egyptians oppress them. (Ex. 3: 7–9)

Throughout the Bible God appears as the liberator of the oppressed. He is not neutral. He does not attempt to reconcile Moses and Pharaoh, to reconcile the Hebrew slaves with their Egyptian oppressors or to reconcile the Jewish people with any of their later oppressors. Oppression is sin and it cannot be compromised with, it must be done away with. God takes sides with the oppressed. As we read in Psalm 103: 6 (JB) "God, who does what is right, is always on the side of the oppressed".

Nor is this identification with the oppressed confined to the Old Testament. When Jesus stood up in the synagogue at Nazareth to announce his mission he made use of the words of Isaiah.

> The Spirit of the Lord has been given to me, for he has anointed me.
>
> He has sent me to bring the good news to the poor, to proclaim liberty to captives and to the blind new sight, to set the downtrodden free, to proclaim the Lord's year of favour. (Lk. 4: 18–19)

There can be no doubt that Jesus is here taking up the cause of the poor and the oppressed. He has identified himself with their interests. Not that he is unconcerned about the rich and the oppressor. These he calls to repentance. The oppressed Christians of South Africa have known for a long time that they are united to Christ in their sufferings. By his own suffering and his death on the cross he became a victim of oppression and violence. He is with us in our oppression.

## Tyranny in the Christian Tradition

There is a long Christian tradition relating to oppression, but the word that has been used most frequently to describe this particular form of sinfulness is the word 'tyranny'. According to this tradition once it is established beyond doubt that a particular ruler is a tyrant or that a particular regime is tyrannical, it forfeits the moral right to govern and the people acquire the right to resist and to find the means to protect their own interests against injustice and oppression. In other words a tyrannical regime has no *moral legitimacy*. It may be the *de facto* government and it may even be recognised by other governments and therefore be the *de iure* or legal government. But if it is a tyrannical regime, it is, from a moral and a theological point of view, *illegitimate*. There are indeed some differences of opinion in the Christian tradition about the means that might be used to replace a tyrant *but* there has not been any doubt about our Christian duty to refuse to co-operate with tyranny and to do whatever we can to remove it.

Of course everything hinges on the definition of a tyrant. At what point does a government become a tyrannical regime?

The traditional Latin definition of a tyrant is *hostis boni communis* – an enemy of the common good. The purpose of all government is the promotion of what is called the common good of the people governed. To promote the common good is to govern in the interests of, and for the benefit of, all the people. Many governments fail to do this at times. There might be this or that injustice done to some of the people. And such lapses would indeed have to be criticised. But occasional acts of injustice would not make a government into an enemy of the people, a tyrant.

To be an enemy of the people a government would have to be hostile to the common good *in principle*. Such a government would be acting against the interests of the people as a whole and permanently. This would be clearest in cases where the very policy of a government is hostile towards the common good and where the government has a mandate to rule in the interests of some of the people rather than in the interests of all the people. Such a government would be in principle *irreformable*. Any reform that it might try to introduce would not be calculated to serve the common good but to serve the interests of the minority from whom it received its mandate.

A tyrannical regime cannot continue to rule for very long without becoming more and more *violent*. As the majority of the people begin to demand their rights and to put pressure on the tyrant, so will the tyrant resort more and more to desperate, cruel, gross and ruthless forms of tyranny and repression. The reign of a tyrant always ends up as a reign of terror. It is inevitable because from the start the tyrant is an enemy of the common good.

This account of what we mean by a tyrant or a tyrannical regime can best be summed up in the words of a well-known moral theologian: "a regime which is openly the enemy of the people and which violates the common good permanently and in the grossest manner" (B. Häring, *The Law of Christ*, Vol. 3, p. 150).

That leaves us with the question of whether the present government of South Africa is tyrannical or not? There can be no doubt what the majority of the people of South Africa think. For them the apartheid regime is indeed the enemy of the people and that is precisely what they call it: the enemy. In the present crisis, more than ever before, the regime has lost any legitimacy that it might have had in the eyes of the people. Are the people right or wrong?

Apartheid is a system whereby a minority regime elected by one small section of the population is given an explicit mandate to govern in the interests of, and for the benefit of, the white community. Such a mandate or policy is by definition hostile to the common good of all the people. In fact because it tries to rule in the exclusive interests of whites and not in the interests of all, it ends up ruling in a way that is not even in the interests of those same whites. It becomes an enemy of all the people. A tyrant. A totalitarian regime. A reign of terror.

This also means that the apartheid minority regime is irreformable. We cannot expect the apartheid regime to experience a conversion or change of heart and totally abandon the policy of apartheid. It has no mandate from its electorate to do so. Any reforms or adjustments it might make would have to be done in the interests of those who elected it. Individual members of the government could experience a real conversion and repent but, if they did, they would simply have to follow this through by leaving a regime that was elected and put into power precisely because of its policy of apartheid.

And that is why we have reached the present impasse. As the oppressed majority becomes more insistent and puts more and more pressure on the tyrant by means of boycotts, strikes, uprisings, burnings and even armed struggle, the more tyrannical will this regime become. On the one hand it will use repressive measures: detentions, trials, killings, torture, bannings, propaganda, states of emergency and other desperate and tyrannical methods. And on the other hand it will introduce reforms that will always be unacceptable to the majority because all its reforms must ensure that the white minority remains on top.

A regime that is in principle the enemy of the people cannot suddenly begin to rule in the interests of all the people. It can only be replaced by another government – one that has been elected by the majority of the people with an explicit mandate to govern in the interests of all the people.

A regime that has made itself the enemy of the people has thereby also made itself the enemy of God. People are made in the image and likeness of God and whatever we do to the least of them we do to God (Mt. 25: 49, 45).

To say that the State or the regime is the enemy of God is not to say that all those who support the system are aware of this. On the whole they simply do not know what they are doing. Many people have been blinded by the regime's propaganda. They are frequently quite ignorant of the consequences of their stance. However, such blindness does not make the State any less tyrannical or any less of an enemy of the people and an enemy of God.

On the other hand the fact that the State is tyrannical and an enemy of God is no excuse for hatred. As Christians we are called upon to love our enemies (Mt. 5: 44). It is not said that we should not or will not have enemies or that we should not identify tyrannical regimes as indeed our enemies. But once we have identified our enemies, we must endeavour to love them. That is not always easy. But then we must also remember that the most loving thing we can do for *both* the oppressed *and* for our enemies who are oppressors is to eliminate the oppression, remove the tyrants from power and establish a just government for the common good of *all the people*.

*A Message of Hope*

At the very heart of the gospel of Jesus Christ and at the very centre of all true prophecy is a message of hope. Nothing could be more relevant and more necessary at this moment of crisis in South Africa than the Christian message of hope.

Jesus has taught us to speak of this hope as the coming of God's kingdom. We believe that God is at work in our world turning hopeless and evil situations to good so that his "Kingdom may come" and his "Will may be done on earth as it is in heaven". We believe that goodness and justice and love will triumph in the end and that tyranny and oppression cannot last forever. One day "all tears will be wiped away" (Rev. 7: 17; 21: 4) and "the lamb will lie down with the lion" (Is. 11: 6). True peace and true reconciliation are not only desirable, they are assured and guaranteed. This is our faith and our hope.

Why is it that this powerful message of hope has not been highlighted in 'Church Theology', in the statements and pronouncements of Church leaders? Is it because they have been addressing themselves to the oppressor rather than to the oppressed? Is it because they do not want to encourage the oppressed to be too hopeful for too much?

As the crisis deepens day-by-day, what both the oppressor and the oppressed can legitimately demand of the Churches is a message of hope. Most of the oppressed people in South Africa today and especially the youth do have hope. They are acting courageously and fearlessly because they have a sure hope that liberation will come. Often enough their bodies are broken but nothing can now break their spirit. But hope needs to be confirmed. Hope needs to be maintained and strengthened. Hope needs to be spread. The people need to hear it said again and again that God is with them.

On the other hand the oppressor and those who believe the propaganda of the oppressor are desperately fearful. They must be made aware of the diabolical evils of the present system and they must be called to repentance but they must also be given something to hope for. At present they have false hopes. They hope to maintain the status quo and their special privileges with perhaps some adjustments and they fear any real alternative. But there is much more than that to hope for and nothing to fear. Can the Christian message of hope not help them in this matter?

There is hope. There is hope for all of us. But the road to that hope is going to be very hard and very painful. The conflict and the struggle will have to intensify in the months and years ahead because there is no other way to remove the injustice and oppression. But God is with us. We can only learn to become the instruments of *his* peace even unto death. We must participate in the cross of Christ if we are to have the hope of participating in his resurrection.

## Challenge to Action

### God Sides with the Oppressed

To say that the Church must now take sides unequivocally and consistently with the poor and the oppressed is to overlook the fact that the majority of Christians in South Africa have already done so. By far the greater part of the Church in South Africa *is* poor and oppressed. Of course it cannot be taken for granted that everyone who is oppressed has taken up their own cause and is struggling for their own liberation. Nor can it be assumed that all oppressed Christians are fully aware of the fact that their cause is God's cause. Nevertheless it remains true that the Church is already on the side of the oppressed because that is where the majority of its members are to be found. This fact needs to be appropriated and confirmed by the Church as a whole.

At the beginning of this document it was pointed out that the present crisis has highlighted the divisions in the Church. We are a divided Church precisely because not all the members of our Churches have taken sides against oppression. In other words not all Christians have united themselves with God "who is always on the side of the oppressed" (Ps. 103: 6). As far as the present crisis is concerned, there is only one way forward to Church unity and that is for those Christians who find themselves on the side of the oppressor or sitting on the fence, to cross over to the other side to be united in faith and action with those who are oppressed. Unity and reconciliation within the Church itself is only possible around God and Jesus Christ who are to be found on the side of the poor and the oppressed.

If this is what the Church must become, if this is what the Church as a whole must have as its project, how then are we to translate it into concrete and effective action?

### Participation in the Struggle

Christians, if they are not doing so already, must quite simply participate in the struggle for liberation and for a just society. The campaigns of the people, from consumer boycotts to stayaways, need to be supported and encouraged by the Church. Criticism will sometimes be necessary but encouragement and support will also be necessary. In other words the present crisis challenges the whole Church to move beyond a mere 'ambulance ministry' to a ministry of involvement and participation.

### Transforming Church Activities

The Church has its own specific activities: Sunday services, communion services, baptisms, Sunday school, funerals and so forth. It also has its specific way of expressing its faith and its commitment i.e. in the form of confessions of faith. All of these activities must be re-shaped to be more fully consistent with a prophetic faith related to the KAIROS that God is offering us today. The evil forces we speak of in baptism must be named. We know what these evil forces are in South Africa today. The unity and sharing we profess in our communion services or Masses must be named. It is the solidarity of the people inviting all to join in the struggle for God's peace in South Africa. The repentance we preach must be named. It is repentance for our share of the guilt for the suffering and oppression in our country.

Much of what we do in our Church services has lost its relevance to the poor and the oppressed. Our services and sacraments have been appropriated to serve the need of the individual for comfort and security. Now these same Church activities must be reappropriated to serve the real religious needs of all the people and to further the liberating mission of God and the Church in the world.

### Special Campaigns

Over and above its regular activities the Church would need to have special programmes, projects and campaigns because of the special needs of the struggle for liberation in South Africa today. But there is a very important caution here. The Church must avoid becoming a 'Third Force', a force between the oppressor and the oppressed. The Church's programmes and campaigns must not duplicate what the people's organisations are already doing and, even more seriously, the Church must not confuse the issue by having programmes that run counter to the struggles of those political organisations that truly represent the grievances and demands of the people. Consultation, co-ordination and co-operation will be needed. We all have the same goals even when we differ about the final significance of what we are struggling for.

### Civil Disobedience

Once it is established that the present regime has no moral legitimacy and is in fact a tyrannical regime certain things follow for the Church and its activities. In the first place *the Church cannot collaborate with tyranny*. It cannot or should not do anything that appears to give legitimacy to a morally illegitimate regime. Secondly, the Church should not only pray for a change of government, it should also mobilise its members in every parish to begin to think and work and plan for a change of government in South Africa. We must begin to look ahead and begin working now with firm hope and faith for a better future. And finally the moral illegitimacy of the apartheid regime means that the Church will have to be involved at times in *civil disobedience*. A Church that takes its responsibilities seriously in these circumstances will sometimes have to confront and to disobey the State in order to obey God.

### Moral Guidance

The people look to the Church, especially in the midst of our present crisis, for moral guidance. In order to provide this the Church must first make its stand absolutely clear and never tire of explaining and dialoguing about it. It must then help people to understand their rights and their duties. There must be no misunderstanding about the *moral duty* of all who are oppressed to resist oppression and to struggle for liberation and justice. The Church will also find that at times it does need to curb excesses and to appeal to the consciences of those who act thoughtlessly and wildly.

But the Church of Jesus Christ is not called to be a bastion of caution and moderation. The Church should challenge, inspire and motivate people. It has a message of the cross that inspires us to make sacrifices for justice and liberation. It has a message of hope that challenges us to wake up and to act with hope and confidence. The Church must preach this message not only in words and sermons and statements but also through its actions, programmes, campaigns and divine services.

*Conclusion*

As we said in the beginning, there is nothing final about this document. Our hope is that it will stimulate discussion, debate, reflection and prayer, but, above all, that it will lead to action. We invite all committed Christians to take this matter further, to do more research, to develop the themes we have presented here or to criticise them and to return to the Bible, as we have tried to do, with the question raised by the crisis of our times.

Although the document suggests various modes of involvement it does not prescribe the particular actions anyone should take. We call upon all those who are committed to this prophetic form of theology to use the document for discussion in groups, small and big, to determine an appropriate form of action, depending on their particular situation, and to take up the action with other related groups and organisations.

The challenge to renewal and action that we have set out here is addressed to the Church. But that does not mean that it is intended only for Church leaders. The challenge of the faith and of our present KAIROS is addressed to all who bear the name Christian. None of us can simply sit back and wait to be told what to do by our Church leaders or by anyone else. We must all accept responsibility for acting and living out our Christian faith in these circumstances. We pray that God will help all of us to translate the challenge of our times into action.

We, as theologians (both lay and professional), have been greatly challenged by our own reflections, our exchange of ideas and our discoveries as we met together in smaller and larger groups to prepare this document or to suggest amendments to it. We are convinced that this challenge comes from God and that it is addressed to all of us. We see the present crisis or KAIROS as indeed a divine visitation.

And finally we also like to call upon our Christian brothers and sisters throughout the world to give us the necessary support in this regard so that the daily loss of so many young lives may be brought to a speedy end.

# Chapter 55

# Carlos Mesters

God's Project

Carlos Mesters is a Carmelite priest who has been involved in the education of basic ecclesial communities, helping them find ways of engaging with Scripture which allow that subtle interplay between the two texts of the Bible and "Life" which is so distinctive of liberationist hermeneutics. For Mesters the Bible is not a history book but a resource which helps to offer an alternative perspective on the world: "the emphasis [in liberationist hermeneutics] is placed not on the text itself but rather on the meaning the text has for the people reading it . . . [it is] understanding life by means of the Bible."

This English translation of God's Project was done in South Africa and is illustrated to help users engage with the reality of the struggle with the apartheid regime. The section included here is the outline of the method of biblical study. In addition the booklet contains an outline of "God's Project" manifest in the Exodus and giving of the Torah as the introduction of an egalitarian society which contrasts with the tyranny and hierarchy of the regime in Egypt.

Source

Carlos Mesters, *God's Project*, Translation: The Theology Exchange Programme, P.O. Box 5, Athlone 7760, RSA.

Further reading

C. Mesters, *Defenseless Flower*, London: Catholic Institute for International Relations, 1989.
N. K. Gottwald and R. Horsley, *The Bible and Liberation*, revised edition, Maryknoll: Orbis, 1993.
C. Rowland, *The Cambridge Companion to Liberation Theology*, Cambridge: Cambridge University Press 1999.
R. S. Sugirtharajah, *Voices from the Margins*, London: SPCK, 1992.

*God's Project*

# INTRODUCTION
We read the Bible not only to **know** the Bible, but mainly to

## LISTEN TO GOD TODAY.
To reach this goal, three things are important:

### I.   *THE BIBLE*

. . . the written text and the historical situation of the people in that time; the study we must do of the text, how to use our own mind and the relevant sciences.

### II.   *THE REALITY*

. . . the things that happen to people today, the facts and the history of our life. It shows us the social place from which the Bible is read.

### III.   *THE COMMUNITY*

. . . The community is the place of faith and prayer where the Holy Spirit, who opens our eyes, is present.

## WE COULD SAY THAT:
* The Bible is like a guitar string
* The Community is the sounding-box
* The Reality is the player
* The Music is God's call to us, today.

## THUS:
The Reality strikes the string of the Bible stretched over the sounding-box of the Community and produces the music which is God's call to us.

The Bible must be read with the "head", with the "heart" and with the "feet". *The feet are very important*. The Bible was written as the product of a journey. It is only by following with our own feet the same journey that we can get to know all the meaning of the Bible for us. And this was the journey of the people.

## SOME IMPORTANT POINTS
1.   To **try to understand the Bible without looking at the reality** of the life of the people of yesterday and today, is the same as leaving the salt out of the food, or the seed out of the earth, or the light under the table.

2.   Why is the reality of life so important for us to understand the Bible? Because the Bible is not the first book God wrote for us, nor the most important one. **The first book is nature**, created by the Word of God; it is the facts, the things that happen, the history, everything that exists and that happens in the life of the people; it is the reality which surrounds us; it is the life we live. God wishes to

speak to us by means of the "book of life". Through this book He sends us His message of love and justice.

3.   But we, men and women, because of our sins, we organized the world in such a way, and we created a society so crooked that we cannot see clearly anymore God's call to us that is present in the life we live. That is why God wrote a **second book**, which is the Bible.

4.   But this second book **did not come to substitute the first one:** the Bible did not come to take the place of life. NO! The Bible was written to help us to understand better the meaning of the life we live and to see more clearly that God is with us inside our reality.

5.   Saint Augustine puts it like this: "The Bible, God's second book, was written to help us to make sense of the world, to give us back the vision of faith and prayerful thinking and to change all reality into a "great revelation of God".

That is why a person who reads and studies the Bible, but does not look at the reality of the people yesterday and today, is unfaithful to the Word of God and does not do the same as Jesus Christ.

# Chapter 56

# The Interpretative Method of "Unlock"

Unlock is a small, interdenominational charity, that was set up in the 1970s, and was then named the Evangelical Urban Training Project (Eutp). It grew out of concern that educational methods and theology passed down through the hierarchy of the established church were inappropriate for those then described as "working class" in urban areas. This concern, together with its continuous struggle for adequate funding, has been a thread throughout its history.

Eutp changed its name to Unlock in 1999, representing its theological and educational method:

- Unlocking real life stories of urban people
- Revealing Good News of the Down to Earth Christ
- Releasing life-changing skills and confidence.

It now works out its mission statement through a network of voluntary workers in a number of urban areas, who provide workshops and consultancy for local churches, and through the sale of "Do It Yourself" resource packs of grassroots Bible study. It also has a role in drawing the needs of those in inner city and housing estate areas to the attention of those who make decisions about education in the church.

Unlock's approach draws heavily on the work of Paulo Freire, its outworking through *Training for Transformation* (Anna Hope and Sally Timmel, Gweru, Zimbabwe: Mambo, 1995–9), and also the clarification of the theological method by Laurie Green in *Let's do theology* (London: Mowbray, 1990). Its resource packs and workshops aim to make this accessible for those in a "tabloid" (non-book), urban culture.


Source

Material from Unlock, 336a City Road, Sheffield.

## Further reading

P. Freire, *Pedagogy of the Oppressed*, Harmondsworth: Penguin, 1972.
Bob Holman with Carol, Bill, Erica, Anita, Denise, Penny and Cynthia, *Faith in the Poor. Britain's poor reveal what it's really like to be "socially excluded"*, Oxford, Lion: 1998.
G. West, *The Academy of the Poor. Towards a Dialogical Reading of the Bible*, Sheffield: Sheffield Academic Press, 1998.
*British Liberation Theology*, ed. John Vincent and Chris Rowland, The Urban Theology Unit, Sheffield, 1995–.

## "Unlock"

### The traditional method of Bible study

The majority of Bible studies begin with a text

| "There was once a man . . ." |

↓

And moves on to an analysis of the text, and the deduction of general principles

| "The Good Samaritan helped his neighbour . . ." |

↓

Finally, there is an encouragement to apply this to life

| "We must help others" |

This style provides a logical framework, within which the person can store the information (in his/her mind, in note form or on disc) for retrieval when it is needed. This requires a way of thinking and communicating which is based on book and lecture methods of learning; it is not the appropriate method for a vast number of people.

## Unlock's method of Bible study

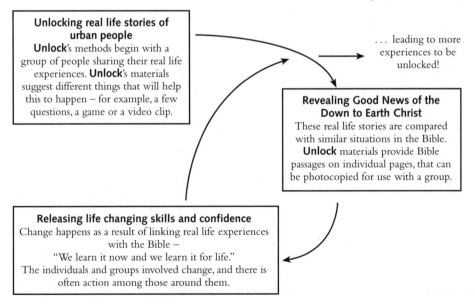

**Unlocking real life stories of urban people**
**Unlock**'s methods begin with a group of people sharing their real life experiences. **Unlock**'s materials suggest different things that will help this to happen – for example, a few questions, a game or a video clip.

. . . leading to more experiences to be unlocked!

**Revealing Good News of the Down to Earth Christ**
These real life stories are compared with similar situations in the Bible. **Unlock** materials provide Bible passages on individual pages, that can be photocopied for use with a group.

**Releasing life changing skills and confidence**
Change happens as a result of linking real life experiences with the Bible –
"We learn it now and we learn it for life."
The individuals and groups involved change, and there is often action among those around them.

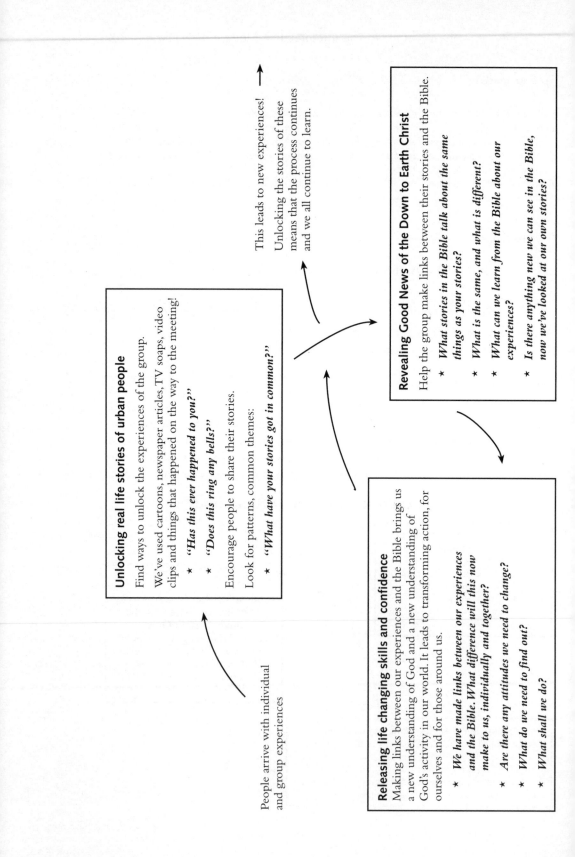

**Unlocking real life stories of urban people**

Find ways to unlock the experiences of the group.

We've used cartoons, newspaper articles, TV soaps, video clips and things that happened on the way to the meeting!

* *"Has this ever happened to you?"*

* *"Does this ring any bells?"*

Encourage people to share their stories.

Look for patterns, common themes:

* *"What have your stories got in common?"*

**Revealing Good News of the Down to Earth Christ**

Help the group make links between their stories and the Bible.

* *What stories in the Bible talk about the same things as your stories?*

* *What is the same, and what is different?*

* *What can we learn from the Bible about our experiences?*

* *Is there anything new we can see in the Bible, now we've looked at our own stories?*

This leads to new experiences!
Unlocking the stories of these means that the process continues and we all continue to learn.

**Releasing life changing skills and confidence**

Making links between our experiences and the Bible brings us a new understanding of God and a new understanding of God's activity in our world. It leads to transforming action, for ourselves and for those around us.

* *We have made links between our experiences and the Bible. What difference will this now make to us, individually and together?*

* *Are there any attitudes we need to change?*

* *What do we need to find out?*

* *What shall we do?*

People arrive with individual and group experiences

# Chapter 57

# Theology from the Perspective of "Third-World" Women

**Aruna Gnanadason,** Women's Oppression: A Sinful Situation **(1988)**
**Chung Hyun Kyung,** Struggle to be the Sun Again **(1990)**

Like their counterparts in the North, women theologians in the South have been committed to challenging the assumption at the heart of the Christian tradition that the male perspective is representative of that of the whole of humanity. Aware that for centuries "theology" (itself a gender-related term) has been monopolized by men, and of the consequences of this for the church, its teaching and for women, feminist and womanist theologians have been doing theology for themselves, telling the half of the story that has so far not been told. At the center of the project is a concern, not to find a space for women within existing (*man*-made) social and ecclesiastical structures, but (as Ann Loades has put it) to bring about "a radical restructuring of thought and analysis which comes to terms with the reality that humanity consists of women and men." In the developing world the influence of this work has been widely felt, and these two extracts are but fragments from an immensely rich body of material reflecting upon the experience of Christian women in Asian, African, and Latin American contexts. It is worth noting that women theologians from the developing world have also challenged their counterparts in the North to acknowledge *their* tendency to universalize their own experience.

Both extracts show the liberating potential for women of a re-reading and re-conceptualizing of the biblical narratives. In the first, Aruna Gnanadason from India reflects on the way Jesus engaged with women he encountered, and in the second Korean theologian Chung Hyun Kyung considers the empowering effect for Asian women of conceiving of God as Mother and Woman.

Sources

Aruna Gnanadason, "Women's Oppression: A Sinful Situation" in V. Fabella and Mercy Amba Oduyoye, eds., *With Passion and Compassion: Third World Women Doing Theology*, New York, 1988, pp. 74–5.

Chung Hyun Kyung, *Struggle to be the Sun Again: Introducing Asian Women's Theology*, London: SCM, 1991, pp. 50–2.

## Further reading

Ursula King, ed., *Feminist Theologies from the Third World, A Reader*, London, 1994.
Elsa Tamez, ed., *Through Her Eyes: Women's Theology from Latin America*, New York, 1989.
V. Fabella, *Beyond Bonding: A Third World Women's Journey*, Manila, 1993.
V. Fabella, et al., eds, *Asian Christian Spirituality: Reclaiming Traditions*, New York, 1992.
G. Dietrich, *Reflections on the Women's Movement in India: Religion, Ecology. Development*, New Delhi, 1992.
R. S. Sugirtharajah, *Voices From the Margin: Interpreting the Bible in the Third World*, London, 1991.
Mary John Mananzan et al., *Women Resisting Violence: Spirituality for Life*, New York, 1996.

## From *Women's Oppression: A Sinful Situation* (1988)

*In Christ: A New Woman*

To women theologians a rediscovery of their biblical heritage has led them to draw strength from the Jesus community, which was an egalitarian, non-hierarchical community. Sinners, prostitutes, beggars, tax collectors, the ritually polluted, the crippled, and the impoverished – in short, the scum of Palestinian society – constituted the majority of Jesus' followers. These are the last who have become the first, the starving who have been satisfied, the uninvited who have been invited. And many of these were women.

Jesus does not waste his time trying to upgrade the feminine role by giving new dignity to the old task. On the contrary, he creates an alternative. A woman's freedom in Christ therefore includes, at the core, her freedom from the system of dominance that diminishes her personhood by imprisoning her womanhood. The Christian feminist viewpoint automatically leads to a critique of historico-cultural traditions that have given women a distorted image of their bodies, their abilities, their roles, their responsibilities, their dignity, and their destiny. Each woman is called to be transformed as person and as woman, not in such a way as to become a "happy slave" seeing blessedness in the subservience demanded by society, but as an individual gifted with human dignity and salvific splendor, no less than her male counterparts.

Women have realized that they derive power from a God who has a definite preference for those who are discriminated against. In a story in the Old Testament (Num. 27:1–8), we see the courage and commitment of five women, the five daughters of a man called Zelophehad who, when their father died, stood up in front of the leader of the Israelites, Moses, and the other leaders of the community and demanded their right to the name and inheritance of their father. Moses, the one in whose hands lay the scales of justice, did not make an arbitrary judgment; he took the case to the Lord (the Bible tells us). And the Lord said that the women were right in their demand! The word of a just God transcended the social and legal practices of those times. Many other examples both from the Old Testament and from New Testament times can be given to show how God intervenes on behalf of the oppressed and changes the course of the traditional practices and laws of the time.

Women's role in church and society is therefore not merely to participate within patriarchal structures of church and society or to perpetuate them (sometimes inadvertently) but to reinterpret the critical-liberating tradition of Christianity, which is the axis on which the prophetic messianic line of biblical faith revolves. Women can participate creatively only when they break through the sinful patriarchal structures (in the family, church, and society) so as to transform relationships based on a subordination/domination ideology into one based on the freedom promised in Christ. In this effort we draw inspiration from Jesus' radical attitude toward women. For eighteen years, the bent-over woman in Luke's story was weighed down by the sinful structures around her but was able to overcome her bent-over state and was recognized as a "daughter of Abraham" by Jesus. To be the daughters of Abraham is to discover the power we derive from Christ.

## From *Struggle to be the Sun Again* (1990)

### God as Mother and Woman

Many Asian women think God as a life-giving power can be naturally personified as mother and woman because woman gives birth to her children and her family members by nurturing them. In many Asian women's writings, God is portrayed as mother and woman. Some Asian women claim that women are more sensitive to fostering life than men because of women's experience of giving birth and nurturing others. A group of Asian women emphasized the point by reflecting on the event of Moses' birth and killing of male infants in Exodus:

> Every woman is close to life and loves her child. Woman is life and love. The killing of the male baby is ironic of the two edged sword that patriarchy has in itself, namely, in male power is also death.

God as mother and woman challenges the old concept which emphasized, along with other attributes, God as immutable and unchangeable. Woman's body grows and changes radically through menstruation and pregnancy compared to the male body. God as mother is more approachable and personable. When Asian women begin to imagine God as woman and mother, they also begin to accept their own bodies and their own womanhood in its fullness. The female God accepts us as we are more than the patriarchal male God. This female God is a vulnerable God who is willing to be changed and transformed in her interaction with Asian women in their everyday life experiences. This God is a God who talks to Asian women, listens to their story, and weeps with them. This God is a God who struggles with Asian women in their claims of power in this world, a God who is growing, changing, and walking with them.

Asian women's trust in this God enables them to trust themselves and to hope in the midst of their hopelessness. The power of God evokes in Asian women a different kind of power, which has been lost in patriarchal religion and society:

> The power that fosters life rather than death
> the power of working together,
> the power of experiencing one's true feelings,
> the power of acclaiming others and
> enabling them to realize their full
> potential as human beings.

With this new power Asian women struggle to be persons with power for self-determination. They dream of a new world where woman is not the moon which has to change according to the sun. Rather they want to become the sun who shines in its own light out of its burning core of life, fostering life on the earth.

> Originally, woman was the Sun.
> She was an authentic person.
> But now woman is the moon.
> She lives by depending on another
> and she shines by reflecting
> another's light.
> Her face has a sickly pallor.

> We must now regain our hidden sun.
> "Reveal our hidden sun!
> Rediscover our natural gifts!"
> This is the ceaseless cry
> Which forces itself into our hearts;
> it is our irrepressible
> and unquenchable desire.
> It is our final,
> complete,
> and only instinct
> through which
> our various
> separate instincts
> are unified.

In Asian women's perspective, knowledge of self leads to a knowledge of God. In their suffering, Asian women meet God, who in turn discloses that they were created in the divine image, full and equal participants in the community with men. To know the self is to know God for Christian Asian women.

# Chapter 58

# Sigqibo Dwane

## Theology and the Context **(1989)**

This short exposition of the nature of contextual theology is written by Bishop Sigqibo Dwane. It is part of a collection published to commemorate the 140th anniversary of the birth of his grandfather, James Matta Dawane. Along with a colleague the elder Dwane formed the Ethiopian Church and then became leader of the Ethiopian movement which was affiliated with the Episcopalian church in South Africa. Ethiopianism is "the nuptials of Christianity and African culture. It demands that Africans must be accepted in the body of Christ on their own terms, and on those of the gospel alone." It has been "one of those little corners in which Blacks have been able to attempt to be themselves, away from the pressures to conform to rigid Western norms and values" (Sigqibo Dwane). The movement reflects a synthesis of orthodox Christian theology which is deeply rooted in African life. The movement began because of a felt and perceived need for the healing of the wounds inflicted by oppression and colonisation. The rights of ordinary people, and especially those of women and children, are championed and defended.

The short essay entitled *Theology and the Context* parallels themes promoted in various examples of Third World theology in which there is the call to do Theology contextually by being attentive to God's voice speaking in and through the persons and events of the contemporary world.

## Source

Bishop Sigqibo Dwane, *Issues in the South African Theological Debate Essays and Addresses in honour of the late James Matta Dwane*, Braamfontein: Skotaville (307 Hampstead House, 446 Biccard Street Box 32483, Braamfontein 2017, 1989).

## *Theology and the Context*

For some time there have been misgivings about the tendency in academic circles to seperate theology from the issues of life. Some theologians have wondered whether they were busy answering questions which weren't being asked. The *Honest to God* debate in the 1960s was a manifestation of this dissatisfaction with the state of affairs. And although a lot of water has gone under the bridge since that debate first made its appearance, nevertheless the attempt by theology to take the context seriously is still at a very early stage.

It is important for those of us who were brought up in the 'old school' to bring ourselves up to date by learning something of the nature of this new approach, and the adjustments it requires us to make in our thinking.

## What is Contextual Theology?

It should be noted at the outset that the designation 'contextual theology', which is frequently used in this connection as a form of shorthand, is not a happy one. There are at least three reasons for this.

The first is that it is misleading because it suggests that in the normal run of things, theology can happily conduct its business in a vacuum, oblivious of the world and its problems, while perhaps on odd occasions the discourse may deviate from its normal practice to deal with real and pertinent questions.

Secondly, Paul Tillich points out that theology is an 'answering discourse'. It attempts to bring revelation face to face with the human situation, as at the incarnation. It is therefore futile to try to do theological reflection away from the arena in which the struggles of life take place.

Thirdly, we need to realise that the pressures of human existence do invariably impinge upon the life of the church, and influence the direction of its teaching. If one looks at even the most universal symbols like the Apostles' or Nicene Creeds, one is faced with the fact that they are products of a particular era, and have evolved in response to certain specific circumstances.

For example, the Apostles' Creed, it is believed, may have had something to do with the need for the instruction of catechumens preparing for baptism.

The origins of the Nicene Creed are of course less obscure, even though there is debate about the text, and about whether the Creed has anything to do with the Nicene (or any other) Council. What we are certain about is the fact that this Creed emerged out of the discussion concerning the divinity of Christ. Athanasius was the champion of this doctrine, while Arius was the villain who advocated all those heretical tendencies of which the *homoousios* phrase ('one substance') is a flat rebuttal.

This observation about the Creeds is true of many other theological formulae or confessions which have now become important historical documents of the church, as well as part of its living tradition. The material is contextual in origin and in the ability of its credal or confessional statements to speak to the church in different places and at different times.

The point at issue here is that theology always happens in a particular context, whether the influence exerted by the circumstances is acknowledged or not. But thanks to the upheaval of the 1960s, the emphasis is changing in theology from the purely academic and deductive approach, towards a more empirical one which sets much store by flexibility and accommodating diversity.

This new emphasis should not only be noted, but highlighted and celebrated. We need to celebrate the fact that theology has consciously opened dialogue with the contexts which make up its environment. This is an exciting new venture whose roots should be firmly secured in order to ensure that the balance is now always maintained between the practical and pastoral on the one hand, and the mental and spiritual discipline on the other.

There will always be a special place of honour for the rigorous discipline of the mind in the study of theology. But we must continue to press for the removal of the barrier which has separated, and continues to separate, doctrine from moral and ethical application, and exegesis of scripture from its practical application.

Of course, the temptation to moralise or preach when theological students should be wrestling with concepts or with the text is a real one. But the dichotomy between the material and the context in which it has to be applied is a very serious one, and one which causes the atmosphere in academic institutions to be rarefied.

It is true that often the academic environment is the matrix of new and creative ideas, but it can become sterile if it gets out of touch with ordinary people's lives. If theology is to be a meaningful discourse, then it has to speak directly and unambiguously to the changing and varied conditions of man. Theology as a whole, and not just certain aspects, should be contextual.

This chapter is an attempt to sharpen the truth that the context is fundamental to theology. Theology has to do with God and His ways among people. As such, it must relate to the world which He created, which He loves, and is the stage of His redemptive work. And this takes us to the next point.

*God and History*

In the previous section we saw that theology has to be relevant to people's needs and that this can come about when their struggles for existence, for justice and human dignity, are taken seriously as the raw materials for reflection and formulation.

The desire to be relevant is by itself sufficient reason for theology to take the context seriously. For we speak in order that we may be heard and understood, otherwise our speech is to no avail.

But there is another and deeper reason for this, which thus far has only been hinted at, but which we must now explore more fully. It has to do with the nature of God's dealing with humanity, a relationship which is grounded and rooted in specific historical events.

Here we need to draw attention to the fact that the crucible of the Old-Testament scriptures is the encounter of God with His people in their suffering as slaves in Egypt, and in all the events of the Exodus which culminated in the covenant and gift of the promised land. Israel's experience of the mighty hand of God, and of His faithfulness to His promise, became the anvil on which the prophetic movement hammered out new ideas as she came into contact with new situations at the time of settlement in Canaan.

Guided by the prophetic movement, and helped by the experience of God's deliverance, Israel's horizons became widened as she began to realise that God is the Lord of the universe, the creator. The mighty hand which had wrought her deliverance was recognised as the same hand which brought creation into being at the beginning. The salvation story, in other words, was extended backwards first to Abraham the patriarch of Israel, and then to Adam the father of the human race.

Theology in this instance, as indeed in others, began in a particular setting, and only on further reflection and application were its boundaries widened. It was the covenant which brought Israel into an intimate relationship with Yahweh. The children of Israel were to be His people, and He their God.

This relationship was nurtured by prayer and worship. The community had at the centre of its life God Himself, whose dwelling among His people was symbolised visibly by the ark of the covenant, and then by the temple in the period of settlement. These symbols were to be a constant reminder that God is Immanuel, and not a hidden God but one who makes Himself known to His people.

In Jesus of Nazareth, the idea of God pitching His tent with His people finds its fullest expression. Jesus is the true and living temple. In Him God not only dwells with His people, but becomes a particular person who is subject to the limitations of time, culture conditioning, and religious belief. Through Him the fulfilment of God's promises to Israel takes place in a particular era and within given historical circumstances.

The earthly ministry of Christ was in response to specific human needs. His passion, death and resurrection were a fulfilment of promises made to Israel of a new beginning, a new Exodus. And as in the Exodus out of Egypt, so in the death and resurrection motif the church has been able to complete the story of man's sojourn on earth. Christ the saviour of the world is also the judge who shall appear in glory at the end to complete His work. He, the second Adam, is the door to God's Kingdom which will embrace all the offspring of Abraham – Jew and Gentile. The particular in Him is also the all-embracing. His original context is the core around which all other human contexts are drawn.

And this is what I want to underline, because it is the crux of the matter. For as the Exodus in the Old Testament and in the New is the centre around which the rest of the material in scripture is organised and given a cohesion, so also the salvation motif in theology is the core around which different human contexts can be pieced together, as the pentecost event so clearly shows. And that takes us to the third point.

## Unity in Diversity

The theme of unity in diversity, the one and the many, is a very ancient one. It is manifested in the history of Israel where Semitic groups of different origins come together in the tribal confederation of Israel and Judah. The outcome of the interaction between God and this motley group of people is of course the Old Testament itself, which is a wide-ranging assortment of literary types, all in one way or another witnessing to Israel's unique religious experience. The golden thread which runs through it all and gives the movement a coherence is the Exodus-covenant motif.

The situation is similar in the New Testament. Firstly, there are the original 12 disciples who were a mixed bag – zealots, fishermen, even a tax-collector – all held together by the charismatic personality of Jesus.

Then in the post-resurrection church there were differences of approach between Peter and Paul, which created serious tensions between the Jewish and Gentile missions. Paul's missionary work had its own tensions caused on the one hand by antinomians, and by adherents of the law on the other. Both were distortions of the gospel of Jesus Christ, and therefore needed correction and rebuke. All these different tendencies were held together, sometimes very delicately, by the experience of easter and pentecost.

Diversity therefore is not a new feature of the Christian life, and need not cause division in the body. What we have to remember is that emphases or particular slants are not the whole truth, but only aspects of it. God alone embraces the whole truth; human beings know only in part. And God in His grace makes provision for unity and wholeness by which all human fragmentariness is overcome.

But how in practice do we contextualise theology? Here I want to throw out a few suggestions for consideration.

Firstly, one should identify the key elements in one's situation. I give my own analysis of the situation I live in as an example.

I am a black person who lives in a township where there is material deprivation, poverty and squalor. The degrading conditions in which people are made to live lead to a loss of self respect in some members of the community, and of hope in others. I see the effects of being discriminated against, and legislated for, in the resentment and anger of young people against the white establishment, and even against white people themselves. I see that so much of township violence is an expression of this.

Often I am painfully aware that the apathy of many older people is a mechanism to cope with the hard facts of life. I see the effects of colonisation and enslavement of people's minds, expressed in their lack of confidence in themselves, and in their feeling of embarrassment about their culture.

Secondly, how do I respond to people in this situation? The question is not what the church should be doing, but rather what I, a member of the body of Christ, am commissioned to do in these circumstances. God the Immanuel stands with His people where they stand, and suffers with them. And He wants each member of His church to be where He is, in order that He may make them His own gift to those who are despondent and need comforting. Certain passages in scripture may provide parallels, and thereby sharpen our vision and articulate our own calling more clearly.

Thirdly, I need to formulate some values to guide me through life's pilgrimage, and these sum up for me what I consider to be the mind of Christ. I may not intend to make decisions in advance, but guidelines are important as a sort of co-ordinating centre, and as a means of eliminating whim or downright folly. If I have a set of guidelines, I can evaluate myself from time to time, not in order to congratulate myself, but that I may see whether my life is patterned on the death, resurrection, and pentecost experience of the community to which I belong.

### Conclusion

God is not a being who sits back and spends all His time contemplating the world, but His nose is always at the grindstone, working for the accomplishment of His purpose.

God is in the world:
  crying for help
  suffering
  dying
  rejoicing at His victory over death and darkness
  loving people to the utmost
  healing, renewing with His spirit
  strengthening people with hope
  preparing for the consummation of His kingly rule.

The call to do theology contextually is the appeal to listen to Him and to respond to His invitation to be with Him in trust and obedience.

# Chapter 59

# Sara Maitland

**Radegund from** Angel and Me **(1995)**

In her introduction to the collection from which Radegund comes Angela West offers a necessary reminder that "the sources of Christianity are largely without abstractions. We have a collection of stories, sayings, parables, letters and poems arising out of living experience. By sucking out – abstracting – the content Western theologians discard context and form as irrelevant and clothe them with the trappings of philosophical knowledge. All other forms of Christian truth are treated as second class. But the biblical texts are artful. The bible's artfulness is our inspiration." Those words are particularly appropriate in a collection of radical Christian writings, reminding us that the neat and the systematic neither best reflects Christianity's foundation texts nor communicates the variety of human experience. Sara Maitland's work captures the biblical artfulness which is a necessary component of radical Christianity.

Sara Maitland writes: St. Radegund (518–587) left her remarkably – even for northern Europe in the sixth century CE – vicious husband, Clotaire of the Franks, and subsequently founded the Convent of the Holy Cross at Poitiers. She became a peace broker among the constantly warring Frankish tribes and in gratitude the Pope presented her with a relic of the True Cross. Her foundation became famous for both the Arts and scholarship. Despite having left her husband she was ordained a Deaconess, and became a patron saint of scholarship (Jesus College Chapel, Cambridge is dedicated to her).

This story was the Tuesday (by tradition the day of the "cleansing of the temple") story in "Sisters of the Spirit," a sequence of narratives for Holy Week; it was published with three other similar sequences as *Angel and Me* (Cassells, 1995) and in a rather different version in *Virtuous Magic: Women Saints and their Meanings* with Wendy Mulford (Cassells, 1998). It is part of my ongoing struggle to create a "hermeneutic of the imagination" or narrative theology – based on the assumption that a theology which does not speak to a whole person is an inadequate theology and that myth, story and poetry are radical tendencies which the present church needs to encourage. More frequently I write novels and other fictions: e.g. *Brittle*

*Joys* (1999) and *Women Fly When Men Aren't Watching* (1993). I am a feminist and a Roman Catholic – and live in Co. Durham, England.


## Source

Sara Maitland, *Angel and Me*, London: Mowbray, 1995, pp. 76–82.


## Radegund

She knew she was dying. She knew it with contentment and peace. Three score years and ten almost precisely measured out and it was time to go. So then. 'Into thy hands,' she murmured, 'into thy hands I commend my spirit.'

'Tonight you will walk with us in paradise,' sing the angels, and if it were not too much effort she would smile.

It was high summer, and they had carried her into the chapel to die. High above her, hazy and shadowed now, the great roof, the ark that had carried her through so many storms, still offered protection. The altar towards which she faced still offered beauty and serenity; the reliquary containing the piece of the True Cross, a gift in her honour sent all the way from Constantinople, for her, shone in glory in its chapel. Around her, her nuns, his sisters, her daughters, prayed with her, so that she did not feel lonely. Out in the guest-house the Frankish Ambassador fumed, needing answers to his now so unimportant questions about the peace treaty, so that she did not feel useless.

Two hundred women, wise and gentle, for whom she had won from foolish and jealous bishops the right to scholarship – enshrined in the rule and blessed by the Bishop of Rome himself, their two hours a day spent not in simpering embroideries but in true study. Two hundred women here in her house in Poitiers.

And he had mocked her barrenness. Silly old fool, she thought now, but quite tolerantly; King Clotaire, son of Clovis, once – and she supposed still – her husband. Ha.

It was high summer. Outside the sun was hot; she could see the sky deep bright blue and the fat white clouds crossing the window. She could hear in the distance the farmers bringing in the grape harvest. This evening the children would squeal and sing as they clambered over the vats and stomped out the rhythms of the pressing dances, and it would be good and sweet, for a little wine was a wholesome thing, and not always the wild dangerous threat that it had been when she was very young.

Tonight at Vespers she will surrender; she will receive the sacrament for the last time, she will bless her sisters, and she will go forth on her long journey. She was ready. She turned her mind to that journey in confidence and serenity.

Then, tugging, distracting, from somewhere deep in the back of her mind, she knew there was something she had not yet done. Something she had promised

. . . promised who? . . . promised herself? . . . something she wanted to do before she died. Something she ought to do.

Her mind scarcely paused at the thought of her escritoire, there was a mass of things undone there, but not anything that mattered. She had laboured for peace this last quarter century and she had not been ineffective, but there was no peace and there would be no peace among the noisy royal houses of Europe, so anything that she might not have had time to finish would not matter too much. An envoy, a truce, a boundary decision might not be made, but she was not going to turn her feet from her journey for that.

Something for the convent. Something for her sisters, something important she had to tell them. She could not remember. Her face furrowed with the effort to remember, her still head moved slightly on its pillow, and at once one of the sisters was there, soothing, wiping her lips with the cool dampness of a linen cloth scented sweetly with lavender from the garden. That warm smell distracted her, and although grateful for the attention, she was irritated by the disturbance.

Her irritation reminded her. She had to tell them about anger, about anger and how sometimes it was good and godly and right. It was not true, women had been deceived, they had been taught that in gentleness, in submissiveness there was power, in giving it up, in throwing it away; that love was simply the ability to suffer and to suffer and suffer. Pah.

Radegund was the daughter of Berthaire, King of Thuringia. Not a childhood to encourage sweetness in any woman – that household of savagery, and intrigue and violence. The war-bands did not disperse during the fighting season, even for banquets. They sat down to eat and they stood up to fight; they would fight with the enemy when there was any around and failing that they would fight with each other and plot and scheme and murder and assassinate. For the royal child it had been exciting; standing beside her mother's chair in the high hall and looking out while men and dogs surged about the hall. Her long blond pigtails had bounced with suppressed excitement and she had been woken in the night more than once because the whole household was on the move again – in fear or in aggression depending on the turn of politics and power.

She was twelve the night of the great raid, when the Frankish soldiers descended on the household, their pine torches smoking and glowing, catching the light of horned helmet, round shield, short sword and bright eyes. If she had stayed in the women's quarters where she belonged she might have been safe; as it was they snatched her in her night shift from the courtyard, galloping, thundering, and then out into the night. She had not been frightened, thrilled rather, just a child.

Thye carried her off to the Frankish Court, to the household of Clovis where she grew up. Her status was strange – she was not slave or prisoner; she was treated with honour; she was held for high ransom at first, which was never paid, and to this day she did not know exactly why. Later she was contracted in marriage to Clotaire, heir of Clovis, and then she was there not as prisoner at all but as the future queen. The household of Clovis was Christian; the future queen, it was decided, should be a Christian also, so they began to instruct her. There was order in that court, order and time and space and women did not mix too much with men, but lived in their own quarters and were treated it seemed to her at first with respect. She was introduced to God, and also to reading and writing and gracious arts. Their God became her god. Christ on the cross dying for her; his presence in the sacrament, in the bread and in the wine. In the singing, so different from the drunken brawlings of childhood; in the poetry and the carved wood, painted and gilded, that was turned into the statues of the saints. A God too whom you could talk with, in the quiet and privacy of your chamber, a God who listened to prayers rather than grew drunk on the blood of slaughtered animals.

All this was so lovely and comforting to her in her loneliness, that she accepted the other bits too. That women can unite with this God only through meekness and obedience; that women have a mission to bring sweetness to the lives of men; that wives must be obedient to their husbands, must keep silent, must honour and obey.

Obeying Clotaire as it turned out was a great deal easier than honouring him. He dealt with the obeying bit, with the back of his hand if all else failed. She struggled unaided with the honouring bit. She was eighteen when they were married and she came to her estate with a glowing heart. She knew he was a wild man, fierce and bloodthirsty and she believed that she could, in the power of Christ – and assisted by her beauty which even she knew, and knew with due modesty, was the kind that sets men's hearts aflame (and, as she learned quickly not just their hearts) – tame this man and make him loving and dutiful.

To this end she directed all her energies. It seemed to her that he devoted what energies he had to spare from pillage, massacre, and debauchery, to her humiliation. He threw her from her own bed at night so that he could lay his mistress there; he made her stand in the hall, in the presence of his war-band, while he berated her for her childlessness. He beat her. He mocked her. And, whenever he felt like it, without warning, without kindness, he raped her.

The priests around her muttered that this was but God's testing of her. She must accept all this in meekness for the glory of God and to save her husband's soul. He must be brought to see that her love was unwavering, that her forgiveness like Christ's was complete. Love would they assured her conquer all so long as she was strong in submission, was humble in humiliation, and was welcoming, warm, tender, sweet, good.

It was right they told her, even that he should interrupt her prayers because a woman came to God only through her husband; that her husband, her king, must be first for her, first even above God.

And she endured it. She believed them and she endured it.

Soft through the castle she went, silent and gentle. When he let her she was generous; and when he forbade it she consented. When he was away from her cavorting with his whores, with his friends, with his horses and hounds, she read and she prayed; when she heard that he was returning she put those things away and attended to his every whim. One day he would turn, one day he would turn and see her, see who she was, see this holy and gentle girl who made his needs her concern, who made his salvation the first matter of her intercession, who loved him and would suffer for and from him, turning her cheek as the Christ did, inviting him to smite the other side.

He killed her brother and made her watch.

He abused her body.

He laughed at her in public.

He burned her books.

She offered it up, she united her sufferings with the sufferings of Christ; she followed the instructions of St Paul and was obedient to him. One day, one day he would turn and love her; one day her long torture would be rewarded. If she were a good enough wife he would change. That was what God wanted. She was being tested. Clotaire and God were testing her. She had to endure in all meekness.

For six years, for six years she endured. She was, they said, as pious as she was beautiful. As good as she was lovely. She was a model of the Christian queen; she gave herself up to her husband's interests as a good woman should. For his political advantage she even consented to the death of her brother; she had left her father and her father's house and cleaved only to her husband in silence and in humility. She was a saint, they said, a banner of Christian womanhood in the dark north.

This did not comfort her.

One evening, late, he came to her chamber drunk, with a drunken comrade, arm in arm. 'Look at my lady wife,' he said with a laugh, 'get you a wife like this, friend. A wife who will do anything. A muling chicken, with the heart of a whore.'

And to her he said 'Take off your clothes.'

'No,' she said. She had not known she was going to say it. She had been ready, waiting, bathed and perfumed for him. She had thought this would be a night like any other. She was as startled as he was to hear her voice saying 'No'. To hear so calm and certain her own mouth say 'No'.

But once it was said, something changed.

She was a Thuringian fury, the dark power of the wild Viking gods of the north was on her; the strength and wrath of the God of the psalmist – the God who blighted Sodom in the night and laid low the walls of Jericho. The God who rode with David against the Philistines, and laid the seven curses on the children of Egypt.

The God who cleansed the temple.

While he stood there blankly, while his friend crept from the room, while his fury tried to gather itself and failed to overcome the stupor of his amazement, she started to speak.

'This, this,' she shouted, banging her own chest, 'this is a temple, a temple of the Holy Spirit, a house of God and you have made it a den of thieves. Enough. Do you hear me, enough. I don't care.'

He took a dazed step towards her and she snatched up the great glazed bowl that stood full of water on her armoire. She hurled it at him, and it crashed, a thousand splinters.

'And now I am leaving. In the morning. Arrange me transport. I am taking the veil, I am going to Noyons and they will make me a deaconess because of your noble name and then you will never be able to touch me again. Never.'

For one moment she saw in his eyes the thing she had debased herself for six years to see; a glimpse of awe, of respect, of admiration. But it was too late. What virtue had not gained her, anger had. What sweetness and suffering had failed to provide, anger did.

She heard the huge stern voice of Jesus saying to her as he had to Lazarus, 'Come out.' Come out of the grave and live.

When she rode away from her husband's house the next morning, setting forth boldly on the long road to Noyons, which would lead in due time to the shorter sunnier road to Poitiers and to her own foundation, her own daughters, her honour and power and glory she heard the cheers of Martha and Mary, and the Lady. She heard the laughter of Thecla, and the merriment of all the martyrs. She heard the voice of Jesus and was surprised but delighted to find that it did not, out from under the shadow of his high hall, sound remotely like the voice of Clotaire.

Life and love were strong and sweet. Her anger had made her a free woman. It was better to be gentle and good; order was better than chaos; peace and study than the wild nights of the war-bands. She was lucky because she was not just pious and beautiful, she was also clever and wise. She never questioned her luck; she never questioned God's kindness to her, but she never questioned the power of anger either. Our Lord in the temple, destroying the tables of the money-changers, is the same Lord as our Lord on the cross. Both.

Especially for women.

She wanted to tell the nuns that, here on this bright summer day, while she was dying. It seemed important.

She searched through her considerable resources of strength and determination. Then she knew that she did not have the time. They would have to learn it for themselves. They could look to her life and work it out.

The lavender-scented cloth moved tenderly across her face again. Fun, that is what she had had since leaving Clotaire. Happiness. Joy. Fun.

She smiled.

The nuns sang. She was ready now.

# Chapter 60

# Kenneth Leech (1939–2015)

The Rebel Church In the Back Streets – Where Are We Now? **(1996)**

Kenneth Leech is a priest in the Anglo-Catholic tradition who believes that "theology is not an activity for academics remote in academic ghettoes, but an activity for Christian people at street level." Born and brought up in Manchester, he has spent most of his adult life in the East End of London, and currently works as a community theologian based at St Botolph's Church, Aldgate. Very much in the tradition of radical East London priests like John Groser and Stanley Evans, whom he mentions in this piece, Leech sees political action as the natural outworking of a belief in the kingdom of God. His own theology has been shaped by his experience, in particular his struggle against racism and his grass-roots pastoral work with drug addicts and homeless people. In 1974 he helped found the Jubilee Group, which describes itself as "a loose network of socialist Christians, mainly within the Anglican Catholic tradition."

In the essay reproduced here, Leech highlights what he believes to be a significant division within the church (as broadly defined), that between those who have accommodated themselves to the world, and those who believe that the coming of the kingdom encompasses a radical transformation of the world and its structures. The latter are characterized by commitment and struggle, which as often as not will take place in the back streets.

Source

Kenneth Leech, "The Rebel Church In the Back Streets – Where Are We Now?", *Christian Action Journal*, Spring/Summer 1996, pp. 15–17.

Further reading

Kenneth Leech, *Soul Friend*, London, 1977.
——, *The Social God*, London, 1981.

——, *Struggle in Babylon*, London, 1988.
——, *Politics and the Faith Today*, London, 1994.
——, *The Sky is Red*, London, 1998.
——, *Through Our Long Exile: Contextual Theology and the Urban Experience*, London, 2001.
Kenneth Brill, ed., *John Groser: East London Priest*, London and Oxford, 1971.
David Nicholls, *Deity and Domination: Images of God and the State in the nineteenth and twentieth centuries*, London: Routledge, 1989.

### The Rebel Church In the Back Streets – Where Are We Now?

I have spent most of my adult life in very localised forms of ministry, reflection and struggle. I came to the East End of London in 1958 as a student and stayed. I now live half a mile from where I lived then. So, at one level, I am a local, backyard, small scale person. On the other hand, I am strongly committed to the 'grand narrative' which, according to the fashionable proponents of postmodernism, is now obsolete. For me, the future of Christian social witness is all about how to relate the concrete struggles of 'the local' to the large scale vision of the Kingdom of God, the reign of justice, love and peace within the created order of people and things. Much of my sense of this interconnectedness has been due to the influence of mentors and comrades in this neighbourhood, both inside and outside the churches.

When I came to the East End, John Groser was coming to the end of his ministry which had begun in 1922. What struck me, first, about Groser was the sheer length of his time here. He arrived in 1922 and left in 1962. He saw the importance of the local community and of long term commitment, in contrast to the situation today (and no doubt in his day too) when clergy tend to move on every few years and get 'promotion'. Groser was concerned with 'the personal as political', a term which only became current after his death. His only book, published in 1949, was called *Politics and Persons*. He was committed to local issues but saw local issues, issues around housing and fascism, for example, in the context of national, international and global ones. He saw the importance of making connections. In contrast to much of the Christian left which was grim and intense, Groser's politics was rooted in worship and dramatic celebration. Following Conrad Noel and the Catholic Crusade, he saw the importance of festivity, colour, music and dancing, in the creation of a Christian social consciousness. Like Emma Goldman, he wanted no part in any revolution which did not include dancing. And, as a deeply traditional Catholic Christian, he saw God, and the orthodox faith in God, as deeply subversive. He wrote in 1927:

> I am known commonly as a socialist of a very advanced type, and although as a matter of fact I belong to no political party, I suppose that would correctly describe me. I took a very active part in the General Strike and would do so again. And this I do, not because I believe that in co-identifying myself with those who are struggling for elementary rights and common justice, I am but following the lead of Jesus . . .

I am suspect in his Body the Church, and I am suspect – not because I deny any doctrine of the Body – but because I affirm them all most strongly and refuse to be tied by the petty conventionalities which govern her. I am not likely to accentuate the misunderstandings and divisions which exist in most dioceses today because I feel that they are mostly about the frills of religion, but I am likely to cause a much more fundamental division.

It is this 'much more fundamental division' with which I too am centrally concerned. In 1956 Stanley Evans, then a parish priest in Dalston, identified the fundamental division within the Christian world as one which did not run along denominational lines but rather divided those Christians in all traditions who believed that the Kingdom of God involved a hope for the transformation of this world and its structures, and those who did not.

In 1962 Evans produced a small book called *The Church in the Back Streets*. It is now largely forgotten and unobtainable. It is also, of course, dated. Yet it remains a seminal work for the church in the inner city. Like Groser, Evans was deeply concerned with overcoming the gulf between the church and the working class. He was a theologian who believed that theology must be done in the back streets and must be localised, that it was a task for the whole people of God or for nobody. He was the key figure in a network of socialist clergy who, until the late 1950s, tended to follow the Communist Party line fairly closely. Today much of his work seems hopelessly dated, yet, in his emphasis on doing theology in local context, and on the parish as a worshipping, theologically alert and servant community and as a force for righteousness in the district, he was way ahead of his time.

Groser and Evans are simply two examples of what I would term back street theology, theology done on the run, theology done often in a hurry, yet good theology, theology in conflict with the dominant structures. Since those days we have had a series of new theological styles – liberation theology, feminist theology, black theology, and so on. But much of this, as it has surfaced in the West, has been elitist and academic, little of it has touched the back streets. It is marketed like any other product, and books on the 'option for the poor' are very expensive and only accessible to the wealthy and intelligentsia. This is not good enough.

Today much of what these old socialist Christians said is common currency in the corridors of power, though much of it only at the level of rhetoric. It is widely assumed that the official church has moved to the left, and it is certainly true that official utterances on social and political issues, whether from Pope John Paul or Anglican bishops or the Methodist Conference, are in sharp conflict with the assumptions of capitalism. There is a good deal of bureaucratic radicalism and many people in key positions in churches who are sometimes unkindly termed 'tenured radicals'. There is much good social theology coming from the various headquarters and from what Henry Clark has termed the 'social action curias', I have no wish to knock the 'trickle down' approach but this really is not good enough either. My own early background as a priest in inner city districts coincided with the emergence of detached youth and community work, and the interaction between theology and youth and community work made me realise how dangerous it is to depend on the utterances from the centre.

If we try to locate this conflict between centre and periphery in some broader historical framework, it becomes clear that since the 1880s there have been two main streams of Christian social action and consciousness, at least within Anglicanism: a genteel, reformist stream, and a more radical, rebel stream. I believe that the social action curias need to be constantly challenged, embarrassed, provoked, disturbed and helped by locally organised movements at the level of the back street church. So let me conclude with some reflections on an experiment in social reflection which has emerged over the last twenty years.

In 1974 a small group of us created the *Jubilee Group* network without intending to do so! All we had in mind was a support group for a group of eight left-wing Anglican priests, mostly East End of London. Within a short time what had emerged was what we now term 'a loose network of socialist Christians, mainly within the Anglican Catholic tradition'. *Jubilee* is an anarchic, disorganised, shambolic phenomenon, more like an atmosphere than an organisation, but seems to have played at least two important roles. First, to create a network of loving support and solidarity for the 'Catholic left', along the lines suggested by Alasdair MacIntyre in *After Virtue* (1981) when he spoke of 'networks of small groups of friends', or by Cornel West and bell hooks in *Breaking Bread* (1991) when they speak of the need for 'a community of comrades who are seeking to deepen our spiritual experience and our political solidarity'.

The second is to develop a form of theological and political reasoning and reflection which is not academic, though it involves academics, and yet does seek to reconnect serious intellectual struggle with commitment, action and struggle at local and national levels. Historically our antecedents are groups such as the Guild of St Matthew (1877), the Catholic Crusade (1916) and the League of the Kingdom of God (1922), but, while we look to tradition and the movements of the past for inspiration and nourishment, we seek to relate Catholic social theology to the issues of the twenty-first century. We have no membership, simply a mailing list and local groups, and all our literature is 'anti-copyright', that is, anyone is free to re-issue it without permission. Our organisation is minimal – an annual meeting and an executive – with the maximum amount of freedom and flexibility. We are a tendency rather than an organisation. There is an important anarchist tradition within the network which produces both a chaotic feel and an ability to act quickly. It also leads on occasions to exaggerated claims by others: thus a briefing to Mrs Thatcher on movements of subversion within the churches in 1990 described us as 'the best known and probably the most influential of these groups'. If only they knew!

We see that the centre of gravity in the Christian world has shifted and that neither the divisions nor the areas of convergence/alliance between Christians any longer run along the old confessional lines. Thus we have found that on many issues we have more in common with the liberation thinkers in the Roman Catholic church or with Mennonites or with the evangelical radicals from Sojourners – or with non-Christians – than we have with other Anglo-Catholics.

So we are strongly committed to alliances including alliances with non-Christian Socialists. We are uneasy at the 'churchy' aspects of much radical Christianity and are committed to our work outside the church structures. At the same time we feel that deeply rooted Catholic theology and spirituality is essential to us for the sustenance and nourishment of radical action, and we are highly critical of liberalism and of the theological reductionism in many 'liberal' Christian circles. We have a strong sacramental thrust and are very strongly socialist, so 'sacramental socialists' would be a good description of our position.

Most of all, and this brings me back to my central point, we believe that social thinking is best done in the course of struggle and movement, a point made powerfully by Stanley Evans in the last paper he wrote and which was delivered after his death in 1965. Here Evans pointed to the debate in the early 60s about old theology and new theology, and he wrote:

> The two theologies, old and new, both seek for an impossible stability. Both think in terms of rest: the one will sound and the other will lie at anchor. But the only purpose of taking soundings is to aid navigation, and they have, in practice, to be taken from a vessel under way. The Pauline vessel in the Sea of Adria dropped its anchors because its navigation had failed, and it was on the verge of wrecking. Navigation is really learned only by those who sail, and this is a fundamental principle of the church. 'He that doeth the will shall know of the doctrine.' We are concerned to discuss faith as a handmaid to the living of the Christian life, as a navigational aid to those who would be in the way that leads to God's kingdom, not as an academic exercise for members of a hydrographical department who have lost their taste for putting to sea, or as a reflective study for those who would spend their days lying quietly at anchor.

# Chapter 61

# Daniel Berrigan (1921–    )

## Jeremiah, the World, the Wound of God **(1999)**

Daniel Berrigan is a Roman Catholic priest, Jesuit, social activist, and poet. He was active in opposing the Vietnam War. With his brother, Philip, he destroyed draft registration files in Catonsville and was sentenced to three years in prison but was sheltered for a time by William Stringfellow. He was arrested regularly for his protest actions at weapons manufacturers. The piece produced here is from his reflections on the book of Jeremiah, one of a series in which Berrigan relates the continuing significance for radical Christianity of the biblical prophetic texts.

## Source

Daniel Berrigan, *Jeremiah, the World, the Wound of God*, Minneapolis: Fortress Press, 1999.

## Further reading

William Stringfellow and Anthony Towne, *Suspect Tenderness: The Ethics of the Berrigan Witness*, New York: Holt, Rinehart, Winston 1971.
Andrew McThenia (ed.) *Radical Christian Exemplary Lawyer: Honoring William Stringfellow*, Grand Rapids: Eerdmans, 1995.
M. Polner and J. O'Grady, *Disarmed and Dangerous*, Oxford: Westview Press, 1998.

## From *Jeremiah, the World, the Wound of God* (1999)

Jeremiah is told: Go then, stand in that place that they declare mine, when in truth it is theirs alone – their nest of illusion, of idolatry. Speak the truth in the place of untruth.

Are they immune in those precincts? Are they safe throughout the land – merely because the Ark of the Covenant is intact? Utter a great no! – unwelcome, unpalatable as the word is bound to be.

*7:5–10.* We are not to conclude that Jeremiah is here (or elsewhere) offering a list of defaults – one among them being worship of false gods. No. Each catalog of crimes ends, in fact, with the name of the greatest of crimes: idolatry.

He digs deep; in truth, idolatry permeates every misdeed. They are unjust toward one another, taking base advantage of widows and orphans, even killing the innocent (v. 6). Such behavior already implies (as insisted on in the same verse) "worshiping false gods."

And so with verse 9: "You put trust in deceitful words, steal, murder, commit adultery, tell lies under oath." And immediately: "You offer sacrifices to Baal, worship gods you have not known before." According to the diatribe, violations of the Decalogue lead to, even as they proceed from, false worship.

The character of Baal? He is a god to whom all things are morally equal. What a convenient deity! No judgment, no accountability – no evil in fact, and no goodness. The categories are irrelevant.

Thus the god stands, along with Astarte, the "queen of heaven" (v. 18), for a world of nature that has been tamed and brought to heel. The seasons are obedient and fruitful in their cycle. No transcendence is implied, no moral consequence. Only give us such gods!

*7:11.* Yahweh's temple, "My temple": Is it to become a place of refuge for thieves? a "den of thieves"? (Matt. 21:13). Jesus, we note, objected forcefully to the huckstering of wares in the precincts.

Here the emphasis is different. Once the presence of Yahweh is ignored, Jeremiah implies, prayer, biblical truth-telling, occasions for repentance, all vanish. The temple is transformed; it is now the refuge of a criminal people.

Then, now, what make of such places?

A story comes to mind. In the National (*sic*) Cathedral in Washington, D.C., a service was held on August 5, 1995. A large congregation from near and far assembled to commemorate the fiftieth anniversary of the atomic destruction of Hiroshima.

A week before the event, we who were invited to speak received a text by mail. We were abruptly informed that words of our own choosing, or overt reference to the great crime of atomic bombing, were disallowed. My text seemed eminently safe, wide of the mark: a selection from a medieval mystic. In the course of the evening, an authority of the cathedral arose, introducing himself as the "ethicist in residence." He recalled the glories of the place: Dr. Martin Luther King had delivered his last sermon there; Archbishop Tutu had preached. Then he added words to this effect: that "the cathedral took no position on the morality of nuclear weapons, or indeed of any other political [*sic*] question."

Martin Sheen, also invited to speak, looked at me in blank disbelief. I arose to my cue, venturing to thank the official for recalling the great spirits who had graced the temple. But I added that I found it difficult to imagine Dr. King ascending the pulpit to declare his peace with a "position of no position, on racism."

I intended to speak in a like vein of Desmond Tutu, and a "no position" on apartheid. But I was interrupted by deafening applause as the congregation rose to its feet, after the first sentence was uttered.

As result of this modest effort at truth-telling, on the following morning several hundred congregants fared forth to the Pentagon demonstration. I suspect that prior to the modest encounter of the previous evening, many among them had not intended to do so.

*7:12.* A bit of history is of help here in decoding the text. Shiloh, the amphictyonic center of tribes, was destroyed during the Philistine Wars. The catastrophe would be remembered in nearby Anathoth, the hometown of Jeremiah. Allusion (he alone makes it) to the catastrophe is even more plausible if Jeremiah is a descendant of the priests who dwelt in Anathoth during the time of exile.

Take it to heart, you people. This is the daring midrash of Jeremiah: the fate of Shiloh can become the fate of "My temple."

But is the vast pile in reality to be thought "Mine"?

"You do those things I hate, and then you come and stand in My presence, in My own temple, and say: 'We are safe.' " Only think: what goes forth, returns. Sacrifice, public behavior, it is all one. The theme will be drummed, century after century, prophet after prophet. As though from hill to hill, heartbeat, soul, were being passed on. The crimes here denounced, renounced, are in reality "never done with." Our crimes, a dark legacy. The sin named original, ever and darkly made new.

As to the temple then, rather than "Mine," awfully – it is "yours," your legacy, your moral void manifest in stone.

"What I did at Shiloh I will do to this temple of Mine, in which you trust." Shocking, on the face of it: the God of the temple threatens the destruction of the temple. And did it not occur?

# Chapter 62

# Gustavo Gutiérrez (1928–    )

The Task and Content of Liberation Theology **(1999)**

Gustavo Gutiérrez is widely regarded as the founding father of liberation theology. His book *A Theology of Liberation* was instrumental in crystallizing a variety of movements in Latin American catholicism in the wake of the Second Vatican Council and the political upheavals of the late 1960s, which saw the sub-continent dominated by military dictatorships. His writings chart the changing fortunes and emphases of liberation theology over the last thirty years. Starting with a clear indebtedness to Marxism and the critical economic theory that criticized the way in which European and North American interests kept the peoples of the so-called Third World in economic impoverishment, liberation theologians, often in dialogue with a highly critical Vatican response, formulated their response as the authentic understanding of the impetus of the Second Vatican Council. Gutiérrez's involvement in parochial ministry in a Lima shanty town epitomizes the emphases of many liberation theologians who have never been armchair radicals but are actively involved as advocates and interpreters of the wisdom of the poor with whom they live and work. Gutiérrez himself has been greatly influenced by Bartolomé de las Casas, the Dominican advocate of the indigenous peoples of the Americas, whose cause he championed with the royal authorities in Spain (see pp. 63–8). Gutiérrez has written extensively on him.

The extract which follows comes from a recent outline by Gutiérrez of the essential features of liberation theology. In it he stresses some of the major differences with the academic concerns of Europe and American academies. The pastoral experience of living and working with the poor gives a different set of priorities to the theological task which makes detachment difficult if not impossible. There is in many respects a harking back to a theological method of an earlier age in which prayer, contemplation, commitment and the service of Christ in the poor and needy are intertwined, so that the theological task cannot be properly understood without reference to all these dimensions.

## Source

C. Rowland, *The Cambridge Companion to Liberation Theology*, Cambridge: Cambridge University Press, 1999, pp. 25–32.

## Further reading

*Gustavo Gutiérrez Essential Writings*, London: SCM Press, 1991.
G. Gutiérrez, *A Theology of Liberation*, rev. edn., London: SCM Press, 1988.
G. Gutiérrez, *Las Casas: in search of the poor of Jesus Christ*, Maryknoll: Orbis, 1993.
R. McAfee Brown, *Gustavo Gutiérrez: An Introduction to Liberation Theology* Maryknoll: Orbis, 1990.
Marc H. Ellis and Otto Maduro, *Expanding the View: Gustavo Gutiérrez and the Future of Liberation Theology*, Maryknoll, NY: Orbis, 1988.

## *The Task and Content of Liberation Theology* (1999)

*Poverty and theological reflection*

At around the middle of the twentieth century, a number of developments helped to revive and to relaunch the theme of poverty within the universal Church. There was a demand for a radical and authentic witness of poverty arising from new religious communities. This came from among those concerned with the growing estrangement from faith evident among the labour movement, in the development of the social teaching of the Church and in some spiritual and pastoral tendencies, especially in Europe. This concern was categorically and prophetically expressed by Pope John XXIII at the Vatican Council: in the call for the Church to become the Church of all, and in particular the Church of the poor (11 September 1962).

Vatican II, for reasons that are well known and easy to understand, did not fully take up John XXIII's proposal, even though this concern was at the fore during much of the work of the Council. However, it was heard, in large measure because of the developments we have already touched upon (albeit not without some reservations and vacillation), where the great majority is both poor and Christian: in Latin America. Alongside the fact of the new presence of the poor, the idea of a Church of the poor stimulated considerable theological reflection.

That is why in around July 1967, a distinction was made between three concepts of poverty:

1   Real poverty (frequently called material poverty), defined as the lack of those goods required to satisfy the most basic needs of human beings. This poverty is an outrage in terms of the message of the Bible. It is a situation wholly contrary to the will of God.
2   Spiritual poverty. This is not primarily the putting aside of worldly goods; it is rather an attitude of openness and acceptance towards the will of God. The

gospel also calls this spiritual childhood, of which the renunciation of worldly goods is a consequence.

3   Poverty as a commitment to be assumed by all Christians, which expresses itself in solidarity with the poor and in protest against poverty. Jesus assumes the sins of humanity in this way, both out of love for the sinner and in rejection of sin.

Such an approach presupposes a particular analysis of poverty and its causes. It also implies a biblical foundation both in relation to a rejection of this inhuman situation as well as towards an understanding of spiritual poverty. Finally it sets out the reasons – leaving aside all idealism – for Christian commitment in this field. This contribution was taken up a year later at Medellín in August and September 1968, and helped clarify the commitment which many Christians had begun to assume.

Closely linked to the theme of poverty emanating from a situation of injustice, a little before Medellín there emerged the theme of liberation, which embodies a number of perspectives. Although the term liberation exists also in the social and political spheres, it comes from a very ancient biblical and theological tradition. It was within this tradition that we sought to locate the term from the beginning. In using the word 'liberation' we distinguished between:

1   Political and social liberation, which points towards the elimination of the immediate causes of poverty and injustice, especially with regard to socio-economic structures. On this basis, an attempt can be made to construct a society based on respect for the other, and especially for the weakest and the insignificant;

2   human liberation, meaning that, although aware that changing social structures is important, we need to go deeper. It means liberating human beings of all those things – not just in the social sphere – that limit their capacity to develop themselves freely and in dignity. Here we are speaking of what Vatican II called a 'new humanism' (cf. *Gaudium et Spes* 55);

3   and, crucially, liberation from selfishness and sin. In the analysis of faith, this is the last root of injustice that has to be eliminated. Overcoming this leads to re-establishing friendship with God and with other people (cf. *Lumen Gentium* n. 1). It is clear that only the grace of God, the redeeming work of Christ, can overcome sin.

Divergent, but at the same time linked, these three dimensions of liberation portray a radical and integral reality, a broad process whose meaning is ultimately to be found in the salvation of Christ. This provides the concept of liberation with its permanent relevance and the demanding appeal, as well as the context for dealing with the issue of poverty.

From the distinctions noted above between notions of poverty, the expression 'preferential option for the poor' emerged from within Christian communities, between the time of the conferences of Medellín and Puebla (1979). Here, the three notion of poverty are bound together with one another, and are made dynamic. *Poor*, here refers to victims of material poverty; *preferential* is inspired by the notion of spiritual childhood or the capacity to accept the will of God in our lives; and *option* relates to the idea of commitment that – as we have suggested – means solidarity with the poor and rejection of poverty as something contrary to the will of God. This option, adopted at the Bishops' conference at Puebla, represents today a point of orientation for the pastoral activities of the Church and an important guideline for being a Christian – in other words, what we call spirituality, one of the fundamental concerns of liberation theology. As is well known, this is a perspective which is widely accepted in the teaching of the universal Church.

All this provides the approach which has become the central plank in the evangelising mission of the contemporary Church in Latin America. It combines a profound sense of the gratuitous love of God with the urgency of solidarity with the 'little ones' of history. These are the two elements, the two pillars of what we call liberation theology. The theme of encounter with our Lord in the suffering faces of the dispossessed and despised of our continent beautifully and concisely expresses a process which has been under way for some years now. It is evident even from the very dawn of Latin American theological reflection inspired by the gospel. We refer to the reflections of the Peruvian Indian Felipe Huamán Poma de Ayala at the beginning of the seventeenth century; to the ideas we find a little earlier in the writing of Bartolomé de Las Casas. Both illustrated their Christian understanding of the cruel predicament facing the Indians through reference to chapter 25 of Matthew's Gospel. This is a text which occupies a central place in the theology of liberation as well, being taken up both in Puebla (1979) and Santo Domingo (1992).

## Theology as critical reflection

The theology of liberation is reflection on practice in the light of faith. In order to understand the scope of such an affirmation, it is helpful to examine the question posed at the outset of this discourse on faith, to see how in this perspective theological method and spirituality interrelate closely; and finally we can set out the present challenges.

### A point of departure

A good part of contemporary theology, since the Age of Enlightenment, appears to take as a point of departure the challenge raised by the (often unbelieving) modern spirit. The modern mentality questions the religious world and demands of it a purification and renewal. Bonhoeffer takes up this challenge and incisively formulates the question that lies at the roots of much contemporary theology: 'how to announce God in a world that has come of age (*mündig*)?'

But in a continent like Latin America and the Caribbean, the challenge comes not in the first instance from the non-believer, but from the 'non-persons', those who are not recognised as people by the existing social order: the poor, the exploited, those systematically and legally deprived of their status as human beings, those who barely realise what it is to be a human being. The 'non-person' questions not so much our religious universe but above all our economic, social, political and cultural order, calling for a transformation of the very foundations of a dehumanising society.

The question we face, therefore, is not so much how to talk of God in a world come of age, but how to proclaim God as Father in an inhuman world? How do we tell the 'non-persons' that they are the sons and daughters of God? These are the key questions for a theology that emerges from Latin America, and doubtless for other parts of the world in similar situations. These were the questions which, in a way, Bartolomé de Las Casas and many others posed in the sixteenth century following their encounter with the indigenous population of America.

This does not mean that the questions posed by modernity are irrelevant for us. It is a question of emphasis, and in this light, poverty without doubt is the most important challenge.

*Reflection on praxis*

How to find a way to talk about a God who reveals Himself to us as love in a reality charcterised by poverty and oppression? From the perspective of the theology of liberation, it is a argued that the first step is to contemplate God and put God's will into practice; and only in a second moment can we think about God. What we mean to say by this is that the veneration of God and the doing of God's will are the necessary conditions for reflection on Him. In fact, only as a consequence of prayer and commitment is it possible to work out an authentic and respectful discourse about God. Through commitment, concretely commitment towards the poor, do we find the Lord (cf. Matt. 25.31–46); but at the same time this discovery deepens and renders more genuine our solidarity with the poor. Contemplation and commitment in human history are fundamental dimensions of Christian existence; in consequence, they cannot be avoided in the understanding of faith. The mystery is revealed through contemplation and solidarity with the poor; it is what we call the *first act*, Christian life, practice. Only thereafter can this life inspire reasoning: that is the *second act*.

Theology, as a critical reflection in the light of the Word adopted through faith on the presence of Christians in a tumultuous world, should help us to understand the relationship between the life of faith and the urgent need to build a society that is humane and just. It is called upon to make explicit the values of faith, hope and charity that that commitment involves. But it also helps to correct possible deviations, as well as to recall some aspects of the Christian life which risk being forgotten in view of immediate political priorities, however charitable those may be. This is the function of critical reflection which, by definition, should not be a Christian justification *a posteriori*. In essence, theology helps the commitment to liberation to be more evangelical, more concrete, more effective. Theology is at the service of the Church's task of evangelisation; it arises out of it as an ecclesial function.

The starting point for all theology is to be found in the act of faith. However, rather than being an intellectual adherence to the message, it should be a vital embracing of the gift of the Word as heard in the ecclesial community, as an encounter with God, and as love of one's brother and sister. It is about existence in its totality. To receive the Word, to give it life, to make it a concrete gesture; this is where understanding of faith begins. This is the meaning of Saint Anselm's *credo ut intelligam*. The primacy of the love of God and the grace of faith give theology its *raison d'être*. Authentic theology is always spiritual, as was understood by the Fathers of the Church. All this means that the life of faith is not only a starting point, it is also the goal of theological reflection. To believe (life) and to understand (reflection) are therefore always part of a circular relationship.

*A way of living and thinking*
The distinction between the two moments (first and second acts) is a crucial point in the method of liberation theology; in other words, the process (method, *hodos*, the way) that should be followed for reflection in the light of the faith. This is indeed more traditional than many think, but what we need to underline here is that it is not only a question of theological methodology, rather it implies a lifestyle, a way of being, and of becoming a disciple of Jesus.

In the book which tells of the Acts of the first Christian communities, this is given a particular and original name: 'the way'. The term is used frequently in an absolute way without qualification. To follow the Way implies a pattern of conduct; the Hebrew word *derek*, which translates into Greek as *hodos*, in fact means both things at the same time: the way and conduct. Christians were characterised by their conduct and by their lifestyle. This is what distinguished the Christian communities in their early years in the Jewish and pagan world in which they lived and bore witness. Such conduct is a way of thinking and behaving, 'of walking according to the Holy Spirit' (Rom. 8.4).

Following Jesus defines the Christian. It is a journey which, according to biblical sources, is a communitarian experience, because it is indeed a people that is on the move. The poor in Latin America have started to move in the struggle to affirm their human dignity and their status as sons and daughters of God. This movement embodies a spiritual experience. In other words, this is the place and the moment of an encounter with the Lord; it represents a way of following Jesus Christ.

This is a fundamental point of reference for the theological reflection taking place in Latin America. It is aware that it is preceded by the spiritual experience of Christians committed to the process of liberation. This encounter with God and the discipleship of the Lord – sometimes extending to surrendering one's life, to martyrdom – has been made more urgent and fruitful by the events of recent years. In the context of the struggle for liberation motivated by love and justice for all, there has possibly opened up a new way of following Jesus in Latin America. There is a new spirituality which, for this very reason, resists clear definition and any attempt to imprison it in description, but which nevertheless is no less real or full of potential.

Following Jesus Christ is the basis of the direction that is adopted for doing theology. For this reason, it could be said that our methodology is our spirituality (in other words, a way of being Christian). Reflection on the mystery of God can only be undertaken if we follow in the steps of Jesus. Only if we walk in the way of the Spirit is it possible to understand and announce the gratuitous love of the Father for all people. Perhaps it is because of this relationship between Christian life and theological method that the Base Ecclesial Communities in Latin America are becoming ever more the agents of such theological reflection.

*A continent of all bloods*

From the outset, Latin American theological reflection raised the question of the 'other' in our society. The inadequacy, and indeed the errors, in the concentration on the reality of poverty adopted at that time made it necessary to analyse first the social and economic reasons for the marginalisation suffered by different categories of the poor (social class, culture, ethnicity and gender). Indeed, although a description of poverty is important, so long as its causes are not identified we are unable to do anything about it, or we are limited to trying to heal social rifts that require much deeper and broader solutions. Many of those causes – although not all – are social and economic. These are most unsettling for the power groups within Latin America and beyond, because they remind them of their responsibility for the conditions in which the majorities live. For this reason, they continually try to ascribe the differences to factors that mask the degree of social injustice. We should not forget this when with the best will in the world – and to some extent correctly – we are sensitive to certain aspects such as the race, culture and gender of the heterogeneous population of Latin America. We need to be clear about the different facets of the problem.

To adopt this perspective, to embark on a structural analysis, was one of the novelties of Medellín. Many of the positions taken in recent years reveal the extent to which this approach has been engraved on the Latin American mind, and has been constantly reworked. At the same time, these positions show with great clarity the need to immerse ourselves in the multifaceted world of the poor, remaining attentive to its cultural and racial dimensions.

Although a longstanding concern, the last few decades have allowed us to become more deeply involved in this complexity. The year 1992 stimulated the need to undertake a critical evaluation of the last 500 years of the continent's history, and helped give more attention to the predicament of the various indigenous nations and to the black population which have been violently incorporated into our world. In many ways we have been witnesses over this period to the force given by the voices of these peoples; they remind us that the expression used by the Peruvian writer José María Arguedas to describe Peru as a country 'of all bloods' can be applied to the whole continent.

All this affects the way of living and announcing the gospel, and certainly the theological reflection that accompanies it. The emphasis that these types of theology adopt, depending on which angle of poverty is the starting point, should not make us lose sight of the global dimension of the issue, nor to forget the horizon of understanding of our languages about God: the language of the marginalised and oppressed, the language of their liberation and the language of the gospel of Jesus.

It is necessary to avoid the possibility that the deepening of reflection on the suffering of the poor in Latin America transforms itself into fruitless searches for theological spaces, anguishing priorities and misunderstandings – with undisguised (in spite of appearances) intellectualist features – that in the long run only undermine the effort of the 'little ones' of history in their struggle for life, justice and the right to be different. We also observe the existence of indigenous groups that are particularly forgotten and excluded. We refer to the aborigines of the Amazon, a region where – as pointed out in one of the texts of the bishops and missionaries – governments are more interested in natural resources than in the inhabitants. This is also the case of the Kunas of Panama and the Mapuche in Chile, amongst others. The distance we need to cover in order to understand these peoples and to express solidarity with them is still long. Nevertheless, these peoples are beginning to make it clear that they live in lands that have always been theirs. This fact is partly a result of the liberating dimension of the gospel. However, it also constitutes a challenge to Christian faith.

What we have just mentioned continues to provide colour and flavour to the new role of the poor we referred to earlier. It too forms part of the – prolonged and stormy – search for identity in a continent of many colours which still finds difficulty in knowing what it is. For this very reason, the state and values of the poor in general, and of indigenous and black people in particular (and among them the women), constitute a challenge for evangelisation in our countries and a stimulus for different types of theological reflection. We face a real upsurge in fruitful understanding of faith, coming from cultural and human backgrounds of great importance. The initial perception of the other thus turns into a much more precise image, providing invaluable enrichment for the theology of liberation. However, much still needs to be done in this area.

*Announcing the gospel of liberation*

To know that the Lord loves us, to accept the gratuitous gift of his love, is the profound source of happiness of those who live according to the Word. To communicate this happiness is to evangelise. Such communication is the purpose of the reflection we call liberation theology. It concerns itself with a proclamation which is, in a way, gratuitous, just as the love which motivates it is gratuitous. What is received free, should be given freely, as the Gospel says. In the starting point for evangelisation there is always the experience of the Lord, a living out of the love of the Father that makes us His sons and daughters, transforming us, making us ever more fully brothers and sisters.

For us, all of this comes together – as we have pointed out – in the question: how to proclaim a God who is revealed as love in a world of poverty and exclusion? How to proclaim the God of life to people who suffer premature and unjust death? How to proclaim the 'Gospel of liberation'?

# Chapter 63

# Thomas Hanks

Matthew and Mary of Magdala: Good News for Sex Workers **(2000)**

Like liberation, feminist, womanist and black theologies, Queer Theology reflects and articulates the experience of a community of Christians traditionally marginalized, silenced, and persecuted by the mainstream church; and just as poor people, blacks and women are "doing theology" and reinterpreting the Scriptures from their own perspectives, so, too, are people who designate themselves as queer – in the main lesbians, gay men, bisexuals, transgendered, and "seeking" people. Reclaiming the Bible is seen as an important task for queer theology, not least since it has so often been used by (usually conservative) Christians to support the stigmatizing and ill-treatment of their queer brothers and sisters. Queer theologians argue that such use of Scripture merely reflects the preconceived notions of the interpreters concerning the "sinfulness of homoeroticism" or "normality of heterosexualism," and (as with other theologies of the same genre), that the unmasking of the link between "pre-conception" and "interpretation" is a crucial strategy for liberation.

The essay reproduced here first appeared in a collection of pieces subtitled "a queer reading of the Bible." In it, Thomas Hanks questions the heterosexual presuppositions behind more traditional interpretations of the Gospel of Matthew, and considers the possibility that Matthew might have been driven into his (despised) line of work as a consequence of his sexual orientation. Hanks' conclusion is that his gospel may be seen as "good news" for sexual minorities. A North American, Hanks has taught in Costa Rica and Argentina, and is executive director of Other Sheep, an ecumenical organization working with sexual minorities in developing nations.

## Source

Thomas Hanks, "Matthew and Mary of Magdala: Good News for Sex Workers" in Robert E. Goss and Mona West, eds., *Take Back The Word: A Queer Reading of the Bible*, Cleveland, Ohio: The Pilgrim Press, 2000, pp. 185–94.

## Further reading

Robert E. Goss and Amy A. S. Strongheart, eds., *Our Families, Our Values: Snapshots of Queer Kinship*, NY, 1997.
Elizabeth Stuart, *Religion is a Queer Thing*, London, 1997.
Gary David Comstock and Susan E. Henking, eds., *Que(e)rying Religion: A Critical Anthology*, NY 1997.
Nancy L. Wilson, *Our Tribe: Queer Folks, God, Jesus and the Bible*, New York, 1995.

## *Matthew and Mary of Magdala*

### *Good News for Sex Workers*

Matthew's gender-bending sexuality surfaces even in his opening genealogy (1:1–17), where he first subverts patriarchy by slipping four women into what was supposed to be a list of male descendants (according to the traditional Jewish literary genre; cf. Luke 3:23–38 with no women before Mary). But Matthew includes only women who were either (unclean) Gentiles or married to (unclean) Gentiles, all of whose irregular sexual unions would be viewed as undermining traditional patriarchal "family values": the harlots, Tamar and Rahab, the Moabitess Ruth (who boldly seduced Boaz), and Bathsheba (adulteress wife of the Gentile Uriah). One expects a certain expertise in simple math from an educated toll-collector-turned-scribe, but Matthew "queers" his math in his genealogy, pretending to find groups of fourteen, when careful counting by scholars reveals that (like militant gays who "can't even march straight") our publican either can't count straight or (like a thoroughbred queer) decides not to (1:14; see the commentaries for various befuddled "explanations") . . .

Just what was Mary of Magdala's profession? Feminist scholarship reminds us that Mary of Magdala, the first witness to the resurrection and "apostle to the apostles," [John 20] did not deny Jesus three times as did Peter. Could not this Mary be a sex worker, repentant of her sin, but not of her sexuality (not even necessarily a sex worker become seamstress)? Why could she not be a church leader on par with Peter and Paul as a woman and as a sexual minority? (Feminist scholars properly remind us of the common white male distortion resulting from always posing questions as either/or instead of both/and.)

In addition to Matthew's emphasis on publicans and sexual minorities (prostitutes, eunuchs, women in irregular unions) and his apparent use of inclusion with Mary of Magdala reechoing the women, including prostitutes, in the opening genealogy, we have the fact that the other women associated with the Magdalene are identified by their "family values" ("mother of . . ." or "wife of . . ."), while Mary of Magdala is simply identified by her city or origin (a port town of ill repute, as feminist scholarship makes clear). Evidently Mary of Magdala had no husband and no children. Unlike Dorcas, the widow-become-seamstress, or Lydia, the seller of purple goods (Acts 9; 16), Mary of Magadala is never explicitly identified as having any respectable profession. No family ties are indicated, yet she is indicated to be a person of considerable economic resources, as sex workers or courtesans often were in her context (Matt. 27:55–56; Mark 15:40–41; Luke 8:1–3).

In a society where "nice" women stayed at home, Mary of Magdala and a few other gender-benders felt free to travel about with a band of itinerant single males and ministered to them from their wealth – a scandalous lifestyle in a conservative patriarchal Jewish environment. The ambitious "mother of the sons of Zebedee" (Matt. 20:20) is never identified as the "wife" of Zebedee since she evidently followed the example of James and John and abandoned her husband to join Jesus in his itinerant ministry (4:21–22; 27:55). Matthew portrays women shattering patriarchal tradition and reclining at table with the men (9:10–13; 11:19; 14:21; cf. Luke 7:36–50). In a society where men were not even expected to talk to women in public (John 4), Mary of Magadala felt free to grasp Jesus' feet (Matt. 28:9), and she even had to be rebuked for clinging to him (the famous *Noli me tangere* of John 20:17). Evidently she was a woman who felt comfortable (not "sexually harassed") with socially disapproved physical contact with males (in fact, Jesus sounds more like the one who is being "sexually harassed"!).

In both Matthew and John, therefore, it is not the male Jesus who takes the initiative in physical contact but Mary of Magdala. This character trait will be viewed as negative only by patriarchal males (who think males should always initiate physical contact with women) or by women who are hypersensitive about physical contact with men (often lesbians or/and victims of male sexual abuse in childhood), who want their ample "space" secure and consider any uninvited physical contact with men as "harassment." Even if not a prostitute, Mary of Magdala might be a good role model for all concerned in cultures where physical touch has become so problematic and litigious . . .

Many gays like myself, impacted by evangelical teaching in our youth, can easily empathize with Matthew's long struggle with the jots and tittles of scripture and his dramatic encounter with a Christ who at times apparently affirms, yet more often transcends, them. Shortly after my own evangelical conversion I left home for Northwestern University and became an active student leader in InterVarsity Christian Fellowship, a student movement with a strong emphasis on inductive Bible study, evangelism, and world mission. After theological studies this led to two decades of submission to ex-gay quackery to "cure" my homosexuality, "marriage" (perhaps more accurately, a failed scientific experiment), and twenty-five years of service with an evangelical mission board in Latin America. Moving from Costa Rica, during our last three years with the mission board (1986–88), in Buenos Aires I began at last to partake of the sacrament of coming out. Like Matthew, I sensed a deep call to follow Jesus in ministry to those marginalized and despised by traditional religions. This led to our resignation from the board (which does not even permit separation, much less divorce). From 1989 until 1991 in my personal crisis (deprived of salary, health insurance, rejected by most friends), I was immensely helped as I worked closely with the Universal Fellowship of Metropolitan Churches (UFMCC) in Latin America. However, my denomination (Presbyterian) did not defrock me, and the UFMCC could not give priority to the trench warfare within the mainline churches. With a few old friends and several new ones who shared a similar vision, in 1992 we sensed God's leading to begin a Multicultural Ministry with Sexual Minorities, which soon took the name Other Sheep.

Our Antioch was St. Louis, but soon from Mexico, John Doner and José Hernández undertook a "Mission Jesus Style" (as a same-sex couple traveling light). Within six months they were able to visit virtually every country in Latin America by bus and established some forty resource centers with Spanish materials for sexual minorities (PFLAG for parents and friends, contemporary scientific materials on homosexuality, Safer Sex, affirming theological and biblical materials). Traditional mainline and evangelical agencies have not even been able to acknowledge the presence of some forty million lesbigays in Latin America, much less work with them. We believe God has raised up Other Sheep as an ecumenical catalyst to respond to needs like this and obey the Great Commission to "teach all nations" (Matt. 28:16–20) to obey Jesus' teachings (often transcending Moses' laws).

In the worldwide struggle of sexual minorities for liberation, freedom, justice, and love, the significance of Matthew's good news to the poor and oppressed is enormous. The Great Commission that concludes the Gospel reminds us that much of primitive Christianity's dynamic growth was due to their capacity to "think globally" as they acted locally. Paul's paradigmatic pioneering efforts to develop a global network of Jesus' followers (envisioned in Matt. 28:16–20) might remind local individuals and groups (in the often isolationist U.S.A.) of their need to show solidarity with sexual minorities in other countries through international entities such as ILGA (International Lesbian and Gay Association) and Other Sheep (Multicultural Ministries with Sexual Minorities).

Matthew's sensitive dialectical deconstruction of cruel legalism shows us how to respect details in the Scriptures dear to the pious – and yet experience that freedom from the yoke of the law (Gal. 5:1; Acts 15:10), for which Jesus and Paul are outstanding paradigms. Above all, the breadth of Jesus' own solidarity with humans in their suffering and oppression (the economically poor, women, the sick and physically challenged, sexual minorities, persons of every culture and color) calls us out of our ghettos and narrow ideological myopia into the kind of global rainbow coalition that can alone challenge and transform the existing international power structures that oppress us. Any attempt to think globally and act locally for human liberation, of course, must begin with a radical personal commitment at first daunting but ultimately affirming of all that we most deeply desire and seek:

"Come to me, all you that are weary and are carrying heavy burdens, and I will give you rest. Take my yoke upon you, and learn from me; for I am gentle and humble in heart, and you will find rest for your souls. For my yoke is easy and my burden is light." (Matt. 11:28–30)

# Index

reason, 39, 121–6, 128–9, 137, 170
reconciliation, 291–2
Reformation, 38, 69–96, 240
repentance, 2–3
revolution, 217, 219, 235–7, 239–40, 275,
    283–4, 288, 297, 328
riches *see* wealth

sexism, 270
Sheffield, 221, 280, 308
Simons, Menno, xxi, 84–5
simony, 51
slavery, xviii, 41, 62–8, 167, 172–5, 177–80,
    182, 184, 234
social analysis, 305
socialism, 193, 199, 218, 327, 329–31
Spirit, xxii, xxv–xxvi, 3, 19, 47–50, 69, 72,
    76–8, 86, 90–1, 93–4, 105, 123, 125,
    127, 128, 130, 146, 160, 165, 218, 262,
    306, 325, 340
Stephen, xix, 149
suffering, 76

Taborite movement, 51
Temple in Jerusalem, xix, 332–4
Temple, William, 199
Teresa of Avila, xxi, 241–2
Tertullian, 4
"third age," 34

tithe, 80, 121, 127, 139
Tolpuddle, 189
trade union movement, 189
Trinity, 34, 42–50, 168–9, 267
Tyler, Wat, 40
tyranny, 68, 119, 198, 130–1, 133,
    299–301, 305

Urban Theology Unit, 280
usury, 75, 80, 206–7
utopia, xxv, 95

Vatican II, 209–10, 221, 262, 277,
    335–7
Vietnam War, 238, 255–6, 332
violence *see* non-violence
visions – *see* Revelation (Scriptural
    Citations)
vocation, xvii, 252

Waldensians, 115, 119
Wallis, Jim, 250
war, 182, 186, 285
wealth, xviii, xxi–xxii, xxiv, xxv, 2, 12–13,
    15–33, 51, 84, 140–1, 143, 158
Wesley, John *see* Methodism
womanist theology, 311, 343
works, 14
Wycliffe, John, 51, 56

# Scriptural Citations